Taking Your iPad to the Max, iOS 5 Edition

Michael Grothaus

Erica Sadun

Apress®

Taking Your iPad to the Max, iOS 5 Edition

ISBN 978-1-4302-4068-6

ISBN 978-1-4302-4069-3 (eBook)

Trademarked names, logos, and images may appear in this book. Rather than use a trademark symbol with every occurrence of a trademarked name, logo, or image we use the names, logos, and images only in an editorial fashion and to the benefit of the trademark owner, with no intention of infringement of the trademark.

The use in this publication of trade names, trademarks, service marks, and similar terms, even if they are not identified as such, is not to be taken as an expression of opinion as to whether or not they are subject to proprietary rights.

President and Publisher: Paul Manning
Lead Editors: Michelle Lowman
Technical Reviewer: Dave Caolo
Editorial Board: Steve Anglin, Mark Beckner, Ewan Buckingham, Gary Cornell,
    Morgan Engel, Jonathan Gennick, Jonathan Hassell, Robert Hutchinson,
    Michelle Lowman, James Markham, Matthew Moodie, Jeff Olson, Jeffrey Pepper,
    Douglas Pundick, Ben Renow-Clarke, Dominic Shakeshaft, Gwenan Spearing,
    Matt Wade, Tom Welsh
Copy Editors: Kim Wimpsett
Compositor: MacPS, LLC
Indexer: BIM Indexing & Proofreading Services
Cover Designer: Anna Ishchenko

Distributed to the book trade worldwide by Springer Science+Business Media, LLC., 233 Spring Street, 6th Floor, New York, NY 10013. Phone 1-800-SPRINGER, fax (201) 348-4505, e-mail orders-ny@springer-sbm.com, or visit www.springeronline.com.

For information on translations, please e-mail rights@apress.com, or visit www.apress.com.

Apress and friends of ED books may be purchased in bulk for academic, corporate, or promotional use. eBook versions and licenses are also available for most titles. For more information, reference our Special Bulk Sales–eBook Licensing web page at www.apress.com/bulk-sales.

Contents at a Glance

Contents

About the Authors

 **Michael Grothaus** is an American novelist and journalist living in London. He was first introduced to Apple computers in film school and went on to use them for years to create award-winning films. However, after discovering many of Hollywood's dirty little secrets while working for 20th Century Fox, he left and spent five years with Apple as a consultant. He's since moved to London and earned his MA in Creative Writing. His first novel, *Epiphany Jones*, is a story about trafficking and America's addiction to celebrity. Currently, Michael is a staff writer at AOL's popular tech news site The Unofficial Apple Weblog (TUAW.com), where he writes about all things Mac. Additionally, Michael has written several other books for Apress, including *Taking Your iPod touch to the Max*, *Taking Your OS X Lion to the Max*, and *Taking Your iPhoto '11 to the Max*. When not writing, Michael spends his time traveling Europe, Northern Africa, and Asia. You can reach him at www.michaelgrothaus.com and www.twitter.com/michaelgrothaus.

Erica Sadun is the bestselling author, coauthor, and contributor to several dozen books on programming, digital video and photography, and web design, including the widely popular *The iPhone Developer's Cookbook: Building Applications with the iPhone 3.0 SDK, Second Edition*. She currently blogs at TUAW.com, and has blogged in the past at O'Reilly's Mac DevCenter, Lifehacker, and Ars Technica. In addition to being the author of dozens of iOS-native applications, Erica holds a Ph.D. in Computer Science from Georgia Tech's Graphics, Visualization and Usability Center. A geek, a programmer, and an author, she's never met a gadget she didn't love. When not writing, she and her geek husband parent three geeks-in-training, who regard their parents with restrained bemusement, when they're not busy rewiring the house or plotting global dominance.

About the Technical Reviewer

 **Dave Caolo** is an author and the Managing Editor at The Unofficial Apple Weblog, TUAW.com. Previous to his career as a writer, Dave spent 8 years as the IT Director at a Mac-friendly residential school in Massachusetts. Today, Dave can be found geeking out with his Macs and spending time with his kids, wife, and Boston Terrier, Batgirl. Learn more at http://davecaolo.com.

Chapter 1

Bringing Your iPad Home

Purchasing your first iPad should be a fun and exciting experience for you. Compared to buying a full-fledged desktop or laptop computer, there aren't as many options to complicate matters. The price tag on an iPad isn't as daunting as that for an Apple MacBook Pro, so the impact to your wallet won't be outrageous even if you don't happen to make the perfect choice. In this chapter, you'll discover what decisions you should make before either heading to your local Apple retailer or ordering an iPad online. You'll learn what you need in addition to an iPad, what you can do if you're not pleased with your purchase or get a faulty unit, and how to get your iPad ready for everyday use. Here are all the basic facts you need to select, buy, and set up your iPad.

Picking Your iPad

Especially at this early stage of the life cycle of the iPad, you have a relatively easy decision to make regarding which model of the device to purchase. There are never that many iPad models available at any particular time, since Apple does a good job of keeping its product lines small and up-to-date. The big questions you'll have to ask yourself are whether you need 3G wireless capabilities, whether your 3G iPad should run on a GSM or CDMA network, how much storage you want in your iPad, and whether or not to purchase a used iPad. Let's look into these four questions in more detail.

Wi-Fi or Wi-Fi + 3G?

The iPad is an Internet-connected device. Sure, it can work as an electronic book reader or a gaming device without an Internet connection, but an iPad without Internet is like a Porsche with a flat tire. Apple gives you two choices: Wi-Fi (wireless network connectivity) models and Wi-Fi + 3G (wireless network plus 3G mobile data connectivity) models. If you ever want an Internet connection away from a Wi-Fi hotspot, you'll need to buy the Wi-Fi + 3G version of the iPad, because you cannot add the functionality to an iPad later.

The Wi-Fi + 3G models are slightly more expensive than the models with Wi-Fi only, to the tune of US$130 more than their Wi-Fi counterparts. What you're paying for is built-in

3G circuitry, a Global Positioning System (GPS) receiver, and an antenna, which is a fancy way of saying that your iPad (with an optional subscription to a data plan with your local wireless carrier) can surf the Web, send and receive e-mail, and connect to the iBookstore from any location with 3G wireless service. Do you need 3G capabilities? Here are some questions you need to ask yourself:

Will you be using your iPad in places where there are no Wi-Fi hotspots? If you plan on using your iPad around your Wi-Fi equipped home and office and if most of the locations that you visit (stores, libraries, coffee shops, airports, and hotels) provide free Wi-Fi, then you might not need the Wi-Fi + 3G model. However, if you often find yourself in need of an Internet connection when you're in your car, on a soccer field, or at some other location without Wi-Fi, then the Wi-Fi + 3G iPad may be the correct choice for you.

Do you have another way to connect to a 3G network? You may already have a different method of accessing a wide-area wireless network. If you have a 3G router such as the Sierra Wireless Overdrive 3G/4G or Novatel MiFi for use with a laptop, then you can use it and your existing wireless data plan to connect to the Internet. If you have an iPhone 4 running iOS 4.3 or newer, you might want to consider using the Personal Hotspot feature on the phone as your gateway to the Internet (a separate data plan is required).

Are you willing to pay extra for both your iPad and the 3G data plan? To begin with, a Wi-Fi + 3G iPad costs $130 more than the corresponding model without 3G. That's not the only additional cost you'll incur, since your wireless carrier is going to charge you for a data plan. In the United States, AT&T provides 3G data service without a contract for $14.99 per month for 250MB of data, or $25 monthly for 2GB of data. The other U.S. carrier, Verizon Wireless, has rates beginning at 1GB of data for $20 per month and up to 10GB for $80 per month. International carriers offer similar plans, so check with your carrier for details about the cost and capacity of data plans in your country.

Do you need to use apps that are aware of the location of the iPad? The Wi-Fi iPad has the ability to determine its location through something called the Wi-Fi Positioning System. This service, provided in North America by Skyhook Wireless, uses the known location of Wi-Fi access points to approximate the location of an iPad. Although this can provide location data to within 20 to 30 meters in crowded population centers in the United States and Canada, it doesn't work at all when the iPad is away from Wi-Fi. The Wi-Fi + 3G iPad contains a full Assisted GPS (A-GPS) receiver for pinpointing the location of the device using GPS. As a result, accurate location can be determined almost anywhere on the planet provided that the Wi-Fi + 3G iPad can "see" the sky.

GSM vs. CDMA

If you decide to purchase the Wi-Fi + 3G iPad, you'll also have to decide what mobile wireless network to run on. In the United States, there are two choices: GSM, the standard used by AT&T Wireless, and CDMA, which is the technology behind Verizon's mobile network. The majority of wireless networks throughout the world use GSM, so frequent international travelers may want to consider that fact when making a purchase decision.

For all practical purposes, the speeds and capabilities of the two 3G networks are similar. The main differentiator for most U.S. iPad buyers is the coverage provided by the two carriers in the area where you live and work. Verizon Wireless customers who are happy with the voice signal quality that they currently get with their mobile phones can stay with their existing carrier for iPad data. Likewise, AT&T Wireless customers with five bars of signal strength and good service may want to stay with their current carrier.

How Much Storage?

Once you've decided whether to purchase the Wi-Fi or Wi-Fi + 3G iPad, your next thought should be about the quantity of built-in storage you want in your iPad. Although the amount of working memory, or RAM, in the iPad is identical across the different models (256MB for the original iPad, 512MB for the iPad 2), the flash drives used for storing applications and data come in three different sizes: 16GB, 32GB, and 64GB. You cannot upgrade the flash drive in the iPad, so you're stuck with whatever you buy. Like any electronic device, the iPad will evolve over time, so larger storage capacities are likely in the future. Also keep in mind that the pre-installed OS and apps on the iPad take up some space already (up to half a GB), so you'll actually have a little less free space on the iPad than stated by Apple.

At the launch of the iPad, the difference between the 16GB and 32GB models was only $100, while maxing out the iPad's storage at 64GB was only $200 more than buying the base model. Before deciding how much storage you want to buy, consider these questions:

> *How big is your music library?* If your library is small and you want to listen to music on your iPad, no problem. If it's large, the extra space on the larger iPad models helps you store additional music and podcasts. Of course, if you already own a music device such as an iPod, you may want to continue using it for listening. iPods come in a variety of capacities and are much more portable than your iPad.

How many videos do you want to carry around? A single two-hour movie may occupy more than a gigabyte of storage. If you travel a lot, especially on airplanes, you may want to pay more to store additional movies and TV shows with those extra gigabytes. In Chapter 7 of this book, we'll talk about using Handbrake to transfer video from DVDs to a format that your iPad can use. Although Handbrake does a great job of compressing video, movies can still be as large as 500MB to 1GB in size. If you also own a second-generation Apple TV, you might consider using Apple's AirPlay and Home Sharing to stream video to your iPad, reducing the need for more storage.

Do you plan to carry lots of pictures? Although many digital pictures are pretty small (a typical photo is 300KB to 1.2MB in size), if you carry a few thousand of them around, they do add up to some serious storage. Do you laugh at the idea of carrying that many pictures around on your iPad? Apple's built-in support for the Mac iPhoto application makes it simple to put years of photo archives onto your iPad with a single synchronization option. Moving photos directly from a digital camera to your iPad is easy using the iPad Camera Connection Kit, so the idea of backing up a trip's worth of memories on your iPad while on vacation isn't entirely out of the question.

Do you need to carry lots of data? You might not think of your iPad as a data storage device, but there are ways to use it (mostly involving e-mailing documents to yourself or using a third-party application) to bring data along with you on the road. If you think you might need to do this, maybe those extra gigabytes could be put to good use.

How long do you plan to use this iPad? If you're an early adopter who plans to trade up at the earliest possible opportunity whenever Apple offers a new unit, you may want to save your pennies now in the hope that a better unit with more memory quickly debuts. If, instead, you want to get the most use out of the iPad for the longest period of time, paying more up front means you won't outgrow the memory quite as fast.

Should You Buy a Used iPad?

Now that the iPad has been on the market for a while, some owners are moving up to newer or more capable iPads, and used devices are often available for less money than new ones. If you don't need the latest and greatest iPad, a used one can be your gateway into the iPad world without impacting your wallet as much.

Believe it or not, Apple is the best vendor for used iPads. The company often makes refurbished iPads available for sale at less than the suggested retail price of new equipment, and the iPad will come with the original factory warranty. You can find the refurbished equipment in the Apple Online Store at http://store.apple.com or on Amazon.com.

eBay is often a good place to purchase used computer equipment, because sellers are given ratings by buyers so that it's possible to see at a glance how others have fared in their transactions with a particular seller. As with any online auction, however, the buyer should beware. Make sure that the seller has pictures of the exact unit you are bidding on, has a return policy, and has a flawless approval rating.

If you're buying an iPad from someone locally, you might want to consider having an Apple Authorized Service Provider (www.apple.com/buy/locator/service/) check the unit over before you make a commitment. While it's easy for you to make a visual inspection of the screen and case for scratches or dents, it's not so easy to see if there is hidden damage caused by water or if there are connectors that have been broken.

Finally, you might be able to afford a new iPad when the next generation is announced (usually in March or April). Retailers need to make room for the incoming iPads and discount their existing stock. Your patience can be rewarded!

Considering System Requirements

Even though you no longer need a computer to set up your iPad, you'll still most likely find yourself using your iPad in conjunction with your Mac or PC. This means your computer will need to have some basic requirements in order for it to talk to your iPad. It will need a USB 2.0 port and an Internet connection running the most recent version of iTunes. Also, the PC needs to be a Mac running OS X 10.5.8 or newer or a Windows computer running Windows XP (Home or Professional with Service Pack 3 or newer), Windows Vista, or Windows 7.

> **NOTE:** If you haven't yet put iTunes on your computer, you can get a free copy from www.apple.com/itunes. It's available for both Mac OS X and Windows systems and is quick and easy to install.

Buying Your iPad

After deciding among the available iPad models, you're probably ready to pull out your credit card and go buy that iPad (see Figure 1–1). Where should you go? To an Apple Store? To an authorized Apple retailer or Best Buy store? Or should you buy online? You might be surprised to learn that there are better and worse choices.

We recommend buying your iPad in person at a store. You can ask questions. You can make human connections. If something goes wrong with your purchase, you have a person who's there to help you work through it. This is not to say that calling Apple's support line is insufficient; it's just that being face to face with a real person makes solutions happen more readily.

The sad fact of the matter is that, on occasion, iPad purchases do not go smoothly. Some people end up with a screen flaw, such as dead screen pixels. It's not an uncommon problem, and if found soon after purchase, it may involve a trade-in for a new unit. Others may have problems connecting to Wi-Fi or 3G networks. The chances of resolving these issues increase significantly when you have a real person to talk to.

As for the question of Apple or other retailers, we lean slightly toward buying at an Apple Store. It's an Apple product you're buying, and the Apple staff members are simply more knowledgeable about that product.

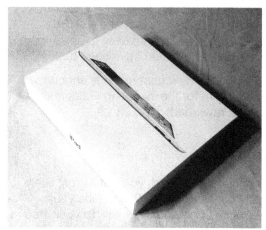

Figure 1–1. *That nice shiny box contains the Apple of your eye, your iPad. Remember to keep all your packaging, receipts, and other purchase information just in case you need to return it to the store.*

Purchasing Your iPad Online

Depending where you live, there might not be a physical store nearby for picking up an iPad. In that case, the Apple Online Store is your best bet for getting your hands on an iPad as soon as possible.

> **NOTE:** There are two quick ways to buy your iPad online. First click the iPad tab at the top of the Apple web site (www.apple.com), and then click the blue Buy Now button. The second way? Point your browser to the iPad page (http://store.apple.com/us/browse/home/shop_ipad/family/ipad) in the Apple Online Store. Be sure to have your credit card ready.

Apple makes it easy for you to purchase your iPad online. The individual models all have their own Select button, and a click brings you to a page that lets you choose which Apple accessories you want to add to your purchase. Adding those accessories to your purchase just requires a click of the radio button near each item, and when you are finally ready to check out, clicking the Add to Cart button displays the contents of your virtual shopping cart as well as a Check Out Now button. An estimate of the shipping date is displayed in your shopping cart next to each item so you know when to start waiting for the delivery truck driver to ring your doorbell.

Repairs, Returns, Warranties, AppleCare, and Insurance

In most situations, the iPad you buy will be in perfect working order, and you should never need to return it to Apple. However, if you do get an iPad that just isn't working properly or that fails during the first year of ownership, there is a tried-and-true process to follow.

First, visit the iPad Support web page (`www.apple.com/support/ipad/`) to see whether you have set up something improperly or whether there is a known issue and solution. If the online support does not resolve the problem, then it is time to either take the iPad to your Apple retailer or send the iPad to Apple.

For iPads that have been purchased at an Apple Store, the easiest thing to do is to grab your receipt, the iPad, the original box, and all the contents of that box, and then head to the store. The Apple Store staff may ask you to work with a person at the Genius Bar in an attempt to resolve the problem, in which case there may be a delay until they can fit you into their busy schedule.

At other Apple authorized retailers, the return policy may be different, so be sure to check that policy when you purchase your iPad.

iPads purchased online from Apple require a Return Material Authorization (RMA). To initiate the return process, call Apple's support phone number at 1–800-275-2273 and speak to an iPad support specialist. If that person determines the iPad is faulty and is eligible for repair or replacement, they will issue an RMA to you.

> **NOTE:** Outside of the United States, you can refer to `www.apple.com/support/`
> `contact/phone_contacts.html` for a list of international phone numbers for Apple Support.

In the first paragraph of this section, we called attention to "the first year of ownership." That's the complimentary warranty period for any iPad. If you want to extend that warranty for another year, you can purchase an AppleCare Protection Plan for iPad for $99. This extends your hardware repair coverage to two years. If interested, you can purchase this option at the online Apple Store. Once the warranty expires, you'll have to pay the going rate for repairs or battery replacements.

American Express cardholders can double their iPad warranty simply by purchasing the device with their Amex card. This Extended Warranty program may be provided by other credit card companies, so be sure to check your card terms and conditions for details.

If you can, make sure to back up your iPad by syncing it to iTunes before bringing it in for service. Apple will usually restore your iPad to factory condition, which means you'll lose any data stored on the iPad during the repair and service process.

Is AppleCare worth buying? In our opinion, it is. In one case, AppleCare more than paid for the replacement of a logic board with a faulty FireWire port on an Apple PowerBook G4 almost three years into the plan.

You're entitled to complimentary phone support for 90 days after the purchase of your iPad. AppleCare extends that period to a full two years, and you can call Apple's experts as many times as you want to get your questions answered.

What about a situation where you find that an iPad isn't what you really needed, or what if you decide that you want the 64GB model instead of the 32GB iPad that you bought? Apple realizes that people change their minds or may be dissatisfied for one reason or another, so you have 14 calendar days to return your purchase. You must return the iPad in the original, unmarked packaging including any accessories (such as the power adapter), manuals, documentation, and registration that shipped with the product. There is a cost for this flexibility, because Apple assesses a 10 percent restocking fee on the return.

Apple does not offer an insurance plan for the iPad, and it's unlikely that the company will do so in the future. Instead, you'll need to call your renter's or home insurance carrier to see how much you'll have to pay for an iPad rider (a rider is placed on top of an existing policy, adding coverage for a specific item not covered under the standard plan).

Unboxing Your iPad

Once you arrive home with your iPad or it is delivered to your door, it's time to unpack it and set it up. iPad packaging (see Figure 1–2) is a small work of art. The iPad ships in a box that contains the device, a Dock Connector to USB Cable, a 10-watt USB power adapter, and a packet of documentation. Each of these items is important and will help you in your day-to-day use.

> *Cable*: The USB cable attaches your iPad to either your computer or the AC adapter. Whether you're charging your iPad for another day of use or you are syncing with your computer to get the latest software update, the Dock Connector to USB Cable is a crucial part of your iPad kit.

> *USB power adapter*: The AC power adapter included with your iPad plugs directly into the wall and allows you to charge your iPad (or any USB device, for that matter). It offers a single USB port. To use it, just connect your iPad to the adapter using the USB cable. It supplies the 5 volts required for powering USB devices.

Figure 1-2. *There's not much inside the iPad box: the iPad, a Dock Connector to USB Cable, a 10-watt AC adapter, and some simple documentation.*

iPad Feature Overview

Once you've unpacked your iPad, take a few minutes to discover more about your new purchase. Figure 1–3 introduces the basic features on your iPad.

The top of the iPad houses a jack into which you can plug your earbuds, a built-in microphone (on the top front of the iPad 2), and a Sleep/Wake button that is used to power on and off certain features. If you purchased a Wi-Fi + 3G model, the top (or left side on the iPad 2) will also house a micro–Subscriber Identity Module (SIM) tray where your phone's micro-SIM card is stored. The bottom of your iPad has a built-in speaker and an indented slot for connecting to the Dock Connector to USB Cable or a dock. The iPad's front has a large touchscreen and a single Home button. You will not see this interactive screen until you have set up your iPad through iTunes.

Newer iPads also feature two cameras: one in the front for playing with Photo Booth or making FaceTime video calls (see Chapter 15) and one in the back that can record high-definition video and take still photos.

On the right side of the iPad (as you look at it from the front), you'll find a volume rocker and an orientation lock slider.

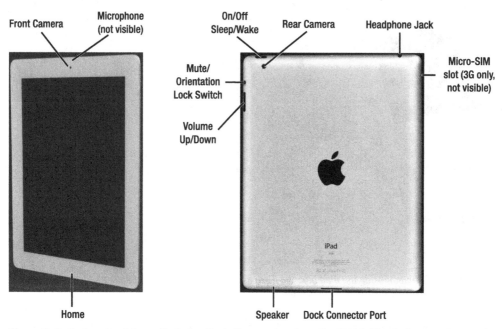

Figure 1–3. *Feature breakdown displaying the buttons and ports on the iPad 2. The dock connector port is on the bottom of the iPad near the Home button.*

Preparing for Setup

You have unpacked your iPad but haven't yet connected it to iTunes. Now is a good time to review the data on your computer. When your iPad is first set up, it will synchronize itself to iTunes and, depending on your computer, to your e-mail accounts, your calendars, and so forth. Before you go forward, here are some items you may want to review and clean up so your iPad starts out its life with the freshest possible data:

> *Contacts*: The iPad can sync with Outlook 2003 or 2007 and Windows Address Book on Windows, Address Book, Outlook, or Entourage on a Mac, and Yahoo! Address Book or Google Contacts on the Internet. To prepare for your first sync, review your existing contacts, and make sure they're up-to-date with current phone numbers and e-mail addresses. If you use another program to manage contacts, consider migrating your contacts to one of these solutions. If you'd rather not, that's OK too. You can add contact information directly to your iPad, although it's not as convenient as having the information automatically loaded for you.

> *Calendar*: Your iPad can synchronize with computer-based calendars just like it does with contacts. The iPad supports iCal, Outlook, and Entourage calendars on the Mac and Outlook calendars on Windows. Get your calendars into shape before your first synchronization, and you'll be ready to immediately manage your schedule both from your computer and from your iPad.

E-mail: Your iPad works with most e-mail providers, including Yahoo! Mail, Google Gmail, and AOL. If your e-mail provider uses the industry-standard POP3, IMAP, or Exchange services, your service will work with iPad. You may want to establish new accounts with these providers before you set up your iPad. That way, they'll load onto your unit the first time you synchronize. You can always add new e-mail accounts later, but it's nice to have them all set up and available for use right away.

Media: Some iPad models offer relatively small storage space when compared to, for example, iPod Classic's generous 160GB hard drive. To make the most of this limited space, set up playlists for your favorite songs, TV shows, movies, and podcasts. Since, in all likelihood, you won't be able to synchronize your entire library to your new iPad, invest time now in weeding through your media to find those items you most want to have on hand.

Software and OS: Update to iTunes 10.5 or newer before you attempt to set up your iPad. If you're using a Mac, make sure you've updated your OS to at least OS X 10.5.8. Windows computers must be running Windows 7, Windows Vista, or Windows XP Home or Professional with Service Pack 3 or newer. You can download the latest version of iTunes from Apple at www.itunes.com/download.

iTunes account: Apple requires a current iTunes account in order to set up your iPad. If you do not already have one, you must sign up for an account with the iTunes Store. If you want to make purchases through the iTunes Store, App Store, or iBookstore, you'll need to have a valid address and credit card. Here are the steps you'll need to follow in order to create that new iTunes account:

1. Launch the iTunes application on your computer, and wait for it to load.

2. Locate iTunes Store in the column on the left side of the window. Click iTunes Store, and wait for the store window to load. You must be connected to the Internet for this to happen, because all the storefront information is stored at Apple.

3. Click the Sign In link at the top-right corner of the screen. iTunes opens the sign-in screen shown in Figure 1–4, which will allow you either to sign in with an existing account or to create a new one.

Figure 1–4. *The iTunes sign-in screen allows you to sign in to iTunes with your existing account or begin the process of creating a new account.*

4. Click Create New Account. The screen clears, and a message welcoming you to the iTunes Store displays. Click the Continue button.

5. Review the terms of service, check the box marked "I have read and agree to these terms and conditions," and click Continue. A new window appears prompting you to create your account.

6. Enter your e-mail address and a password (you must enter the password twice for verification). Also enter a question and answer that will help verify your identity, as well as the month and day of your birth. Review the other options on the page, and adjust them as desired before clicking Continue. Again, the screen will clear, and you'll move on to the final account creation step.

7. Enter a valid credit card and the billing information for that credit card. These must match to finish creating your account. When you have entered the information, click Continue.

After following these steps, you will receive a confirmation e-mail at the address you specified while signing up. The e-mail welcomes you to the iTunes Store and provides you with the customer service web address (www.apple.com/support/itunes/store).

You don't need a credit card to get an iTunes App Store account. If you're planning on only downloading free apps and don't have a credit card, there's a way to create an iTunes App Store account from your iPad. The following instructions assume that you don't already have an account and that you've already unwrapped your iPad. Don't worry; you can always come back to these instructions later if you'd like to wait.

1. Launch the App Store app on your iPad by tapping its icon.

2. Look for a free app. It can be anything, but just make sure that the price is listed as Free. Tap the Free button to start the "purchase" process; then tap Install App.

3. A dialog appears asking you to sign into the iTunes App Store by using an existing Apple ID or by creating a new Apple ID. Tap the Create New Apple ID button.

4. You'll be asked to choose a country or region for the store that matches the billing address for your payment method. Select one from the list that appears when you tap the country name next to the word *Store*; then tap the Next button.

5. Agree to the iTunes Store Terms & Conditions.

6. Now you're asked to enter new account information, including your e-mail address, a password, a secret question and answer, and your date of birth. When you've entered that info, tap Next.

7. On the Billing Information screen, tap the name next to the word *Credit Card*, and select None as your billing method. Enter a valid name and billing address, and then tap Next.

8. At this point, an Email Verification screen should appear. Tap Finish, and then open Mail on your iPad (that's assuming it's already set up; if not, you can do this part on another computer).

9. Open the e-mail from Apple, and tap the Verify Now link. You're asked to sign in to complete the account creation.

10. Tap the Use Existing Account button, enter the username (e-mail address) and password that you just created, and then tap OK.

11. You'll see a message telling you that your iTunes Store account has been successfully created. Tap the Done button, and then you can start downloading any free apps, books, music, or videos from iTunes, the App Store, or the iBookstore. Read more about these stores in Chapter 8.

Configuring Your iPad

With iOS 5, Apple has cut the cord from your iPad to your computer. This new "PC free" world of iOS devices is a new era in computing technology. Oh, you still have to plug the iPad into your computer or charger to recharge the battery all right, but now you no longer need to plug the iPad into your computer to begin using it. You can buy it in the store, open it up right there, and go through a simple setup procedure right on the iPad.

Follow the steps in this section to set up your iPad right out of the box:

1. Take your iPad out of its packaging.

2. Press the power button on top of the iPad to turn it on. You'll see the screen in Figure 1–5. If your iPad does not automatically power on and display this screen, press and hold the Sleep/Wake button. With the main screen facing toward you, you can find this button at the top left of the iPad. After a few seconds, the iPad should wake up and display the white Apple logo as it powers on. If the iPad does not respond and does not display either the white Apple logo or the Connect to iTunes screen, contact the store where you purchased the iPad.

Figure 1–5. *The iPad setup welcome screen*

3. Slide the configure slider to begin setting up your iPad.

4. Select your language on the next screen.

5. On the screen that appears with the panning globe, select your country or region.

6. On the next screen you'll get a choice to enable or disable Location Services. Location Services allows the iPad and its apps to estimate your current location. After you have chosen to enable or disable Location Services, tap the Next button.

7. The Wi-Fi Networks screen appears next. Select your wireless network, enter your Wi-Fi password, and tap the Join button. This will allow you iPad to join your Wi-Fi network and make use of its Internet connection for a number of things, such as connecting to iCloud or using the Maps app.

8. On the next screen you can choose to set up your iPad as a new device or restore it from an iCloud or iTunes backup. If you've never owned an iPad before, select Set Up as New iPad. If you are restoring from a previous iPad, select the iCloud or iTunes backup option (see Figure 1–6).

Figure 1–6. *The iPad restore option screen*

9. On the next screen, enter your Apple ID. You have an Apple ID if you've ever bought anything from the iTunes Store. If you don't have an Apple ID, tap the Create a Free Apple ID button. Alternately, you can skip this step. When finished entering your Apple ID, tap the Next button. You'll have to agree to Apple's Term and Conditions. Read them if you want; then tap Next again.

10. Once you've entered your Apple ID, you are taken to the Set Up iCloud screen. We'll talk all about iCloud in Chapter 2. For now, just choose whether you want to use iCloud or not; then tap Next.

11. If you've chosen to use iCloud, the backup screen appears next. Select whether you want to back up your iPad to iCloud or to your computer; then tap Next.

12. As part of iCloud, Apple lets users track their iOS devices and Macs using a feature called Find My iPad. Select whether you want to allow you iPad to be found using your iCloud account. This free service is part of your iCloud account and allows you to track down your iPad should it become lost or stolen. We'll talk more about Find My iPad in Chapter 12. Click Next after you've made your selection.

13. On the next screen, choose whether you want to send anonymous diagnostics to Apple to help the company improve the iOS and iPad experience. Tap the Next button after making your selection.

14. After you've successfully navigated all those setup screens, you'll see the one pictured in Figure 1–7. Congratulations! You've set up your iPad. Simply tap the Start using iPad button to begin playing with your new favorite toy!

Figure 1–7. *Completing the iPad setup process*

Once you've set up your iPad, you can begin using it right away if you have most of your media stored in the cloud through iCloud. However, if you are still storing most of your media on your computer, you'll need to pair your iPad with your computer in order to get your music, movies, and TV shows on it.

Pairing Your iPad to Your Computer

As we mentioned earlier, a big feature of iOS 5 is that it's "PC free." That means it has the ability for your iPad to sync wirelessly with your computer. But before you can sync wirelessly, you must pair your iPad to your computer. This must be done through the USB cable that came with your iPad. You need to do this only once.

To pair your iPad to your computer, follow these steps:

1. Locate the two ends of the USB cable that was included with your iPad. One is thin and marked with a standard three-pronged USB symbol. The other is wide and marked with a rectangle with a line in it.

2. Orient your iPad. On the back of your iPad, the Apple logo and the word *iPad* show you which way is up. The dock connector is at the bottom of your iPad.

3. Connect the wide end of the USB cable to the bottom of your iPad. Be gentle but firm, without twisting or forcing the connection. Connect the thin end to a spare USB 2.0 port on your computer (for a direct-connected sync) or a USB power adapter (for a Wi-Fi sync).

4. iTunes launches, and your iPad chimes softly.

5. Since this is the first time you are pairing your iPad with your computer, the iPad Setup Assistant appears in iTunes (Figure 1–8). This screen allows you to name your iPad and choose what items to automatically sync to it. If you want to name your iPad something other than "your name's iPad," enter a new name into the "The name of my iPad is" field. Do not press Enter or Return, and do not click the Done button. We recommend you uncheck both boxes: "Automatically sync songs to my iPad" and "Automatically sync photos to my iPad." It's far easier to manage these choices manually.

6. Click the Done button. iTunes closes the Setup Assistant.

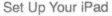

Set Up Your iPad

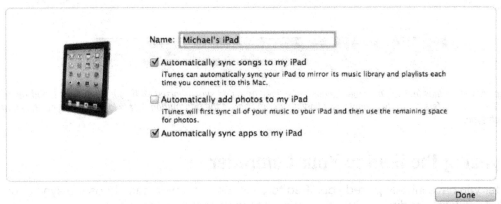

Figure 1–8. *The iPad Setup Assistant lets you name your iPad and decide which items to automatically synchronize to it.*

Once you've paired your new iPad, you're ready to perform your first synchronization. In the iTunes source list, which is the light blue column on the left side of the iTunes screen, locate the Devices section, and click the name of your iPad. This opens its Preferences window (see Figure 1–9). The tabs along the top of the Preferences window allow you to set each of the options associated with your iPad. We go into what each of these tabs does in detail in Chapter 2.

> **TIP:** Click your iPad's name a second time to open a text edit field that allows you to edit the name. You can name your iPad more creatively than the default (your name and "iPad").

Figure 1–9. *iTunes lets you manage the content loaded onto and synchronized with your iPad. Each tab at the top of the screen offers a variety of controls, allowing you to choose the information that is loaded onto your touch at each sync.*

Syncing the iPad to Your Computer

After you have initially paired your iPad to your computer, you can choose to sync your iPad wirelessly or directly (by connecting it to your computer) for all future syncs. However, if you want to sync wirelessly, you first have to enable wireless syncing.

Do this by checking the box that says "Sync with this iPad over Wi-Fi" (Figure 1–10) on your iPad's Summary page in iTunes. After you've done this, the steps to sync your iPad wirelessly or through a USB cable are pretty much the same.

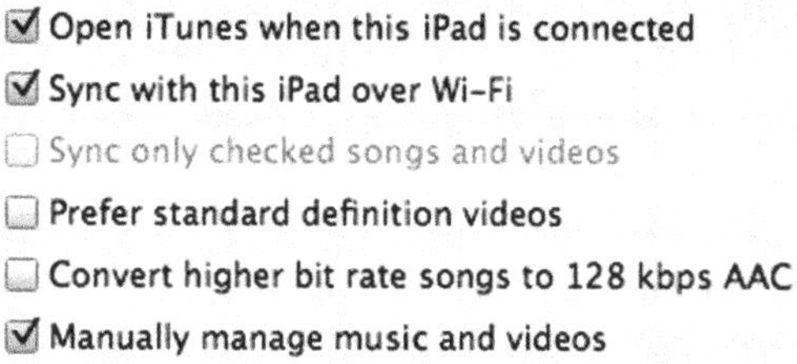

☑ Open iTunes when this iPad is connected
☑ Sync with this iPad over Wi-Fi
☐ Sync only checked songs and videos
☐ Prefer standard definition videos
☐ Convert higher bit rate songs to 128 kbps AAC
☑ Manually manage music and videos

Figure 1–10. *Check "Sync with this iPad over Wi-Fi" to enable Wi-Fi syncing.*

To sync via a USB cable, follow these steps:

1. Plug your iPad in to your computer via the USB-to-dock connector cable. Your iPad begins syncing.

2. Unplug the iPad when the sync is finished.

To sync wirelessly, follow these steps:

1. Both your iPad and computer must be turned on and connected to the same Wi-Fi network.

2. When your iPad appears under the Device header in the iTunes source list, click the Sync button in iTunes to begin your sync.

3. Don't leave the Wi-Fi network until the sync notification in your iPad's status bar disappears (Figure 1–11). When it does, you know your sync is complete.

Figure 1–11. *The rotating arrows in the status bar tell you your iPad is syncing to your iTunes library.*

No matter which way you choose to sync, you can continue to use your iPad while it syncs to your library. We discuss all your syncing options in detail in the next chapter.

Accessorizing Your iPad

If you purchase your iPad in an Apple Store, your Apple sales associate will show you many accessories that are available for it. These accessories are from Apple and third-party sources, and they provide your iPad with protection and added functionality.

Apple sells iPad docks to make charging and syncing your iPad a snap. The $29 iPad Dock and iPad 2 Dock support your iPad in an upright position and work with other accessories and optional audio cables. For the original iPad, text entry into iPad apps is enhanced with the iPad Keyboard Dock ($69), which charges the iPad as you type.

For protection of the iPad 2, Apple provides the iPad Smart Cover ($29; Figure 1–12), which can also be folded into a variety of positions for supporting the iPad 2 on flat surfaces. The colorful Smart Cover attaches to the iPad 2 magnetically and automatically turns the iPad's display on when opened or off when closed.

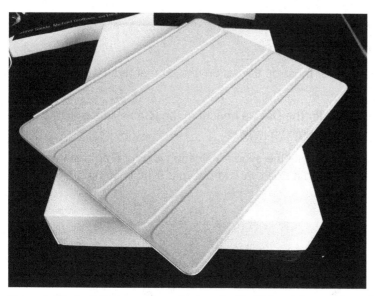

Figure 1–12. *Available in a rainbow of colors, the iPad 2 Smart Cover protects the iPad's display while adding very little weight or thickness.*

Photographers will want to buy the iPad Camera Connection Kit ($29; Figure 1–13), which includes two adapters—one for connecting a camera through a USB 2.0 cable, the other for reading SD memory cards. The USB adapter can also be used to connect USB headsets and keyboards to the iPad.

Figure 1–13. *The iPad Camera Connection Kit includes two adapters. The one on the left connects to a standard USB cable for direct connection to a digital camera, while the adapter on the right can be used to read or write SD memory cards.*

Since you might want to show slide shows or Keynote presentations from an iPad, Apple sells the iPad Dock Connector to VGA Adapter ($29). The VGA end of the adapter can be connected to external monitors, some TVs, and PC projectors. On the iPad 2, whatever is on the screen can be mirrored to an external display, while the original iPad is limited to displaying only apps that have been specifically written to provide video-out capabilities.

The Apple Digital AV Adapter ($39) is perfect for putting slides, movies, photos, and anything else visible on your iPad onto your HDTV. This adapter provides a standard HDMI connector as well as a dock connector port for charging your iPad while it is connected to your display.

The Apple Component AV Cable ($39) and Composite AV Cable ($39) also work with the iPad, providing two more methods of linking external monitors and projectors to the device. The same application limitations apply with these cables as well.

Finally, the Apple Wireless Keyboard ($69) and most other Bluetooth keyboards are iPad-compatible, providing an alternative way of entering text into iPad applications.

Summary

In this chapter, you've seen how to select and purchase your iPad. You've discovered what's involved in setting up an iTunes account, activating your iPad, and pairing your iPad to your computer. To wind things up, here is a quick overview of some key points from this chapter:

- There are several models of the iPad, but whichever unit you choose, you'll probably want to buy it in person at a store, unless you need an online-only feature such as engraving.

- To use your iPad, you no longer need to own a computer. You can buy your iPad and configure it right out of the box. However, it's always helpful to sync your iPad with iTunes on a computer so it is loaded with all of the media you already own.

- iPads are not cheap. Protect your investment by insuring your touch, and consider adding AppleCare for two years of coverage (from the date of purchase) against hardware repairs.

- Your iPad purchase entitles you to one complimentary support incident within the first 90 days of product ownership.

- There are almost as many accessories for the iPad as there are songs in the iTunes Store. You may have to do a lot of browsing before you know which accessories are right for you.

Putting Your Data and Media on Your iPad

So, you've unboxed your iPad and connected it to iTunes. Now what? Chapter 1 briefly introduced the basics of syncing your iPad with your music, movies, photos, and other data via iTunes. Now this chapter explores the options you have for syncing your data with your iPad. Whether you've bought your songs and videos from the iTunes Store or have imported them into the program from CDs and DVDs, iTunes can synchronize your iPad to nearly any content in its library. If you want a rich media and applications library on your iPad, you need to sync those contents from the library on your computer.

iTunes determines which app, music, and video files transfer to and load onto your iPad. You're about to discover how to bring all this content together in iTunes and send it to your iPad via the USB Dock Connector data cable. You'll see how to choose which items you want to synchronize and how to keep your iPad content fresh and up-to-date.

Working with iTunes

Before you begin to choose which songs, videos, podcasts, and audiobooks will be synchronized, you must first physically connect your iPad to your computer and launch the iTunes application. Use the USB cable that shipped with your iPad (or an equivalent dock) to connect your iPad to a spare USB port on your system. Launch iTunes by clicking the iTunes application icon on your computer. If your iPad uses a lock code, you must unlock your device before iTunes can connect to it (see Figure 2–1).

NOTE: It's best to connect using USB 2.0. USB 2.0 provides superior bandwidth and better connectivity. Although USB 1.1 is supported, iTunes will complain if you attempt to sync using USB 1.1 and will recommend that you switch to a USB 2.0 port. Your iPad generally will not be able to recharge while syncing. Do not be alarmed by the Not Charging message that appears at the right of your iPad's topmost status bar. Instead, use the 10-watt wall plug connector included in the iPad package to provide the power level your iPad needs to charge. Your iPad has a phenomenal onboard battery. You will find that, unlike other mobile devices, you need to recharge it only every day or two. Yes, you can sync more often, but you don't really have to if your only concern is to keep the charge ready for use.

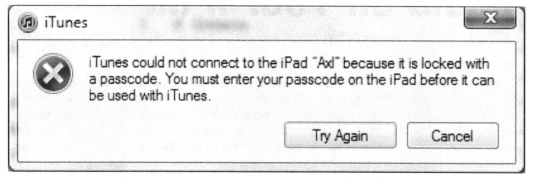

Figure 2–1. *iTunes prompts you to unlock your iPad before it will connect to the device.*

Once connected, your iPad appears in the list on the left side of the iTunes window. This light blue column, called the *source list*, is divided into several sections for your media library, the iTunes Store, devices, and playlists. The iPad, along with any other devices connected to your computer, is listed under the Devices header, as shown in Figure 2–2.

If you do not see your iPad in this list, make sure you've physically connected your iPad through the USB cable and that the cable is firmly inserted into both the computer and the iPad. Next, make sure your iPad is powered on. Your iPad is listed when it's active or asleep, but it won't show up when it's powered down. If your iPad is correctly connected and powered on but still does not appear, do a Google search for *disappearing iPads*. There are known (however occasional) support issues with iOS devices not appearing in iTunes. You will find that others have experienced the same problem, and you might be able to find a solution.

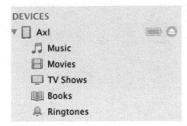

Figure 2–2. *Your iPad appears in the Devices section of the iTunes source list. The items listed under the device (which you can view by toggling the hide/reveal triangle to the left of the device name) will vary based on the items you have chosen to synchronize to your device. Notice how the image to the left of your iPad's name looks like a tiny iPad. In iTunes, device pictures look like the actual device in use.*

The iPad iTunes Settings Pane

When you select your iPad in the iTunes source list, you are presented with a settings pane that contains a series of tabs. These tabs allow you to customize the way your device connects to and synchronizes with your iTunes media. Each tab provides a different way to customize your iPad's contents, allowing you to set options associated with your iPad.

The tabs you'll see (from left to right) include Summary, Info, Apps, Music, Movies, TV Shows, Podcasts, iTunes U, Books, and Photos (see Figure 2–3). If you're already an iPhone or iPod touch user, the iPad settings pane will look very familiar, though it does have some options that are not available with the iPhone or iPod touch. If your iPad is your first Apple touch device, don't worry—you don't need any knowledge of the iPhone or iPod touch to navigate the tabs. You'll be up to speed after you read this chapter.

> **NOTE:** If you see a Ringtones tab in iTunes for your iPad, do not be alarmed. It sometimes shows up for devices that don't actually have telephony capabilities.

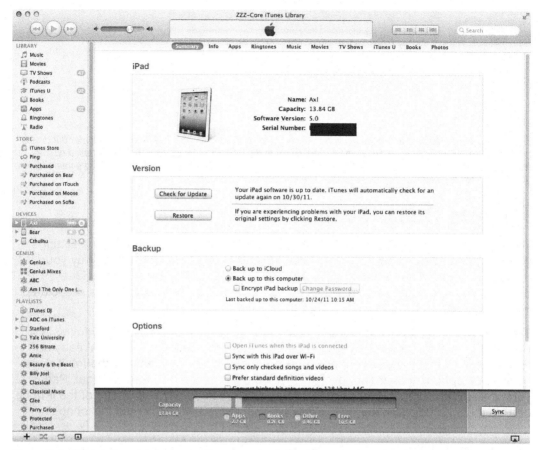

Figure 2–3. *iTunes allows you to manage the content loaded onto and synchronized with your iPad. Each tab running along the top of the settings pane offers a variety of controls, allowing you to choose what information gets loaded onto your iPad at each sync. The iPad figure in the top section of the Summary pane should match the model and color of your device.*

Running along the bottom of the iPad settings pane, you'll find a long, colorful Capacity bar (see Figure 2–4). This bar appears regardless of which tab you have selected. Your iPad's total storage capacity is shown on the left, and the amount of data you have on the iPad for different types of files is broken down into color-coded segments. Blue is for audio, purple is for video, orange is for photos, green is for apps, lighter purple-pink is for books, yellow is for other stuff (mostly data and the operating system), and gray is for the remaining free space you have on your iPad. The key just below the Capacity bar shows what each color segment represents and the amount of space occupied per category.

Figure 2–4. *The Capacity bar is a visual representation of the different types of files occupying space on your iPad.*

> **NOTE:** The Capacity bar breakdown is pretty self-explanatory. Still, some people are thrown by yellow—the color that represents "Other." What is "Other," exactly? This includes database files (which keep track of your music, video, and podcast libraries), which can be 100MB to 200MB in size; album artwork (which can be 500KB per track); and preference files for the applications you have on your iPad. Preference files let the apps remember in-app settings you've configured every time you launch them. If you store a lot of data inside your applications, the green Apps segment increases accordingly.

A Word on Syncing Your Data

iPad storage starts at just 16GB of data. Many of us have music or movie libraries that are far larger than even the greatest of the iPad's storage options. If you have a 16GB iPad and a 20GB music library, not only will you not be able to fit all your music, but, even if you settle for 16GB of your music library, you won't have room for photos, movies, books, or apps. Recognizing this reality, Apple devised the settings preferences to help you organize and select your most important data and bring it to the iPad. The following tabs that we discuss will help you select what to sync to your iPad.

> **NOTE:** Applications like Air Video, Dropbox, LogMeIn, and Air Sharing Pro provide ways to offload local storage to remote servers, letting you free up space on your iPad. Instead of synchronizing entire movies, Air Video streams media from your home computer to your iPad wherever you have an available Internet connection. Dropbox, LogMeIn, and Air Sharing Pro each let you transfer data to and from remote servers (Dropbox and Air Sharing Pro) or your home- or office-based desktop (LogMeIn and Air Sharing Pro).

Do note that although you most likely will not be able to fit all of your music, photos, and movies onto the iPad, you can easily change what you have on the iPad. For example, once you've watched a movie on your iPad, you can remove it and replace it with another one. Also, some files are larger than others. Movies are typically the largest and thus are good candidates for removal if you need space. Contacts, calendars, and book collections are all text-based files, and text takes up very little space, so don't worry about syncing all of these onto your iPad.

Where Do You Get Media From?

The iPad is a great leisure device for consuming media. But where do you get that media? The easiest and most direct way to get movies, music, TV shows, and books onto your iPad is through the iTunes Store on your computer (see Figure 2–5). In the iTunes Store you can buy music by the song or album, rent or purchase movies, download your favorite TV shows by the episode, or subscribe to a Season Pass and download free podcasts and iTunes U content.

Figure 2–5. *The iTunes Store is the world's largest music store. You can also download movies, TV shows, apps, podcasts, and books from it.*

You can also import music and movies from your own collections. Importing music from CDs is straightforward using iTunes, and importing video isn't hard either. One way to get movies onto your iPad is to rip them from your DVD collection.

> **NOTE:** *Ripping* a DVD means copying content from the disc into a format that's playable on other devices, including iPads. To load video from your DVDs onto your iPad, download a copy of HandBrake from http://handbrake.fr (for both Windows and Mac) and convert your DVD content to an iPad-friendly format. HandBrake is free and easy to use. Insert your DVD into your computer, run the application, and follow the directions in the program. After your movie has finished ripping, you can either add it to iTunes automatically (check your settings) or manually drag and drop it into iTunes.

To get applications, you must use the iTunes App Store. There's no other way to add new software items to your iPad. You can easily browse for apps from the desktop version of iTunes or in the dedicated App Store app on the iPad, which is covered further in Chapter 8.

You can build your iPad e-book library in a variety of ways. Perhaps the easiest is to buy titles through Apple's iBookstore (see Chapter 8 for details), which is part of Apple's free-to-download iBooks app. You can also take advantage of the more than 33,000 free e-books at Project Gutenberg (www.gutenberg.org) by downloading books to your downloads folder and then dragging them into iTunes. There are also many e-book stores and publishers that sell e-books directly online. For a good list of web sites that sell e-books, go to www.epubbooks.com/buy-epub-books.

iBooks also supports PDF files. You can purchase inexpensive PDF versions of popular titles from many vendors. Some publishers, like Baen Books, sell DRM-free PDF editions directly on their web site. Baen also offers an extensive free e-book collection (www.baen.com/library/) that's well worth checking out.

> **NOTE:** E-books come in many formats. The formats that are compatible with the iPad's iBooks app are ePub (offering fully interactive book features, including font resizing and page re-layouts) and PDF (with simple document display; what you get is what you see). Make sure when buying an e-book outside the iBookstore that it is in ePub or PDF format, or else you'll need to find another app that reads the format your e-book is in or use a converter such as Calibre (http://calibre-ebook.com). For example, books from Amazon's Kindle Store can be read on the iPad but not in the iBooks app. You need to download Amazon's free Kindle for iPad app (from the iTunes App Store) to read Kindle-formatted e-books purchased from Amazon.

Remember to Apply Your Changes

After you change iPad settings in iTunes via the settings pane (as described in the following sections), they do not become finalized until you click the gray Apply button to the right of the Capacity bar (see Figure 2–6). If you forget to click it, iTunes will automatically remind you before you navigate away from the iPad settings pane. If you make a change in the settings pane by mistake, simply click the Revert button that sits above the Apply button. Note that the Capacity bar will grow and shrink as you opt to add and subtract media; this happens before you sync, allowing you to monitor how much of your iPad's storage you'll be using once you commit the sync.

Figure 2–6. *The Revert and Apply buttons allow you to accept or negate any of the changes you have made in iTunes' iPad settings pane.*

The Tabs

The tabs (see Figure 2–7) running along the top of the iPad settings pane are how you navigate all your iPad settings. The tabs you'll use include Summary, Info, Apps, Music, Movies, TV Shows, Podcasts, iTunes U, Books, and Photos. To begin configuring the settings on any tab, just click the tab to select it.

Summary   Info   Apps   Music   Movies   TV Shows   Podcasts   iTunes U   Books   Photos

Figure 2–7. *Each setting tab offers a different way to control the way that iTunes synchronizes your iPad to your home media library.*

The Summary Tab

The Summary tab (see Figure 2–3) is the first tab you see in the iPad settings pane. It displays your iPad's overview, including the iPad's name, capacity, currently installed firmware version, and serial number. From this page, you can check for firmware updates; restore your iPad to a pristine, factory-installed condition; and set options to help you manage the way your data is backed up and synced. The page is broken up into several boxes: iPad, Version, Backup, and Options.

iPad Box

In this box, an image of your iPad is displayed along with its name, capacity, software version, and serial number, which are described in the following list. The iPad image should match the model and color of your device.

> *Name*: This is whatever name you have given your iPad. To rename it, click the iPad in the source list. This opens a text edit field around the name. Edit the name as desired (see Figure 2–8), and then press Return or Enter to confirm your change.

> *Capacity*: This number indicates the actual data capacity of your iPad. As with all data storage, the advertised capacity (16GB, for example) never quite matches the actual capacity (14.03GB).

NOTE: The difference between the actual data capacity and the advertised capacity is because the advertised capacity uses base 10; Apple and other manufacturers talk about a gigabyte as 1,000,000,000 bytes. In computer terms, this decimal number is worthless. Computers use base 2. To a computer, a gigabyte is 1,073,741,824 bytes, so the advertised 64,000,000,000 bytes for a 64GB iPad get cut down to about 59.6 computer-sized gigabytes. Add in some overhead for the operating system's file structure, and boom, you're down to those 59.42GB that your iTunes screen mentions for your 64GB iPad. All sorts of useless lawsuits have been filed over this issue throughout the years, and this is still the way things are done in the mass-storage industry.

Software Version: The iPad regularly updates its software with bug fixes and improvements. iTunes indicates which firmware release is currently installed on your iPad. Click Software Version to switch to the Build Version display, showing which firmware build you are using. As this book is being written, the latest iPad software is release 4.3.1, with build 8G4.

Serial Number: This unique serial number identifies your iPad to Apple. Click Serial Number to reveal your unit's unique device identifier (UDID).

TIP: Use the serial number to check your current warranty status at the Apple Self Solve web site (https://selfsolve.apple.com/GetWarranty.do). There, you can see whether you have properly registered your device, whether you have active telephone technical support service, whether you are covered for repairs and service, and the details about your AppleCare protection plan. If you have not yet signed up for AppleCare service for your new iPad, you can do so directly at the Self Solve site. It prompts you for billing information and processes your credit card payment. AppleCare extends your iPad coverage to two years from the purchase date of your hardware.

NOTE: You can use the UDID to register your iPad for certain developer beta tests (called *ad hoc builds*). Copy this value to memory via **Edit ➤ Copy** and then paste it into an e-mail to send your UDID to a developer. Although your UDID is not a particularly sensitive piece of information, you probably should not share it freely with others, just in case some as-yet-unknown exploit finds a use for UDIDs. Send it only to trusted developers, who will register it at Apple to enroll you in its ad hoc distribution program. Another, simpler, way to share your UDID with others is to download the free Ad Hoc Helper application from the App Store. You can get to the proper iTunes page by loading this URL into your web browser: http://itunes.apple.com/app/ad-hoc-helper/id285691333?mt=8.

In general, the only things that could change in the iPad box are your iPad's software version number and your iPad's name. When you perform a software update to the iPad, this field matches its new version number. This provides an easy way to determine what version of the iPad OS you are using. If you change the name of your iPad by clicking its name in the iTunes source list and then editing the text (see Figure 2–8), the Summary tab reflects that change. Your iPad's capacity and serial number will never change.

Figure 2–8. *Click your iPad's name in the iTunes source list to rename it to anything you want. The name change will be reflected on the Summary tab.*

Version Box

The Version box allows you to manually check for iPad OS software updates by clicking the Check for Update button. Next to the button you will see text notifying you whether your iPad software is up-to-date or an update is available. Sometimes iTunes will notify you that there is a software update available before you've even clicked the Check for Update button. It knows this because iTunes automatically checks for iPad OS updates once a week. The text next to the button also tells you when iTunes will next automatically check for an update.

> **NOTE:** If an iPad software update is available, you should install it. Sometimes updates provide new features; other times they provide simple bug fixes. Apple rigorously tests these updates before releasing them to the public, so it's safe to assume the updates will make your device better (whether you notice it or not). Confused between the Restore and Update options? Updates offer newly released firmware from Apple. Installing an update leaves your data and applications unchanged. Restoring your iPad returns it to a factory-fresh state, removing all apps and data.

Below the Check for Update button is the Restore button. You may experience problems with your iPad at some point and need to restore your unit to its factory-fresh settings. To do this, click the Restore button and follow the prompts (see Figure 2–9). Backing up your unit saves both your settings and your data to your computer. The restore process wipes all information from your iPad and reloads the most recent firmware. After restoring, use your backup data to reload your personal settings, contacts, bookmarks, and photos to your iPad.

You can, if needed, restore your iPad to a firmware version other than the current one. Select which iPad firmware to restore to by pressing the Shift key (on Windows) or Option key (on a Mac) while clicking the Check for Update button or the Restore button. iTunes opens a file dialog box in which you can navigate to the .ipsw file (which stands for iPad software; these files are actually renamed ZIP archives, which you can unzip and explore if you're so inclined) you want to use, select it, and perform your update or restoration.

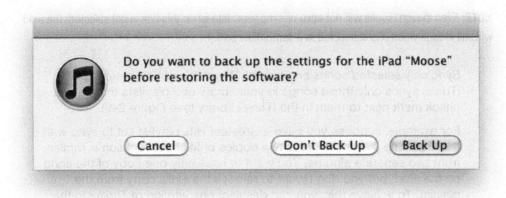

Figure 2–9. *After a restore, you'll have the option of putting back all your data on the iPad as it was before.*

Backup Box

This box allows you to choose how you want to back up your iPad system and application data. You can back up to Apple's iCloud or to the local computer. Apple offers 5GB of cloud storage for free. You can easily consume that with backed-up data, let alone with application cloud-based documents. Additional iCloud storage costs $20/year for 15GB total (including your free 5GB), $40/year for 25GB total, and $100/year for 50GB total.

If you back up to your computer instead of the cloud, you'll save a bit of space and potentially a bit of money. At the same time, you'll lose the "it just works" convenience of that backup. Also, if your computer dies for any reason, you will not have the off-site security of knowing your data is safe in the cloud. You'll need to tether your iPad to your computer and allow the backup to occur during a tethered sync.

You may want to encrypt your iPad backup by checking the "Encrypt iPad backup" option. This allows you to set a password for your backed data. Be aware, if you lose that password, your data will be gone. You cannot recover your password through e-mail.

Options Box

You have several preferences in the Options box. To enable or disable any of the features, simply select or deselect the check box next to it.

> *Open iTunes when this iPad is connected*: This option is selected by default. It tells your computer to open iTunes when it detects your iPad is connected via USB. If this option is deselected, iTunes will not open when you connect your iPad, and no data will be synced to your device until you manually open iTunes and click the Sync button next to the Capacity bar.

> **NOTE:** Even though iTunes will not open or sync your data when this box is not selected, the iPad will still charge when it is connected to a compatible port.

Sync only selected songs and videos: When this option is selected, iTunes syncs only those songs in your library and playlists that have a check mark next to them in the iTunes library (see Figure 2–9).

For example, suppose you have a Greatest Hits playlist set to sync with the iPad. The playlist includes two copies of Michael Jackson's *Thriller* from two separate albums. You want to have only one copy of the song on the iPad, but you don't want to remove the extra copy from the playlist. To achieve this, you can deselect one version of *Thriller* in the playlist and enable "Sync only selected songs and videos." The playlist will sync to your iPad minus the extra *Thriller*, but the alternative track will remain in your playlist and in your iTunes library.

Prefer standard definition videos: With this selected, iTunes will sync only the standard-definition version of a video to your iPad if you have both the high-definition and standard-definition versions. You sometimes get both versions when you buy a movie or TV show from the iTunes Store. Choosing to sync only the standard-definition version saves storage space on the iPad. HD is all the rage at the moment, and although the quality of HD video *is* superior to SD, if you use your iPad to watch videos only occasionally and not as your main video consumption device, you'll probably want to opt for the SD version. The quality is fine, and you'll be able to fit more video on your iPad for those long road trips.

Convert higher bit rate songs to 128 kbps AAC: Digital music comes in many formats and sizes, with the most popular being MP3 and AAC. Depending on how you obtained your music, whether by buying it from the iTunes Store or ripping it from old CDs, your songs will likely have different encoding settings. A song encoded at 256KBps takes up twice the space as a song encoded at 128KBps. With the "Convert higher bit rate songs to 128 kbps AAC" option selected, any music synced to your iPad will be converted on the fly to 128KBps AAC files. This saves a lot of space on your iPad by reducing higher bit rate songs to a perfectly acceptable 128KBps.

> **NOTE:** Unless you are an extreme audiophile with a gifted ear, you likely will not notice a difference between a 128KBps AAC file and a 256KBps version of that file.

TIP: If you have an iPhone or iPod touch that you frequently carry around with you, you may want to opt to not put any music on your iPad at all. You'll save a lot of space, and you'll always have your music with you on your other device. Use that extra space on your iPad to fill it with video and books, taking advantage of the iPad's relatively large screen.

Manually manage music and videos: With this option selected, music and videos aren't automatically synced with your iPad. You choose exactly which items you want on your iPad by dragging the songs or videos from the iTunes library onto the iPad in the iTunes source list. You manage those songs and videos by clicking the drop-down triangle next to the iPad in the iTunes source list. To remove a song or video file, you navigate to your music, movies, or TV shows playlist, select the song or video file, and press the Delete key on your computer's keyboard.

NOTE: Manually adding music or video to or removing it from your iPad does not affect the files on your computer. Whenever a file is added to or deleted from the iPad, it is just a copy of the file in your iTunes library. The original file will always reside in your iTunes library until you delete it from there.

Encrypt iPad backup: Each time your iPad syncs with iTunes, a backup of all the files and settings on your iPad is created. This backup is handy if you ever need to restore your iPad. Once the restore is complete and you've synced your iPad to iTunes again, you have the option of restoring the iPad from this backup, which, once completed, will enable you to retain all your old settings and files on your newly restored iPad.

With the "Encrypt iPad backup" option selected, your backups, and thus all your data, are encrypted and protected by a password. To back up from an encrypted data file, the user must know the password to the file. Next to this selection is a Change Password button. This allows you to change the password to your encrypted data at any time.

NOTE: Do not forget your password! If you encrypt your backups and forget your password, you will not be able to restore your backup data. You will have to resync all your data from scratch. You'll also have to reconfigure all the settings on your iPad to the way you had them, including rearranging the iPad's app icons. If you have lots of custom settings on your iPad, this can take a long time. Remember your passwords!

Configure Universal Access: The last thing you will see on the Summary page is a Configure Universal Access button. Clicking this button opens a Universal Access box (see Figure 2–10) that allows you to set seeing and hearing device assistance options for people who are hard of sight or hearing. The options are as follows (only one of the three Seeing radio buttons can be selected):

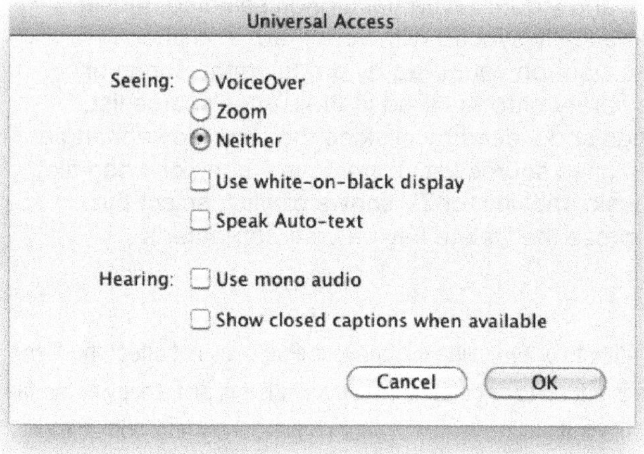

Figure 2–10. *The Universal Access settings*

- *Voice Over*: Makes your iPad speak its interface, saying the names of buttons, reading the contents of text fields, and otherwise describing on-screen elements in a way that transforms a visual presentation into a spoken description.

- *Zoom*: Allows the user to magnify portions of the screen that normally don't support a built-in zoom function. When this option is selected, the user can double tap any part of the iPad's screen with three fingers to automatically zoom in 200 percent. When zoomed in, the user must drag or flick the screen with three fingers. When the user navigates to a new screen, zoom always returns to the top middle of the screen.

Use white-on-black display: Selecting this option will invert the colors of the iPad's screen so text appears white on a black background. The iPad's entire screen will look like a photograph negative, providing greater contrast for visually challenged users.

Speak Auto-text: With this option selected, any autocorrection text (such as the spell-check pop-ups that appear when you are typing) is spoken aloud to the user.

Add contacts created outside of groups on this iPad to: When this check box is selected, you'll have access to a drop-down list of all your address book groups. If you create a new contact on your iPad and don't assign the contact to a group, that contact will be automatically put in the group you select here.

Sync Yahoo! Address Book contacts: When this check box is selected, you can automatically sync your Yahoo! Address Book contacts with your iPad address book. You first have to agree to the pop-up box that asks you to acknowledge you are allowing your iPad to sync to your Yahoo! account. Next, you are prompted to enter your Yahoo! ID and password. Once you've done this, your contacts are set to sync. Clicking the Configure button will allow you to enter a different Yahoo! ID.

Sync Google Contacts: When this check box is selected, you can automatically sync your Google contacts with your iPad address book. You first have to agree to the pop-up box that asks you to acknowledge you are allowing your iPad to sync to your Google account. Next, you are prompted to enter your Google ID and password. Once you've done this, your contacts are set to sync. Clicking the Configure button will allow you to enter a different Google ID.

Sync iCal Calendars

To sync your calendars, you need to be using one of the following: iCal or Microsoft Entourage on a Mac, or Microsoft Outlook on a Windows computer.

To sync your calendars, select the Sync iCal Calendars check box (see Figure 2–11). Just like with contacts, you then have the option of syncing all your calendars or just selected ones.

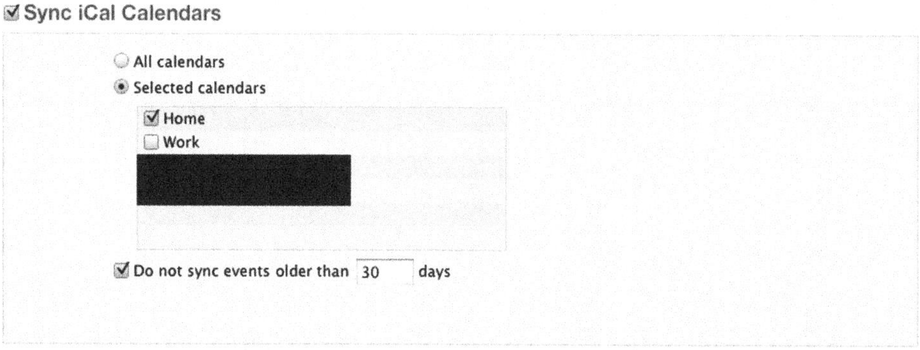

Figure 2–11. *Your calendar syncing options*

If you check the "Do not sync events older than" check box, iTunes does not synchronize events that are more than a certain number of days old. The default number of days is 30, but you can enter anything up to 99,999 days.

NOTE: A great place to find premade calendars for holidays, school events, or your favorite sporting teams is at www.icalshare.com.

Sync Mail Accounts

Each mail account you have set up in Mac OS X's Mail or Microsoft's Outlook appears here (see Figure 2–12). After you select the Sync Mail Accounts check box, you have the option of selecting or deselecting any account. Accounts not selected will not appear in the iPad's Mail app. This option does not sync your mail messages, just the account settings.

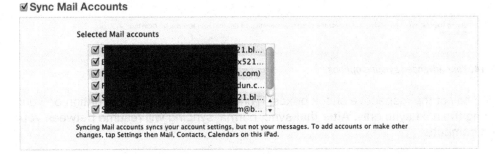

Figure 2–12. *Your e-mail account syncing options*

Other

Apple should really have named this section "Bookmark and Notes Syncing," but it opted for "Other." Here you can sync your web bookmarks from your browser on your computer to the Safari web browser on your iPad (see Figure 2–13). Again, if you have an iCloud account, your bookmarks will be synced over the air. If not, select the Sync Bookmarks check box, and if applicable, choose your browser from the drop-down menu. On the Mac, bookmark syncing supports Safari. On a Windows computer, bookmark syncing supports Safari and Microsoft Internet Explorer.

Other

- ☐ Sync Safari bookmarks
- ☐ Sync notes

Figure 2–13. *Your bookmarks and notes syncing options*

This section also allows you to sync your notes to your iPad. Note syncing works only with the Mac OS X Mail application or, on a Windows machine, Microsoft Outlook. To enable note syncing, select the check box.

Advanced

This section allows you to replace your contacts, calendars, mail accounts, bookmarks, and notes on the iPad with information from your computer (see Figure 2–14). This is a handy feature if your information gets out of sync and you want to make sure that everything you see on your computer matches with what's on the iPad.

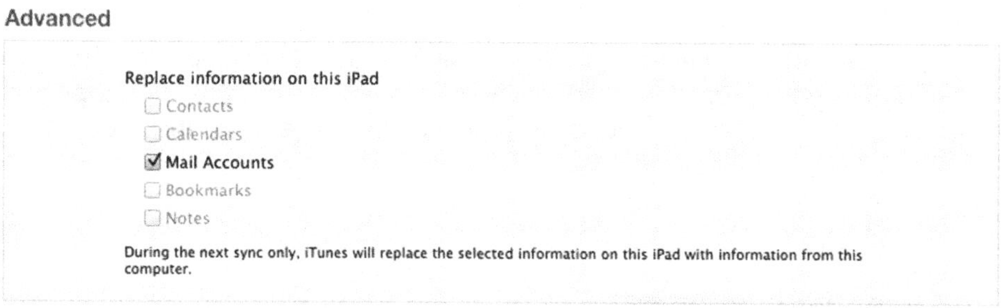

Advanced

Replace information on this iPad
☐ Contacts
☐ Calendars
☑ Mail Accounts
☐ Bookmarks
☐ Notes

During the next sync only, iTunes will replace the selected information on this iPad with information from this computer.

Figure 2–14. *Your advanced syncing options*

When you select the respective check boxes, iTunes will replace the information on your iPad during the next sync only. After that sync, normal syncing will resume between your iPad and computer.

> **NOTE:** If your calendars and contacts are being synced via iCloud, you will not be able to select their check boxes in the Advanced section.

The Apps Tab

This tab is the place where you get to decide which apps you want to put on your iPad and allows you to arrange them with drag-and-drop simplicity. This tab is composed of two main sections: Sync Apps and File Sharing.

Sync Apps

Under the Sync Apps heading, shown in Figure 2–15, you'll see a scrollable list of all the applications you have in your apps library in iTunes. You can sort the list by name, by kind, by size, by category, or by date downloaded.

In the apps list, you'll see a check box on the left of each app's icon. To the right of each icon is the app's name, and below that are the app's category listing and the file size of the individual application. Any app that has a selected check box means the app is set to sync with the iPad.

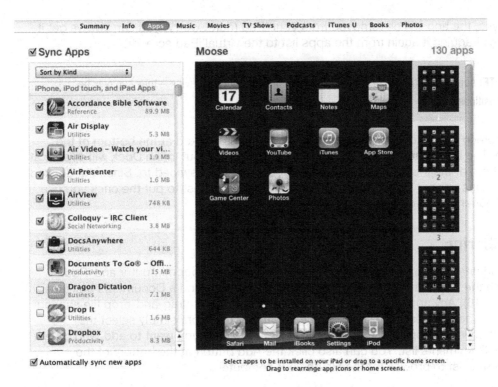

Figure 2–15. *The Apps tab is where you choose what apps to put on your iPad and in what order to arrange them in.*

> **NOTE:** Whenever you download a new app in iTunes, it will automatically sync with your iPad on the next sync. You can, of course, simply remove the app after the sync or deselect the "Automatically sync new apps" option shown in Figure 2–15.

Next to the apps list you'll see a visual representation of your iPad desktop, and next to that you'll see one or more black screens with icons that are already on, or set to be synced with, your iPad. You'll also see a completely gray screen below the last black one.

The easiest way to get apps on your iPad is to find them in the apps list and simply drag them onto the virtual iPad screen. As soon as you do, the app's check box is automatically selected in the apps list.

You can drag around the apps on your virtual iPad screen until you've arranged them in the order you like. You can also grab the smaller black screens and move them up or down in the list, rearranging entire pages of apps on your iPad. The black screen at the top of the list will be the home page on your iPad, and each one below that will be a subsequent swipe away. The gray screen at the bottom is an extra screen that you can use to create a new screen with apps.

To remove an app, simply hover the mouse over the app, and you'll see a little X appear in the upper-left corner. Click the X, and the app disappears from the screen. On the next sync, the app will be removed from your iPad (don't worry, you can always get it back by dragging it again from the apps list to the virtual iPad screen).

> **NOTE:** Apps shipped with the iPad cannot be removed from the device—they can only be repositioned.

Each screen can hold 20 apps in addition to the ones docked at the bottom of the screen. The Dock can hold up to six apps. Any apps you put in the Dock will appear at the bottom of the iPad no matter what app screen you've swiped to. Since the docked apps always appear at the bottom of any app page, it's best to put the ones you use most frequently down there for quick access.

File Sharing

The iPad introduced an easy way to share files between your computer and iPad. Beneath the File Sharing heading you'll see an Apps box and a Documents box (see Figure 2–16). Any apps currently on your iPad that support drag-and-drop file sharing appear in the Apps list here. To get a file into the application, simply select the application in the Apps list, find on your computer the file you want to add, and drag it into the Documents list. You can also click the Add button at the bottom of the Documents list to browse for the file on your computer.

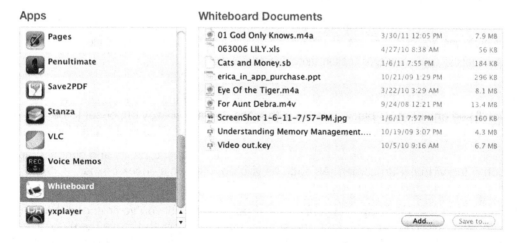

Figure 2–16. *Apps that support drag-and-drop file sharing and their enclosed documents*

If you've created a completely new file on your iPad, say in Apple's text editor Pages, and want to transfer that file to your computer, select the file in the Documents list, click the "Save to…" button below the list, and choose where on your computer you want to save the file. Alternately, you can simply drag the file from the Documents list to your desktop.

To delete a file from the app that contains it, select the file in the Documents list and press the Delete key on your keyboard. A pop-up window appears asking if you really want to delete the file. Click Delete to complete the deletion.

As long as a file is shared inside an app, that file is always backed up as part of app backups when you sync your iPad to your computer.

> **NOTE:** Just because you can drag a file to an app's document box doesn't mean the app can open it. Apps are limited to working with files that the iPad supports. For example, the iPad does not natively support Microsoft's WMV video files. If you drag a WMV movie to an app, the app will contain it but will still not be able to play it unless support is built into that application itself. Pages wouldn't be able to open a movie document, for instance.

Synchronization Options

In each of the remaining tabs, iTunes offers a primary check box allowing you to sync items. You can sync music, movies, TV shows, podcasts, iTunes U classes, books, and photos. For the first four of these, you'll be given the option to synchronize items automatically.

To choose that automatic option, check the appropriate box in each tab (Sync Music, Sync Movies, and so on), check the automatic box ("Automatically include"), and then choose how you want iTunes to select those items.

> *Recent items*: Select some number of recently added items (typically 1, 3, 5, 10, or all) to synchronize to your iPad.

> *Unplayed or unwatched items*: When this is selected, you can choose from all unplayed/unwatched items or some. Pick some number of the most recent selections or, if you want to catch up with media that's been sitting around for a while, the least recent unplayed selections.

> *New items*: These work in much the same way as unplayed items in that you can pick a certain number of items. The difference between new and unplayed/unwatched is that an item is considered "unplayed" (or "unwatched") until it's been fully listened to or watched. After that, it is played/watched. New means the item has never been accessed at all. This ensures the material synced to your iPad is completely fresh.

Further automatic options allow you to decide whether these choices are selected from the entire collection or from selected items. This varies by tab.

To choose items manually, uncheck the "Automatically include" option and use the on-screen selection elements for each tab to pick which items you want to synchronize to your iPad.

The Music Tab

The Music tab is essentially self-explanatory (see Figure 2–17). Ensure the Sync Music check box is selected at the top. In the box below it, you will see two radio buttons and several check boxes.

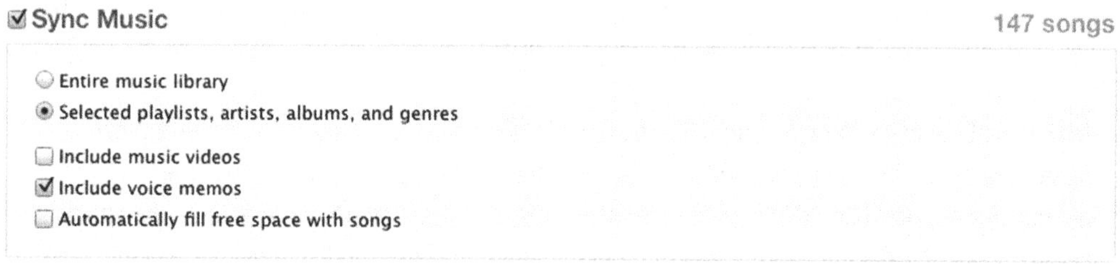

☑ Sync Music   147 songs

○ Entire music library
◉ Selected playlists, artists, albums, and genres

☐ Include music videos
☑ Include voice memos
☐ Automatically fill free space with songs

Figure 2–17. *The Music tab allows you to select which playlists, artists, albums, and genres you want to sync to your iPad.*

Entire music library: When this option is selected, your entire music library will be synced to your iPad, but only if you have the storage space available on your iPad. If you have more music than iPad storage capacity, the remainder of the music will stop syncing once the iPad is full.

Selected playlists, artists, albums, and genres: If you select this option, you will see four boxes appear listing all the playlists, artists, albums, and genres you have in your iTunes library (see Figure 2–18). Go through and select the check boxes of the playlists, artists, albums, and genres you want on your iPad.

Include music videos: If you select this check box, any music videos associated with playlists, artists, albums, or genres will be transferred to the iPad.

Include voice memos: If you select this check box, any voice memos you have stored in your iTunes library will sync with your iPad.

Automatically fill free space with songs: This check box appears only if you've selected the "Selected playlists, artists, albums, and genres" radio button. If selected, once all your other files (movies, books, photos, and so on) have been synced to your iPad, any leftover free space will be filled with music until your iPad can't fit anything else on it. We don't recommend selecting this option. It severely limits your ability to create any new documents on your iPad since it won't have any space left to store them. This is a feature better suited to the music-based iPod touch than the application-centric iPad.

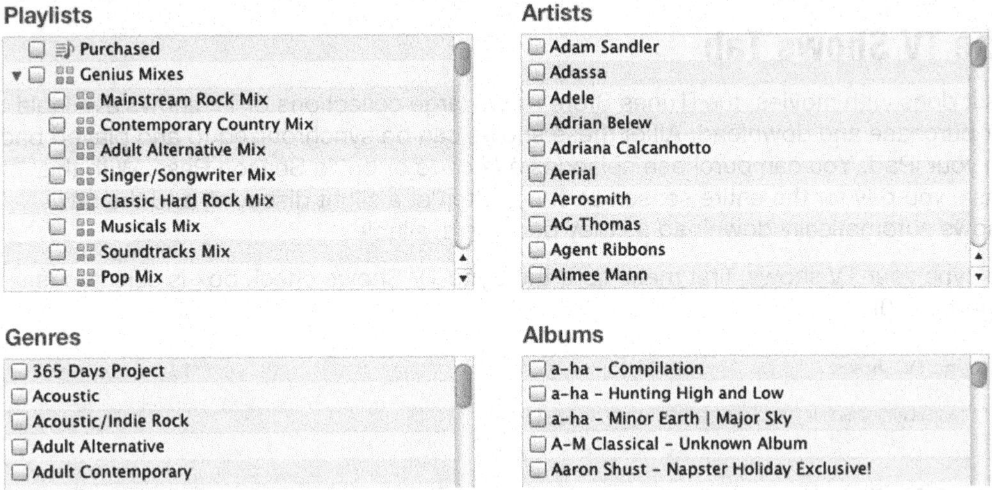

Playlists
Purchased
Genius Mixes
Mainstream Rock Mix
Contemporary Country Mix
Adult Alternative Mix
Singer/Songwriter Mix
Classic Hard Rock Mix
Musicals Mix
Soundtracks Mix
Pop Mix
Artists
Adam Sandler
Adassa
Adele
Adrian Belew
Adriana Calcanhotto
Aerial
Aerosmith
AG Thomas
Agent Ribbons
Aimee Mann
Genres
365 Days Project
Acoustic
Acoustic/Indie Rock
Adult Alternative
Adult Contemporary
Albums
a-ha - Compilation
a-ha - Hunting High and Low
a-ha - Minor Earth | Major Sky
A-M Classical - Unknown Album
Aaron Shust - Napster Holiday Exclusive!

Figure 2–18. ***Select the playlists, artists, albums, and genres you want to sync with your iPad.***

The Movies Tab

The iTunes Store offers a large collection of movies available for rent or purchase that you can download and sync to your iPad. The Movies tab, shown in Figure 2–19, gives you several ways of getting your movies onto the iPad.

Summary
Info
Apps
Music
Movies
TV Shows
Podcasts
iTunes U
Books
Photos
Sync Movies
2 movies
Automatically include
all
movies

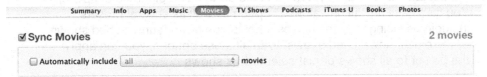

Figure 2–19. ***The Movies tab allows you to select which movies you want to sync to your iPad.***

To sync your movies, first make sure the Sync Movies check box is selected. You'll see a check box on the Movies tab. If you leave this check box empty, iTunes will not synchronize movie content to your iPad:

> *Automatically include ... movies*: If this check box is selected, you'll be able to access a drop-down list of preset options to make your movie syncing experience easier. From the drop-down list, you can select to sync all your movies (not a good idea, because one hour of video can take up to half a gigabyte of space); or, if you'd like to go the space-saving route, select the 1, 3, 5, or 10 "most recent movies" preset. You also have the option of selecting the "all unwatched" movies preset, which will add all the movies in your library that you have not watched yet. Other preset options include syncing 1, 3, 5, or 10 of your "most recent unwatched movies" or 1, 3, 5, or 10 of your "least recent unwatched movies."

The TV Shows Tab

As it does with movies, the iTunes Store offers large collections of TV shows available for purchase and download. All of these shows can be synchronized to and played back on your iPad. You can purchase episodes *à la carte* or buy a Season Pass. With this pass, you pay for the entire season at once, often at a slight discount, and the new shows automatically download as they become available.

To sync your TV shows, first make sure the Sync TV Shows check box is selected (see Figure 2–20).

☑ **Sync TV Shows**   1 episode

☐ **Automatically include** [all unwatched   ‡] **episodes of** [all shows   ‡]

Figure 2–20. *The TV Shows tab allows you to select which shows you want to sync to your iPad.*

The following options appear on the TV Shows tab:

> *Automatically include … episodes of …*: If this check box is selected, you'll be able to access a drop-down list of preset options to make your TV show syncing experience easier. From the drop-down lists you can select to sync all your TV shows (again, not a good idea if you have a lot, because one hour of video can take up to half a gigabyte of space). You also have an "all unwatched" option as well as several presets, including syncing only the newest shows, the newest unwatched shows, or the oldest unwatched shows. With all these options, you can apply the preset to all shows or just selected TV shows.

> *The Shows and Episodes boxes*: If the "Automatically include" check box is selected and set to anything but "all," you also have the option of selecting additional TV shows from your iTunes library in these boxes (see Figure 2–21). With the "Automatically include" check box deselected, you'll be able to manually select as many or as few of your TV shows as you want in these boxes.

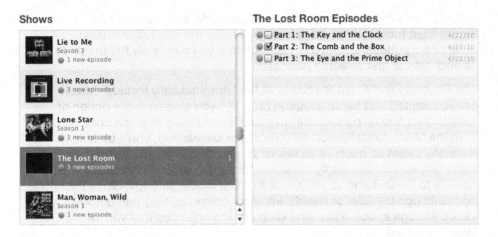

Figure 2–21. *The Shows box allows you to select TV series to sync to your iPad. In the Episodes box to the right, you can select which episodes of the series to sync.*

The Podcasts Tab

Many people use iTunes to subscribe to their favorite podcasts. *Podcasts* are audio programs delivered over the Internet, much as TV shows are delivered over the airways. Numerous podcasts are available these days, including entertainment, advice, how-to shows, and much more. iTunes monitors your podcast subscriptions and can automatically download new shows when they become available. The Podcasts tab lets you control which shows are synchronized to your iPad.

The Podcasts tab, as shown in Figure 2–22, has a similar look and feel as the Movies and TV Shows tabs.

Figure 2–22. *The Podcasts tab allows you to select which podcasts you want to sync to your iPad.*

To sync your podcasts, first make sure the Sync Podcasts check box is selected. You'll find these items on the Podcasts tab:

> *Automatically include ... episodes of ...*: If this check box is selected, you'll be able to access drop-down lists of preset options to make your podcasts syncing experience easier. From the right drop-down list, you can select to sync all your podcasts or selected items. Syncing all your podcasts won't take up as much room as syncing all your movies or all your TV shows will if the podcasts in question are audio-only. However, if you are downloading video podcasts, the same space requirements apply as with movies. In addition to the "all"/"selected" option, the left drop-down offers "all unplayed" and "all new" options as well as several

presets, including syncing only the newest podcasts, only the most recent/least recent unplayed podcasts, or only the most recent/least recent new podcasts. With all these options, you can apply the preset to all podcasts or just selected podcasts.

The Podcasts and Episodes boxes: If the "Automatically include" check box is selected and set to anything but "all," you also have the option of selecting additional podcasts from your iTunes library in these boxes. With the "Automatically include" check box unselected, you'll be able to manually select as many or as few of your podcasts as you want in these boxes. You can apply the same "five most recent" and similar options to these items as you can with other media settings. Since many podcasts update daily or weekly with new episodes, they can quickly eat up storage space. Plus, why keep around episodes that you've already listened to?

The iTunes U Tab

iTunes U is a free service offered by Apple and a wide range of educational institutions to disseminate educational tools such as class lectures and language courses. iTunes U operates much like podcasts, and getting them onto your iPad works in a similar way.

To sync your iTunes U items, first make sure the Sync iTunes U check box is selected (see Figure 2–23).

Figure 2–23. *The iTunes U tab allows you to select which iTunes U collections you want to sync to your iPad.*

You'll find these items on the iTunes U tab:

Automatically include… items of …: When this check box is selected, you'll be able to access drop-down lists of preset options to make your iTunes U syncing experience easier. From the right drop-down list you can choose to sync all your iTunes U items or selected items. In addition to the "all" option, the left drop-down offers "all unplayed" and "all new" options as well as several presets, including syncing only the newest iTunes U items, the most recent/least recent unplayed items, or the most recent/least recent new items. With all these options you can apply the preset to all items or just selected items.

The Collections and Items boxes: If the "Automatically include" check box is selected and set to anything but "all," you also have the option of selecting additional items from your iTunes library in these boxes. With the "Automatically include" check box deselected, you'll be able to manually select as many or as few of your iTunes U lessons as you want in these boxes.

The Books Tab

One of the big features of the iPad is the ability to buy and read e-books in the new iBooks app. You'll delve into the iBookstore and the iBooks app in Chapters 8 and 9, respectively; for now all you need to know is that the Books tab in the iPad settings pane is where you control what books get synced to your iPad (see Figure 2-24).

Make sure the Sync Books check box is selected at the top. In the box below it, you will see two radio buttons. "All books" syncs every book in your iTunes library. "Selected books" allows you to sync only the books you choose in the Books box further down the page.

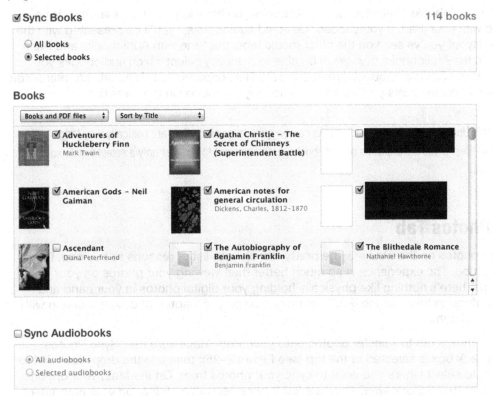

Figure 2-24. *The Books tab allows you to select which books you want to sync to your iPad.*

> **NOTE:** Even if you have 300 books in your iTunes library, you might as well sync them all. An e-book takes up hardly any space. As a matter of fact, *War and Peace*, one of the largest books out there (and also one of the greatest), takes up only 1.2MB of disk space. That's more than 50 percent less than a single 128KBps AAC music file. Of course, illustrated books will take up more space, but even then they still shouldn't take any more room than a few MP3s would. Don't worry about a cluttered library, either. You'll learn how to organize your books in Chapter 9.

Below the Books box you will see a Sync Audiobooks check box (see Figure 2–24). Again, there are two options: "All audiobooks" or "Selected audiobooks."

With "All audiobooks" selected, any audiobooks you have in your iTunes library will be synced with your iPad. If you choose "Selected audiobooks," you'll be presented with the familiar layout you've seen on the other media tabs, this time with Audiobooks and Parts boxes. In the Audiobooks box, you'll be able to manually select which audiobooks you want to sync. Some audiobooks have separate files, or *parts*, that designate chapters. You can select only the parts you want to sync for any audiobook in the Parts box.

> **NOTE:** Unlike with e-books, audiobooks can be quite large since they are basically very long audio files. If you have dozens of audiobooks, you may want to transfer only a select few to save space.

The Photos Tab

Viewing photos on the iPad may be pretty low on your list of reasons to buy one, but it shouldn't be. The experience is so much better than viewing your photos on your desktop. There's nothing like physically holding your digital photos in your hand and swiping through them on the iPad's gorgeous display. (Chapter 13 covers working with photos in depth.)

Use the Photos tab to transfer photos onto your iPad. Make sure the "Sync Photos from" check box is selected at the top (see Figure 2–25); then use the drop-down list to the right to select where you want to sync your photos from. On the Mac, your options will be iPhoto 4.0.3 or newer, Aperture 3.0.2 or newer, or any folder on your computer. On a Windows machine, your options will include Adobe Photoshop Elements 3.0 or newer or any folder on your computer.

Figure 2–25. *The Photos tab allows you to select which photos you want to sync to your iPad.*

the Devices icon. Click the Devices icon (it looks like an iPhone), and you'll be presented with the Devices settings pane, as shown in Figure 2–26.

Figure 2–26. *The iTunes Devices settings pane*

Here you'll find settings for devices that interact with iTunes. These devices can include iPads, iPods, iPhones, and AirPort Express devices.

> *Device backups*: Any time you sync your iPad, iTunes creates a backup of its contents. Any backup of iPods, iPhones, or iPads can be seen here. You'll see the name of the device along with the date it was last backed up. Hover your mouse over the name of the iPad to be presented with its serial number.
>
> iTunes keeps multiple device backups at a time, but you can choose a backup to restore from by selecting a device in the source list and right-clicking (Ctrl-clicking) it. Choose Restore from Backup and select the backup you want to restore from. iTunes places backup files in the following locations:
>
> - *Mac*: ~/Library/Application Support/MobileSync/Backup/ (Use the Option key when choosing Finder's Go menu to access your Library.)

- *Windows XP*: \Documents and
  Settings\(username)\Application Data\
  Apple Computer\MobileSync\Backup\

- *Windows Vista and Windows 7*:
  \Users\(username)\AppData\Roaming\Apple Computer\
  MobileSync\Backup\

The list of information iTunes backs up is a long one:

- Safari bookmarks, cookies, history, and currently open pages

- Map bookmarks, recent searches, and the current location
  displayed in Maps

- Application settings, preferences, and data

- Contacts

- Calendars

- CalDAV and subscribed calendar accounts

- YouTube favorites

- Wallpapers

- Notes

- Mail accounts

- Autocorrect dictionaries

- Camera roll

- Home screen layout and web clips

- Network settings (saved Wi-Fi hotspots, VPN settings, network
  preferences)

- Paired Bluetooth devices (which can be used only if restored to
  the same iPad that did the backup)

- Keychain (This includes e-mail account passwords, Wi-Fi
  passwords, and passwords you enter into web sites and some
  other applications. The keychain can be restored only from
  backup to the same iPad. If you are restoring to a new device,
  you will need to fill in these passwords again.)

- Managed configurations/profiles

- MobileMe and Microsoft Exchange account configurations

- App Store application data (except the application itself, its tmp
  and Caches folders)

- Per-app preferences allowing use of location services

- Offline web application cache/database
- Autofill for web pages
- Trusted hosts that have certificates that cannot be verified
- Web sites approved to get the location of the device
- Most (although not all) in-app purchases

To delete an iPad backup, select the backup from the Device backups list and click the Delete Backup button. Confirm the deletion by clicking the Delete Backup button in the window that pops up.

Prevent iPods, iPhones, and iPads from syncing automatically: Select this box if you want to disable automatic syncing when you plug your iPad into your computer. To sync, you'll need to manually click the Sync button at the bottom of the iPad's iTunes settings pane.

The only other option relevant to the iPad in the Devices settings pane is the "Look for iPod touch, iPhone, and iPad Remotes" check box, which is not shown in Figure 2–26. Apple makes an iPhone app called Remote. This app allows you to use your iPod touch, iPhone, or iPad as a remote control for your home computer's music library. In other words, you can be sitting on your couch and navigating your entire iTunes library on your Mac or Windows computer (or Apple TV) right from your iPad. All you need is the free Remote app, the iPad, and your computer to be on the same Wi-Fi network. If this box is deselected, your iPad will not be able to pair with your iTunes library. Clicking the Forget All Remotes button will make iTunes unpair with every iPod touch, iPhone, or iPad that it allowed to be used as a remote.

Restoring

If you are ever experiencing problems with your iPad, you can choose to restore it. iTunes offers two options of restoring your unit: restore to the factory defaults or restore from a backup. The factory default method will restore your iPad to its original factory settings—as if you've just turned it on for the first time. Restoring from backup will restore the iPad from its last saved backup file.

To restore to factory settings, in iTunes on your computer select the iPad from the Devices list, select the Summary tab, and click Restore (this deletes all the data on the iPad and restores it to the factory settings). When prompted by iTunes, select the option to restore your settings.

To restore from backup, in iTunes on your computer right-click (or Ctrl-click) on the iPad in the Devices list, choose Restore from Backup, and select a backup to restore from. The iPad will then be restored from the backup listed in the Device backups list.

NOTE: If you've set up password encryption on your iPad backups (discussed earlier in this chapter), you will not be able to restore from the encrypted backup if you forget the password. Be sure to write it down!

Summary

In this chapter, you've explored the options you have for syncing your media and data with your iPad. You've discovered where to get your media and how to make sure your iPad/iTunes sync preferences stick. To wind things up, here is a quick overview of some key points from this chapter:

- The way your iPad connects with iTunes and the settings pane you are presented with will be familiar to you if you've used an iPhone or iPod touch; however, there are some important differences with the iPad.

- The Capacity bar will always be visible in the iPad settings pane and is an easy indicator to see how much space you have left on your iPad.

- No change you make to your iPad setting pane is complete until you click the Apply button. Likewise, if you accidentally make a change you don't want, you can always click the Revert button.

- It is important to manage what data you sync with your iPad. If you sync all your music, you might not have room left over for syncing your photos and videos.

- Syncing apps can be fun and easy using the visual representation of your iPad on the Apps tab. However, sometimes app syncing can be a slow process if you have a lot of apps. Waiting can be a pain, but it's best never to interrupt a sync.

- Syncing your movies, music, TV shows, podcasts, iTunes U items, books, and photos is pretty straightforward, and once you've mastered how to sync one form of media, syncing the rest of the forms is easy.

- iCloud offers mobile sync of photos via Photo Stream.

Exploring the iPad Hardware

Now that you've purchased your iPad and have had a chance to sync it with iTunes, it's time to get a bit more familiar with the actual hardware. In this chapter, we'll talk about the various hardware controls on your iPad and how to use them. We'll discuss the care and maintenance requirements of your new device, and we'll explore the details of some of the more widely used Apple accessories for iPad. Grab that iPad, any Apple accessories you may have purchased, and perhaps a refreshing beverage, and let's take a quick tour of the hardware.

The Bits and Pieces of an iPad

In Chapter 1, you were briefly introduced to the names and locations of some of the switches and ports that decorate the outside of your iPad. In this chapter, we explain *how* those switches and ports are used.

On/Off Sleep/Wake Button

On the top-right corner of the iPad is one of the more important buttons on this little slab of glass and aluminum: the On/Off Sleep/Wake button (see Figure 3–1). That's kind of an odd name for a button, but it describes the function quite clearly.

When your iPad has been totally powered down, you'll need to press and hold this button for two or three seconds to turn it back on. A white Apple logo will appear, followed shortly by either the Home screen of your iPad or the Passcode Lock screen.

Figure 3–1. *The Sleep/Wake button is used for powering the iPad on or off and for putting it to sleep when it's not being used.*

If you don't plan on using your iPad for a few hours, you have your choice of either waiting for it to automatically lock and go to sleep (if that option has been turned on in Settings) or manually putting it to sleep. To do the latter, give the button a quick, firm press, and the screen goes dark. When the sound on your iPad is turned up, you'll even hear a click as an audible verification that the device has been put to sleep.

You can wake up the iPad either by giving the On/Off Sleep/Wake button another quick press or by pressing the Home button. Once again, if you have enabled a passcode lock, you need to enter that passcode correctly before you can use the iPad.

Occasionally, you may want to shut off your iPad completely. This means, of course, that it won't be magically picking up e-mail, waking to display alarms, or doing anything else. It will be totally shut down. This is handy when you're not going to be using the iPad for a long time (for example, you leave it home while on a trip) and don't want the battery to drain.

To shut off the iPad, simply hold down the On/Off Sleep/Wake button for about five seconds. The iPad will display a black screen with a Cancel button at the bottom in case you really don't want to shut it off and a red button near the top labeled "Slide to power off." Sliding your button to the right with your finger shuts off power to the device.

This trick can be useful on those rare occasions where an iPad app simply won't respond to your touch and the entire device is locked up. To turn it back on, press the On/Off Sleep/Wake button one more time.

With an iPad 2 adorned with a Smart Cover, there's another way to sleep and wake the iPad: just open the Smart Cover to wake the iPad, or close it to put it back to sleep.

Mute/Screen Rotation Lock

Moving to the right side of the iPad (as oriented with the Home button and Dock Connector port at the bottom and the screen facing you), the next switch is the mute/screen rotation lock (see Figure 3–2). The name of this switch describes the two functions it performs; by default, it is used to mute the iPad, turning the sound on the device completely off. But the mute/screen rotation lock switch can also be used to keep your iPad's screen from changing orientation.

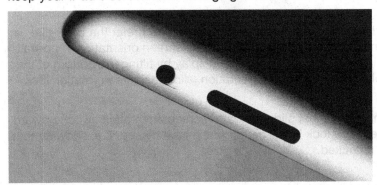

Figure 3–2. *The mute/screen rotation lock (the small switch) and the volume toggle (the larger button)*

When the button is used to mute your iPad, moving the switch from the top position to the bottom turns off the sound on the device and briefly displays a mute icon (see Figure 3–3) on the iPad screen to signify that the sound has been turned off. Muting your iPad can be very useful if you're trying to play Angry Birds while attending an important meeting.

Figure 3–3. *When you flip the mute/screen orientation switch to the down position, this mute icon displays.*

New iPad users can sometimes get frustrated when they're reading or playing a game, tilt the iPad a little too far in one direction or another, and have the screen change its orientation from portrait to landscape, or vice versa.

That's where the screen rotation lock comes in handy. It's the second use of the switch on the side of your iPad. To allow the switch to lock the rotation of your iPad screen, go to Settings ➤ General, and set "Use Side Switch to:" Lock Rotation. When you move the switch to the down position, an icon showing a circular arrow with a lock in the middle of it (see Figure 3–4) appears on the screen momentarily. The same icon in miniature form appears in the right corner of the status bar at the top of the screen. Now you can turn the iPad any way you want, and the screen always stays in the same orientation.

Figure 3–4. *No matter how your iPad is oriented, the display will remain in the same orientation if the screen rotation lock is enabled.*

For example, if you're reading a book in iBooks and find that you prefer the book-like feel of reading in portrait mode, you might want to lock the screen orientation in portrait mode. To lock the screen in portrait mode, orient the display by tilting the bottom of the iPad down. When the display is in the proper orientation, slide the screen rotation lock button down.

To turn the screen rotation lock off, just slide the mute/screen orientation switch upward toward the top of the screen. The lock in the center of the icon disappears, showing that the screen rotation is now unlocked.

Volume Toggle

Continuing our tour around the perimeter of the iPad, the next button encountered is the volume toggle. As the name implies, it is used to turn the volume up or down or to shut off sound completely. You can see where the volume toggle is located in Figure 3–2.

Increasing the volume of the speaker in the iPad (or any headphones attached through the headphone jack) just requires a push on the top part of the toggle. One push brings the volume up a notch; holding down on the toggle quickly takes the iPad to top volume.

Bringing the volume down requires pushing on the other end of the volume toggle. If you push and hold the volume toggle on its lower end, your iPad's sound is shut off. That's handy for those situations where you need to quickly turn off the volume on Pandora when the phone rings.

Whenever you touch the volume toggle, a visual indication of volume appears in the center of the iPad display (see Figure 3–5). If you have a set of Apple headphones with a volume switch on the cord plugged into your iPad, you can use that switch in a similar manner to adjust volume without touching the iPad.

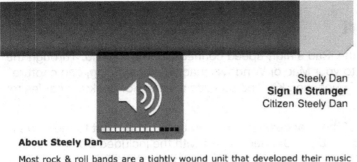

Steely Dan
Sign In Stranger
Citizen Steely Dan

About Steely Dan

Most rock & roll bands are a tightly wound unit that developed their music
years of playing in garages and clubs around their hometown. Steely Dan r
subscribed to that aesthetic. As the vehicle for the songwriting of Walter B(
Donald Fagen, Steely Dan defied all rock & roll conventions. Becker and Fa
truly enjoyed rock -- with their ironic humor and cryptic lyrics, their eclecti

Figure 3–5. *This transparent icon appears when you adjust the volume on your iPad with either the volume toggle
or headphones with a volume switch.*

Speaker

Speaking of sound volume, the next item on the iPad tour is the speaker. It's hidden on
the bottom of the iPad (see Figure 3–6) and blasts out various system beeps, music, and
movie soundtracks through a grid of tiny holes in the curved aluminum bottom of the
iPad 2. On the original iPad, it's a set of three tiny oblong openings behind mesh grills.

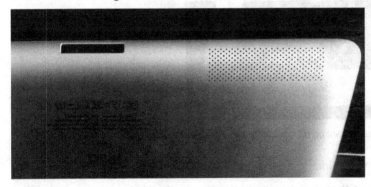

Figure 3–6. *The iPad speaker openings (right) and Dock Connector port (left)*

There's not much to say about the speaker, other than if you're purchasing or making a
case for your iPad, be sure that it has an opening in the proper location so that the
sound isn't muffled. One more hint: be sure to keep liquids away from the speaker and
the Dock Connector port (see the following section), because even a slight splash may
void your iPad warranty.

Dock Connector Port

The Dock Connector port is the iPad's high-speed connection to the world. Through the port, your iPad can connect to your Mac or Windows machine for syncing, can capture photos through the Camera Connection Kit, and can use a variety of docks or cables for charging the battery.

We'll be talking about many of those accessories later in this chapter, but for now, we're going to just talk about using the Dock Connector port with the included Dock Connector to USB cable.

You can find instructions on how to plug the cable into the Dock Connector port in Chapter 1. When plugging the cable into your iPad, be sure to have the side with the small gray icon (it's a rectangle with a line in it) facing up, and also make sure that you push the cable in squarely. In other words, don't have the cable connector angled up, down, or sideways, because that can cause undue wear on the Dock Connector port.

Home Button

To quote Dorothy from *The Wizard of Oz*, "There's no place like home." The Home button (see Figure 3–7) is undoubtedly the most heavily used physical button on the iPad.

Figure 3–7. *The Home button, centered here on the bottom of the iPad 2, has many uses.*

It is used for a number of actions, including the following:

- Quitting an application that is in use and returning to the Home screen.

- Waking a sleeping iPad.

- Displaying all of the apps that are currently running on your iPad. This feature, which was added with iOS 4 (the fourth iteration of Apple's mobile device operating system), is enabled by double-clicking the Home button. The iPad's display becomes transparent, and the active apps are displayed in the row of icons at the bottom of the screen.

One fascinating thing about the iPad is that, depending on how you're holding it, the Home button can be on the top, bottom, left, or right side of the display. In most situations, however, it is in the standard bottom side of the screen.

Headphone Jack

On top of the iPad on the left side is the headphone jack (see Figure 3–8).

Figure 3–8. *The headphone jack on an iPad 2 Wi-Fi + 3G*

The headphone jack accommodates any standard 3.5mm stereo headphone connector, so you have thousands of choices for headphones to enhance your listening pleasure. Apple sells two headphones: the Apple Earphones with Remote and Mic and the Apple In-Ear Headphones with Remote and Mic. Both of these headphones provide a way for you to control music volume as well as play, pause, rewind, advance, or skip through music or video.

Remember earlier in this chapter, when you were warned about getting water into the speaker or Dock Connector? That warning goes for the headphone jack as well. In that jack is a small liquid sensor. If you ever get your iPad wet, the liquid sensor changes color. This indicates to any Apple technician who is disassembling your iPad that the iPad was wet at one point or another, and it voids your warranty. Unfortunately, some people have found that the liquid sensor may show "water damage" even if the iPad has just been exposed to extremely humid conditions.

If this happens to you, it's within your rights as a consumer to insist on having the technician open the iPad, because there is a second internal sensor that is less susceptible to humidity.

Microphone

The iPad's microphone is probably the most invisible piece of equipment on the device. On the first-generation iPad, it's a tiny hole located right next to the headphone jack. The second-generation iPad moved the microphone to the front of the iPad, where it is a miniscule circular array of microscopic dots arranged above the front-facing camera.

If you're using an iPad application to record a lecture or conversation, you can enhance the sound recording slightly by orienting the mic directly toward the person(s) speaking. When you're recording your own voice, either of the Apple headphones with microphones discussed in the previous section provides clear reproduction of your speech without picking up a lot of background noise. Also available from many sources professional-quality mics such as the $60 iRig Mic from IK Multimedia (ikmultimedia.com/irigmic/) that plug into the headphone jack.

USB headsets also work well for listening to and recording on the iPad when connected through the USB adapter that is part of the iPad Camera Connection Kit. We'll discuss the Camera Connection Kit later in this chapter.

Micro-SIM Port (Wi-Fi + 3G iPad Only)

There's one more port on the Wi-Fi + 3G iPad that doesn't exist on the Wi-Fi model: the micro-SIM port (see Figure 3–9).

Every device that is connected to a GSM-based mobile phone system anywhere in the world uses a small card called a *subscriber identity module* (SIM) card. Your 3G iPad cannot access the Internet through a 3G network without an SIM card, so each 3G iPad comes with one pre-installed. Apple uses a smaller SIM card form factor in the iPad called *micro-SIM*.

On occasion, SIM cards may be defective and require replacement. For that purpose, there is a tiny door on the left side of the 3G iPad. On the original iPad, it's located on the lower part of the left side, while it's near the top of the second-generation iPad. That door has a miniscule hole in it, which you can think of as the lock for the door (see Figure 3–9).

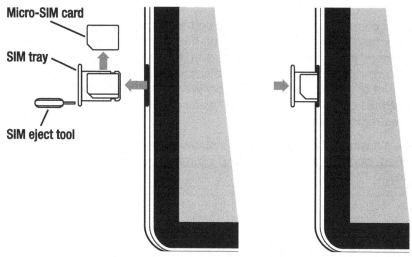

Micro-SIM card

SIM tray

SIM eject tool

Figure 3–9. *The micro-SIM card, the SIM tray, and the SIM eject tool are found only on the Wi-Fi + 3G iPad. On the second-generation iPad, the port is located near the top of the left side of the device.*

The 3G-enabled iPad also comes with a SIM eject tool, which is a small oblong aluminum piece with a small protrusion on one end. To open the SIM door, take the SIM eject tool and put the protruding piece into the hole in the door. Apply pressure to the tool, and the door will pop up from the surface. It is quite easy to lose the SIM eject tool, so in a pinch you can use a small paper clip bent to resemble the tool.

Grasping the top of the door with your fingers, pull the micro-SIM out of the iPad. It rests in a small tray, and it can be popped out and replaced with a new micro-SIM. To put the new SIM into the iPad, simply push the tray back into the iPad until the door is flush with the side of your device.

Care and Maintenance of Your iPad

Although an iPad isn't as expensive as MacBook Pro, you'll still want to keep it around as long as possible. With a little loving care, your iPad can serve you for many years to come. In this section of Chapter 3, we'll tell you how to maintain your iPad for long life and years of loyal service.

Cases

As with the iPhone before it, the iPad is creating its own economy with a plethora of accessories being produced for it. Some of the hottest products for iPad are cases that protect the device from scratches, water, dirt, and accidental drops. Although we're not going to list every possible case in this section, we'll talk about the different types of cases and who they're for.

Sleeves

An iPad sleeve (see Figure 3–10) is usually made of a soft material with a nonscratch lining. The iPad is placed into the sleeve, and then it's commonly put into another carrying case—a backpack, a purse, a briefcase, or a laptop bag.

Figure 3–10. *The Targus Hughes Leather Portfolio Slipcase iPad sleeve by Targus. Image courtesy of Targus.*

More than anything, sleeves are designed to protect the iPad from scratches when it is placed into another bag. They can be made of a variety of materials (there are sleeves made of leather, fleece, cork, neoprene, nylon, and hemp, for example), and prices are also all over the map.

Examples of sleeves are products from Targus (www.targus.com) and Booq (booqbags.com).

Bags

Bags for the iPad (see Figure 3–11) are meant not only to protect the iPad but to be the primary form of transportation for it as well. As such, they're usually equipped with a handle or strap of some sort for easy carrying. Price-wise, bags are usually more expensive than sleeves, but they also provide more protection. Often there's some sort of padding provided, as well as a stiff insert to protect the screen.

Figure 3–11. *The attractive and functional iPad Travel Express bag from WaterField Designs. Image courtesy of WaterField Designs.*

Several stylish bags are made by WaterField Designs (sfbags.com) and Tom Bihn (www.tombihn.com).

Skins

If you want to protect the surfaces of your iPad without a lot of extra weight, consider a skin. These are usually made of a thin material that might not protect your iPad against a drop but will keep scratches away. Zagg's Invisible Shield for iPad (www.zagg.com) and Fusion of Ideas' Stealth Armor (www.fusionofideas.com/sa-ipad/index.html) are two perfect examples of skins that provide scratch protection with little or no bulk.

Book-Style Cases

The iPad is an excellent electronic book reader, so why not make it look like a book? The first case of this type was developed by San Francisco-based DODOcase (dodocase.com), a company that fused high-tech and old bookbinding skills and came up with a good-looking and protective iPad case. Other companies have followed suit, with the Twelve South BookBook for iPad (twelvesouth.com/products/bookbook_ipad/) being a clever and beautiful example of this genre of iPad case (see Figure 3–12).

Figure 3–12. *Make your e-book reader look like a book with a clever and beautiful book-style case like the Twelve South BookBook for iPad. Photo courtesy of Twelve South.*

Caring for the Battery

One great thing about the iPad is the battery life. It's not uncommon to go for days without charging the battery, and the thought of being far from a power outlet will no longer cause you to panic. A good rule of thumb is that, for normal usage, the battery level drops about 10 percent for each hour of use. If you're playing games with some heavy graphic and sound demands, your battery may not last as long on a charge. On the other hand, if you're reading an e-book, the iPad battery may last longer.

However, your iPad battery won't last forever without a charge, so you'll want to charge it on a regular basis. You do this by connecting the iPad to a power outlet using the Dock Connector to USB cable and the 10W USB power adapter or by connecting the cable to a high-power USB 2.0 port.

What do we mean by high-power USB? Generally, that means plugging either directly into a port on your computer or into a powered USB hub. Plugging your iPad into a port on a USB keyboard or into an unpowered USB hub won't charge it. Instead, you'll see the message "Not Charging" in the status bar next to the battery icon. We recommend plugging the iPad into the power adapter every night to receive a full charge.

If your iPad is *very* low on power, you may see one of the images in Figure 3–13 on the screen. These mean that the device needs to be charged for at least ten minutes before you can use it. If the battery is extremely low or completely drained, you may not see these images for up to two minutes after plugging the iPad into a power source.

 or

Figure 3–13. *If you see either of these symbols on your iPad screen, stop using it, and plug it into a power source as soon as possible.*

With constant usage, your iPad battery may eventually get to the point where its capacity to hold a charge has depleted 50 percent or more from the original specification. You'll be able to tell this is the case if your iPad is constantly running out of power or if it never shows that it is completely recharged after being plugged in for a long time. In this case, you may need to have your battery replaced by an Apple-authorized service provider. If you purchased an AppleCare Protection Plan for your iPad and you've owned it for less than two years, you may be able to have Apple replace the battery at no cost.

There are some simple steps you can take to stretch your battery life that can be useful in situations (international flights, for example) where you cannot readily recharge your battery:

> *Turn off push notifications*: Some apps use Apple Push Notifications to provide alerts. These tend to decrease battery life when frequently used, so you can disable push notifications by going to **Settings ➤ Notifications** and turning Notifications to Off.

> *Turn off Wi-Fi*: When you're not using Wi-Fi, turn it off to save power. Go to **Settings ➤ Wi-Fi** and set Wi-Fi to Off.

> *Have a Wi-Fi + 3G iPad*? Using 3G networks tends to drain battery power faster than connecting via Wi-Fi. If you're in a zone with low or no 3G coverage, turn off 3G to improve your battery life. There are two ways to do this. First, choose **Settings ➤ Cellular Data**, and set Cellular Data to Off. The second method is to simply turn on Airplane Mode, which is accomplished by going into Settings and setting Airplane Mode to On.

> *Minimize use of location services*: iPads can determine where they are by two methods: by Wi-Fi location through Skyhook Wireless's database of Wi-Fi hotspot locations or by Assisted GPS (A-GPS) on Wi-Fi + 3G iPads. Both of these methods can reduce battery life. If you don't need to know where you are or where you're going, disable location services. Go to **Settings ➤ Location Services** and slide the Location Services switch to Off.

Adjust the brightness of your screen: The iPad normally has Auto-Brightness turned on, which means that it will brighten the screen in bright ambient light conditions and darken it in darker rooms. You may want to adjust brightness yourself by going to **Settings ➤ Brightness & Wallpaper** and dragging the slider to the left to lower the default screen brightness. Less brightness results in better battery life.

Know your downloaded applications: Some apps that you run on your iPad may be eating your battery life. Games that prevent the screen from dimming automatically are a common culprit, as are apps that need to run continuously for location updates. Geotracking apps that poll the GPS position of a Wi-Fi + 3G iPad are known to pull the battery life down quickly.

Keep your iPad out of temperature extremes: Apple recommends keeping your iPad out of direct sun and hot cars. Extreme heat can cause decreased battery life and may also result in other issues we'll discuss shortly. Apple's recommended temperature ranges for the iPad are 32° to 95° F (0° to 35° C) in operation and -4° to 113° F (-20° to 45° C) when it is turned off.

Set your iPad to turn off after a short amount of inactivity: The Auto-Lock feature, which can be set by going to **Settings ➤ General ➤ Auto-Lock**, will automatically turn off your screen after a preset amount of time. For best battery life, set the interval to a short time like one or two minutes.

Caring for the Screen

Unlike the easily scratched displays on early mobile devices like the Apple Newton MessagePad or Palm Pilot, the iPad's screen is made of a very durable and extremely hard glass. Although it will resist most scratches, eventually something may scratch the screen. Except in extreme situations, this should not harm the screen, and you should still be able to use your iPad with no difficulties.

Probably the biggest issue you'll have with an iPad display is that it tends to pick up fingerprints. The iPad screen has an oleophobic (oil-repelling) coating on it, but it still picks up smears and fingerprints quite easily.

Cleaning fingerprints and smears off of your iPad screen can get to be a bit of an obsession. Fortunately, about the only time that they're readily visible is when the iPad is turned off, so you shouldn't need to get obsessive about fingerprints. On those occasions where the smearing is really interfering with your iPad use, Apple recommends turning off the iPad completely, unplugging all cables, and then using a soft, slightly damp, lint-free cloth. We recommend using a RadTech ScreenSavrz cleaning cloth (`www.radtech.us`), dampening the cloth slightly with water, and then squeezing it until almost all the water is gone.

Some iPad users claim that baby wipes work well to clean the iPad screen. They're inexpensive, convenient, and easy to use. After cleaning the screen, just wipe any remaining dust or liquid residue with a soft cloth.

Next, use the cloth to wipe the screen. Make sure that you avoid any openings on the iPad, such as the headphone jack, Dock Connector port, and speaker.

Never use window cleaners, liquid eyeglass cleaners, household cleaning sprays, alcohol, ammonia, or any abrasives to clean the iPad, because they may damage the screen.

Heat: The iPad's Worst Enemy

In the previous section about battery life, we mentioned Apple's recommendation that you keep the iPad out of hot conditions in order to optimize battery life. There's another good reason to make sure you keep your iPad cool—it may shut off if it gets too hot.

Apple designed the iPad without a built-in cooling fan so that you wouldn't be bothered by the noise and power consumption of a fan. Unfortunately, that means the only way your iPad can keep itself cool is by transferring heat to the surroundings through conduction.

Some iPad users reported that when their device experienced conditions with a high ambient temperature, a warning appeared on the screen and the iPad shut down. To bring your iPad "back to life," it's necessary to bring it into a cool place out of direct sun until it can cool down. This seems to be a more common occurrence during summer and when the iPad is being used in direct sunlight.

Apple Accessories for iPad

It's been two years since the first iPad come out, and there are thousands of third-party accessories available for it and the new iPad 2. For many iPad buyers who will be making their purchase from a nearby Apple Store or through the Apple Online Store, Apple accessories may be their first choice.

In this section, we'll describe the iPad accessories made by Apple and how they can be used to enhance your user experience. You've already been introduced to these accessories in Chapter 1; here, we provide more details about how each of these items can be used with your iPad.

Smart Cover

We mentioned the Apple Smart Cover for iPad 2 earlier in this chapter as a way to protect the screen of your device from scratches. The Smart Cover is useful in many other ways as well.

The Smart Cover is made of either leather ($69.00) or polyurethane ($39.00), which means that when your iPad is wearing the Smart Cover it is easier to grip. We find the "naked" iPad to be somewhat slippery, so having the Smart Cover has probably kept us from dropping the iPad at least once.

The Smart Cover is attached to the iPad 2 with very strong and strategically placed magnets. There's only one right way to attach the cover, and when you get the cover into the proper orientation, it actually installs itself.

The Smart Cover has one magnet that works with a small microswitch inside the iPad 2 to wake the device when the cover is lifted or put it to sleep when the cover is closed. That feature makes it unnecessary to press the On/Off Sleep/Wake button to bring the iPad to life.

Our favorite feature of the iPad Smart Cover is that it folds origami-like into a handy stand, as shown in Figure 3–14. There's a steel plate inside one of the folds in the Smart Cover that is attracted to an array of magnets. When folded into a triangular tube shape, the Smart Cover acts either as a prop for easier typing on the iPad or for convenient viewing of movies.

Figure 3–14. *The iPad 2 Smart Cover acts as a screen protector, a handy stand, and a sleep/wake button.*

iPad 2 Dock

The Apple iPad 2 Dock ($29.00) provides a docking base for charging and syncing your iPad 2 (see Figure 3–15).

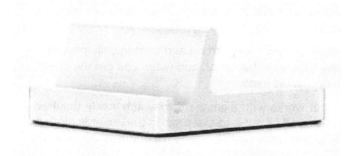

Figure 3–15. *The Apple iPad 2 Dock is plain and functional.*

There's a similar dock available for the original iPad, and many other vendors have created docks that are equally functional and less expensive. The iPad 2 Dock provides access to a Dock Connector port and an audio line-out port. It holds your iPad at one fixed angle, and there's no way to adjust the angle. For those who want to use a Bluetooth keyboard with the iPad, the iPad 2 Dock is a perfect way to hold the iPad in a useful configuration for typing.

iPad Camera Connection Kit

For photographers, a very useful accessory from Apple is the iPad Camera Connection Kit (see Figure 3–16). The kit consists of two separate connectors that plug into the iPad's Dock Connector port. The first has a slot for a Secure Digital (SD) memory card like those used in many digital cameras and camcorders. When you want to move photos or movies from your camera to your iPad for sharing or touch-up, you simply plug in the Camera Connection Kit's SD adapter, remove the SD card from your camera, and insert it into the SD slot on the Camera Connection Kit.

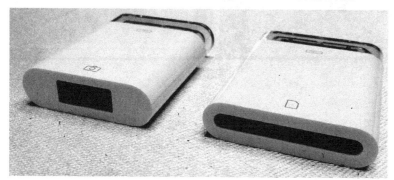

Figure 3–16. *The iPad Camera Connection Kit consists of a USB adapter (left) and an SD memory card reader (right).*

Even more useful is the second connector, which provides the iPad with a USB port. What can you connect to the USB port? A digital camera or camcorder, of course, but you can also attach most USB keyboards, USB headsets, and even an iPhone or iPod touch. If you're using your iPhone or iPod touch as a camera and want to move your photos or video to the iPad for editing, the Camera Connection Kit USB adapter and the regular iPhone sync cable make beautiful music together.

The ability to add a USB headset to an iPad makes it a great portable workstation for Skype voice chats, and if you have a favorite USB keyboard that you just can't part with, you'll now be able to use it with your iPad.

iPad 10W USB Power Adapter

The iPad comes with a 10W USB power adapter for charging, but you may want a second adapter for travel or so you can charge up both at home and at work. The iPad 10W USB Power Adapter has one additional piece that's not included with the standard adapter that you get with your iPad—it's a 6-foot-long power cord, so you don't need to be right next to the power outlet to get a charge.

Apple VGA Adapter

When Steve Jobs announced on the iPad on January 27, 2010, he also announced the availability of iWork for iPad. iWork consists of three powerful apps: Pages, Keynote, and Numbers.

Apple's Keynote is presentation software, so for those of us who give presentations as part of our work life, this was exciting news. What we needed, however, was some way to get the image from the iPad to a standard PC projector or large monitor.

Minutes later, Jobs announced the Apple VGA Adapter (see Figure 3–17), which provides exactly that capability. For the original iPad, the VGA Adapter works with only certain apps that have been written to include a set of special drivers. On the iPad 2, the VGA Adapter provides true mirroring of everything on the screen to an attached display or projector.

Figure 3–17. *The iPad Dock Connector to VGA Adapter is useful for displaying Keynote presentations on an external monitor or PC projector.*

This adapter is a godsend for presenters who don't want to lug a laptop around. With Keynote for iPad, the adapter, your iPad, and a PC projector, you're ready to wow the crowd with your presentation.

Apple Digital AV Adapter

With the introduction of the second-generation iPad, Apple introduced a new cable: the Digital AV Adapter. The purpose of this cable is to let your iPad connect to the many high-definition displays and TVs that use the HDMI connector standard.

This adapter features a dock connector on one end to plug into the iPad, and an HDMI cable port on the other end. The HDMI side also has another dock connector in case you want to power your iPad while using it to pump video to your HDTV. The Digital AV Adapter mirrors content on your iPad 2 screen to an HD display but works only with apps that specifically support video-out on the original iPad.

Apple Composite and Component AV Cables

Not every PC projector or TV uses the VGA standard for the input of video signals, so Apple made sure that the Apple Component and Composite AV cables worked with the iPad. Unlike the VGA and adapter, which will work in video mirroring mode on an iPad 2, these cable works only with applications that have been written to take advantage of the video-out capabilities of the iPad. We hope more iPad programmers will support video-out in their applications in the future.

Apple Wireless Keyboard

The Apple Wireless Keyboard is another Apple product that can be used with the iPad. This diminutive keyboard is comfortable and has good tactile feedback for touch-typing.

The keyboard uses Bluetooth wireless connectivity to converse with the iPad and has two AA batteries that provide power to it. If you have an existing Apple Wireless Keyboard and want to use it with your iPad, you will need to pair the keyboard with the iPad only—you cannot use it for both your Mac and your iPad unless you go through the pairing process each time you want to use it.

The best thing about the keyboard is that it is not attached to anything, so you can use it in front of your iPad, in your lap, or up to 30 feet away from the iPad.

As we mentioned earlier, just about any third-party Bluetooth keyboard will work with the iPad. There are a number of vendors who are producing iPad cases that incorporate a Bluetooth keyboard, such as the ZaggMate (http://zagg.com/accessories/zaggmate-ipad-case) and the Kensington KeyFolio case (http://kensington.com)

Apple Earphones with Remote and Mic

Although the iPad essentially uses the same operating system software as an iPhone, it's not designed to make or receive phone calls. Even the iPad Wi-Fi + 3G can't make voice calls except by using FaceTime or Voice over IP (VoIP) software like Skype (http://skype.com) or Line2 (www.line2.com).

Even though you can't make phone calls with your iPad like you can on any iPhone, you'll still want to listen to music, watch movies, or even take part in the occasional FaceTime chat. For that reason, you may want a good set of headphones. The Apple Earphones with Remote and Mic have a small switch on one of the earphone cables that acts as a remote control for iTunes. If you need to fast-forward to the next song, pause, turn the volume up or down, or rewind, you can do it with the remote.

The remote switch also includes one important component—a small directional microphone for picking up your voice. Since these are the same headphones that are included with each iPhone, you can use them with your iPad by simply plugging them into the headphone jack.

Apple In-Ear Headphones with Remote and Mic

The last Apple accessory for the iPad that we'll discuss is another headphone. The Apple In-Ear Headphones with Remote and Mic are virtually identical to the previous entry, but with one important difference. These headphones actually fit inside your ear canal so that you get better sound quality and isolation from outside noises.

Summary

This chapter introduced you to the user-controllable hardware of your iPad by taking you on a tour of the various switches, buttons and ports you'll use on a daily basis. You also became familiar with the care and maintenance of your iPad and found out more about the iPad accessories that you can purchase from Apple.

Here are some key points from this chapter:

- For ease of use, the iPad has very few physical switches and toggles. Most interaction with an iPad is done through the touch screen. The true buttons and switches consist of the On/Off Sleep/Wake button, the Home button, the volume toggle, and the mute/screen rotation switch.

- There are many ways to extend the battery life of your iPad for those rare occasions where you'll be away from a power outlet for a long time. On those long international flights, consider dimming the screen, lowering the volume, and turning off all wireless services (Wi-Fi, 3G, and Bluetooth).

▓   Extreme temperatures are the enemy of your iPad. Chances are, if you're feeling uncomfortable, your iPad is too! Keep it at a temperature you'd feel comfortable at, and you shouldn't run into any problems.

▓   Never get liquids into any of the ports on your iPad, especially the headphone jack. Exposure to liquids can void the iPad warranty.

▓   If you plan on using any of the Apple cables or adapters to connect your iPad to a projector, TV, or home theater system, understand that not all apps may support those cables.

Chapter 4

Interacting with Your iPad

For those of you who have used an iPhone or iPod touch, you'll already have some idea of how to interact with your iPad. However, because of the iPad's large screen, you'll find some subtle differences between the iPhone and your iPad. Never used an iPod touch or iPhone before? That's OK too, because you are absolutely going to be blown away by the iPad's Multi-Touch screen. The iPad responds to the language of your touch. Its vocabulary includes *taps*, *drags*, *pinches*, and *flicks*. With these actions, you control your iPad as easily as using a mouse to control your personal computer. And there's a lot more to interaction than just drags and taps. Your iPad offers Multi-Touch technology. That means it can recognize and respond to more than one touch at a time.

In this chapter, you'll discover all the different ways you can interact with your iPad—from zooming into and out of pictures to using the iPad's large built-in keyboard to setting Accessibility options. You'll also look at the iPad's new Notification Center, which allows you to view all your app notifications in one place. Let's get started.

Interaction Basics

Personal computers have mice. Personal digital assistants (PDAs) have styluses. The iPad has your fingers. It does not work with mice or styluses. It requires real finger contact. Your iPad does not just sense pressure points. It detects the small electrical charge transferred from your fingers. That means you can use your iPad with your fingers, your knuckles, or even—if you're feeling up to it—your nose, but you cannot use it with pencil erasers, Q-Tips, or those PDA styluses. The electrical charges in your touch make it possible for the iPad to detect and respond to one or more contacts at a time, that is, to use Multi-Touch technology.

> **TIP:** If you're feeling really adventurous, you can use a frozen hotdog in place of your finger. Korean winters are very cold, and people were getting frostbite on their fingers from removing their gloves to use their iPhones outside. Some enterprising people in Korea discovered that you could use a frozen hotdog in lieu of your finger and still be able to interact with the iPhone's touch screen, all while keeping their gloves on. Theoretically, a frozen hotdog should work with the iPad's screen as well.

The iPad Language

How you touch your iPad's screen provides your communication vocabulary. Here's a quick rundown of the basic ways you can speak to your iPad:

Pressing the Home button: The Home button lives below the touch screen and is marked with a white square. Press this button at any time while in an app to return to your Home screen with its list of applications. Double-pressing the Home button while on a Home screen or while inside an app will bring up the multitasking bar. We'll talk more about multitasking later in this chapter.

Tapping: Tap your iPad by touching your finger to the screen and removing it quickly. Tapping allows you to select web links, activate buttons, and launch applications. When typing text, you may want to tap with your forefinger or, if it's more comfortable, your thumb.

Double-tapping: Double-tapping means tapping your screen twice in quick succession. Double-clicking may be important on your personal computer, but double-tapping is not actually used all that much on your iPad. You can double-tap in Safari (the web browser that ships on your iPad) to zoom into columns and double-tap again to zoom back out. In Photos (the iPad's built-in photo viewer), use double-tapping to zoom into and out from pictures.

Two-fingered tapping and dragging: The iPad's Multi-Touch technology means you can tap the screen with more than one finger at a time. A few applications respond to two-fingered gestures. To do this, separate your forefinger and middle finger and tap or drag the screen with both fingers at once. For example, in Safari, a double-fingered drag allows you to scroll within a web frame without affecting the page as a whole.

Holding: At times, you'll want to put your finger on the screen and leave it there until something happens. For example, holding brings up the spyglass while you're typing, and in Safari, it brings up URL previews.

Dragging: Drag your finger by pressing it to the screen and moving it in any direction before lifting it. Use dragging to scroll up and down in Safari and Music (the application that plays your iTunes songs). Some applications offer an index on the right side, like the one shown for the iPad app in Figure 4–1. To use this index, drag along it until the item you want comes into view.

Figure 4–1. *The index bar (boxed) to the right of the Music app*

Flicking: When you're dealing with long lists, you can give the list a quick flick. Place your finger onto the screen, and move it rapidly in one direction—up, down, left, or right. The display responds by scrolling quickly in the direction you've indicated. Use flicking to move quickly through your e-mail contacts list, for example.

TIP: Flicking and dragging will not choose or activate items on the iPad's display. Try this yourself by dragging and flicking on the Home screen.

Stopping: During a scroll, press and hold your finger to the screen to stop scrolling. Apple's legal text provides a great place to practice flicking, dragging, and stopping. To get there, select **Settings ➤ General ➤ About ➤ Legal**. Have fun with its endless content of legalese that you can flick, drag, and stop to your heart's content. If you don't want to stop a scroll, just wait. The scroll will slow and stop by itself.

Swiping: To swipe your iPad, drag a finger from the left side of the screen toward the right. Swiping is used to unlock your iPad and to indicate you want to delete list items.

Pinching: On the iPad, you pinch by placing your thumb and forefinger on the screen with a space between them. Then, with your fingers touching the screen, move them together, as if you were pinching the screen. Pinching allows you to zoom out in many iPad programs, including Photos and Safari.

Unpinching: To unpinch, perform the pinch in reverse. Start with your thumb and forefinger placed together on your screen and, with the fingers touching the screen, spread them apart. Unpinching allows you to zoom into those same iPad applications where pinching zooms out.

Orientation

In most images of the iPad, you'll notice it's in portrait orientation with the physical Home button on the bottom bezel. However, there's actually no "right" way to hold the iPad. Apple designed the iPad as an orientation-agnostic device. What this means is you can hold the iPad in portrait or landscape mode and still interact with the device (Figure 4–2). As a matter of fact, you could completely flip the iPad upside down and still see what's on your screen as right side up.

Figure 4–2. *The iPad in portrait and landscape modes*

Although there's no right way to hold your iPad, some apps do offer additional features when you flip the iPad into landscape or portrait mode. For instance, if you are in Mail in portrait mode, you will see only the currently selected e-mail on your screen. To see a list of other e-mails, you need to select the inbox in a drop-down menu in the header bar. If, however, you rotate your iPad to landscape orientation, you'll be presented with a list of all your e-mails alongside the currently selected e-mail. We'll discuss orientation-specific features of various apps later in this book.

> **NOTE:** Although most apps will display in either orientation, some will not. Many games force you to use the iPad in landscape mode.

The Lock Screen

If you've just turned on your iPad or when your iPad has been idle for a while, it automatically locks, and the screen goes dark. When this happens, press the Home button. The locked iPad screen appears, as shown in Figure 4–3. To unlock your iPad, swipe the slider from the left to the right. The locked screen clears, and the Home screen springs into place.

Figure 4–3. *The iPad lock screen*

You can set how long the iPad should wait before locking itself. Go to **Settings** ➤ General ➤ **Auto-Lock**, and choose the number of minutes you want your iPad to wait before locking. To disable auto-locking, choose Never—and make sure you have a good power source available nearby. Auto-locking is a power-saving feature. Disabling it means your iPad runs through its battery more rapidly.

For security, you can assign a passcode for your iPad. You can choose between a regular passcode and a simple passcode. A *simple passcode* is just like a four-digit PIN you have for your debit cards. Go to **Settings** ➤ General, tap Passcode Lock, and then tap Turn Passcode On at the top of the screen. Next, tap Simple Passcode so it's switched to On to establish a new simple passcode. Your iPad prompts you to enter a four-number code, as shown in Figure 4–4.

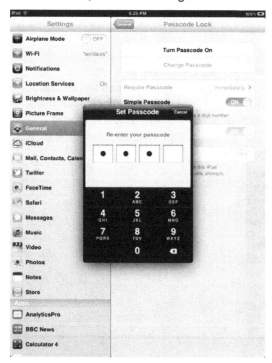

Figure 4–4. *Setting your simple passcode*

Enter a code, or tap Cancel to quit without entering a code. After you enter the code, the iPad prompts you to reenter it and then enables further Passcode Lock settings. Those settings include setting how long the iPad needs to be idle before it's locked down, setting whether the picture frame will be displayed while the iPad is locked (more on the picture frame in Chapter 13), and setting whether all the data on the iPad should be erased after ten failed passcode attempts.

To enter a regular passcode, which is effectively a password using any combination of letters, numbers, and symbols, go to **Settings** ➤ General, tap Passcode Lock, and then tap Turn Passcode On at the top of the screen. Next, tap Simple Passcode so it's switched to Off to establish a new complex passcode. Your iPad will display a keyboard for you to type your complex passcode in on.

To test your passcode (either simple or complex), click the Sleep/Wake button once (to put your iPad to sleep) and again (to wake it up). The passcode challenge screen greets you, as shown in Figure 4–5. Enter your passcode, and your iPad unlocks.

Figure 4–5. *The passcode lock screen displaying the keyboard for you to enter a complex passcode on. A simple passcode will show a number pad.*

To remove the passcode from your iPad, go back to the Passcode Lock settings screen (Figure 4–4). Choose Turn Passcode Off, and reenter the passcode one more time to confirm that it's really you making this request.

So, what happens if you lose your passcode or a mean-spirited colleague adds one to your iPad without telling you? You'll need to connect the iPad to your home computer and use iTunes to restore the iPad software. You can restore your iPad by selecting the Summary tab in iTunes and clicking Restore. For more information about restoring your iPad, see Chapter 2.

On the lock screen, to the right of the Slide to Unlock bar, you'll notice there is a small icon of a flower inside a box (see Figure 4–3). This is the Picture Frame button. Tap this to turn your iPad into a digital picture frame. The iPad will display your photographs one after the other on the screen until you choose to stop it by tapping the screen and tapping the Picture Frame button again or sliding the Slide to Unlock bar. You'll learn more about the picture frame function of the iPad and its settings in Chapter 13.

The lock screen can also perform one last function: controls for the iPad's music player. If music is playing on the iPad when the screen is locked, you can double-press the Home button to display music controls at the top of the screen. You'll learn more about these controls in Chapter 7.

The Home Screen

As discussed, when you turn on your iPad, you'll be presented with a lock screen. Depending on whether you have a passcode set on your iPad, either you'll swipe the Slide to Unlock bar and be presented with a numeric or qwerty keypad or you'll be immediately taken to your iPad Home screen.

The iPad Home screen (see Figure 4–6) is the first page of apps you have on your iPad. Depending on how many apps you have, you may have several pages that will show in subsequent order when you swipe to the left.

Figure 4–6. *The iPad Home screen*

> **TIP:** Since the Home screen will be the first page you're taken to when you unlock your iPad, it makes sense to keep your most frequently used apps on the Home screen for easy access.

From the top of the screen down, you'll see the following elements:

Status bar: A thin, black bar runs along the top of your iPad Home screen. This status bar, shown in Figure 4–7, will display on every page of your iPad Home screen.

Figure 4–7. *The status bar*

The status bar can show many icons, but the standard layout you'll most likely see is the following: in the upper-left corner, you'll see the word *iPad* or *iPad 3G* (depending on which model you have), next to a Wi-Fi icon. The Wi-Fi icon shows you that you are connected to a wireless hotspot and also tells you the strength of your wireless signal. If you have an iPad 3G, you'll also be presented with the name of your 3G service carrier. In the middle of the status bar, you'll be presented with the current time. On the right corner of the status bar, you'll see a battery meter icon, next to the percentage of the battery remaining.

The status bar can also show other status icons. These include the following:

Airplane mode: With airplane mode, you can't access the Internet or use Bluetooth. Other functions of your iPad are available.

E: This stands for EDGE, a cellular data network that's slower than 3G. Many times E will appear when you are outside your 3G network. You can connect to the Internet using EDGE; just keep in mind it's slower than 3G (available on iPad Wi-Fi + 3G only).

o: This little symbol stands for GPRS. If 3G is a race car and EDGE is a bicycle, GPRS is a turtle. Think 1994 dial-up slow (available on iPad Wi-Fi + 3G only).

Activity: The activity icon looks like a sun. You'll see the activity icon whenever network activity (such as downloading data) is occurring on your iPad.

VPN: This shows you are connected to a virtual private network (VPN). Many companies use VPNs so you can log in securely to their e-mail systems or private networks from your home.

Lock: This padlock tells you your iPad is locked. You'll only ever see this icon on the lock screen.

Screen Rotation Lock: This signifies that the screen rotation is locked. See Chapter 3 for more details.

Play: This icon tells you a song, podcast, or audiobook is playing.

Apps page: Below the black status bar you'll see a series of app icons (see Figure 4–8). Each page can hold up to 20 apps in addition to the ones found in the Dock. As we'll discuss shortly, apps can be deleted and rearranged without the need to plug your iPad into iTunes.

Figure 4–8. *A page full of apps*

Page dots: Just above the app icons in the Dock, you'll see a series of small, white dots (see Figure 4–9). This series of dots begins with a tiny magnifying glass. We'll get to the magnifying glass shortly. The dots next to the magnifying glass signify the number of pages of apps you have on your Home screen. If you see five dots, it means you have five pages of apps. The dot that is the brightest signifies the location of the page you are currently on among all your pages of apps.

Figure 4–9. *The dots signify how many pages of apps you have.*

The Dock: At the bottom of every page of the Home screen is a long, gray slate known as the Dock (see Figure 4–10). The Dock can contain up to six apps. No matter what page of apps you swipe to, the Dock will always show the same apps. The advantage of this is that if you have ten pages of apps but frequently check your e-mail, no matter what page of apps you're on, you'll always have quick access to your Mail app if you've placed it in the Dock.

Figure 4–10. *The Dock can hold between zero and six apps.*

> **NOTE:** Unlike with some apps, no matter if you are holding your iPad vertically or horizontally, all the elements of the Home screen, including how you interact with it, always remain the same.

Manipulating the Home Screen

There are several ways you can interact with your iPad Home screen:

> *Navigating the apps pages:* If you are on your first page of apps, swipe your finger to the left to reveal the next page of apps. Keep swiping your finger to the left to proceed navigating through all your app pages. To go back to the previous page of apps, simply swipe your finger to the right. Alternately, you can drag your finger to the left or right to go for the slow reveal of the next page of apps.

> **NOTE:** The pages of the Home screen move only left or right. Unlike in many apps, they do not move up or down.

> *Launching apps:* To launch an app, simply tap its icon. To return to the Home screen, press the round, physical Home button on the iPad's bezel.

> *Manipulating app icons:* This is fun. Let's say you want to rearrange the icons on your Home screen but aren't near your computer to do it through the iPad's iTunes preferences page that we discussed in Chapter 2. Simply touch and hold any icon on the Home screen. After a few seconds, you see all the icons on the page start to jiggle like they're little mounds of gelatin (see Figure 4–11). You can now remove your finger from the app. The icons will continue to jiggle. While jiggling, you can touch and hold any app icon and then simply drag it to a new position on the page. You can also drag icons to and from the Dock.

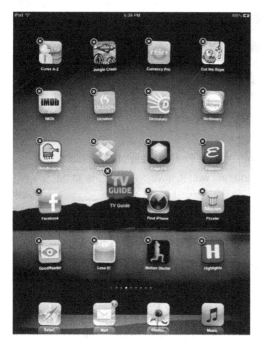

Figure 4–11. *Jiggling icons. In this example, the TV Guide app is being moved.*

You can go ahead and swipe to a new page of apps while they are all jiggling and rearrange the apps on that page. You can also transfer apps between pages. Simply touch and hold the app you'd like to move to a different page and drag it toward the side of the screen where the page is located. After a brief pause, the next page will automatically swipe over, and you can drop the app anywhere you want it. If that page is already full of 20 apps, the app in the lower-right corner will be pushed to the next page automatically.

NOTE: If your Dock already has six apps on it, you must remove an app first before adding a new one to the Dock. Unlike with home pages, apps in the Dock will not automatically be pushed to a new page if you try to add a new app to a full Dock.

Creating folders of apps: In Chapter 2 we talked about how to create folders full of apps on your iPad using iTunes, but you can also create folders of apps right on your iPad. Simply touch and hold an app icon until all the apps are jiggling (see Figure 4–11). Once they are, drag an app onto another app icon and hold it there. After a second or two, an app folder will appear. Drop the app inside the folder so it appears next to the app icon you held it over (see Figure 4–12).

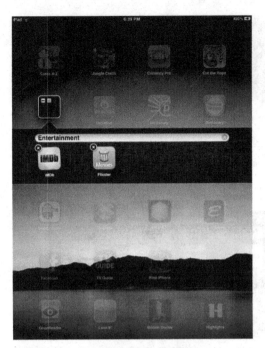

Figure 4-12. *Creating a folder full of apps*

You can arrange the apps in this new folder any way you want. You can also name the folder whatever you want. A cool thing Apple did was give the folder the ability to guess the name you want it to be. In the example in Figure 4–12, we created a folder with two movie apps inside. The iPad knew both apps were entertainment-related and named the folder Entertainment, appropriately. You can always change the name of the folder, however. Tap anywhere outside the folder to return to the normal apps screen. Drag any app to an existing folder to add it to that folder.

Folders appear as gray boxes with multiple app icons inside (see Figure 4–13). Folders can contain up to 20 apps and you can have up to 26 folders on a page (20 on a page plus 6 folders can be stored in the dock). To open a folder, simply tap it, and its contents will expand while the rest of the outside app icons are grayed out (see Figure 4–13). To exit a folder, tap anywhere outside of it.

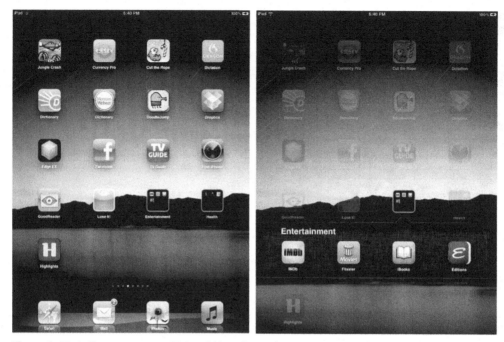

Figure 4–13. *Left, an apps page with two folders, Entertainment and Health. Right, the same apps page with the Entertainment folder open.*

Removing apps: In Chapter 2 we told you how to remove apps from your iPad using iTunes. You can also remove an app from the iPad right on the iPad. To do this, simply touch and hold any icon on the Home screen and wait for them all to begin jiggling like they did when you were rearranging apps (see Figure 4–14).

Figure 4–14. *While an app is jiggling, tap the X to remove it.*

Notice how some of the apps have a little black and white *X* in their upper-left corner? Tapping that *X* will delete the app. Don't worry if you accidentally delete an app from your iPad. The apps are always store in your iTunes library, and you can reinstall them at any time.

> **NOTE:** Although you cannot delete any Apple apps that were factory installed on your iPad, you can actually hide some of their icons from appearing on the Home screen. To do this, go to **Settings ➤ General ➤ Restrictions**. Under the Allow header, any app that is switched to Off will cause that app to be hidden on the Home screen. Using this method, you can hide Safari, YouTube, Camera, FaceTime, and iTunes.

To delete an app, simply touch the *X*. A pop-up will appear on the screen asking whether you want to delete the selected application. You'll also see a note saying deleting the app "will also delete all of its data," as shown in Figure 4–15. *This is important!* If you've created a new document inside the app or achieved a new high score on a game and delete the app before syncing it to iTunes, any new data associated with that app will be deleted. So, if you've created a new documents in Pages and decide to delete the Pages app, your new document will be forever lost if you don't sync your iPad before deleting Pages. Any documents the Pages app contained before the last sync will be available to you again if you resync the Pages app from iTunes.

Figure 4–15. *The deletion warning pop-up*

> **NOTE:** If you delete an app accidentally and need it back right away but are not near your computer, you can simply use the iPad's built-in App Store app to download the app again. If it was a paid application, don't worry; you won't be charged a second time. Your iTunes account will know you've already paid for it.

If you are sure you want to delete an app, go ahead and tap the Delete button. If you've changed your mind, tap Cancel. When an app is deleted, all the other apps on the page will shift one position to fill the space of the deleted app.

Multitasking and Managing Background Apps

Starting with iOS 4, Apple introduced multitasking features to the iPad. Multitasking means you can have more than one app running at a time. In other words, you could be browsing the Web in Safari, but in the background you could have an instant messaging app running. Even though your entire iPad's screen would be devoted to the Safari app, you would still be online and notified of new instant messengers in the IM app.

As we've mentioned before, to leave an app, you press the Home button to return to the Home screen, and then you find the next app that you want to launch and tap its icon. With the multitasking features built into iOS 5, you don't have to return to the Home screen every time you want to launch a different app. Now, no matter what app you are in, pressing the Home button twice will bring up a row of all the apps that are currently running in the background (see Figure 4–16). These apps are referred to as *background* apps. Any app you have launched on the iPad since turning it on will run as a background app until you close the app for good (discussed in a few pages). This background app bar is a very handy feature, but there is one small caveat: all the apps you see there might not actually be running in the background. Apple also uses this bar to show recently used apps, so even after a reboot, you might see several apps in the bar even though you have not launched them since rebooting.

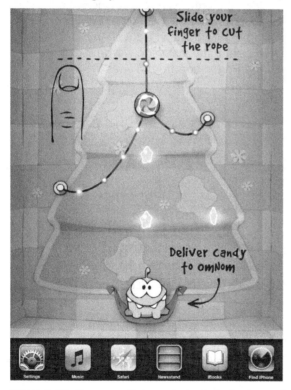

Figure 4–16. *Some apps that are running in the background while we are currently in the Cut the Rope game*

In Figure 4–16, you can see we are in a fun game called Cut the Rope. By double-pressing the Home button twice, the multitasking bar slides the screen up, and you can scroll through all your other open, or background, apps. To see more currently running background apps, slide your finger over the row of apps. To quickly switch to another background app, tap its icon, and it will swap places with the current app you are in (see Figure 4–17).

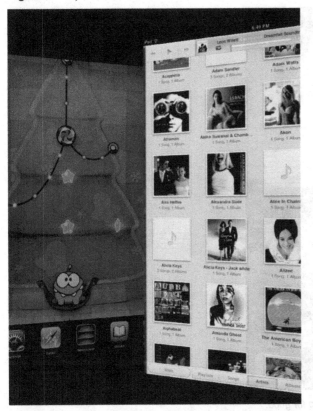

Figure 4–17. *The Cut the Rope app swapping places with the Music app via the iPad's multitasking features*

Closing an App for Good

The iPad's Home screen allows you to launch any application with a single tap. Once you've launched that app, it remains open in the background even if you return to the Home screen. To close the app for good, double-press the Home button to open the background apps bar. Swipe through the row of apps until you've found the one you want to close. Now touch and hold the app's icon until it and the other apps in the bar start to jiggle. You'll notice red circles with white minus signs have appeared in the corner of all the apps in the bar (see Figure 4–18). Tap the red circle to close the app. To reopen the app, you'll need to launch it from the Home screen again.

Quitting applications instead of letting them remain open in the background lowers your CPU usage, keeps your iPad slightly cooler, and puts a little less strain on your battery.

Remember how we mentioned that Apple also uses this background multitasking bar to show recently used apps? Well, if the app isn't running, tapping the minus sign will remove the recently used app from the bar. The way Apple has this implemented, you can't really tell just by looking through the bar which apps are running and which are just recently used apps.

Figure 4–18. *Tap the red circles to close an app for good.*

Force Quitting an App

The iPad's Home screen allows you to launch any application with a single tap. When in an app, press the iPad's Home button to return to the Home screen at any time. If, for some reason, a program hangs and your iPad becomes unresponsive, you can press and hold the Home button for six to ten seconds to quit that program and return to the Home screen.

> **TIP:** A Back button appears in the upper-left corner of many iPad screens while inside an app. Tap this button to return to the previous screen in the app. This is different from pressing the Home button. The Back button moves you between screens within an app. The Home button leaves an app and returns you to the Home screen.

Multitasking Gestures

As you can now see, the iPad has wonderful multitasking capabilities built in. But users aren't limited to accessing the multitasking features by double pressing the Home button. They can use gestures as well.

To enable multitasking gestures, go to **Settings ➤ Multitasking Gestures** and toggle it to On. Once multitasking gestures are enabled, you can use four- or five-finger (whichever is more comfortable for you) gestures to do the following:

> *Pinch to the Home screen*: In any app, simply use four or five fingers to make a pinching motion. You'll see the current app shrink into the home page as app icons on the home page return to view, as if you were going through a star field.

> *Swipe up to reveal multitasking bar*: Using four or five fingers, swipe up from the bottom of the screen to reveal the multitasking bar (see -16).

> *Swipe left or right between apps*: Using four or five fingers, swipe left or right between apps. You'll be able to move through them in the order that they are arranged in the multitasking bar.

You'll want to get familiar with multitasking gestures because they make for a fluid and seamless experience in navigating your Home screen and apps. They also make clicking the Home button unnecessary.

Spotlight Search

At this point, you've explored everything the iPad Home screen offers save one important feature. Earlier we mentioned a small gray magnifying glass icon next to the row of dots that represent the pages of apps that you have (see Figure 4–19). This magnifying glass icon represents the iPad's powerful search feature, named Spotlight.

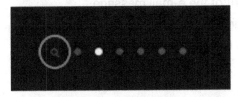

Figure 4–19. *The Spotlight magnifying glass icon (circled) at the bottom of every home page*

To access Spotlight, simply swipe to the right of the first page of your Home screen. You'll be taken to a page that displays a small, white search field at the top with the words *Search iPad* in it. At the bottom of the page, you'll be presented with the built-in keyboard.

Simply begin typing any search query into the search field and the space between the search field, and the keyboard will begin populating with results (see Figure 4–20).

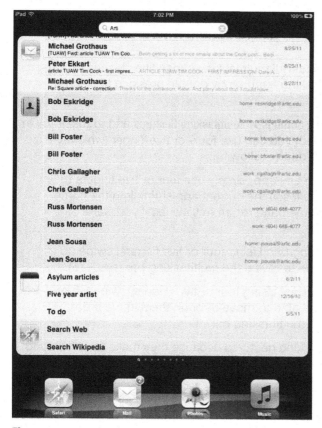

Figure 4–20. *The Spotlight search results page*

Currently, Spotlight is capable of searching the following:

> *Contacts:* First, last, and company names.
>
> *Mail:* To, From, and Subject fields; content of the e-mail message.
>
> *Calendar:* Event titles, invites, and locations.
>
> *Music:* Song names, artists, and albums. Podcast and audiobook titles and names.
>
> *Notes:* Note title and content.
>
> *Events:* Event title and content.
>
> *Videos:* Video name.
>
> *Applications:* App name.
>
> *Podcasts:* Podcast name.
>
> *Audiobooks:* Audiobook title.
>
> *Reminders:* Reminders name and content.
>
> *Messages:* Messages content.

To select a result, simply tap it, and you'll automatically be taken to the document or file in the app it's found in. At the bottom of the Spotlight results you have the option to search the Web for your query and also search Wikipedia. Tapping either of those options will open the Safari web browser and take you to your default search engine page or the Wikipedia search results page.

Although Spotlight is a nice feature, it does have some limitations. Perhaps the biggest limitation is that you can't search for text in the body of an e-mail. Also, Spotlight isn't smart enough to recognize misspellings, so anything that is mistyped in a note or e-mail subject won't be found.

> **NOTE:** If you have dozens and dozens of apps, instead of swiping through all the Home screen pages, you can simply go to Spotlight and search for the name of the app. When its icon appears, simply tap it to launch it.

Spotlight Settings

Go to **Settings** ➤ **General** ➤ **Spotlight Search**, and you'll find a list of the things Spotlight searches through on your iPad. You can deselect apps to eliminate them from Spotlight search (for example, tap Music to deselect it, and names of songs won't show up when you're searching). You can also use the grip icon to the right of the screen to rearrange the order that search groupings appear in.

iPad Settings

The iPad has myriad settings allowing you to customize how your iPad works and looks. You can find all of these settings in the Settings app on your iPad Home screen (Figure 4–21).

Figure 4–21. *The Settings app icon*

Tap the Settings app, and on the left side of the screen, you'll see a list of settings for the iPad and any Apple iPad apps that shipped with the iPad (see Figure 4–22). Below those, you'll see an Apps heading. Any apps you've downloaded from the iTunes Store will appear here if they have customizable settings. To select an app's setting, tap the name of the app.

Figure 4–22. *The general settings selections*

Although we'll go into greater depth about Apple's built-in app's individual settings throughout the book, for now let's get acquainted with the iPad's General settings:

About: This shows you how many songs, videos, photos, and applications you have on your iPad. It also shows you your iPad's total storage capacity and how much you have left. Your iPad's OS version number, model, and serial numbers can be found here, along with your Wi-Fi and Bluetooth IDs. At the very bottom, you'll see links to Apple's legal and regulatory documentation.

Software Update: New in iOS 5 is the ability to update the iOS software without having to plug your iPad into iTunes and download the software from there. Now any time a software update is available for iOS, a red badge will appear on the corner of the Setting icon. You can also manually check for iOS software updates by navigating to **Settings ➤ General ➤ Software Update**. Any available iOS software updates will be found there.

Usage: Usage is another new Settings preference that allows you to see how much storage each app on your iPad is taking up.

If you tap the Edit button on any app's Usage screen, you can selectively delete any of the items to free up space. You can even delete entire apps (but not the ones that shipped on your iPad) to free up all the space they take up.

Usage is handy if your iPad is almost full but you want to download a movie at the airport to watch on the plane. You can delete some songs or other content in apps to get enough space to download that movie.

Usage also allows you to toggle the battery's percentage display. Choose whether to display the percentage of battery power you have left next to the icon of the battery in the status bar.

Sounds: This area gives you a slider to adjust the volume on your iPad and set your ringtone. It also enables you to turn on or off sounds for e-mail, calendar alerts, lock sounds, and keyboard clicks. It also allows you to set the sounds for your ringtones and Tweets.

Network: This displays your network settings. See Chapter 3 for details.

Bluetooth: This allows you to turn the iPad's Bluetooth signal on or off. If you aren't using any Bluetooth devices with your iPad, keep Bluetooth turned off. It'll save you battery life.

iTunes Wi-Fi Sync: As we discussed in Chapter 2, you can now sync your iPad wirelessly when it's in range of your computer on the same Wi-Fi network. When you plug in your iPad to a power source, it will automatically sync. However, you can initiate a sync from your iPad at any time by going to **Settings ➤ General ➤ iTunes Wi-Fi Sync**. To initiate a sync, simply tap the *Sync Now* button.

Spotlight Search: The settings for iPad's Spotlight search features.

Auto-Lock and Passcode Lock: As we talked about earlier, this is where you configure your lock settings.

Restrictions: If you share your iPad among your family or buy one for your children, you may want to limit what they can do on it. The Restrictions settings will let you limit access to Safari, YouTube, and the iTunes Store app. In addition, you can restrict users from installing new apps and using location services. You can also choose what content you want allowed on the iPad. Settings include restricting In-App purchases and limiting access to movies, music, TV shows, and apps that surpass your chosen ratings.

Use Side Switch To: Set the function of the iPad's physical side switch. Choose from between making it a rotation lock witch or a mute switch.

Multitasking Gestures: Switch multitasking gestures on or off.

Date & Time: This allows you to select a 24-hour clock as well as set your time zone and set the date and time manually.

Keyboard: This is where you control all your keyboard settings. We'll go through them in the next section.

International: Use this settings pane to select your preferred language and region formatting for addresses and phone numbers.

Accessibility: This is where the settings for the sight and hearing impaired are. We'll go into these in detail later in the chapter.

Reset: Reset All Settings lets you set your iPad's settings to factory default. Erase All Content and Settings works like Reset All Settings but also erases all your personal data. This section also allows you to reset your network, keyboard, Home screen layout, and location settings to the iPad's factory defaults.

The Keyboard

Like the touch keyboard on your iPhone? You haven't seen anything yet. Using the iPad's keyboard for the first time is nothing short of an epiphany when you realize what a large-screen, Multi-Touch device is capable of.

The keyboard, shown in Figure 4–23, will display automatically when you are in any app that needs to have text input. It is important to note that the software keyboard will not display if the iPad is paired to an external Bluetooth keyboard. (Refer to Chapter 3 for Bluetooth pairing.)

Figure 4–23. *The iPad's Multi-Touch keyboard. Note the keyboard button in the lower-right corner.*

For this section, we'll look at using the on-screen keyboard in Apple's Notes app that comes on every iPad.

Open Notes, and click the + button in the upper-right corner to create a new note. At the bottom of your iPad's screen, you'll see the keyboard automatically appear (see Figure 4–24). Alternatively, you can tap and hold the keyboard button (the key in the lower-right corner of the keyboard) and drag the keyboard up to split it. This split keyboard enables *thumb typing*, using your thumbs to type while holding the iPad. Many people find this split keyboard a lot more comfortable to type on because of the awkwardness of holding a device you are typing on. To join the keyboard again, tap and hold the keyboard button and select the Dock and Merge button that pops up.

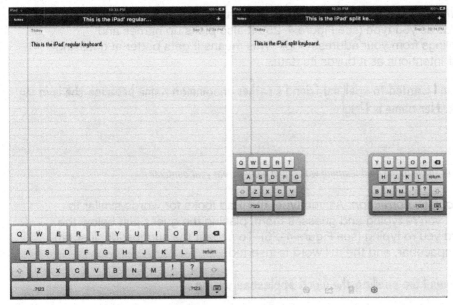

Figure 4–24. *The standard keyboard appears at the bottom of the iPad's screen (left). Or you can split it and position it anywhere up or down the screen you want (right).*

> **NOTE:** Using the keyboard in portrait orientation gives you a smaller keyboard but more space to see what you're typing on-screen. If you switch to landscape orientation, you'll have a larger keyboard but less space to see what you've typed. Play around to see what works best for you.

Though Apple has outdone itself in designing the iPad's keyboard, many people still think it's the hardest thing to get used to on their new iPad. Making the switch to a touch-screen keyboard can be difficult, but it does get much better over a relatively short amount of time. The keyboard gets easier to use the more you use it, not just because you get used to it, but because it has a secret, and it's not just that you can split it in two.

The secret is that the keyboard, shown in Figure 4–23, is smart—so smart that it corrects for a lot of typos and misaligned fingers. It automatically capitalizes the start of sentences. It suggests corrections for misspelled words. It uses predictive technology to make it easier to hit the right keys. So, within a few weeks, you'll master the keyboard's quirks. You can also use Apple's iPad Smart Cover (mentioned in Chapter 1) to give the iPad a better angle for typing. A cover folds back into a triangle and forms a wedge that tilts the iPad at a comfortable angle so you can type and look at the screen above the keyboard at the same time. The angle of the case makes it easier to avoid mistakes touch-typists make on the iPad's on-screen keyboard, namely, resting palms and fingers on the screen.

Here are some of the key technologies that make the iPad keyboard work:

Dictionary: The iPad has a built-in dictionary that learns frequently used words as you type (see Figure 4–25). It also picks up names and spellings from your address book. This means it gets better at guessing your intentions as it builds its data.

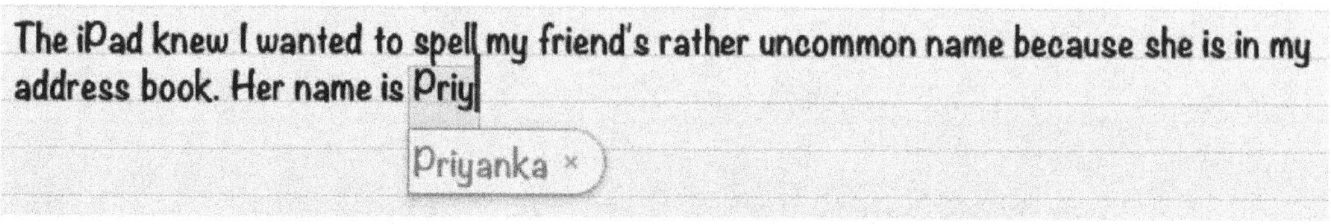

The iPad knew I wanted to spell my friend's rather uncommon name because she is in my address book. Her name is Priy

Priyanka ×

Figure 4–25. *An example of the iPad learning words and names from your contacts*

Automatic correction: As you type, the iPad looks for words similar to what you're typing and guesses them, placing the guess just below the word you're typing (see Figure 4–26). To accept the suggestion, just tap the spacebar, and the full word is inserted.

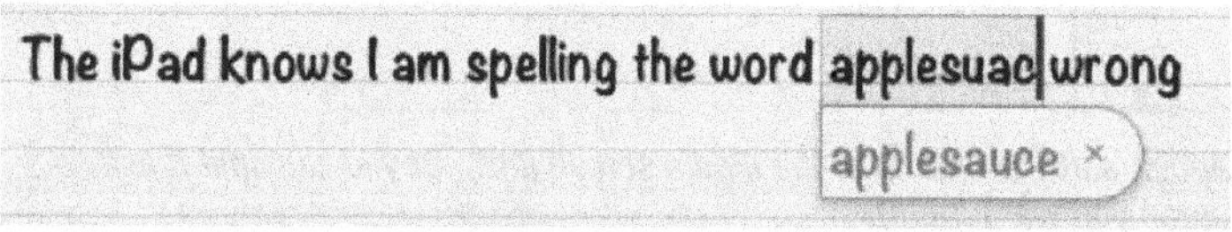

The iPad knows I am spelling the word applesuac wrong

applesauce ×

Figure 4–26. *An example of the iPad's auto-correction features*

Spell check: If you do spell a word wrong or the iPad doesn't recognize it, you'll see a red line appear below the word. When you tap the word, one or more alternate spellings will appear above it (see Figure 4–27). Simply tap the right word, and it inserts itself into the text.

technology

If I spell techknology wrong, I'll see a red line under it. If I tap the word I'll get possible spelling corrections.

Figure 4–27. *An example of the iPad's spell-check feature*

Predictive mapping: The iPad uses its dictionary to predict which word you're about to type. It then readjusts the keyboard response zones to make it easier for you to hit the right letters. Likely letters get bigger tap zones; unlikely letters get smaller ones.

More Keyboards

Thought the iPad had only one keyboard? Think again. It has more than a dozen (in different languages). It also has two other keyboards you'll frequently access from the primary keyboard on your screen.

On the primary keyboard (shown earlier in Figure 4–23), you'll notice the comma, exclamation point, question mark, and period next to the Shift key. Below that is the *.?123 key* (in some applications it's the @123 key). Tapping the .?123 key automatically switches your QWERTY keyboard into a numeric keyboard with further punctuation symbols, an "undo" option, and another keyboard modifier key labeled #+= (see Figure 4–28).

> **TIP:** You don't need to use the "undo" button to undo something. You can simply shake your iPad. (Not too hard! You don't want to look like you've lost your marbles!) An undo pop-up will appear on the screen giving you the option of undoing your last action or canceling the undo.

Figure 4–28. *The .?123 keyboard*

Tapping the #+= key takes you to a third keyboard with more punctuation and a "redo" button (see Figure 4–29). Redo, if the app supports it, will repeat the last action performed. So if you've copied and pasted text, tapping the redo button will paste the text again.

Figure 4–29. *The #+= keyboard*

Getting Started

When you're new to the iPad, start by typing slowly. Typing with the iPad in your hands can be difficult because of the device's size. For optimal typing experience, place the iPad on a table or prop it in your lap. At first, you may be typing by using your index fingers on each hand, but the more you use it, the more you'll typing as you do on a physical keyboard. Whatever method you use, make sure to go at a pace that allows you to keep track of what you're typing and make corrections as you go. Here are a few typing how-tos:

Summoning the keyboard: To open the keyboard, tap in any editable text area.

Dismissing the keyboard: To make the iPad's keyboard go away, tap the bottom-right key (you can see the key in Figures 4–23, 4–28, and 4–29). It's the button with the picture of a keyboard and a down arrow on it. To get the keyboard back, simply tap in any editable text area again.

Accepting or rejecting automatic corrections: The iPad displays suggested corrections just below the word you're typing, as shown earlier in Figure 4–25. To accept the suggestion, tap the spacebar. (You don't need to finish typing the word; the iPad puts it in there for you.) To decline the correction, tap the word itself. The iPad will not make a substitution, even when you press the spacebar.

Using the spyglass: While you're typing, you can adjust the cursor by using the iPad's built-in spyglass feature, as shown in Figure 4–30. Hold your finger somewhere in the text area until the spyglass appears. Then use the magnified view to drag the cursor exactly where you need it.

If I spell technology wrong, I'll see a red line under it. If I tap the word I'll get possible spelling corrections.

Figure 4–30. *The spyglass gives you pinpoint precision for cursor placement.*

> **NOTE:** If you are going to be doing a lot of typing on your iPad (like writing a book, for instance), you may want to look into getting the iPad Keyboard Dock or the Apple Bluetooth keyboard we told you about in Chapter 3. A physical keyboard turns the iPad into more of a traditional computer. Plus, if you are a touch-typist, you'll probably type much faster on a physical keyboard because you can feel its presses and hear its clicks. You aren't limited to an Apple Bluetooth keyboard either. Several third-party keyboards work with the iPad. Contact the manufacturer to find out what their Bluetooth keyboards do.

iPad Typing Tricks

Once you get the hang of the keyboard, the iPad offers several other ways to make typing easier. This section describes a few of these handy iPad typing tricks.

Contractions

When you want to type a contraction like *can't* or *shouldn't*, don't bother putting in the apostrophe. The iPad is smart enough to guess that *cant* is *can't* (Figure 4–31). Of course, if you're typing about the British Thieves' language, make sure to tap the word to decline the change from the noun to the contraction.

When you're typing in a word like *we'll*, where the uncontracted *well* is a common word, add an extra *l*. The iPad corrects *welll* to *we'll* and *shelll* to *she'll*.

Figure 4–31. *"Cant" becomes "Can't."*

> **TIP:** Other contraction tricks include *itsa*, which gets corrected to *it's*, and *weree*, which gets corrected to *we're*.

Punctuation

When at the end of a sentence, tap the punctuation key, then tap the item you want to use (such as a question mark or period), and finally tap the spacebar. The iPad is smart enough to recognize the end of a sentence and put you back in alphabet mode. During normal typing, you can also double-tap the spacebar to add a period followed by a space. This double-tap trick is controlled in your settings via **Settings ➤ General ➤ Keyboard ➤ "."** Shortcut.

Accents

Tap and hold any keyboard letter to view inflected versions of that letter. For example, tapping and holding e presents the options of adding e, é, or ê (among other accents), as shown in Figure 4–32. This shortcut makes it much easier to type foreign words. To select a non-English keyboard, go to **Settings ➤ General ➤ International ➤ Keyboards** and choose from your iPad's long list of foreign-language variations.

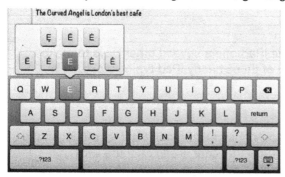

Figure 4–32. *iPad handles accents like a pro.*

Caps Lock

To enable the Caps Lock function, go to **Settings ➤ General ➤ Keyboard Preferences**. When this function is enabled, you can double-tap the Shift key to toggle the lock on and off.

Word Deletion

When you press and hold the Delete key, the iPad starts off by deleting one letter and then the next. But if you hold it for longer than about a line of text, it switches to word deletion and starts removing entire words at a time.

Auto-capitalization

Auto-capitalization means the iPad automatically capitalizes the word at the beginning of a sentence. So, you can type *the day has begun*, and the iPad is smart enough to capitalize *the*, as in, *The day has begun*. This means you don't need to worry about pressing the Shift key at the beginning of every sentence or even when you type *i*, because *i went to the park* becomes *I went to the park*. Enable or disable auto-capitalization in **Settings ➤ General ➤ Keyboard Preferences**.

Shortcuts

iOS 5 allows you to specify text shortcuts that expand into full words or phrases. For example, typing "omw" expands into "On my way!" You can add any kind of text shortcuts you want. Go to **Settings ➤ General ➤ Keyboard ➤ Add New Shortcut** and type in the phrase you'd like to add and its shortcut text. Adding your own shortcuts can save you retyping common phrases you use in e-mail or text messages.

Copy and Paste

Apple has created an easy and intuitive way to select a word or block of words, copy them, and then paste them into another location.

Let's copy some text from a web page in iPad's Safari web browser. Before you can copy a word, you'll need to select it. To do that, press and hold your finger over a word. A black contextual menu will pop up that gives you the Select and Select All options. Select will highlight just the single word. Select All will highlight all the words on the page. No matter which you choose, you'll be presented with a grab point at the beginning and end of the selected text (see Figure 4–33). These grab points allow you to adjust which text is selected.

Figure 4–33. *Grab points allow you to select a single word, a sentence, or a whole paragraph to be copied.*

> **NOTE:** If you've selected text to copy in an editable document, you'll see a contextual menu that says Cut, Copy, or Paste. Selecting Cut will remove the text. Selecting Copy will copy it, and if you already have text copied, you'll be able to paste it over your current selection.

Once you have selected your text, you'll see another contextual menu that says Copy. Tapping Copy will copy the text and make it available in any app that support text input.

Now let's go back to the note in the Notes app. To paste the text you copied from Safari into your note, simply press and hold your finger on the screen until the spyglass pops up. Use the spyglass to adjust the cursor to the location where you want to insert the copied text and let go. You'll see another contextual menu pop up that gives you three options: Select, Select All, and Paste. Tap Paste, and your copied text will be instantly inserted (Figure 4–34).

Figure 4–34. *Simply tap Paste, and your text is inserted automatically.*

Undo and Redo

As mentioned earlier, the iPad's keyboard sports undo and redo buttons. Tapping the undo button undoes the last action you performed. So if you've copied and pasted text, tapping the undo button will unpaste the text but leave it copied on your clipboard. Remember that you can also shake your iPad to display an undo pop-up that will ask you whether you want to undo the last action you performed.

Redo, if the app supports it, will repeat the last action performed. So if you've copied and pasted text, tapping the redo button will paste the text again.

Dictionary Lookup

iOS 5 allows you to look up any word in a note, e-mail, or web page. Simply select the word and then tap Define in the contextual menu popup. The dictionary panel will display the definition of the word. Click the Done button to exit the dictionary panel.

Notification Center

A major new feature in iOS 5 is the Notification Center. As its name suggests, this is a central location where you can see all of your notifications in one place. This includes new e-mails, reminders, tweets, messages, Facebook posts, and more. Basically, if an app can send you any kind of notification, it'll appear in the Notification Center.

To access the Notification Center, simple swipe down with one finger from the top of your iPad's screen. It doesn't matter where you are—on a Home screen, in an app or game, or even on the iPad's lock screen. Wherever you are simply swipe down with one finger and the Notification Center appears.

Alternately, notifications will appear on the iPad's lock screen if you so choose. When a notification appears on the iPad's lock screen, you can touch and hold the icon next to the notification, which represents which app sent the notification, and slide it to the right across the notification. This will unlock the iPad and take you immediately to the app that sent the notification.

In Figure 4–35 you can see that the Notification Center on the Home screen is displaying the select notifications we have set up to be alerted to. In this case, those notifications are FaceTime calls, Weather Channel alerts, Calendar events, and Mail messages.

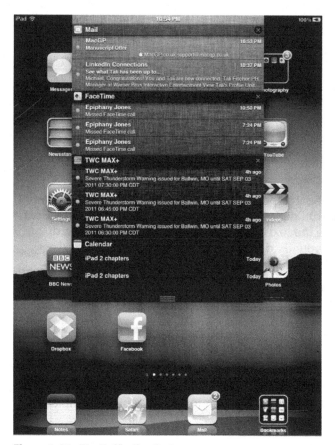

Figure 4–35. *The Notification Center*

To scroll through the Notification Center, simply swipe up or down with your finger. Tap any notification in the Notification Center to be taken directly to the app that sent the notification. For example, in Figure 4–35 if you tap the FaceTime missed call notification, you will automatically be taken to the FaceTime app and initiate a return call. Tapping the weather alert takes you to the Weather Channel app. Tapping an e-mail notification takes you right to that e-mail. Pretty cool, huh?

To close the Notification Center, touch the three grab bars at the bottom of its screen and swipe up.

Types of Notifications

There are many types of notifications in iOS 5 on the iPad. They all perform the same task—notifying you of an event—but they all notify you in a different way:

> *Banners*: Banners appear at the top of your screen and go away automatically after a few seconds. They're a short visual cue that lets you see you have a notification without interrupting your work. The banner notification in Figure 4–36 tells us we've just received an e-mail from "MacGP" and the subject of the e-mail is "Manuscript Offer."

> *Alerts*: Alerts are more abrupt than banners. An alert is a pop-up dialog box that requires you to take some action before the alert will disappear. You can see an example of an alert in Figure 4–15.

> *Badges*: Badges are red icons that appear in the corner of an app's icon. Badges often contain numbers. For example, in Figure 4–35 the "2" badge on the Mail icon means there are two new e-mails waiting.

> *Sounds*: Sounds are audible notifications of an event. You might hear a "ding!" when you get a new e-mail, for example.

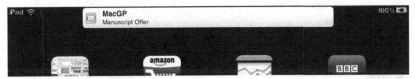

Figure 4–36. *The banner type of notification.*

Now that you are familiar with the types of notifications, let's look at how to configure them for each app and configure what notifications appear in the Notification Center.

Setting Up Notifications and the Notification Center

To configure notifications, go to Settings ➤ Notifications (Figure 4–37). You're presented with a list of all the apps that offer notifications. Beneath an app's name are labels telling you what types of notifications that app is sending you. As you can see, a single app can send you multiple types of notifications.

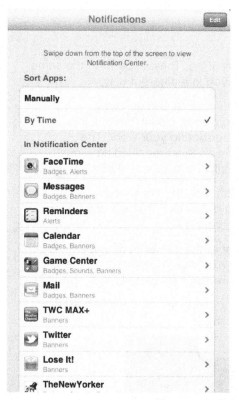

Figure 4–37. *Notifications settings*

The Notifications settings screen allows you to sort the order of the apps that appear in your Notification Center. Tap By Time to show the most recent notification at the top of the Notification Center. If you select Manually, you can then tap the Edit button and drag the apps up or down the list. The order that you put them in will be the order that they appear in the Notification Center.

The Notifications setting screen also shows you two lists. The first is In Notification Center, and the second is Not in Notification Center. Apps appearing in the In Notification Center list will appear in the actual Notification Center you access by swiping down from the top of your screen. Apps appearing in the Not In Notification Center list will still send you notifications; they just won't appear in the Notification Center list.

There's an advantage to not having all your notifications show in the Notification Center: it reduces clutter. After all, you might not care to see all the Twitter @mentions you've received in your Notification Center, but you may want to still have notifications enabled for the Twitter app, such as badges, which will appear on the app icon itself.

Each app has its individual notifications settings. To access them, simply tap the name of the app in the notification settings (Figure 4–37). The app's individual notification settings will appear (Figure 4–38).

Figure 4–38 shows the notification settings for the Game Center app. These notification settings are a good representation of the settings you'll find for other apps, but be aware that settings can vary from app to app.

> *Notification Center*: Toggle this to show or hide the app's notifications (Game Center's in this case) in the Notification Center.
>
> *Show*: Select how many notifications from the app to show in the Notification Center.
>
> *Alert style*: Choose from between none, banners, or alerts.
>
> *Badge App Icon*: Toggle this to show or hide red badge notifications.
>
> *Sounds*: Toggle this to hear/mute audible notifications.
>
> *View in Lock Screen*: When set to on, an app's notifications will appear on the iPad's lock screen. If this is set to Off, the app's notifications will not appear on the lock screen but will appear in the Notification Center when viewed from elsewhere in iOS. Apple gives users this option in order to hide sensitive information (such as e-mails) from prying eyes.

Figure 4–38. *Selecting an app's notification settings.*

Accessibility

Apple wanted to make sure everyone could use the iPad as easily as possible. To that end, Apple offers accessibility features to help people with disabilities use the iPad. We briefly touched on the iPad's accessibility options in the iPad iTunes settings pane in Chapter 2. The iPad features more accessibility options than the ones you see in the settings pane, however. To see all the accessibility options, tap the Settings icon on the iPad's Home screen. Under General settings, tap Accessibility. You'll see the Accessibility settings slide onto the screen (see Figure 4–39). Let's go through these settings one by one.

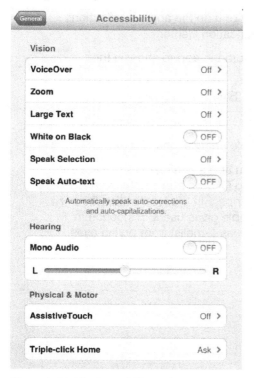

Figure 4–39. *The Accessibility settings*

VoiceOver

With VoiceOver turned on, the user can simply touch the screen to hear a description of what is beneath his finger. They can then double-tap to select the item. With VoiceOver enabled, the iPad will speak when the user has a new e-mail message and can even read the e-mail to the user.

Zoom

Zoom allows those hard of seeing to magnify their entire screen. This is different from the standard pinch and zoom features of the iPad's regular software. Accessibility Zoom will magnify everything on the screen, allowing the user to zoom into even the smallest of buttons. When this option is selected, the user can double-tap any part of the iPad's screen with three fingers to automatically zoom in 200 percent. When the screen is zoomed in, you must drag or flick it with three fingers. Also, when you go to a new screen, zoom will always return to the top middle of the screen.

Large Text

This lets you increase the size of text in Contacts, Mail, and Notes. You can choose from 20-point text, 32-point, 40-point, 48-point, and 56-point.

White on Black

For some people with seeing difficulties, inverting the color of a computer screen so it resembles a photographic negative allows them to read text better. Turning White on Black does this.

Speak Selection

With this option selected, any selected text (such as the text you select when copying and pasting) will be spoken aloud.

Speak Auto-text

With this option selected, any auto-correction text (such as the spell-check pop-ups that appear when you are typing) will be spoken aloud.

Mono Audio

With this selected, the stereo sounds of the left and right speakers or headphones will be combined into a mono (single) signal. You can then choose which speaker, the left or the right, you want to hear the mono audio come from. This option lets users who have a hearing impairment in one ear hear the entire sound signal with the other ear.

Assistive Touch

Apple recognizes that for people who have motor skills, using a multitouch screen like the one found on the iPad could be difficult. With this in mind, Apple created Assistive Touch. When Assistive Touch is enabled a black and white dot will always show on the iPad's screen (Figure 4–40).

Figure 4–40. *The Assistive Touch dot resides anywhere you put it along the edge of the iPad's screen. Tap it to bring up the Assistive Touch menus.*

Tapping the dot will display an on-screen menu overlay (Figure 4–41) that allows users to tap icons that represent gestures. So instead of tapping or swiping with two fingers, Assistive Touch allows the user to simply tap a button, which will then perform the gesture automatically.

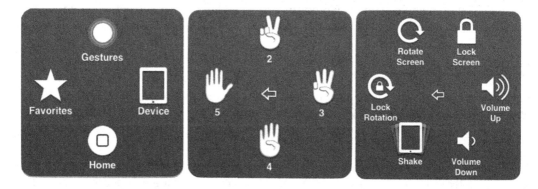

Figure 4–41. *The Assistive Touch on-screen menus*

Triple-Click Home

If you are sharing an iPad in a house with someone with disabilities, selecting this option will allow users, by triple-clicking the iPad's physical Home button, to quickly toggle VoiceOver, Zoom, White on Black, or Assistive Touch on or off (Figure 4–42). You can also set it so triple-clicking the Home button causes a pop-up to appear on-screen asking what accessibility feature to turn on.

Figure 4–42. *The Accessibility Options pop-up window*

> **NOTE:** With the exception of the triple-click Home feature, all of these accessibility settings can also be configured from within the iPad iTunes settings pane on the Summary tab (see Chapter 2).

Summary

This chapter explored all the ways you can interact with your iPad, from taps to buttons to pinches. You read about the touch screen and how you can communicate with it. You discovered how to access your Home screen, how to lock it, and how to rearrange its icons. You explored your iPad's General settings, and you learned tips and tricks to using the iPad's virtual keyboard and setting accessibility options. In short, you were introduced to all the basic ways you and your iPad can communicate with each other. Here are a few key lessons for you to carry away with you:

- Build up your working iPad interaction vocabulary. You will be surprised how often one of the rarer gestures, like the two-fingered tap, can prove useful.

- If you are using your iPad in an area where your data's security is an issue, be sure to set a passcode lock.

- The Notification Center shows you all your alerts and notifications in one easy to access place.

- Spotlight is a powerful search tool on the iPad and offers you another way to quickly launch your apps.

- The iPad supports more than a dozen keyboard languages as well as physical hardware keyboards.

- Don't worry about typing perfectly on the iPad. Its smart keyboard will correct most of your mistakes automatically.

■   Just because you have a disability doesn't mean you can't use the
iPad. The iPad has many accessibility features to help the those with
sight or hearing issues.

Chapter 5

Connecting to the Internet

Although your iPad can theoretically be used unconnected with no real links to the outside world, it's designed to be an Internet-ready tool. It offers built-in Wi-Fi or Wi-Fi + 3G connectivity, and most of the default apps are useless without having an Internet connection of some sort.

Without the Internet, you'd have no need for Mail to send and receive messages, and there would be no reason for the Safari web browser. You wouldn't be able to pull up maps, YouTube would just be a bland icon taking up space on your Home screen, and you couldn't buy apps from the App Store, books from the iBookstore, or music, movies, and videos from iTunes. Facebook and Twitter? Forget about them without that Internet connection.

Fortunately, Apple makes it simple for you to connect to the Internet. In this chapter, we'll tell you how to make and troubleshoot Internet connections through Wi-Fi and 3G and discuss an alternative to the built-in 3G.

Connecting with Wi-Fi

Wi-Fi is the common name for wireless networking based on the IEEE 802.11 standard. Although Wi-Fi has its roots in the early 1990s, it has really taken off in the past ten years, with Wi-Fi access points now available in many public places such as hotels, libraries, restaurants, and even buses and airplanes.

For many people, Wi-Fi access points were a godsend for home networking because it meant that computers and printers could be connected to each other without the expense and inconvenience of installing cabling. In most cases, a Wi-Fi router is attached directly to a home cable or DSL Internet modem to provide wireless Internet to any computer within range.

Your iPad supports Wi-Fi connections under the 802.11b/g/n standards. It's not necessary to know what each of these standards means, other than that the maximum raw data rate (the speed at which data is pumped to your iPad) increases with each successive standard. The iPad and Wi-Fi router will communicate with each other based on the highest common standard, so if your Wi-Fi router supports only 802.11b, the rate at which the two devices will talk will be limited to 802.11b speeds. Likewise, if you have one of the newest Apple AirPort Extreme Wi-Fi routers, your iPad communicates with it using an implementation of the fast 802.11n standard.

Authentication and Encryption

One important factor for all Wi-Fi networks is the use of encryption. Encrypted networks require that a password or passphrase be entered when joining the network for the first time. The password not only authenticates your iPad to the network, essentially making sure that you are allowed to use that network, but is used as a key to encrypt any data that is transferred between your iPad and the router.

Both authentication and encryption are important for any wireless network. Setting up authentication on your home or office network ensures that no unauthorized person can use your wireless network without your permission. This is important, since providing access to your Internet connection to anyone who happens to be in the area can be considered a breach of the terms of service with many Internet service providers. In addition, if anyone commits a crime from a computer connected to your wireless network with or without your knowledge, you can be held accountable.

Likewise, encryption makes it difficult for hackers to intercept and decode transactions between your iPad and any other computer. This is extremely important when you're performing monetary transactions. Three major types of encryption are in place on most home, office, and public Wi-Fi networks at this time: WEP, WPA, and WPA2. WPA2 is the successor to the WPA encryption standard and is considered (when used with a strong passphrase) to be extremely secure.

Why discuss authentication and encryption in a book about iPads? Well, if you're unfamiliar with Wi-Fi networks, the topic will definitely come up when you try to connect your iPad to the networks.

Setting Up Wi-Fi

Establishing a Wi-Fi connection is part of your iPad's initial setup procedure. The first time you use your iPad with iOS 5, it walks you through the process of selecting a network and, if needed, authenticating with a password (see Figure 5–1).

Figure 5–1. *Establishing a Wi-Fi connection is part of the standard iOS 5 setup procedure.*

You'll need to know your network password or passphrase, as well as the name of the network to which you want to connect. Knowing the name can be very important if you live in an apartment building where there are many wireless networks within range. A pop-up appears on the screen asking you to enter the network password, and once you've entered it correctly, iOS connects you to the network.

You can also connect to a Wi-Fi network at other times and places, using the built-in Settings application. The settings pane allows you to enable and disable Wi-Fi and to select and customize your connections.

In Figure 5–2, there are two networks within range of the iPad. The lock icon signifies that you need to enter a password or passphrase before you can connect to the network, while the AirPort icon (the fan-shaped icon to the right of the lock) indicates the relative signal strength of the network. Here, SadunNet is coming in loud and clear; the CCWC connection is much weaker.

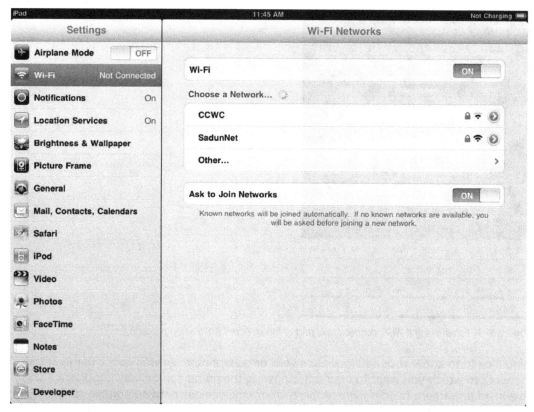

Figure 5–2. *In the Settings app on an iPad with Wi-Fi only, the top switch allows you to toggle Wi-Fi settings on and off.*

To enter the password and join the network, tap the network name, and a password screen appears. Type in your password or passphrase, and then tap the Join button on the iPad's virtual keyboard. If you've entered the password correctly, the network name turns blue and a check mark appears next to it, indicating that it is the selected network. If you didn't enter the correct password, you'll see an error message similar to the one in Figure 5–3. Tap the Dismiss button, and try again.

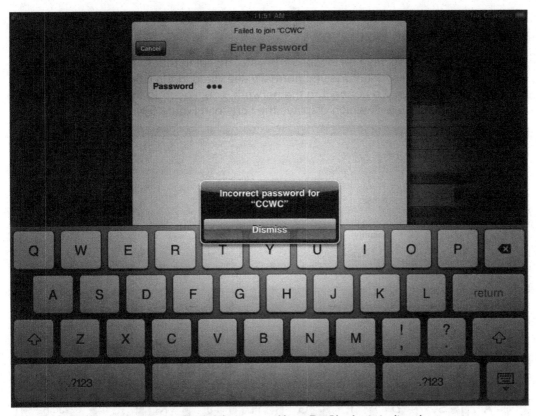

Figure 5–3. *It looks like somebody mistyped the password here. Tap Dismiss to try it again.*

If your iPad Wi-Fi is not enabled, you can turn it on by going to Settings ➤ Wi-Fi and sliding the button marked Off so that it displays On.

Your iPad remembers networks that you've joined so that you don't have to reenter network information every time you move to a new wireless network. If there is no known network nearby, either you have to manually select the new network or you'll be asked if you want to join a new network. What's the difference? It all depends on whether the Ask to Join Networks button (see Figure 5–2) is set to On. If it isn't, you have to manually select the network, and if it is, your iPad will ask you whether you want to join the new network.

When you are connected to a Wi-Fi network, the Wi-Fi icon in the status bar displays your connection strength. More full bars (up to five) indicate a stronger connection.

Troubleshooting Wi-Fi Connection Issues

There are some common issues that new iPad owners may run into. Here's a brief discussion of some of them that you may encounter.

No Network Name Displayed

In this case, the network may be closed or private, meaning that the service set identifier (SSID), which is the network name you normally see listed in the Choose a Network list, has been set as hidden. To connect to the network, you'll need to tap the Other button, shown earlier in Figure 5–2, which displays the screen in Figure 5–4.

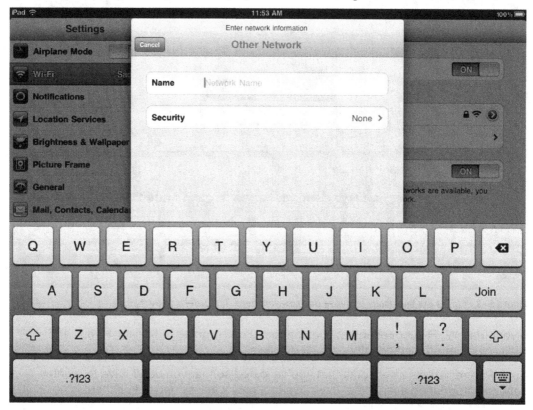

Figure 5–4. *Entering information about hidden networks is useful when using iPads in corporate environments.*

Ask your network administrator the name of the network, and enter that in the Name field. It's also a good idea to ask them what type of security has been set up on the network, since you'll need to choose that by tapping the Security button and then tapping the corresponding button on the Security screen, shown in Figure 5–5.

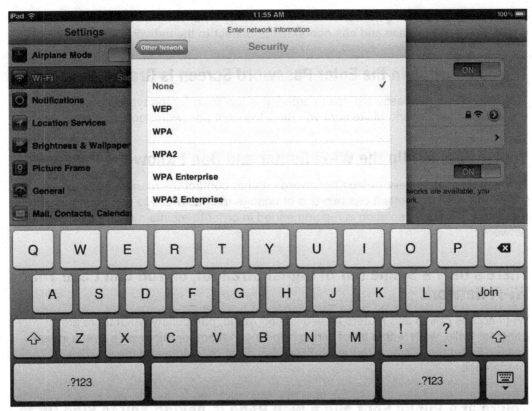

Figure 5-5. *The iPad uses settings to define the type and level of encryption used to keep your data from prying eyes.*

What do these acronyms stand for? Wired Equivalent Privacy (WEP) is an aging method of securing wireless networks. Then why is WEP available on the nice, new iPad? It exists primarily for the benefit of people who haven't upgraded their Wi-Fi access points to newer, more secure technology.

WPA stands for Wi-Fi Protected Access, another aging security technology. WPA Enterprise was a standard encryption algorithm with additions that made it more "bulletproof" for corporate use.

If at all possible, you should use WPA2 or WPA2 Enterprise security to ensure that your data is protected in transit. WPA2 is the most secure existing Wi-Fi security method at this time. It's recommended that you use a truly random passphrase of 13 or more characters for even better security, although it may be more useful to just use a longer—but more memorable—passphrase.

What does memorable mean? Something that *you* can easily remember but would be very difficult for someone else to guess. For example, a passphrase of "ilovemydogfredandhesmyfavoritepet" or even "ilmdfahmfp" (i.e., the first letters of the words of that same phrase) is much easier to remember than "X1F39%@233.abc$@#@."

Once you've entered the network name and security type, you'll be asked for the password or passphrase and can continue to connect to the network.

The Join Button in the Enter Password Screen Is Grayed Out

This means that the password you're entering is too short for the type of security enabled on the network. Make sure you have the right password, and then try again.

You've Just Set Up the Wi-Fi Router and Don't Know the Password

Some Wi-Fi routers have default passwords. Either contact the manufacturer's web site to find out what the default password is or change the password to something you can remember. The latter solution is recommended in order to maintain security on your network.

There's Only a Single Bar of Signal Strength, or You Can't See Your Wi-Fi Network

Wi-Fi access points and routers have a limited range, particularly when there are concrete walls, walls with a lot of wiring or piping in them, or microwave ovens in use nearby. Either move closer to the Wi-Fi access point or try to avoid the sources of interference.

You're at a Public Spot and a Web Page Is Asking You to Sign On to the Network

This is quite normal with public Wi-Fi networks, including the AT&T wireless hotspots in U.S. Starbucks locations. If you're in a location that requires you to pay for Wi-Fi, a login screen may appear into which you'll have to enter subscription information or purchase access time. If it does not appear, open the Safari web browser on your iPad, and the screen should appear.

Your Wi-Fi Connection Is Showing Five Bars, but You're Not Connecting to the Internet

Make sure that you are connecting to the correct Wi-Fi network and not another one nearby. If you are trying to connect to the proper Wi-Fi network, then the connection from your Wi-Fi access point or router to your cable or DSL modem may be down. If that connection looks fine, then your Internet service provider may be having issues. You can test this by checking other computers at your location to see whether they're able to use the Internet.

All the Wi-Fi Networks Have the Same Name

This is more common than you'd imagine. Many people purchase Wi-Fi access points or routers and never change the name from the factory-set one. In heavily populated areas, it's not uncommon to see a number of networks named "Linksys." If you're in this situation, contact the router manufacturer for information on uniquely naming your Wi-Fi network.

None of These Solutions Have Worked

It may be time to reset the network settings on your iPad. To reset network settings, tap **Settings ➤ General ➤ Reset ➤ Reset Network Settings**. A dialog box appears, warning you that you're about to delete all network settings, returning them to factory settings. Tap Reset. This will restart your iPad, and when it comes back up, all saved networks, Wi-Fi passwords, and other settings will be gone. Try to locate and join the network again.

If you can't connect to your network, then try to see whether your iPad can connect to a publicly available network. For instance, if you have an Apple Store close by, try connecting to their network. At least if that doesn't work, you can always confer with the Apple Genius Bar at the store.

Special Wi-Fi Settings

For most people, the default Wi-Fi settings work perfectly. However, there may be situations where you are connecting to a network that requires special settings. In this case, you may be asked to change those settings on your iPad.

You can access special Wi-Fi settings by going to **Settings ➤ Wi-Fi** and then tapping the blue arrow icon to the right of the network name. A much more detailed listing of network settings appears (Figure 5–6).

The first thing you may be asked to change is the way in which your iPad receives an Internet Protocol (IP) address. Most of the time, that's done through something called Dynamic Host Configuration Protocol (DHCP). When your iPad is set up to get a network address using DHCP, it asks for an address when it joins a network and is then given a "lease" that lasts a certain amount of time. That lease usually renews automatically. If you ever need to renew the DHCP lease manually, there's a Renew Lease button on the DHCP tab of the Settings screen you can tap to do that.

Another way to get an IP address is through Bootstrap Protocol, or BootP (Figure 5–7). The BootP tab shows information that may need to be changed for your iPad to receive an address from a pool of addresses registered on a configuration server.

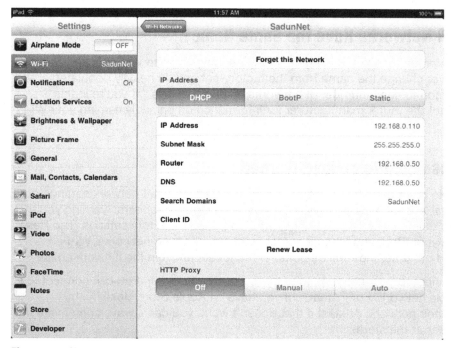

Figure 5–6. *You may never need to change or view your network settings. This is where you can control those settings in those cases where it's necessary.*

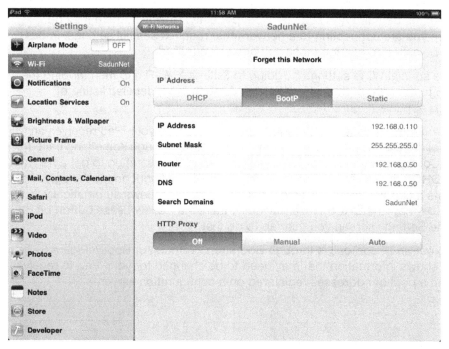

Figure 5–7. *The BootP configuration display*

Finally, some networks require a fixed, or *static*, IP address (Figure 5–8). In this case, you're usually given a static IP address, a subnet mask, and router and DNS server addresses to enter into the appropriate fields in order to connect to the network. Check with your system administrator to find out these values in advance.

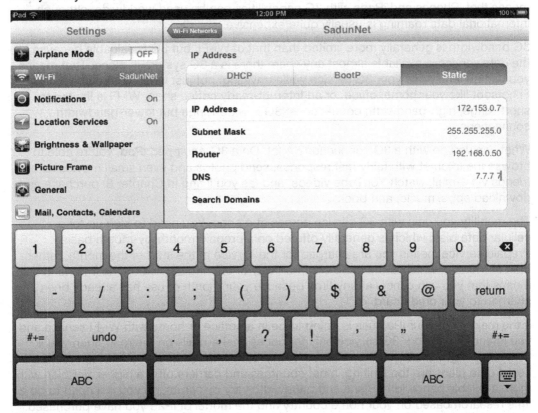

Figure 5–8. *Static IP settings on the iPad*

On each of the three tabs of the Settings screen (DHCP, BootP, and Static), you will find three buttons for HTTP Proxy. These are visible in Figures 5–6 and 5–7. In Figure 5–8, the HTTP Proxy section is hidden by the keyboard. A *proxy server* is a computer system that acts as an intermediary between your computer and some other server. Many companies, for instance, require all web traffic from computers to pass through a proxy server to log or audit usage. If you need to enter proxy information, your system administrator will give you instructions on the settings needed.

Connecting with 3G

The iPad ships in both Wi-Fi only and Wi-Fi + 3G models. 3G models are now available in the United States from supported carriers. Outside the United States, other carriers provide 3G cellular data service on a country-by-country deployment.

3G is a family of mobile telecommunications standards allowing simultaneous voice and data services. Apple has chosen to follow the Global System for Mobile Communications (GSM) standard in its telephony products, the iPhone family, and the iPad Wi-Fi + 3G. This standard predominates world mobile telephone systems, which means that iPhones and iPads with 3G capabilities can be used worldwide, although international data roaming is usually quite expensive.

3G bandwidth is generally more limited than that of Wi-Fi, but 3G is valuable because the data service is available almost anywhere there is a 3G system in place. That means you can generally use your 3G service while traveling, not just when you're at a local Wi-Fi hotspot like your home, office, or an Internet-ready coffee shop. Wi-Fi is limited to short-range, high-bandwidth connections; 3G is wide-range but lower-bandwidth connections.

What can you do with a 3G connection? A lot. On a 3G-equipped iPad, you're able to browse the Internet with fairly fast response, send photos and even small movies to friends via e-mail, watch YouTube videos, and (as you'll find in Chapter 8) purchase and download apps, music, and books.

The mobility you gain with 3G service comes at a price. You need to sign up for a cellular data plan, which is generally offered on a prepaid month-by-month basis. Prepaid service means you are charged for the service at the start of the month, rather than at the end, which is the more common way of offering service on the iPhone. It also means that you can cancel at any time because your month of use has already been charged to your credit card.

If the majority of your iPad use is going to be in an office or home with Wi-Fi service and you intend to use your 3G service only for occasional e-mails on the road, then you'll probably be good with a more-rationed, lower-bandwidth plan. If you find that the lower-tiered data plans are too limiting, most countries and carriers offer a higher-tier plan with more available bandwidth. Plans and bandwidth vary by carrier, so you will need to do a little research based on your home country and the model of iPad you have purchased. For example, in the United States, you cannot switch service for a Verizon-ready iPad to AT&T service. The hardware limits you to a carrier because of the way the unit connects to the cellular data network.

To determine what your 3G usage is at any time after you've signed up for a monthly plan, go to **Settings ➤ Cellular Data ➤ View Account**. This information, as well as the reminders that are sent out by carriers when you're nearing a data usage limit, can be very helpful in keeping an eye on how many megabytes you're actually consuming.

Setting Up 3G

There's a very easy way to tell you have a Wi-Fi + 3G iPad in your hands without looking at the box; when you turn it on, the left side of the status bar shows the name of the 3G carrier and the signal strength at your location (Figure 5–9).

Figure 5-9. *The iPad with Wi-Fi + 3G shows the carrier name and signal strength, as well as the network type (3G, EDGE) on the left side of the status bar.*

Setting up your 3G data plan is fast and requires only a credit card. With your iPad turned on, tap **Settings ➤ Cellular Data.** If 3G isn't turned on, sliding the Cellular Data button to On activates the built-in radio. If no Cellular Data Account has been set up, you're asked to choose a plan and sign up for the service right on your iPad. The details for signing up will vary by carrier, but as a rule, you will have to enter your first and last name, a contact telephone number, an active e-mail account, and credit card information.

Moving along through the form, you'll come to the terms of service. Read through them if you desire, and then tap the Agree button to move through the process. The terms of service will vary by carrier as well.

Some carriers allow you to add a one-time international plan as well. These plans are very expensive. Make sure that the countries you plan to travel to are supported by the international plan. Select the date that you want to start your international plan, and then tap the Done button. If you're not going to be traveling abroad soon, don't tap any of the plans, and just tap Done to continue.

Generally, a few minutes after signing up for a data plan, a notification (Figure 5–10) appears on the iPad display telling you the data plan has been activated. That means you're all set for wandering around town with your iPad, free from the restrictions of needing to be near a Wi-Fi access point. In the United States, if you're now an iPad data customer, you will receive free Wi-Fi at either any carrier-supported hotspot, depending on your subscribed service.

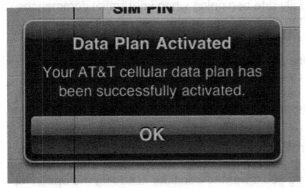

Figure 5-10. *Congratulations! Your iPad is now ready to connect to the world through 3G.*

Data Roaming

When you're using your iPad internationally, it's a very smart idea to know what cellular company or companies your international plan uses and how to turn off data roaming. If data roaming is turned on, your device may connect to a cellular carrier that does not have an agreement with your home carrier, in which case you'll be charged an even higher rate. To disable data roaming, select **Settings** ➤ **General** ➤ **Network** and switch your data roaming option to Off.

For GSM iPads such as the AT&T iPad 2, research your carrier's international roaming partners. Go to the carrier's web site and look up the partner carriers, the technologies used, and the frequencies.

When traveling with a Verizon iPad (or, should one debut, a Sprint one), its CDMA service makes connecting to local data more difficult. Because of this, you may want to consider renting a small mobile Wi-Fi unit like the Novatel Wireless MiFi hotspot. MiFi hotspots provide portable networks that you can connect to from your GSM or CMDA iPad or laptop without using your iPad's built-in data service. You need not enable data roaming on your iPad to access the Internet through a MiFi's cellular data.

XCom Global is one vendor that rents MiFi units for international use. For about $18 a day, you gain access to local data, which is easily served over Wi-Fi to your iPad or laptop. You can, of course, purchase your own unit directly and then shop for SIMs while on the go, but having a preprovisioned device that works directly out of the box is a big win for many travelers.

The coverage areas and expected bandwidth vary. For example, you can expect 7.2Mbps in the United Arab Emirates but only 1Mbps in Guam. Check the coverage maps at the XCom site to make sure the areas you are visiting will allow service.

If you are traveling between countries, you can set up multiple unit rentals through XCom Global. You are still charged a daily rate beginning when your travel commences and ending when you return to the United States. The company's FAQ page answers many common questions about their service.

While traveling, your data usage is unlimited. So, what does "unlimited" data mean? Check out XCom's "fair use" terms. Providers in various countries may cap usage or throttle bandwidth for users who draw heavily on data, but for normal computing needs (assuming you're not downloading several multigigabyte movies per day), you should be covered.

Rent for 7 days, and XCom throws in free shipping (normally $29.90 for FedEx 2Day; you will pay extra for overnight regardless). If you are renting for more than 14 days, the daily rate goes down to $16.15/day. One thing you'll want to consider is adding the option for the $2.50/day battery booster pack. MiFi works best when it's always on—a battery pack offers a way to avoid switching it on and off (although it will get quite warm, so be sure to keep it in a ventilated bag or pocket). Alternatively, you can supply your own battery pack.

We recommend the ZAGGsparq battery pack. This $100 device is international-aware, allowing you to charge from 220V sources; you don't need a voltage converter, because a simple outlet adapter is fine. This will save you the rental fees and provide handy power on the go even when you're back at home (it's rated to recharge an iPad four times over).

Also, you may consider opting for the insurance. At about $4/day, it covers up to three devices, allowing you to worry less about pickpockets and lost equipment. With insurance, you will pay a $160 deductible per unit rather than the $800 XCom normally charges. Three devices, $480, which is quite a bit less than the $2,400 you're on board for.

Together all these charges do add up to a hefty $25/day or so, not counting possible shipping costs, but as a business expense, that's relatively little compared to what you'll be spending on flights, hotels, food, and incidentals. It's unquestionably a much better deal than paying roaming data charges.

Summarizing this section, the key things to know when you're taking your iPad Wi-Fi + 3G overseas are to turn off data roaming and to "know before you go."

Changing Account Information or Adding Data

Your iPad is very helpful in letting you know when you're getting close to the bandwidth limit on your data plan. It notifies you when you have 20 percent left, when you have 10 percent remaining, and when your plan has run out of data. You can decide to either stop using data at this point, purchase another data plan, or (when available, as carrier offers do vary) upgrade your plan for a higher bandwidth allotment.

To upgrade your data plan, change a credit card, edit your address information, or buy an international data plan, select **Settings ➤ Cellular Data**. Tap the View Account button, and you'll be able to make any changes instantly on your iPad.

Airplane Mode

When you're flying with an iPad with Wi-Fi + 3G, it's just as if you have a large mobile phone in your possession. Although airlines are much happier with Wi-Fi these days, with many actually providing in-flight Wi-Fi service, you'll still find that 3G and other mobile connections are frowned upon while you're in the air.

Like an iPhone, the iPad with Wi-Fi + 3G has controls for being switched into Airplane Mode. To turn on Airplane Mode when the flight attendant makes the announcement that "all cellular phones must be turned off," launch Settings. The first control available at the top of the page (Figure 5–11) is the Airplane Mode switch.

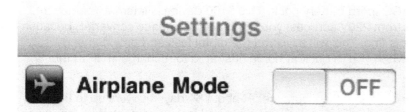

Figure 5–11. *Apple knows how important it is to turn off that 3G radio in your iPad during a flight. That's why Airplane Mode is the first setting available in the Settings app.*

Slide the Airplane Mode switch to the right so that the switch turns to On and disables Wi-Fi, 3G, and Bluetooth. When you want to use Wi-Fi during a flight, you can do that by tapping the Wi-Fi Settings button located just below Airplane Mode and then enabling Wi-Fi, separate from any 3G service.

The Alternative to Built-in 3G

One way of getting mobile connectivity without built-in 3G in your iPad is to use a mobile broadband router. These devices are available from a number of cellular carriers and are small boxes that attach to a 3G network and then allow up to five devices near the box to share the 3G connection.

In the United States and Canada, mobile broadband routers are available from Novatel Wireless (brand name MiFi) and Sierra Wireless (brand name Overdrive). These petite boxes are available from Sprint and Verizon, which are oddly enough not carriers associated with the GSM standard used by the iPad.

Sprint's Overdrive 3G/4G Mobile Hotspot (Figure 5–12) is an example of the mobile broadband routers that can be used with your iPad. The interesting thing about the Overdrive is that it works with the Sprint 4G network that is beginning to be rolled out to major cities in the United States. The 4G network is up to ten times faster than 3G service, meaning that you could conceivably use your iPad at speeds that would be similar to those achieved by a Wi-Fi network.

Several mobile phones (the Palm Pre Plus, for example) can be used as mobile hotspots, so check with your cellular carrier for information about this possibility. In many countries, including the United States, carriers allow *tethering* to an iPhone—that is, using a 3G iPhone as a mobile broadband router. However, if tethering your iPhone while traveling, you will need to arrange for data roaming just as you would on the iPad.

Figure 5–12. *Want to connect at speeds faster than 3G and share your wireless broadband connection with friends? A wireless broadband router such as the Sprint Overdrive 3G/4G Mobile Hotspot can do that for you. Image courtesy of Sprint.*

Summary

In this chapter, you read about the process of connecting to the Internet both through Wi-Fi and through 3G data connections. You learned some valuable troubleshooting tips for those times that you can't connect to Wi-Fi networks. Here we summarize some of the most important ideas in this chapter:

- Your iPad communicates with the world through Wi-Fi and (if you have an iPad with Wi-Fi + 3G) 3G cellular connections. Without Wi-Fi or 3G, you have no connection to the Internet.

- Security is very important when using Wi-Fi. To achieve the highest levels of wireless security, use WPA2-level encryption.

- Because of the expense, data roaming should be turned off when you're traveling internationally. Instead, either use GSM roaming partners and sign up for an international data plan *or* rent a mobile hotspot that offers Wi-Fi access for your iPad and other mobile devices.

- Be sure to put your 3G iPad into Airplane Mode when you're using it on an airplane to comply with federal and international regulations.

Browsing the Internet with Safari

When Apple introduced the iPhone in 2007, Steve Jobs said it was like having the Web in your pocket. The Safari web browser on the iPhone was revolutionary. It allowed you to literally touch the Web like never before. Take the iPhone Safari experience, magnify it by ten, and you'll have some idea of what browsing the Web is like on the iPad. Web pages on the iPad's screen are large and show you more than ever before with a clarity you've never imagined. It's like the iPad turns the Web into an interactive magazine in the palm of your hands.

In this chapter, you'll discover how to get the most from Safari and all its awesome powers. You'll learn how to navigate web pages, manage bookmarks, and use both Portrait and Landscape orientations. You'll also discover some great finger-tap shortcuts, bookmarking tips, and Safari's handy Reader and Reading List functions. Read on to learn about all this and more.

Getting Started with Safari

Tap the Safari application icon to launch the program. By default, Apple places it in the bottom left of the Dock. It's marked with a white compass on a blue background (see Figure 6–1). Once tapped, the Safari application opens a new window.

Figure 6–1. *The Safari icon*

Safari's Browser Window

Many elements on the Safari window may look familiar, especially to anyone experienced in using web browsers or Safari on the iPhone or iPod touch. Familiar elements include the Address bar, the Reload button, and the History navigation arrows. Figure 6–2 shows a typical Safari browser window.

Figure 6–2. *The Safari window displays many familiar features, including the Address bar and the Back, Forward, and Bookmarks buttons.*

Let's look more closely at the top of a Safari page. Atop every Safari window, you'll see the Navigation bar (see Figure 6–3). The Navigation bar contains common buttons and tools found on any modern web browser. From left to right, they are as follows:

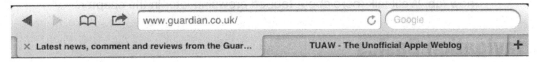

Figure 6–3. *The Safari Navigation bar*

The Back button: This takes you back one page in your browsing history.

The Forward button: If you've gone back one page, the Forward button will move you one page forward in your history.

> **NOTE:** When the back and forward buttons are grayed out, you haven't yet created a history. The arrows turn from light gray to dark gray once you start browsing, and you can move back and forth through your history to the previous and next pages. Each page maintains its own history. You can't use these buttons to go back to a page you were viewing in another window (see the Pages button discussion next).

The Bookmarks button: Tap the book-shaped icon to open your Bookmarks screen. The Bookmarks screen also contains your complete browsing history for Safari as well as your Reading List. We discuss Reading List later in this chapter.

The Share button: This button looks like an arrow breaking out of a box. Tapping it displays a menu that allows you to add a bookmark of the current page, add the current page to your Reading List, add a shortcut to the page on your Home screen, mail a link to the page, tweet the page, and print the web page displayed. We'll talk more about this button later in this chapter.

The Address bar: Use the Address bar at the top center of the Safari window to enter a new web address (web addresses are uniform resource locators, also known as a URLs).

The Reload button: The arrow bent in a semicircle in the Address bar is the Reload button. Tap it to refresh the current screen.

The Stop button: As a page loads, Safari replaces the Reload button with a small *X*. If you change your mind after navigating to a page, tap this. It stops the current page from loading any further.

The Search bar: Tapping this gives you quick access to Google search.

Tabs: Below the menu bar you'll find tabs. If you're used to using a modern web browser, you'll be familiar with tabs. Tabs are a way to have multiple web pages open in the same window. You can quickly switch between web pages by tapping the page's tab. To the right of the last tab is a plus (+) button. Tapping this allows you quickly create a new tab. We'll talk more about tabbed browsing later in the chapter.

Navigation Basics

iPad's Safari lets you do all the normal things you expect to do in a browser. You can tap links and buttons. You can enter text into forms and so forth. In addition, Safari offers iPad-specific features you won't find on your home computer: tilting the iPad on its side moves it from Landscape to Portrait view and back. The following sections guide you through Safari's basic features.

Entering URLs

Tap the Address bar to open the URL-entry window (see Figure 6–3). The Navigation section appears at the top of your screen, and a keyboard opens from below. Between these, the screen dims, and you can still see part of the page you were on (see Figure 6–4).

Figure 6–4. *The Safari window you see when operating in the URL or search fields*

NOTE: If you decide you want to remain on the page you are on, simply tap the dimmed area between the Navigation bar and keyboard, and you'll be taken back to the page. Alternatively, you can tap the Hide Keyboard button in the lower-right corner of the keyboard.

You'll also see a Bookmarks bar appear below the URL field and above your tabs (see Figure 6–5). These aren't all of your bookmarks but a select few you've decided to add to the Bookmarks Bar folder that's located in your collection of bookmarks. Bookmarks are generally used for quick access to your most frequently visited web sites. To activate a bookmark in the Bookmarks bar, simply tap it, and you'll be taken to its web page.

Figure 6–5. *The Bookmarks bar gives you quick access to some of your bookmarks.*

If the current URL field is empty, simply tap it and begin typing. You'll briefly see a contextual menu saying Paste, but don't worry about that. Just start typing, and the contextual menu will disappear (or hit the Paste button if you want to paste a URL that you've copied previously).

If the current URL field is populated (e.g., if you are already on a site and not a blank page), simply tap it. You'll see a small gray *X* appear where the Refresh button normally appears (see Figure 6–5). Tapping this *X* will clear the contents of the URL field. Additionally, if you'd like to copy the current URL, tap anywhere in the URL field, and you'll get a pop-up menu that says Select, Select All, and Paste. Tap Select All, and then tap Copy in the pop-up field that appears.

Don't worry about typing http:// or even www; Safari is smart enough to know that those are required and will add them automatically. A handy feature on the iPad's keyboard in Safari is the dedicated .com button (see Figure 6–6). This single button makes your fingers perform four keystrokes less work. What's even cooler is that, when you press and hold the .com button, you'll be presented with a pop-up field allowing you to select .edu, .org, .us, and .net.

Figure 6–6. *Safari's keyboard, complete with .com, .edu, .org, .us, and .net buttons*

As you type, Safari matches your keystrokes to its existing collection of bookmarks. A pop-up field will appear and display a list of possible matches from both your bookmarks and your history (see Figure 6–7). To select one, just tap it. Safari automatically navigates to the selected URL.

When you are done typing in a URL, tap Go, and Safari will navigate to the address you've entered. To return to the browser screen without entering a new URL, tap anywhere between the keyboard and the Navigation bar.

> **TIP:** When you see a white *X* in a gray circle in a text-entry field, you can tap it to clear the field.

Figure 6–7. *The URL entry window allows you to enter the address that you want Safari to visit.*

Entering Text

Many times you'll have to fill in user names or passwords on a web page to log in, or you may be on a page that asks you to fill in other forms. To edit the contents of any text-entry field, simply tap it, and Safari will open a new text-entry keyboard.

Although this keyboard is superficially similar to the one shown in Figure 6–5, it presents a few differences. These differences include the Previous and Next buttons atop the keyboard that search for other text fields on your web page (see Figure 6–8). These buttons let you fill out forms without having to go through tedious tap/edit/done cycles. Simply enter text, tap Next, enter more text, and so forth.

Figure 6–8. *The text-entry keyboard for web page forms. Notice the Previous, Next, and AutoFill buttons at the top.*

Another difference from the text-entry features in Safari is the AutoFill button. Tapping the AutoFill button will automatically populate the text fields with information from your personal contact card in your address book. It will also enter stored user names and passwords. We'll talk about setting up AutoFill features later in this chapter.

To submit a form after you've entered all the text, tap Go or Search. This is like pressing the Enter or Return key on a regular computer.

Searching the Web

From any Safari window, you'll just be a tap away from a web search. As shown in Figure 6–5, a Google search field lies just to the right of the URL field. Tap this search field to bring up the keyboard and enter a term you want to search for in Google.

The search field elongates while the URL field shortens, and the Go button on the keyboard switches to a Search button. Type a word or two, and you'll see a pop-up box appear with Google-suggested search terms based on what you've typed (see Figure 6–9). To select one of the Google-suggested terms, you can simply tap it in the list or just finish typing what you are looking for and tap Search on the keyboard. Safari will navigate to www.google.com (no matter what page is currently displayed) and search for your queried term.

Figure 6–9. *The search field, complete with suggested keywords*

If you'd rather use Bing or Yahoo! search than Google search, you can navigate to **Settings ➤ Safari** to change your default search engine (we'll go through all of Safari's settings later in this chapter).

Searching for Text on a Web Page

Safari also allows you to search for specific text on a web page. You can search for text in two ways. First is via the Google (or Yahoo! or Bing) search field. Tap inside the Google search field and enter the word or words on the web page that you are looking for. Tap where it says *Find*; next, tap the text you entered in the bottom of the search suggestion pop-up field (see Figure 6–10).

Figure 6–10. *Searching for text on a web page*

After you tap the Find command, Safari will zoom into the section of the web page with the first occurrence of the text you are looking for and highlight it in yellow (see Figure 6–11). Then, using the Search text bar at the bottom of the page, you can tap the previous or next arrow buttons to find more instances of the text on the web page. You can also refine your keyword search using the search field in the Search text bar at the bottom of the page. Tap Done or anywhere on the web page to exit text search.

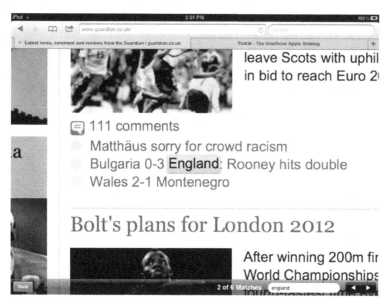

Figure 6–11. *Text search results displayed in Safari*

The second way to search for text on a web page is just to tap Safari's search field and then enter the text you are looking for in the Find on Page search field above the keyboard that appears on screen (Figure 6–9).

Following Links

Hypertext links are used throughout the World Wide Web. Text links are marked with underlines and usually involve a color change from the main text. Image links are subtler, but they can also move you to a new location.

Tap these links to navigate to new web pages or, for certain special links, to open a new e-mail or view a map. When a link leads to an audio or video file that the iPad understands, it will play back that file. Special links include `mailto:` (to create Mail messages), `tel:` (for phone calls, if you have Skype installed on your iPad), and automatic recognition of Google Maps URLs (which will take you to the iPad's Maps app).

> **NOTE:** Supported audio formats include AAC, M4A, M4B, M4P, MP3, WAV, and AIFF. Video formats include h.264 and MPEG-4.

You have other options than simply tapping a link to get to a new page. To preview a link's address, touch and hold the link for a second or two. An address pop-up field will appear next to the link (see Figure 6–12). Below the link's full address, you'll see three buttons, which behave as follows:

The Open button: Takes you to the link as if you simply tapped it instead of touching and holding it

The Open in New Tab button: Takes you to the link in a new Safari tab

The Add to Reading List button: Adds the current link to your Reading List

The Copy button: Copies the link so you can paste it later into an e-mail message or URL field

To cancel any of these options and stay on your current page, simply tap your finger anywhere on the screen.

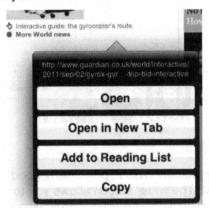

Figure 6–12. *Options when touching and holding a link: Open, Open in New Page, Add to Reading List, and Copy*

TIP: To detect image links on the screen, tap and hold an image. If it turns gray, it's a link. If it remains at the same brightness, it's just a plain image. When you tap and hold a linked picture, you'll have the same options as you do with a text link. You'll also have one additional option: Save Image. This will save the image to your Photos app on the iPad.

Changing Orientation

One of the iPad's standout features is its flexible orientation support. When you turn your unit on its side, the iPad flips its display to match, as you can see in Figure 6–13. A built-in sensor detects the iPad's tilt and adjusts the display to Landscape orientation. Tilt back to vertical, and the iPad returns to Portrait orientation. It takes just a second for the iPad to detect the orientation change and to update the display. Don't forget you can always lock your screen's orientation by sliding the screen Orientation Lock button on the side of the iPad; however, you should sure you have the button set to lock the orientation and not to mute the iPad. To do this, go to **Settings ➤ General** and then set the Use Side Switch to: option to Lock Rotation.

Figure 6–13. *Safari can display web pages using both Portrait and Landscape orientations.*

The iPad's Landscape view offers a significantly wider display. This is particularly good for side-to-side tasks such as reading book-width text. The wider screen allows you to use bigger fonts and view wider columns without scrolling sideways. The Portrait view provides a longer presentation. This is great for reading web content with more narrow columns, like news feeds. You don't have to scroll quite as much in Portrait view as you do in Landscape view.

Whether in Landscape or Portrait view, Safari features work the same, including the same buttons in the same positions. In Landscape view, you enter text using a wider, sideways keyboard.

Scrolling, Zooming, and Other Viewing Skills

Safari responds to the complete vocabulary of taps, flicks, and drags discussed in Chapter 2. You can zoom in on pictures, squeeze on columns, and more. Here's a quick review of the essential ways to interact with your screen:

> *Drag*: Touch the screen and drag your finger to reposition web pages. If you think of your iPad as a window onto a web page, dragging allows you to move the window around the web page.

> *Flick*: When dealing with long pages, you can flick the display up and down to scroll rapidly. This is especially helpful when navigating through search engine results and news sites.

Double-tap: Double-tap any column or image to zoom in, auto-sizing it to the width of your display. Double-tap again to zoom back out. Use this option to instantly zoom into a web page's text. The iPad recognizes how wide the text is and perfectly matches that width.

Pinch: Use pinching to manually zoom in or out. This allows you to make fine zoom adjustments as needed.

Tap: Tap buttons and links to select them. Tapping allows you to move from site to site and to submit forms.

Page down: When zoomed in onto a column, double-tap toward the bottom of the screen while staying within the column. The page recenters around your tap. Make sure not to tap a link!

Jump to the top: Tap the very top of the screen (just below the time display) to pop instantly back to the top of the page.

Stop a scroll: After flicking a page to get it to scroll, you can tap the page at any time to stop that movement. Don't forget that you can also manually drag the screen display to reset the part you're viewing.

> **TIP:** Some web pages have text boxes in them, which have their own scrollbars, separate from the scrollbars of the web page. If you come across a web page with a text box while using Safari on the iPad, you can scroll through the text box on the page without scrolling through the entire page. To do this, swipe up or down with two fingers inside the text box. Only the contents of the text box will scroll, and the main page will stay in place.

Tabbed Browsing

Safari offers tabbed browsing, allowing you to keep multiple web pages open in the same window and quickly switch between them. Tabbed browsing is a godsend if you often browse multiple web sites at the same time.

By default, Safari always has one tab open. It's the current web page you are on. You can see what one tab looks like in Figure 6–13. It's the long bar beneath the URL field with the name or header of the web site in the tab. You can have a maximum of nine tabs open at one time. If you create a new tab with nine tabs already open, it will replace the oldest tab. To see what Safari looks like with multiple tabs open, check out Figure 6–14.

You can interact with tabs in several ways:

Opening a new blank tab: To open another blank tab, tap the plus (+) button below Safari's search field. Doing so will bring up a new tab in the tab bar. You can then enter in the web address in the URL field.

Open a link in a new tab: Tap and hold on any web link on a web page. The pop-up menu will appear as shown in Figure 6–12. Tap Open in New Tab, and the link will open in a new tab.

Rearrange tabs: You can move tabs around to arrange them in the order you want. To do this, simply tap and hold a tab with your finger and then drag it to the left or right of the next tab to move it.

Close a tab: Tap the small x button that appears to the left of a web site's name or header on the currently selected tab.

View recently closed tabs: Tap and hold the plus (+) button below Safari's search field as if you were going to create a new tab. But hold it instead of letting go. A pop-up menu will appear with the history of your recently closed tabs. Tap a page from the list to open it in a new tab.

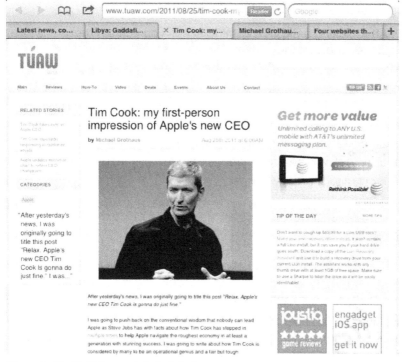

Figure 6–14. *Multiple open tabs in Safari*

Working with Bookmarks

One of the great features of the iPad is that it lets you take your world with you: contacts, calendars, e-mail accounts, and bookmarks. You don't have to reenter URLs for all your favorite pages on the iPad. It loads these bookmarks whenever it syncs, provided you have enabled this feature in the iTunes iPad Preferences window (see Chapter 2).

Selecting Bookmarks

A bookmarks collection can contain hundreds of individual URLs, which is why people really appreciate the iPad's simple bookmarks browser (see Figure 6–15). When you tap the Bookmarks button in the Navigation bar, a simple Bookmarks pop-up window appears. It uses the same folder structure that you've set up on your personal computer. You can tap folders to open them and tap the Back button (top-left corner) to return to the parent folder.

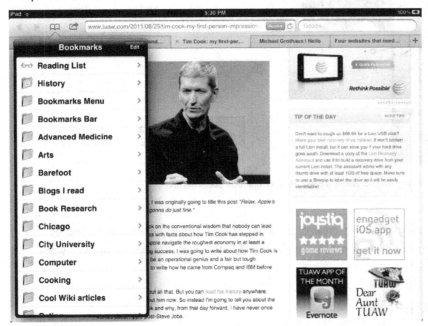

Figure 6–15. *Use iPhone Safari's interactive Bookmarks navigation menu to locate and open your favorite bookmarks.*

Identifying bookmarks is easy. Folders look like folders, and each bookmark is marked with a small open book symbol. Tap one of these, and Safari will take you directly to the page in question. If your list of bookmarks is long, simply flick or scroll through the list.

When you are on the first level of your bookmarks, you'll notice a History folder at the top. Tap it, and you'll be taken to all the pages you've visited in Safari since you last cleared the history. To clear the history, tap the Clear History button, and you'll be asked to confirm. Tap the red Clear History button to confirm (Figure 6–16).

You'll also see a folder labeled Bookmarks Bar. Any bookmarks placed in this folder will appear in the Bookmarks bar that shows below the bottom of Safari's Navigation bar when you are entering a URL (shown earlier in Figure 6–5).

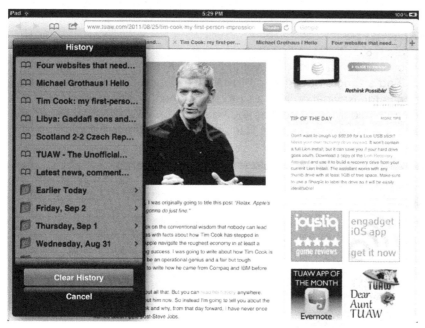

Figure 6–16. *Safari's History folders and the Clear History deletion confirmation*

> **NOTE:** The history of your desktop browser and iPad's Safari browsers do not sync. Any pages you navigate to on your iPad will not show up on your desktop's browsing history, and vice versa.

Editing Bookmarks

As Figure 6–15 shows, an Edit button appears at the top right of the bookmark's pop-up field. Tap this to enter Edit mode (see Figure 6–17).

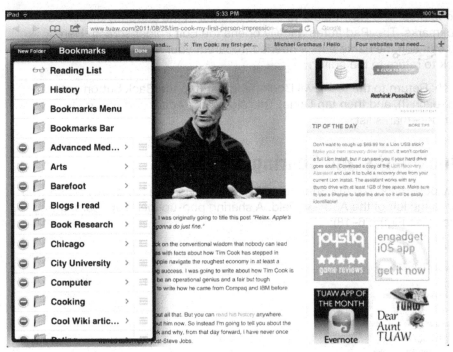

Figure 6–17. *Safari contains a built-in bookmark-management system that allows you to edit and reorder your bookmarks.*

Edit mode allows you to manage your bookmarks on your iPad just as you would on your personal computer:

> *Delete bookmarks*: Tap the red Delete circle icon to the left of a bookmark to delete it. Tap Delete to confirm or tap elsewhere on the screen to cancel.

> *Reorder bookmarks*: Use the gray grab handles (the three lines on the far right) to move folders and bookmarks into new positions. Grab, drag, and then release.

> *Edit names*: Tap the gray Reveal arrow (the sideways V symbol to the right of each name) to open the Edit Bookmark or Edit Folder screen. Use the keyboard to make your changes and tap the Back button to return to the Bookmarks editor.

> *Re-parent items*: You can move items from one folder to another by tapping the parent folder field below the Name edit field. Select a folder, and then tap the Back button to return to the Bookmarks editor. Unfortunately, you don't get the same wild animation that you do in Mail when you send an item to a new folder, but at least it works reliably.

Add folders: Tap New Folder to create a folder in the currently displayed bookmarks. The iPad automatically opens the Edit Folder screen. Here, you can edit the name and, if needed, reparent your new folder. Tap Back to return to the editor.

Finish: Return to the top-level Bookmarks list (tap the Back button until you reach it), and then tap Done. This closes the editor and returns to your bookmarks list.

Saving Bookmarks and Sharing Web Pages

To save a new bookmark, tap the Share button in the Navigation bar of any Safari web page. It's just to the left of the Address field. A sharing pop-up menu appears, giving you six choices (see Figure 6–18):

Figure 6–18. *Tap the Share button to see all the ways you can share a web page.*

Add Bookmark: Tapping this lets you enter a title for the bookmark and then optionally select a folder to save it to (see Figure 6–19). Tap the currently displayed folder to view a list of all available folders. The root of the bookmark tree is called Bookmarks. After making your selection, tap Save. Safari adds the new bookmark to your collection. If you want to return to Safari without saving, tap Cancel.

Add to Reading List: Tapping this adds the current page to your Reading List. We'll talk about Reading List in a moment.

Figure 6–19. *Add Bookmark allows you to rename the bookmark before you save it.*

Add to Home Screen: This is a cool feature. Tapping this adds an icon of the web page to your iPad Home screen. Apple calls these web page icons *Web Clips*. Before you save a Web Clip, you have the option of renaming it. Keep the names short, so you can see the entire name under the Web Clip icon on the Home screen.

NOTE: Some web sites will have an iPad-optimized site icon when you add a Web Clip to your Home screen. Others will just show you a thumbnail of the page in the shape of an iPad icon.

Web Clips look just like app icons and allow you to simply tap to open Safari and automatically be taken to the web page. We keep a Home screen on the iPad full of our favorite Web Clips so we can quickly navigate to our most frequently visited sites (see Figure 6–20). We find this much quicker than using the Bookmarks feature in Safari.

Figure 6–20. *A series of Web Clips on the iPad Home screen. You can see which sites have dedicated Web Clip icons and which ones make iPad use a thumbnail of the web page.*

In iTunes the Web Clips will appear in the virtual iPad screen on the Apps tab (see Chapter 2). Note that you can only rearrange Web Clips within iTunes, not delete them. To delete a Web Clip icon on the iPad, press and hold it until it jiggles, and then tap the *X* in the upper-left corner.

> *Mail Link to this Page*: Tapping this button opens a new Mail message window in Safari and automatically inserts the link into the body of the message.

> *Tweet:* Tapping this button will compose a Twitter message that you can send out to all your followers (Figure 6–21). You must have a Twitter account to use this feature.

Figure 6–21. *Tweeting a link from Safari to your Twitter account*

Print: Tap this button to bring up the Print menu (Figure 6–22). The Print menu allows you to select which wireless AirPrint printer you want to print to, as well as the number of copies you want to print. After you have made your choices, click the Print button.

Figure 6–22. *Printing a web page from Safari*

Eliminating Clutter with Reader

Safari has an awesome built-in feature that all other mobile web browsers lack. It's called Reader (not to be confused with Reading List, another awesome feature that we'll talk about shortly). Reader allows you to eliminate all the clutter on web pages, such as the ads, the comments, and the banners, and read the content of that page as if you were reading it from a piece of paper. You can see Reader in action in Figure 6–23.

Figure 6–23. *Safari's Reader feature. Left: a web page as it normally appears. Right: the same web page when viewed through Reader.*

As you can see in Figure 6–23, viewing the text on a web page through Reader is much easier because all the distractions are eliminated. To activate Reader, click the gray Reader button that appears in the Address bar. The Reader document will slide up onto screen. To exit Reader mode, click the now purple Reader button in the URL field. Notice that the Reader button appears only when you are on a web page that has a single article. You will not see a Reader button on the front page of the *New York Times* web site, for example; you'll see it only when you view single articles on the site.

Building Up Your Reading List

Reading List is another new feature of Safari in iOS 5. It allows you to save web pages to read when you have the time. I know, that sounds a lot like adding a bookmark, right? It's similar, but Reading List is more of a temporary bookmark. It's for that cool article we find about a small town in Andorra, which we want to read but don't have time right now. It's not a bookmark we want to keep forever; it's just something we want to make sure we return to read. You can think of reading list almost as tearing an article out of a newspaper you want to read later.

To add a page to your Reading List, tap the Share button at the bottom Safari's window. The Sharing menu appears (see Figure 6–18). Tap Add to Reading List. Your web page has now been added to your Reading List.

To access your Reading List, tap the Bookmarks button in Safari. In the bookmarks screen you'll see a folder labeled Reading List with a pair of eyeglasses as an icon at the top (Figure 6–15). Tap it to view your Reading List. The Reading List panel (Figure 6–24) contains all the web articles you've added to it. If the Reading List menu is open and you are on a web page that has not been saved to it, you can tap the plus (+) button that appears in the upper-right corner of the Reading List menu.

Figure 6–24. *Safari's Reading List*

In the Reading List menu you can tap a tab to see all the articles you've ever added or just the ones you haven't read yet. Simply select an article in the Reading List to load it in Safari and read the saved web page.

Any saved page will disappear from the Unread section of Reading List after you have scrolled through its entirety; however, it will always show in the All section until you manually remove it. To remove pages from Reading List, simply swipe right over the article and tap the red Delete button that appears.

One of the best features about Reading List is that is synced across all your computers and iOS devices (like the iPad and iPhone) that use Safari. This allows you to find an interesting article on Safari on your iPad, save it to Reading List, and then read it on your Mac or iPhone. Just open up Safari, and the article will appear in Reading List no matter what device you are on. Safari accomplishes this by syncing Reading List via your iCloud account.

Safari Settings

Like many apps on the iPad, Safari can be customized to a degree. Customize your Safari settings by navigating to the Settings app on your iPad Home screen and tapping Safari. This screen, shown in Figure 6–25, allows you to control a number of features, mostly security related. Here's a quick rundown of those features and what they mean:

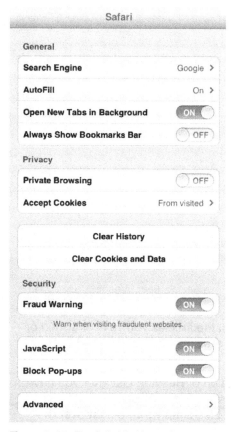

Figure 6–25. *The Safari Settings window is primarily concerned with security features.*

Search Engine: This setting determines which search engine is used for the search field you saw in Figure 6–3. Choose from Google, Bing, or Yahoo!

AutoFill: This allows you to turn on AutoFill for use in filling out forms on web pages. In the My Info box, select your address book card to take the AutoFill information from. Here you can also choose to turn on Names & Passwords. With this feature on, Safari will remember login names and passwords to web sites you visit. Tap Clear All to wipe all saved names and passwords from your iPad.

Open New Tabs in Background: When this is set to On, any links opened in new tabs will open in the background. This means you'll remain on the page from where you opened the link in a new tab. You won't be automatically taken to that page unless you turn this option Off.

Always Show Bookmarks Bar: Turn this on, and you'll always see the Bookmarks bar below Safari's Navigation bar; otherwise, this bar appears only when you select the URL field (see Figure 6–5).

Private Browsing: When private browsing is enabled, your web history will not be saved, nor will any of the user names, passwords, web searches, or text you enter on a web page.

Accept Cookies: Cookies refer to data stored on your iPad by the web sites you visit. Cookies allow web sites to remember you and to store information about your visit. You can choose to always accept cookies, never accept cookies, or accept cookies only "From visited" web sites.

Clear History: Tap and confirm to empty your page Navigation history from your iPad. This keeps your personal browsing habits private to some extent, although other people can still scan though your bookmarks.

> **CAUTION:** Clearing your Navigation history does not affect Safari's Page history. You can still tap its Back button and see the sites you've visited.

Clear Cookies and Data: Tap and confirm to clear all existing cookies and cache from your iPad. Your iPad's browser cache stores data from many of the web sites you visit. It uses this to speed up page loading the next time you visit. As with cookies and history, your cache may reveal personal information that you'd rather not share. Tap Clear Cache and Confirm to clear your cache.

> **TIP:** Clearing your cache may also help correct problem pages that are having trouble loading. By clearing the cache, you remove page items that may be corrupt or only partially downloaded.

Fraud Warning: Turn this preference on, and you'll be presented with a warning before navigating to a potentially fraudulent web sites. Unfortunately, fraudulent sites are rampant on the Internet (like bogus PayPal sites). This feature helps you recognize and avoid those sites.

JavaScript: JavaScript allows web pages to run programs when you visit them. Disabling JavaScript means you increase overall surfing safety, but you also lose many cool and worthy web features. Most pages are safe to visit, but some, sadly, are not. To disable JavaScript, switch this from On to Off.

Block Pop-ups: Many web sites use pop-up windows for advertising. It's an annoying reality of surfing the Web. By default, Safari pop-up blocking is On. Switch this setting to Off to allow pop-up window creation.

Advanced: This preference gives you control over databases and debugging. Most people will never need to use it. Some sites like Gmail use databases. These databases store local information on your iPad for offline browsing. Emptying databases can clear up problems you may be having on certain web sites. The debug consol helps developers optimizing their web sites for the iPad.

The iPad and Flash Videos

If you've ever watched a video on the Web, chances are it was encoded using Flash. Ever since Apple unveiled the iPhone to the world, there has been growing tension between Apple and Adobe. The reason for this: Apple does not allow Adobe's proprietary Flash plug-in to run on the iPhone—or the more recent iPad.

Flash, in Apple's estimation, is a slow, buggy, and archaic technology. Steve Jobs himself even posted a letter on Apple's web site effectively telling the world the same thing (www.apple.com/hotnews/thoughts-on-flash/). His letter was the final word for anyone hoping to see Flash on the iPad or iPhone. It's just not going to happen.

What many people misunderstand when they hear "no Flash on the iPad" is that they think the iPad can't play web videos. Nothing could be further from the truth. Sure, if a video is encoded in Flash, you can't view it on the iPad. And while most videos on the Web (about 75 percent of them, Steve Jobs said) are encoded in Flash, most are also available in a new, universal web standard called HTML5. HTML5 videos don't require a plug-in to play. HTML5 is also much less power hungry than Flash—an important feature when dealing with mobile devices that consume battery power.

The world is moving to HTML5, and Apple chose to support it—and open standards—instead of Adobe's aging and proprietary Flash. Most of YouTube's videos have already been re-encoded to support HTML5, and many other major web sites have chosen to drop Flash in favor of the new HTML5 web standard.

Summary

The iPad turns browsing the Internet from something you did at your desk to something you can do in the comfort of your lap as leisurely as if you were flipping through a magazine. In a way, browsing the Internet on the iPad gives web pages a tangibility they've never been capable of before—you can just reach out and touch them. It's very likely that, after using Safari on iPad to surf, you'll never want to explore the Web any other way.

Here are a few tips to keep in mind as you move on from this chapter:

- iPads work in more ways than the traditional vertical, or Portrait, orientation. Go ahead and flip your iPad on its side to view web pages in Landscape mode. Your Safari pages will adjust.

- Nope, there's no Flash support. There never will be. And you don't need it.

- Web Clips are a great way to access your favorite web sites right from your iPad's Home screen.

- Tap the top of any Safari page (right below the clock in the Status bar) to quickly return to the top of the web page.

- Safari's tabbed browsing lets you navigate back and forth between multiple web pages at once, just like you can on desktop web browsers.

- Don't confuse Reader and Reading List. Reader lets you strip away ads and read a web page's text as if you were reading a newspaper. Reading List allows you to save interesting articles to come back to at your leisure.

Touching Your Music and Video

The iPad offers new ways to interact with your media. The iPad provides a magnificent dedicated music player, and with just a few touches, you can access that same audio from a wide variety of other applications, allowing you to enjoy your tunes as you play and work. When you watch a TV show, a movie, or a quick video on your iPad, its wide-screen video playback capabilities and superb television integration provide beautiful, clear images that are larger than ever before. What's more, the iPad's wireless Internet capabilities allow you to access a huge range of content—from YouTube to embedded video on the Internet to your own personal computer—and to share the content already on your device out to external players. This chapter introduces the primary applications that let you enjoy music and video on your iPad: Videos, YouTube, Safari, and Music.

Watching Video on the iPad

Video forms such a basic component of your iPad that you shouldn't think about it as just a single application. Apple provides the base technology used by several built-in apps that support video playback of third-party media. The following list provides a quick overview of those Apple-supplied apps (see Figure 7–1).

> **NOTE:** Chapter 15 discusses how you can record and play your own homebrew video using the iPad's built-in camera system.

Figure 7–1. *Videos, YouTube, and Safari all feature video playback capabilities on the iPad.*

Videos: The Videos application appears on the Home screen of your iPad. The icon looks like a traditional clapperboard, with a black-and-white striped top over a blue base. This application plays back the TV shows, movies, podcasts, iTunes U lessons, and music videos you've synchronized from your home iTunes library.

YouTube: You'll find the YouTube app icon next to the Videos app icon in Figure 7–1. The icon looks like an old-fashioned TV, complete with a greenish screen and brown dials. YouTube connects to the Internet and allows you to view videos from YouTube.com. You can navigate to www.youtube.com in Safari on the iPad and browse YouTube videos that way, but the iPad's YouTube app wraps www.youtube.com in such a nice and easy-to-navigate package that you'll find it's leaps and bounds better than using YouTube in a web browser.

Safari: Safari, which you read about in depth in Chapter 6, offers a third way to view videos. Like its computer-based equivalents, the Safari app allows you to watch embedded movie files. Safari's icon looks like a light blue compass with a needle pointing to the northeast.

In addition to the three apps that play video that ship with the iPad, thousands of other apps play video. You can discover all these apps in the iTunes Store. Some of my personal favorites are YXPlayer, which allows me to view videos from my family's personal camcorder (it records in AVI format), the BBC News app to view news footage, and the Weather Channel app to watch weather-related news stories and Doppler video.

For all that the iPad brings to video, it has limits. Your iPad's built-in applications play files using H.264 MPEG-4 video and its immediate family, and that's pretty much it. You cannot use your iPad's standard apps to view Flash/Shockwave videos or animation or play AVI videos or DivX, Xvid, Matroska video, or any of the other dozens of popular formats. If your video isn't in MPEG-4 H.264 format, by default, your iPad won't understand it without help.

Fortunately, the App Store helps you work around this limitation. Some third-party apps enable you to watch videos using formats that the iPad does not officially support. Video-playing applications include such titles as CineXPlayer, yxplayer, and Azul Media Player. These viewers work with a wide variety of content including WMV, AVI, DivX, and Flash FLV formats, among others. Because these applications work outside of Apple's built-in media support, you will generally have to preload your content to each app. Use iTunes' Apps tab, in the File Sharing section, to add and remove video files.

Some applications also let you access media directly from web URLs, even allowing you to play Flash video (FLV) embedded in web pages (rather than URLs that link directly to FLV assets). Custom web browser Skyfire offers Flash video playback support by using edge cases. It isn't always successful, because some monetized sites like Hulu currently disable iPad video access through any solution outside their own custom player (the Hulu Plus player in Hulu's case). Even if Flash-on-iPad limitations were removed, Hulu's own restrictions mean that it will not freely distribute video to mobile browsers.

The general consensus on the matter is that although Adobe has had Flash technology ready to roll out for iPad and iOS in general for some time, relations between Adobe and Apple have kept that technology off the platform.

> **NOTE:** Apple's iPad officially supports H.264 video, up to 1.5Mbps, 1024 by 768 pixels, 30 frames per second, and 720p in M4V, MP4, and MOV file formats.

Video Playback

The iPad is an orientation-agnostic device: you can interact with it in portrait or landscape mode. That's no different for playing video. When you watch a video on the iPad, you can watch it holding the iPad in portrait mode or in landscape mode. Depending on the app you are watching it in, you may see more options for the video being played or indeed for the app itself.

However, most apps display the video interface with all the same elements, meaning once you know how to control video playback in one app, you know how to do it in the rest of them. Here is a quick overview of those controls, which are shown in Figure 7–2.

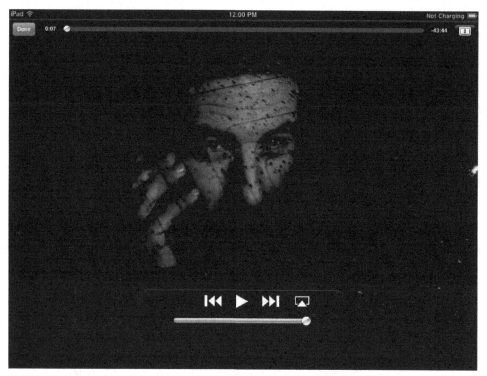

Figure 7–2. *The iPad's video playback controls allow you to control playback as you watch.*

Play/Pause: Play/Pause appears as either a right-pointing triangle (Play) or a pair of vertical lines (Pause). Tap this button to pause or resume video playback.

Rewind: The Rewind button appears as two triangles pointing left to a line. Tap it to return to the start of the video, or press and hold the button to scan backward.

Fast-Forward: The reverse of Rewind, the Fast-Forward button's triangles point to the right instead of the left. Press and hold this button to scan forward. Tap it to skip to the next video track.

AirPlay: A rectangle with an embedded upward-pointing triangle, AirPlay allows you to redirect over-the-air playback to other devices. At the time this book was being written, AirPlay receivers were limited to second-generation or later Apple TV units and third-party applications like Banana TV (http://bananatv.net).

Volume: The volume control is the large line below the Play/Pause button. Drag the volume control knob to adjust playback volume. Of course, you can always use the dedicated physical volume button on the side of the iPad as well.

Scrubber bar: The scrubber bar appears at the top of your screen. It is a long line with a small knob that you can drag. (The volume control is the thicker bar at the bottom.) Drag the playhead along the scrubber bar to set the current playback time.

Zoom: The Zoom button looks like two arrows in a white box pointing away from each other, at the top right of your screen. Either double-tap the screen or tap the Zoom button to switch between full-screen mode and the original aspect ratio. To get back into the original aspect ratio's view, double-tap the screen again, or tap the Zoom button again. You'll note that the Zoom button changes slightly when viewing a video full-screen: the arrows turn into a letterbox icon. When viewing in full-screen mode, you use the entire iPad screen, but some video may be clipped from the top or sides of the video. In the original aspect ratio, you may see either letterboxing (black bars above and below) or pillarboxing (black bars to either side), which results from preserving the video's original aspect ratio.

Audio tracks and Subtitles: If alternate audio tracks or subtitles are available in the video you are watching, you'll see an icon that looks like a speech bubble appear in the controls. Tap this icon to select from a pop-up list of audio tracks and subtitles.

Done: The Done button appears on all video application screens. Tap Done to exit video playback. Press the physical Home button on the iPad's bezel to quit the app and return to your Home screen.

While you're playing a video, the iPad automatically hides your video controls after a second or two. This allows you to watch your video without the distraction of on-screen buttons. Tap the screen to bring back the controls. Tap the screen again to hide them; or leave them untouched for a few seconds, and they once again fade away.

Videos App

To launch the Videos app, tap its blue clapperboard icon. When the app opens, you'll be presented with a list of media items synchronized to your iPad. These items are organized into categories by tabs, including items such as movies, TV shows, podcasts, and so forth (see Figure 7–3). As long as you've already synced videos from your iTunes library (see Chapter 2), you'll see them appear here. Tap through each tab to find a complete selection of synchronized media.

Figure 7–3. *The Videos app offers separate tabs of movies, TV shows, podcasts, music videos, and iTunes U lessons you've synchronized to your iPad.*

Playing a Video

As you can see, the Videos interface shown in Figure 7–3 couldn't be simpler. Its thumbnail images represent the items you've copied to your iPad. (Synchronizing these items is discussed in Chapter 2.) Navigate between your various video media categories by tapping the category tabs that run along the top of the screen (see Figure 7–4). If you have a lot of videos in a specific category, you can flick your finger to quickly scroll through the list.

Movies	TV Shows	Podcasts	Music Videos	iTunes U

Figure 7–4. *Navigate your video categories by tapping the appropriate category tab at the top of the screen.*

Tap any video thumbnail to open it. The item's icon flies forward as gray panels unfold from behind it like origami. You'll be presented with the information page that displays the name of the video and the year it was made, along with other information that could include the length, dimensions, file size, codecs, and copyright notice, but generally it simply includes an extended episode or movie description (see Figure 7–5). Tap "more" to see the entire write-up.

If you are viewing a video with chapters, such as a TV show (each episode in a season is considered a chapter), podcast, or movie, you'll see a list of chapters. If it's a podcast or TV show, you'll be presented with the episodes you have on your iPad, including the name, a summary, ratings, and the length of each episode.

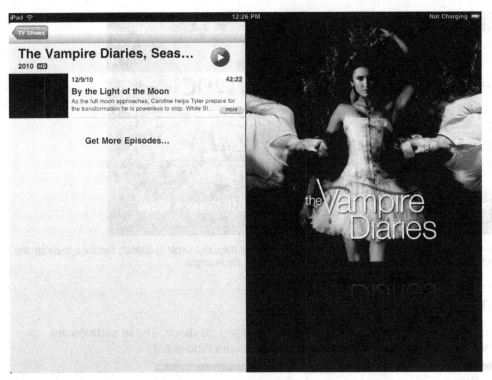

Figure 7–5. *Information screens for movies and TV shows*

To begin video playback, tap the circular Play button in the top right of the screen, or if your video has a list of chapters, tap a chapter from the list. Your screen clears, and the video loads and automatically begins playing. Tap Done to return to the information page.

Deleting Videos

If you want to delete a video from your iPad, touch and hold the video thumbnail until a circle with a white *x* appears in the corner of the video's icon (see Figure 7–6). Tap the *x* to delete the video. With the exception of videos rented from the iTunes Store, deleting a video from the iPad will not delete it from your computer. You'll be able to sync it again from your iTunes library should you choose to do so.

Figure 7–6. *Tap and hold a video's thumbnail icon, and wait for the x in a circle to appear. Tap the x to delete the video. Time to delete those old out-of-date WWDC 2010 videos, for example.*

Video Settings

You can adjust several settings that affect your video playback. These settings are accessed through the iPad's Settings application (see Figure 7–7).

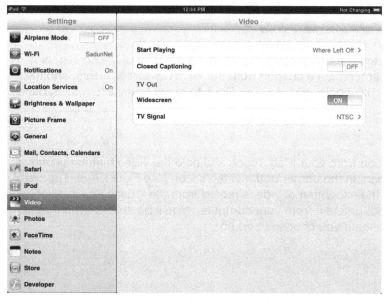

Figure 7–7. *The Videos preferences*

Start Playing: This setting allows you to choose whether to start playing videos from the beginning or from where you left off. Being able to start from where you left off is terrific when you're trying to work through a movie or TV episode in short snippets. You might prefer to always start product demonstration videos at the beginning, however.

Closed Captioning: If your video contains embedded closed captions, you can view them by switching this option from Off to On. Closed captions are not just helpful for the hard of hearing. They provide an excellent way to augment your video-watching experience in noisy conditions when on the subway or at a busy cafeteria.

The iPad's Video app also lets you play content from it through your home television. You'll need to buy some extra cables for this, which you can read about later in the "Video Accessories" section of this chapter, but the Video settings is where you can choose the following options:

Widescreen: Turn this on to force wide-screen videos to be played in wide-screen on your TV. This preserves their original aspect ratio.

TV Signal: Choose either NTSC or PAL. If you are in North America or Japan, you'll most likely have an NTSC TV. In Europe, Australia, and New Zealand, it's PAL.

YouTube

Discovering, navigating, and watching YouTube videos on the iPad is an experience that's light years beyond watching them on your computer while sitting at your desk. The iPad turns watching YouTube videos into a fantastic leisure experience that you can enjoy from the comfort of your couch.

Unlike the Videos app, the YouTube app requires an Internet connection. As long as you have at least a Wi-Fi connection, you're all set. At the time this book was being written, YouTube allows you to watch videos using 3G connections as well (if you have a 3G iPad); the application automatically downgrades video quality to put less strain on your bandwidth allocation. The lower-quality videos won't look quite as good as they will over a Wi-Fi connection, but they won't deplete your account quite as fast.

To take full advantage of the YouTube app, you'll want to have a YouTube account. You don't *need* one to use the app, but having one makes the app that much more powerful. With a YouTube account, you can view and bookmark your favorite videos; subscribe to YouTube users' videos; see with a tap of a button all the videos you've uploaded to YouTube; and share, rate, and flag videos—all from within the YouTube app. Creating a YouTube account takes only a few minutes and can be done at www.youtube.com/create_account.

To launch the YouTube app, tap the YouTube icon; it looks like a retro-styled TV set (shown earlier in Figure 7–1). When launched for the first time, the application displays the Featured screen, as shown in Figure 7–8. This screen showcases videos chosen by YouTube's staff.

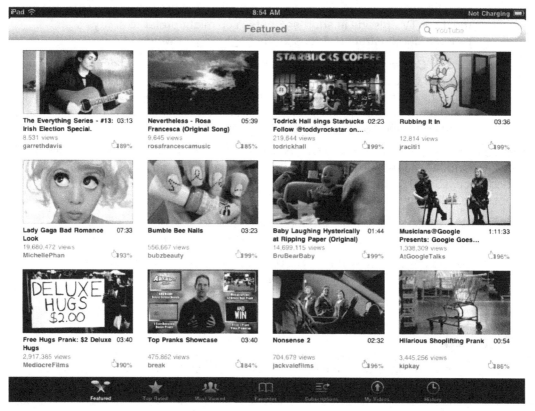

Figure 7–8. *YouTube's Featured screen provides a video showcase.*

Navigating and Finding YouTube Videos

Key elements of the YouTube app include a search field in the upper-right corner of the app and a row of seven buttons at the bottom of the screen. Each button (see Figure 7–9) offers a different way to discover and enjoy YouTube videos.

Figure 7–9. *The YouTube navigation bar*

> *Featured*: This screen displays videos reviewed and recommended by YouTube staff. You'll often find some worthwhile viewing here that you might otherwise miss.

Top Rated: This screen displays videos that have the highest ratings on YouTube. You can choose to show the highest-rated videos for the day, the week, or all-time. Viewers assign ratings, and the videos with the highest votes are collected here.

Most Viewed: This screen displays videos that have the most views on YouTube. You can choose to show the most-viewed videos for the day, the week, or all-time. Here's where you'll discover videos that have gone viral, passed from viewer to viewer by e-mail, Twitter, and Facebook recommendations.

Favorites: This screen displays all the videos you've added to your Favorites list on YouTube. This screen will also show you a list of any playlists and their videos when you tap the Playlists tab at the top of the screen. This is one of the features of the YouTube app that requires you to have a YouTube account. To sign into your account, tap the Sign In button in the top-left corner (see Figure 7–10). You'll be prompted to enter your user name and password. Once you do this, any videos you've favorited will be displayed.

Figure 7–10. *The Sign In/Sign Out button is located in the top-left corner of the Favorites, Subscriptions, and My Videos pages. Tap it to log into your YouTube account.*

To remove a bookmarked video, tap the Edit button in the top gray bar. All your bookmarked videos will display a circled *x* in their top-left corner. Tap the *x* to remove the video from your favorites. When you are finished deleting favorites, tap the blue Done button. (When you delete your last favorite, and there are no favorites left, the iPad automatically returns you to the Favorites screen without having to tap Done.)

> **NOTE:** Removing a video from your YouTube favorites on the iPad also removes it from your YouTube account, meaning it will no longer be displayed in your favorites, no matter what device you log into YouTube from. You cannot undo removing favorites.

Subscriptions: YouTube allows you to subscribe to another YouTube user's videos so you can keep up-to-date with the latest videos they've posted. Any subscriptions you have will show up on this screen. Tap the name of the user to see all their videos displayed to the left of the list. This feature requires you to be logged into your YouTube account.

My Videos: This screen displays all the videos you've uploaded to YouTube. This feature requires you to be logged into your YouTube account.

History: This screen displays the videos you have viewed on your iPad. The history does not reflect the videos you've viewed on your computer while logged into your YouTube account. To clear your history, tap the Clear button in the top-left corner.

You can also use the search field, found in the upper-right corner of any of these screens, to search YouTube's library of videos.

Viewing YouTube Videos

After finding a video you want to watch, what do you do next? This is one of the situations where the next step depends on whether you're holding the iPad in landscape or portrait mode. If you tap the video thumbnail in portrait mode, the video's information screen will appear, and the video will automatically begin playing in the information screen. If you tap the video thumbnail in landscape mode, the video will begin playing full-screen, and you'll need to tap the Done button to view the video's information screen.

Video information screens provide detailed information for each video. Depending on which orientation you are holding your iPad in—landscape or portrait—you'll see that information laid out slightly differently, but either orientation gives you the same information. Figure 7–11 shows the same info screen in both landscape and portrait modes.

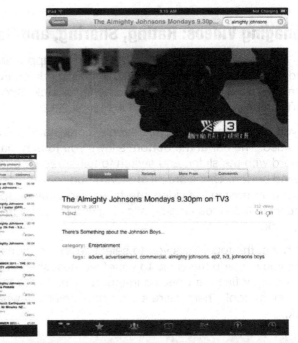

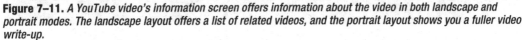

Figure 7–11. *A YouTube video's information screen offers information about the video in both landscape and portrait modes. The landscape layout offers a list of related videos, and the portrait layout shows you a fuller video write-up.*

On the video information screen you'll find the name of the video, its rating (in stars, from zero to five, when applicable), the number of times the video has been viewed, its run time, and more. You'll also see tabs labeled Related, More From, and Comments.

> *Related*: Shown by default, this tab lists videos related to the one you're watching. YouTube uses some clever tricks to match names, themes, and uploaders, among other aspects, to provide a list of videos that are most related to the one that you're currently watching.

> *More From*: Tap this tab to see more videos from the YouTube user who uploaded the video you are currently watching. From this tab you can also tap a Subscribe button to subscribe to the user's video feed. The user's YouTube name and videos will show up on the Subscriptions page.

> *Comments*: Tap this tab to read comments left by other YouTube users about the video you are watching. You can also tap the "Add a comment" field to write your own comment. You must be logged into your YouTube account to write a comment.

Managing Videos: Rating, Sharing, and So On

You can do more with videos in the YouTube app than just sort and view them. While in a video's information screen, you can bookmark, share, rate, and flag the video, as well as move from embedded to full-screen playback. Simply tap the video to bring up its YouTube control overlay, shown in Figure 7–12.

As you see in Figure 7–12, the overlay consists of opaque bars at the top and bottom of the video. The bar at the bottom allows you to play/pause the video, scrub backward or forward with the slider, and switch to full-screen mode by tapping the double-arrow expand button. These are all standard controls and operate exactly as you'd expect them to, matching the video interface used in other applications. The double-arrow also appears in full-screen mode, allowing you to return from full-screen to embedded playback.

The bar at the top allows you to select several options for managing the video. From here, you can add the video to your favorites, share it with others, vote on the video (like or dislike), or flag the video as inappropriate. All the top-bar options require a YouTube account to apply them. Here's a quick overview of what the options are and how they work.

Figure 7–12. *Tap a video in the video information screen to overlay it with a number of management options.*

NOTE: You must be viewing the video in its information screen (i.e., embedded mode) to rate the video, share it with others, and so forth. The managing video toolbar does not show up when you are playing a video in full-screen mode. The only exception is bookmarking. In full-screen mode, a bookmark icon appears next to the volume slider at the bottom of the screen. Tap it to add the video to your favorites.

Add: Tap this to bookmark the video to your favorites. If you have more than one Favorites list, you'll be able to select the list you'd like to add the video to. The video will immediately appear under the Favorites button in the YouTube app.

Share: Tap this to send a link to the video in an e-mail message. Without taking you out of the YouTube app, an e-mail compose window will pop up with the name of the video in the Subject field and a link to it in the body of the message. Just enter the e-mail address of the person you want to send it to, and you're done! You can also add your own text to the body of the e-mail like any other e-mail.

Like/Dislike: Tapping either button flags the video as one you like (thumbs up) or dislike (thumbs down).

Flag: Tapping this button will display a red Flag as Inappropriate button. Tap that to send a notification to YouTube. They will review the video and pull it from the site, if they deem it necessary. Be warned: don't flag videos just because you don't like the content. Flagging is meant only for objectionable content. If you falsely flag too many videos, you could have your YouTube account suspended.

NOTE: The Rate and Flag buttons will be grayed out when you've already rated or flagged the video.

YouTube Tips

Here are some tips for using the YouTube application:

- Use the Clear button at the top-right corner of the History screen to erase your YouTube viewing history. People don't have to know you've been watching that skateboarding dog.

- Don't overlook the Related Videos list. Scroll down on the video information screen to find related videos that you may want to view. YouTube is pretty clever about adding listings that you may actually want to see.

■ While navigating videos on the Featured, Top Rated, and Most Viewed pages, scroll all the way down, and you'll see a gray video icon with the words "Load More…" on it. Tap this to load more videos on the selected page.

■ You can play your YouTube videos out to TV either by connecting your iPad through a supported video cable (composite, component, VGA, and HDMI cables are all available through the Apple Store) or by selecting an AirPlay destination such as an Apple TV or a third-party player like Banana TV.

Watching Videos on the Web with Safari

Video on the iPad isn't limited to special-purpose applications. You can also watch MPEG-4 movie files with the iPad's Safari application. Chapter 6 introduced Safari. Here you'll see how you can connect to video on the World Wide Web and watch it in your Safari browser.

Many web sites besides YouTube feature embedded video. For example, go to virtually any news site, and you're sure to find embedded video. As mentioned in Chapter 6 and earlier in this chapter, the iPad, and thus Safari, does not support Flash playback, which limits the iPad's ability to display every single web video (see Figure 6-20 to see what happens when a Flash video is displayed on a web site in iPad's Safari). However, many web sites serve HTML5 and MPEG-4 videos, and they are fully iPad-compliant. You can also use a third-party application like the Skyfire Mobile Browser to view Flash video on the Web.

For example, the web site TED (www.ted.com), where you can watch videos of some of today's greatest minds talk about science, education, technology, and art, is fully iPad-compatible. Figure 7–13 shows playing back in the iPad's Safari web browser this site's video of author Elizabeth Gilbert talking about creativity.

You simply tap an embedded video to begin playback. Depending on the speed of your Internet connection, it may take a few seconds before the video begins playing. You can watch the video in-page or full-screen. To navigate between the two views, tap the video, and a navigation bar appears along the bottom of it. It displays the Play/Pause button, the navigation scrubber, and the familiar full-screen double-arrow button at the very right. Tap the double arrows to enter full-screen view. To exit full-screen view and return to the web page, tap the Done button on the video playback screen.

> **NOTE:** Disabling YouTube via restrictions hides its icon and prevents children (and others) from freely browsing YouTube content. Choose **Settings ➤ General ➤ Enable Restrictions**. Switch YouTube from On to Off.

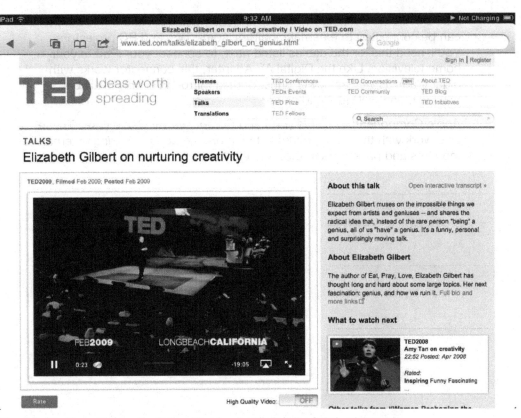

Figure 7–13. *Many videos on the Web can be played natively in the Safari web browser.*

Video Accessories

If you are going to be watching a lot of videos, there are several iPad accessories you should consider purchasing:

Stands: Several companies make them, and they range in price from $5 to $100. Whatever stand you choose, make sure it holds the iPad in landscape mode, because that gives you maximum screen real estate to watch your videos. Some cases also double as an iPad stand. Apple's iPad 2 Smart Cover ($39) folds into a stand.

Apple Digital AV Adapter ($39): Use this adapter (see Figure 7–14) to connect your iPad to any television using an HDMI connection. The dual-port design allows you to charge your iPad through the second port at the same time as you display video. The iPad 2 offers screen mirroring, but the adapter can be used with older iPads for applications that support video-out, including Videos, Photos, and YouTube.

iPad Dock Connector to VGA Adapter ($29): The VGA end of the adapter can be connected to external monitors, some TVs, and PC projectors. You'll need this, or the cables listed next, to connect your iPad to your home television. Like the Digital AV Adapter, this connector works with older iPads as well as newer ones. Screen mirroring is only available, however, on the iPad 2 and newer.

Apple Component AV Cable ($49) and *Composite AV Cable* ($49): These also work with the iPad, providing two more methods of linking external monitors and projectors to the device.

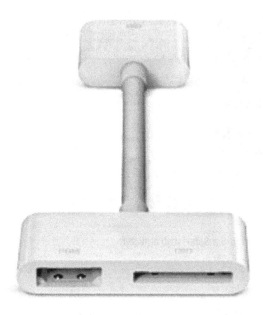

Figure 7-14. *Apple's new Digital AV Adapter provides HDMI connectivity from your iPad. The second connector outlet allows you to charge your iPad at the same time as you display video.*

Don't worry if you don't know the difference between VGA, HDMI, Composite, and Component. All three are types of physical video connectors that link devices to TVs.

- *VGA* is a 15-pin connector that you can still find on the back of many PCs. It supports resolutions up to 2048×1536.

- *HDMI*, also known as the High Definition Multimedia Interface, is a digital audio/video connector (it carries both signals at once) that provides high-definition signal support up to 2560×1600 across a single digital link.

- *Composite* is a video connector that channels three video source signals through a single connection. It's the oldest of the four technologies, but it still supports a resolution of up to 720×576i.

- *Component* is a video connector that takes three video source signals (red, green, and blue) and outputs them through three different connections. It's basically an RCA cable with three heads like the composite cable, but Component offers a much better resolution, up to 1920×1080p (otherwise known as *full HD*).

Many modern TVs support all these connections. Check your TV's manual to see which yours supports.

Projecting Video

Although Apple's connector cables allow you to direct your iPad video to televisions, a number of innovative third parties provide video solutions as well. Take the $430 Cinemin Slice (www.wowwee.com) from WowWee, for example. It's a video system that allows you to dock your iPad (see Figure 7–15) and project video to any screen or wall. With it, you can avoid a lot of awkward cabling when making presentations on the go, plus you don't have to arrange in advance for an HDTV. Instead, you can carry this relatively small unit along with you and display to any large flat surface, including the ceiling, if needed—the projector head is on a hinge that can rotate forward and upward.

The Slice works with iPad 2's screen mirroring. If you need to project in landscape mode rather than portrait, which most business folk probably prefer, you can purchase a $40 connectivity pack to use with your Apple-branded VGA video cable. If you need to use wireless mirroring, you'll need to connect an Apple TV unit to your projection system.

Figure 7–15. *The $430 Cinemin Slice product offers a highly portable way to project iPad 2 screens for on-the-go presentations.*

Listening to Music on the iPad

When Apple introduced the iPad, many people started complaining on the Internet that it was nothing more than a big iPod touch, even though most of them hadn't yet tried the iPad. There's even a popular parody video that shows joggers carrying an iPad instead of an iPod on their morning run. By now you've discovered that the iPad is much more than just a big iPod touch, but it also *does* play music like an iPod. (Just don't go jogging with it; or, if you do, get a Bluetooth headset and throw the iPad in a backpack, so you don't look silly running with something the size of a laptop screen in your hands, or, worse yet, attached to your arm.)

When it comes to the iPad, the Music app allows you to browse your audio libraries and select items to play. This app brings all the functionality and ease of use you expect from an iPod, but it delivers that functionality in a distinctive iPad package.

If you are used to listening to music on an iPod, iPod touch, or iPhone, you may expect the iPad to have the same kind of interface for its music player. In actuality, the iPad's music player provides a complete big-screen redesign. This is great news, because if you are used to using iTunes on a Mac or a Windows computer, you'll be instantly familiar with the basic functionality of the iPad's music player app. The iPad's easy-to-understand interface highlights its music features in a way that's simply not possible on a smaller screen.

NOTE: Do not confuse the Music and iTunes applications on your iPad. Music is used to play back your music tracks. iTunes connects you to the mobile iTunes Wi-Fi Music Store and is not a general music player.

Navigating the Music Library and Playlists

Tap the Music icon (see Figure 7–16) on your iPad's Home screen to launch the app. The Music icon is bright orange and has a picture of a musical note.

Figure 7–16. *The Music icon*

The first thing that you'll notice about the Music app (see Figure 7–17) is that its functionality is similar to that of iTunes. Not only can you listen to music in the app, but you can easily create and edit playlists like you would on your desktop. If you've played music on an iPhone or iPod touch, you'll be struck by how much more open the layout of the iPad's Music app feels. There's so much more space on the iPad that you can see more music at once. Instead of popping up and down long sequences of menu screens, the iPad presents more options and more music in one place, making it much easier to find and enjoy your tunes.

TIP: You can search for songs without opening the Music app. Use the iPad's Spotlight feature to the left of the Home screen to search for a song; then tap it to begin playing.

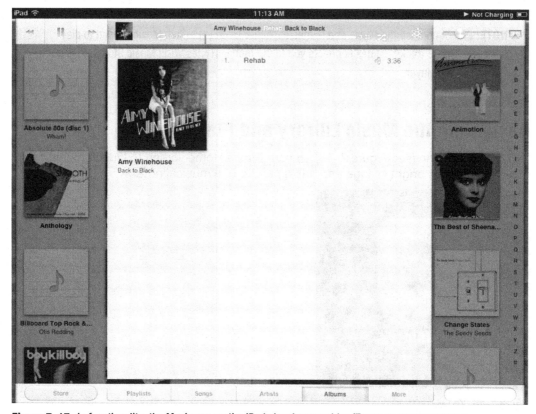

Figure 7–17. *In functionality, the Music app on the iPad closely resembles iTunes on your computer.*

The Music window is composed of elements that help you choose and play your music:

> *The play bar*: This runs along the top of the app and, when playing music, contains Play/Pause, Forward, and Rewind buttons; the playback scrubber; and the volume control. An optional AirPlay button may appear here if you can connect to a valid AirPlay audio destination on your local network.

> *Store button*: Found at the bottom-left of your screen, this button offers one-click access to the iTunes mobile music store.

> *The category list*: In the bottom row you'll see your music separated into different categories, depending on the items you have synced to your iPad (see Figure 7–17). Tap any category to see its contents.

> ▪ *Playlists*: Presents your music organized by playlists. Tap a playlist (it looks like a stack of albums) to navigate to a list of the songs contained within. Then tap any song to begin playing it.

> ▪ *Songs*: Contains all the music on your iPad in an alphabetic list.

■ *Artists*: Presents your music on an artist-by-artist basis. Tap an artist to see all their albums and the songs on each album. Tap any song to begin playing it.

■ *Albums*: Presents your music album by album. Tap an album cover, and it springs forward and flips around to reveal a full album view. Tap a song to begin playing it.

■ *More*: Offers other categories such as by-genre-ordering and via composers. Tap a genre cover or composer name to see all the albums and the songs per album that match your choice.

Searchbox: This field allows you to search through your currently displayed music collection by entering text to search for.

Between each of these elements, you'll find all your individual content. The displays will vary, however. On the Playlists screen, each item is represented as a pile of albums. In the Songs view, iTunes offers you a list of songs. The remaining options (Artists, Albums, Genres, and so on) are presented in tiled views, letting you choose each item as desired, navigating to the list of elements that make those up with a tap. As you use this app, you'll find these presentations become more and more natural to use as they closely match how you think about and play your music.

Playing Audio from the Music Library and Playlists

Whether you are in your main music library or a playlist, to start playing a song, simply tap it. Figure 7–18 shows the Music app's Now Playing screen. You arrive at this screen whenever you start playing a song and then tap the small album icon in the top bar on your screen. To return to the library, tap the album icon again.

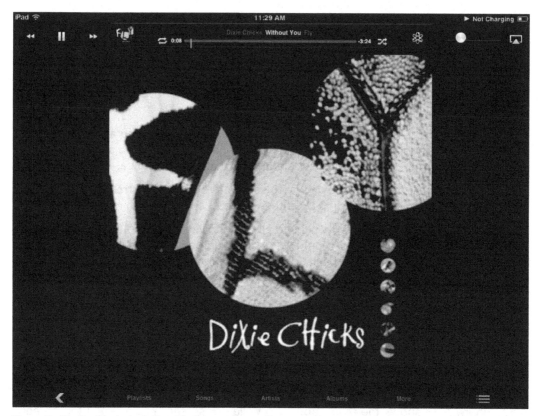

Figure 7-18. *The Music app's Now Playing screen provides an interactive screen that controls playback for the currently playing item. From this screen, you can adjust the volume, pause and resume playback, and loop the current track.*

When playing music, you'll also notice that a Play indicator has appeared in the iPad's status bar (see Figure 7–19). The right-pointing Play indicator at the top right of the screen (just left of the battery status) appears universally when you're playing back music. This tells you at a glance that music is playing. You'll find this especially helpful when you've removed your earbuds and placed the iPad on a table. It alerts you that your battery is gleefully emptying itself as your iPad plays music that no one is hearing.

Figure 7-19. *The Play indicator is next to the battery status in the iPad's status bar.*

Now Playing Screen

The Now Playing screen (see Figure 7–20) is divided into several sections. Here's a rundown of each of those sections and what kinds of information and controls you'll find there.

Title Bar

The title bar (see Figure 7–20) is the central bar at the top of the Now Playing screen and contains the following items:

Figure 7–20. *The title bar on the Now Playing screen*

Rewind: The Rewind button looks like a line followed by two left-pointing triangles.

- Tap to move back to the beginning of the currently playing song.

- Double-tap to move to the previous song in the album or playlist. If you are already at the start of the song, a single tap moves you back; if you're already at the first song, this works as if you had pressed the Back button—you return to the most recent album or playlist screen.

- Touch and hold to rewind through the current song. You'll hear very short snippets as you move backward through the song. This feature proves especially handy while listening to audiobooks.

Play/Pause: Play looks like a right-pointing triangle. Pause looks like a pair of upright lines. Tap this button to toggle between playback and pause modes.

Forward: The Forward button looks like the Rewind button in a mirror. The line is to the right, and both triangles point right instead of left.

- Tap once to move to the next song in the album or playlist. If you're at the last song, tapping Forward moves you back to the album or playlist.

- Touch and hold to fast-forward through your song.

Now Playing Album cover: Offers one-tap navigation between the now-playing screen and your music library. Alternatively, tap the back arrow at the bottom-left of the Now Playing screen.

Loop control: This control, which looks like a pair of arrows pointing to each other in a circle, appears when you tap album art.

- Tap once to loop the currently playing album or playlist. After the last song plays, the first song starts again.

- Tap a second time to loop just the current song. The number 1 appears on the loop, telling you that the loop applies to just this song.

- Tap once more to disable looping.

- A blue loop (both the regular loop and the loop with the number 1) indicates that looping is enabled. A white loop means looping is switched off.

Scrubber bar: The scrubber bar appears to the right of the loop control. Tap the album cover to make this control appear; tap again to hide it.

- The number at the left of the bar shows the elapsed playback time. The number at the right shows the remaining playback time.

- Drag the playhead to set the point at which your song plays back. You can do so while the song is playing, so you can hear which point you've reached.

Shuffle: The shuffle control looks like two arrows making a wavy *X*. It appears to the right of the scrubber bar and, like the loop and scrubber controls, appears only after you tap the album cover.

- When the shuffle control is off (white), album and playlist songs play back in order.

- When the shuffle control is selected (blue), the Music app randomly orders songs for shuffled playback.

Genius: Looking like a futuristic atom, the Genius button creates a collection of songs from your library that go great together and adds it to your Playlists collection.

Volume slider: Drag along the slider to adjust the volume. You can also use the iPad's physical volume button to adjust the volume. If you've attached an external speaker or remote control, you can use its switches to control the playback volume as well.

AirPlay button: When music-capable AirPlay receivers are available on your home network, an AirPlay button appears just to the right of the volume slider. Tap the button and select a receiver to redirect your music to. Because of Apple's highly encrypted AirTunes protocol, AirPlay for music and audio was limited to Apple-branded receiver equipment until spring 2011, when it was finally reverse engineered to allow access by third-party applications.

Artist, song, and album: These items appear at the top middle of the screen and are for information only. Tapping them does nothing.

> **NOTE:** If you are using Apple's iPhone earphones with a remote and mic to listen to music on your iPad, all the buttons and click features of the iPhone's earbuds work just fine (despite Apple not listing the earbuds as an official iPad accessory). Click to play/pause a song. Double-click to skip to the next song. Triple-click to return to the previous song. Tap the + or – button on the earphone control to increase or decrease the volume. The microphone on the iPhone earbuds also works fine with the iPad. The Apple Earphones with Remote and Mic cost $29 at the Apple Store.

Album Cover

Below the scrubber bar, you'll notice the song's album art taking up a majority of the display (see Figure 7–18). When you've downloaded album art, the cover image appears just below the top bar and occupies most of your screen. (When the iPad cannot find album art, it instead displays the same light gray music note on a white background.)

Double-tap the album to flip it over to the song-by-song album listing. Tap any song to switch to playing it. Here, you can also add song ratings for the current song using the star control, just under the scrubber bar. A single-tap returns you to the album cover art.

If you tap the album instead of double-tapping it, it zooms to fill the entire screen. Tap it again to return to the normal view.

Bottom Bar

At the bottom of the Now Playing screen you'll see a two buttons, one on each side of the screen, with grayed-out categories between them:

> *Back button*: Tap the Back button (the arrow pointing left) at the bottom left of the screen to return to your library.

> *Album View button*: This button looks like a three-item bulleted list and appears at the bottom right of the screen. Tap this to switch between your Now Playing screen and its Album view. This works the same as double-tapping the album cover.

Album View

Album view is a powerful and fun way to navigate your music. You can access Album view in two ways, both from the Now Playing window.

- Double-tap the album art area to reveal Album view. The cover art will flip around, and you'll be presented with the full list of songs from that album.

■ Tap the Album View button in the thick bottom bar of the Now Playing window. The cover art of the current song will flip around, and you'll be presented with the full list of songs from that album.

Why use Album view, as shown in Figure 7–21? Pretend you are listening to a playlist and a song comes on you haven't heard in a while. It's a great song, and you want to check out what other songs are on the album. Album view lets you do this without leaving the playlist. Simply access it by using either of the methods mentioned earlier, and you'll be presented with a screen that shows a track list of all the songs from that album along with their names and durations. Scroll up and down the track list to see all the items on the current playlist or album. Tap any item to start playback.

Figure 7–21. *Album view shows a list of tracks and durations for the current music.*

Album view also allows you to rate your songs. Use the star control that appears below the scrubber bar to rate the current song, from zero to five stars. Drag your finger along the stars to set your rating. These ratings sync back to your computer. Rating your music is a good thing to do because it lets you keep track of songs you really like. You can create smart playlists to contain all of your five-star songs, enabling you to access them all in one place instantly.

Also, if you use the iTunes DJ feature in the desktop version of iTunes, higher-rated songs will be played more often. iTunes DJ is an iTunes feature that picks songs from your library and creates an endless playback of music. It's great when you are having a party. iTunes DJ is not a feature of the Music app on the iPad.

Creating Playlists

Playlists you've chosen to sync from iTunes will automatically appear in your Music app. But you aren't limited to creating playlists on your computer. You can create standard and Genius playlists right from your iPad, allowing you to build audio-listening experiences on the go.

Creating a Playlist

To create a standard playlist, tap the New button at the top-right of the Playlists tab. A pop-up appears, asking you to name the playlist. Enter a name, and tap Save. Immediately after, a list of all the songs on your iPad slides up the screen. Select the songs you want to include in your playlist by tapping the + button next to each track. When you select a song, it will appear grayed out. You'll also find an Add All Songs option at the top of your list of songs. Adding all the songs in your library defeats the purpose of a playlist, however.

If you select a song by accident, you cannot unselect it at this point, but you can easily remove it later.

While adding songs to a playlist, you have several options to navigate your library to find the songs you want (see Figure 7–22). At the bottom of the Add to Playlist screen, you'll see the category views of the Music app: Songs, Artists, Albums, Genres, and Composers. Select any of these to sort through your song library, and then click the appropriate song to add it to the playlist.

Tap the Done button at the top right when you are finished adding songs.

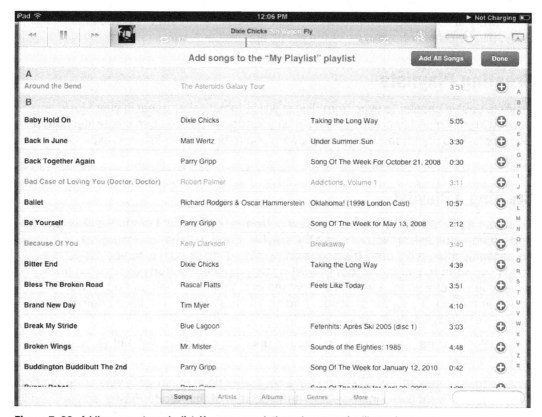

Figure 7–22. *Adding songs to a playlist. You can search through your entire library for songs.*

Editing a Playlist

When you are finished adding songs to your new playlist and tap the Done button in the upper-right corner, you are taken to the playlist edit screen (see Figure 7–23). This screen allows you to add, delete, rearrange, and shuffle songs.

Figure 7–23. *The playlist edit screen allows you to further customize your playlists after their creation. As you can see here, the playlist creation tool allows you to add song duplicates. If this happens, use the edit screen to remove those (unless you really want songs to repeat.)*

You can access the playlist edit screen from any existing playlist by tapping the gray Edit button at its top-right corner. This playlist edit screen allows you to do the following:

> *Add songs*: Tap the Add Songs button to be presented with the Add to Playlist screen again, and follow the previous steps until you've added the items you want; then tap the Done button again.
>
> *Delete songs*: Tap the white and red minus (–) button to remove a selected song. Tap the red Delete button that appears to the right of the song to confirm deletion. Removing a song from a playlist will not delete it from your music library on your iPad or on your computer.
>
> *Rearrange songs*: Tap and hold the grip bars to the right of a song, and drag to rearrange it in the playlist.

NOTE: You can edit only standard playlists. If you have synced a smart playlist (the kind with the icon of a machine's cogwheel next to it in iTunes) from your computer, you won't be able to edit it.

Deleting Playlists

In iOS 5, you delete playlists in the Playlists tab by tapping and holding the album pile until a small circled X appears at the top-left of that playlist. Tap the X. You will not receive any further confirmation, and the playlist will be removed from your iPad. So, do this carefully.

Creating a Genius Playlist

Genius is a feature in iTunes that finds songs in your music library that go together. It does this by matching rhythm, beat, artists, genres, and Internet data. A Genius playlist is a list of songs that results when you choose to run the Genius feature on a song you are listening to.

You can create Genius playlists in iTunes on your computer or on the iPad. However, to enable the Genius feature, you need to turn it on through iTunes on your computer first. To do this, launch iTunes on your computer, go to the Store menu, and select Turn on Genius. You'll need to log in with an iTunes Store account (see Chapter 8 for creating an iTunes account) to access the Genius features. Enter your user name and password, agree to the terms and conditions, and sit back as Apple analyzes your music library.

You can create or update your iPad's Genius playlist by tapping the Genius icon in the bar at the top of the screen. The currently playing song acts as the seed for this list.

A new playlist named Genius Playlist appears in your music library. In its list of songs, you can scroll through to see what Genius has picked out. The playlist offers options via buttons at the top of the song list:

> *Refresh*: Tap Refresh to rebuild the Genius playlist around your original song. This allows you to retain the same playlist styling with an updated selection of tracks matching that theme. This is a great feature if you're exercising and finish the playlist but want to keep going with the same kind of songs you just listened to.

> *Save*: Did Genius generate an absolutely awesome collection of songs that you want to keep around to play over and over again? Tap Save to keep your Genius playlist for later. After tapping Save, the name of the playlist changes from Genius to the name of the song you chose to create the playlist.

Editing a Genius Playlist

Genius playlists offer the following two management options. Both appear as buttons above the song list when the Genius playlist is selected.

Refresh: Tapping Refresh populates the Genius playlist with all new songs seeded by your original selection. Keep your theme while switching up the music with this option. All songs previously on the playlist are removed but remain in your music library.

Edit: Tapping Edit prompts the white and red minus (–) button to appear next to the name of each item in the Genius playlist, and grip bars to appear to the right. Make your updates and then tap Done to finish your edits.

Playing Podcasts, Audiobooks, and iTunes U Lessons

If you've synced podcasts, audiobooks, and iTunes U lessons to your iPad, their categories will show up in the categories list at the bottom of the screen in the More section. To view the items available in each category, simply select the category name from that More menu.

For podcasts and iTunes U lessons, tap the series or class, and then select the episode or lesson to begin playing back that item. To play an audiobook, tap your chosen audiobook in the list.

Displaying Music Playback Controls When in Another App

We've already mentioned how your music, podcasts, and audiobooks will keep playing even when you leave the Music app. The good news is that you don't need to go back into the Music app to change tracks. Simply double-tap the iPad's physical Home button in quick succession to reveal the recent apps list, and then swipe to the right to find your iPad playback controls (see Figure 7–24). From this small pop-up, you'll be able to navigate through songs, adjust the volume, or select an AirPlay destination. To close this panel, tap anywhere on the main screen. Tap the Music icon at the right to move immediately into the Music application. (When you're in the middle of watching YouTube or Videos, this icon may change to that app.)

Hey, Mr. Good Looking Guy

Figure 7–24. *These iPad controls appear to the left of your recently used applications. Swipe to the right to uncover this little gem.*

You can also access these controls when your iPad is locked. Simply double-tap the iPad's Home button, and the Music navigation bar appears at the top of the display (see Figure 7–25).

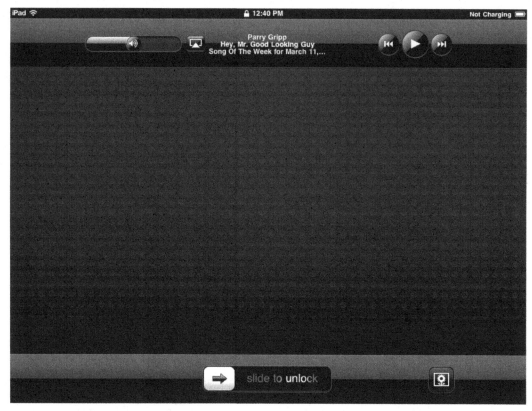

Figure 7–25. *With a simple double-tap of the iPad's home button, music options appear on the iPad's lock screen. Use these buttons and sliders to control music playback even when your iPad is locked.*

Music app Settings

Surprisingly, for a feature-rich application like Music, the iPad provides just a few settings for its music player. You'll find these in **Settings ➤ Music** (see Figure 7–26), and they work as follows:

> *Sound Check*: Say you're listening to a song that was recorded way too low. So, you crank up the volume during playback. Then when the next song starts playing back, *boom!*—there go your eardrums. Sound Check prevents this problem. When you enable Sound Check, all your songs play back at approximately the same sound level.

TIP: You can also use Sound Check in iTunes. **Choose Edit ➤ Preferences ➤ Playback ➤ Sound Check** (Windows) or **iTunes ➤ Preferences ➤ Playback Sound Check** (Mac).

EQ: The iPad offers a number of equalizer settings that help emphasize the way different kinds of music play back. Choose from Acoustic, Dance, Spoken Word, and many other presets. To disable the equalizer, choose Off.

Volume Limit: Face it, personal music players bring your audio up close and very personal—so up close, in fact, that your hearing may be in peril. Though not a dedicated music player, the iPad is no different. We strongly recommend you take advantage of the iPad's built-in volume limit to protect your ears. Tap Volume Limit, and adjust the maximum volume using the slider. All the way to the left is mute—sure, you'll protect your ears, but you won't be able to hear anything. All the way to the right is the normal, unlimited maximum volume. If you're super paranoid or, more usually, if children have access to your iPad, tap Lock Volume Limit to open a screen that allows you to set a volume limit passcode. No one may override your volume settings without the correct passcode.

Group by Album Artist: Choose this to override the artist metadata when you want to give priority the artist listed on the album rather than the artist listed in each track.

TIP: If your songs don't have lyrics embedded in them, you can add them yourself. In iTunes, select a song, and then press Cmd+I (Mac) or Ctrl+I (Windows). On the song's Get Info screen, navigate to the Lyrics tab. You can paste in the lyrics field any lyrics you have for the song. There are also a number of apps that search your iTunes songs and automatically add lyric information. Try Get Lyrical (www.shullian.com) on the Mac and SoundCrank (www.soundcrank.com) on the Windows computer.

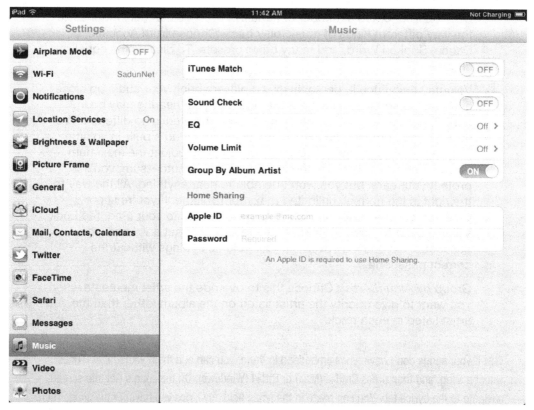

Figure 7–26. *The Music app's Settings screen allow you to set EQ and adjust volume limits, as well as add credentials for iTunes' new Home Sharing feature.*

Setting Up Home Sharing

Home Sharing allows you to play music on your iPad that is stored on your home computer. It's pretty much the opposite of AirPlay, where you send music and videos from your iPad out to other devices for playback. For Home Sharing to work, your computer and your iPad must be sharing the same Wi-Fi network, and iTunes has to be running on your computer. Home Sharing is a feature of the iTunes application itself, and it has to be able to serve that data out to the network and from there to your iPad.

Enable Home Sharing by entering your Apple ID and password in settings. You must use the same Apple ID and password that your home computer is signed into. If you fail to do so, you won't be able to access your music.

On your home computer, launch iTunes, and select **Advanced ➤ Turn On Home Sharing**. Enter your Apple ID and password, then click Create Home Share.

From the iPad side of things, you can access Home Sharing media by tapping the Library item at the top of the Music app's sources list (see Figure 7–27). Select the shared library you want to browse from the pop-up. Once selected, it may take a minute or two for the library contents to load (there is eventually a progress wheel that fills to let you know how long it will take). Once loaded, the Home Shared library replaces the current library, and the check mark in the Home Sharing pop-up switches to the library in use. You can return to your onboard library at any time by selecting your iPad from the Home Sharing pop-up.

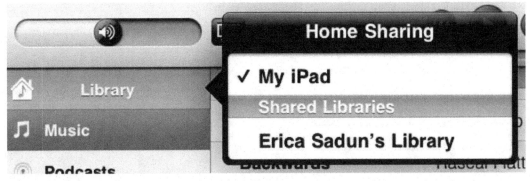

Figure 7–27. *Access shared libraries from the Music app's Library item at the top of the sources list.*

Summary

In this chapter, you learned how to watch videos through the YouTube and Videos apps, as well as in the Safari web browser. You also learned how to browse and play back your music and podcasts using the Music application and Home Sharing.

Here are a few points you should take away and consider:

- Video playback is consistent across applications. If you can handle video in YouTube, you'll know how to use it in Safari. The changes between the screens are minor and easy to follow.

- Set up a free YouTube account to enjoy the YouTube app even more. You'll be able to bookmark your favorite videos, subscribe to video feeds, and rate and share your favorite clips.

- The Music app playlists are a lot of fun. The Music app lets you create and edit two kinds of these: standard, which lets you manually add songs to it, and Genius, which automatically generates a list of songs based on a single song you choose in your music library.

- Save your ears. Adjust your playback volume using the built-in volume controls and limiters. You can find out more about the increasing occurrence of noise-induced hearing loss at www.cdhh.org/resources.php.

- Don't forget about double-tapping the Home button to pull up music controls, regardless of your current application.

- Home Sharing currently can be used only when your iPad and computer share the same Wi-Fi network. Ideally, Apple will extend this to remote access in future updates. Forcing you to authenticate with your Apple credentials suggests that that feature remains just around the corner.

Chapter 8

Shopping for Apps, Books, Music, and More

You might think of your iPad as an Internet-connected computer, but it's much more than that. It's also a software store, a bookstore, a music store, a game store, and a place to buy videos and movies. Why drive to that Redbox kiosk to rent a movie or wait for a Netflix DVD to show up in the mail when you can rent a movie on your iPad and watch it immediately?

The iPad builds upon Apple's history of building electronic storefronts that make it easy to purchase digital content. This started with the iTunes Music Store on April 28, 2003, resulting in Apple becoming the number-one seller of music in the United States just five years later. Now known as the iTunes Store, Apple's digital store accounts for 70 percent of all worldwide digital music sales.

Through the iTunes Store, you have access to more than 11 million songs available worldwide. Your iPad, if it is using the U.S. iTunes Store, provides access to more than 1 million podcasts; 40,000 music videos; 3,000 TV shows; 20,000 audiobooks; 2,500 movies; and close to 300,000 iPhone and iPad apps.

You don't need to visit a physical store to buy those apps—they're all available from an application included with every iPad called the App Store. The App Store is analogous to a software-specific department in the overall iTunes Store, and the App Store app provides a quick way to search for, learn about, and purchase apps from your iPad.

Starting with the launch of the iPad on April 3, 2010, Apple opened the virtual doors of a new store, the iBookstore. Although it doesn't yet have the selection of Amazon's Kindle Bookstore, a large number of classic and new titles are available.

In this chapter, we'll take you on a virtual shopping spree buying apps, music, movies, videos and TV shows, and books, all while sitting with your iPad in front of you.

The App Store

The App Store opened its virtual doors on July 11, 2008, and as of the printing of this book, more than 10 billion apps have been sold. Most of those apps were written for the iPhone and iPod touch but can run on an iPad unchanged. Many apps have been written especially to take advantage of the larger screen and faster processor of the iPad, and some apps run on both platforms but have improved capabilities that appear only when viewed on the iPad.

When you activated your iPad in Chapter 1, you were asked either to enter an existing Apple ID or to sign up for one. By doing this, Apple set up both the payment and authorization mechanism that is used by all of the on-device stores. That means you're ready to make purchases in any of the Apple stores directly from your iPad.

When you launch the App Store on your iPad, you're greeted with a screen that looks like Figure 8–1.

Figure 8–1. *The iPad App Store*

By default, the App Store initially shows you featured apps. How can you tell? There are six icons at the bottom of the App Store page: Featured, Genius, Top Charts, Categories, Purchased, and Updates.

Featured Apps

At the top of the store you'll see three buttons: New, What's Hot, and Release Date. Each one of these buttons displays a slightly different view of the inventory of the App Store. Start by looking at the New view.

New

At the top of the page is an ever-changing sample display of new apps. These apps have been highlighted by the App Store staff as being either unique or best-selling. When you see an app that you'd like more details about, just tap it, and a detailed app description appears (see Figure 8–2).

Figure 8–2. *Detailed description of an app in the App Store*

The app description screen displays a large version of the icon that appears on your iPad screen, as well as the price, the category that the app is in, information about the latest release, compatibility, and customer star ratings and reviews. Want to tell a friend about the app that you found? Tap the Tell a Friend link, and the App Store creates an e-mail that you can send to your buddy.

> **NOTE:** If you have purchased an app and have problems with it, tap the Support button at the bottom of the Featured and Top Charts pages, and you can let both Apple and the developer know about the issue. This button provides a link to Apple's support web pages concerning iTunes, and under the heading App Store and iBooks are links that display common troubleshooting tips and an Email Us button. Apple responds to most queries with 24 hours, which makes this the most direct way to get an answer. You can also tap the App Support button on the left side of an app description page (see Figure 8–2) to contact the developer directly.

The description of an app shows a maximum of about five lines of information on the iPad screen. To read more, tap the More link to expand the description (see Figure 8–3).

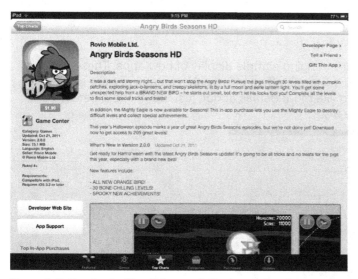

Figure 8–3. *Tapping the More link expands the description of an app. Compare this description with the five-line description shown in Figure 8–2.*

Buttons on the left side of the screen provide direct links to the developer's web site and support page. The images displayed on the screen scroll, so to see all of them, just drag the visible picture to the left.

We recommend reading the customer ratings and reviews at the bottom of the app description page, although they can sometimes be misleading. We find that the reviews often point out common issues that other users may be having with the app, so you can decide whether to purchase the app now or wait for a revision. When you buy an app, you can also rate it and write a review for others to read. Ratings are applied by clicking anywhere from one (bad) to five (good) stars. If you choose to write a review instead, note that you'll be asked to sign into your iTunes account once more and told your review will be screened by Apple prior to publishing.

When you've decided to purchase an app, all you need to do is tap the price. The price turns to a green Install App button, which you then tap. A dialog box appears on your iPad screen asking you to enter your iTunes password and then tap OK. Once you've done that, the app is downloaded and installed onto your iPad. You'll receive an e-mail receipt from Apple outlining your purchase within a few days.

> **NOTE:** When you tap OK and the download begins, the App Store closes, and the Home screen of your iPad appears. Don't be alarmed; this is normal. This also happens when you're updating apps.

Let's go back to the App Store for a few minutes and talk about the other areas on the New screen. Below the spotlighted section is a New and Noteworthy section of apps (see Figure 8–4). Apple's staff chooses this crop of apps from new entries to the App

Store, and the apps are often unique and fun. To scroll through the New and Noteworthy apps, tap the white arrows on the left and right sides.

Figure 8–4. *New and Noteworthy apps are singled out for extra attention in the App Store for interesting functionality, fun game play, or tremendous value.*

Next on the screen is usually a small group of icons, pointing to an App of the Week, groups of similar apps (apps for kids or music creation apps, for example), or apps that deserve special attention.

Continuing down the App Store screen, there's a selection of Staff Favorites (see Figure 8–5). These may not necessarily be new apps, but they've captured the hearts of the App Store staff, and they'd like for you to know about them. As with the New and Noteworthy apps, you can browse through the selection by tapping the white left and right arrows.

At the bottom of the App Store is a set of Quick Links. If your account currently has an unspent balance, that amount is listed. By tapping that balance, you can view or change any of your iTunes account information. If you don't have a balance, that information is available by tapping the Account button at the very bottom of the App Store screen.

See that Redeem button in Figure 8–6? That's a fun way to buy apps on someone else's dime. You may be lucky enough to get a "promo code" from a developer. That's a code that can be redeemed for a free copy of an app. When you tap Redeem, a dialog box appears into which you can enter that code, an iTunes Gift Card code, or a gift certificate code number. Enter the code and tap Redeem, and then enter your iTunes password. If you've entered a promo code for a specific app, that app is downloaded and installed. If you've entered a gift card or certificate code, then your iTunes account is credited for the value of the card or certificate.

Figure 8–5. *Staff Favorites, Quick Links, and the common App Store buttons are found at the bottom of the App Store screen.*

Figure 8–6. *Redeeming promo codes, gift cards, and gift certificates is a nice way to buy many apps.*

The last button on the bottom of the App Store screen is for Support. Tapping this button directs you to the iTunes support web page (www.apple.com/support/itunes) in the Safari web browser.

The answers to many common questions are found on the iTunes support page, so be sure to browse through the information before requesting further help. If you don't see an answer for your questions about iTunes, the App Store, the iBookstore, or purchases of music or videos, there's a button for sending an e-mail to the iTunes Store support team. In most cases, you'll receive a response within 24 hours.

What's Hot

The What's Hot screen displays a similar layout to New, except with a listing of What's Hot apps in place of New and Noteworthy. This screen also displays a frequently updated compendium of apps that are of particular interest to iPad users. Shortly after the release of the iPad 2, for example, this section highlighted apps that had been specially enhanced for the new device.

Release Date

Finally, the Release Date button on Featured provides a scrolling look at all apps that have been released, in reverse chronological order. For each day, the apps are listed alphabetically. First you'll see apps released today listed in alphabetic order, then apps for yesterday also listed in alpha order, and so on.

> **NOTE:** The descriptions of the virtual stores on the iPad are based on how they appeared during the writing of this book. Apple frequently changes the design of the stores, so specific details described in this chapter may be different by the time you read this.

Top Charts

Whenever we want to see what's popular on the iPad, we start up the App Store and immediately tap the Top Charts button at the bottom of the screen. A list of the Top Paid iPad Apps and a list of the Top Free iPad Apps are displayed (see Figure 8–7). Scrolling further down the screen, there's a list of top-grossing iPad apps.

Figure 8–7. *The Top Charts screen in the App Store displays the top paid and free iPad apps.*

Apple defines Top Paid and Top Free iPad Apps by the number of downloads of each app, while the lower list is calculated on the total revenue generated by apps. That means if a high-priced app sells well in the App Store, it's going to top the Top Grossing iPad Apps list.

Categories

Sometimes you don't want to browse through hundreds or thousands of iPad apps, and you'd much rather just see all apps that pertain to a specific category. The Categories button at the bottom of the App Store displays a set of buttons that lead to app listings by category (see Figure 8–8).

This is a great way to find the top entries in a particular category of app. For example, let's assume that you're looking for an iPad app to help you balance your checkbook and home budget. The most likely category for an app of this type would be Finance.

A quick tap on the Finance button displays a familiar-looking screen (see Figure 8–9) with a list of new or recently updated iPad apps in the Finance category. These apps are sortable by three criteria—Name, Most Popular, and Release Date—by tapping the Sort by button and selecting the appropriate sort type.

Figure 8–8. *Looking for a specific type of app? The category listing groups apps with similar functionality.*

Figure 8–9. *Viewing the most popular apps in the Finance category of the App Store*

By using categories, you've reduced the number of apps to look through to a manageable number. It's a great way to make the best use of your App Store shopping time.

Searching

What if browsing through the App Store just isn't leading you to the one product you're looking for? If that's the case, then it's time to do a search.

The search box is in the upper-right corner of the App Store screen. To search for a keyword, type it into the search box, and then press the Search button on the iPad's virtual keyboard. You'll notice that as you're typing your keyword, the App Store app provides a list of suggestions (see Figure 8–10).

Searching can be very useful when you know part of the name of an app but can't remember the exact spelling. For instance, one of us was trying to find a note-taking app for the iPad recently. He knew that it was called either DeskPaper or PaperDesk but couldn't remember for sure. Typing **paper** into the search box brought up a number of suggestions, and sure enough, PaperDesk for iPad was listed. He tapped the suggestion, which took him right to the description of the app.

Figure 8–10. *As you type a word into the App Store search box, suggested apps are listed.*

Downloading Updates and Previously Purchased Apps

Developers are always updating their apps. Updates can include major new features or just subtle performance tweaks. How do you know when there's an update to one of the apps you've downloaded? A red badge with a number appears in the corner of the App Store icon on the iPad Home screen (Figure 8–11). The number in the red button tells you how many of your apps have available updates.

Figure 8–11. *When you have an app update available for download and installation, a red notification circle will appear on the App Store icon on your iPad.*

That same number appears on the Updates button in the App Store. To install the updates, open the App Store, and tap Updates. A listing of all the available updates occupies the screen, and there's an Update All button in the upper-right corner of the screen (see Figure 8–12). Tap that button to begin the download and installation of the app updates.

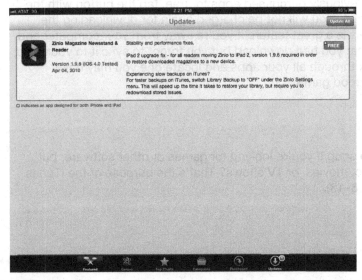

Figure 8–12. *When there are app updates available, tapping the Update All button downloads and installs all of them.*

You'll be prompted to enter your iTunes password in order to validate your request. Once that's been done, the application downloads and installs. If the application update is more than 20MB in size and you're using an iPad with Wi-Fi + 3G, then a warning appears noting that you must be connected to the much faster Wi-Fi network before downloading the update. Any smaller updates are downloaded and installed immediately, even over the 3G network.

> **Note:** If you start downloading an app that's greater than 20MB in size and then leave the Wi-Fi network before it finishes, the download will pause, and you'll be able to resume once you rejoin a Wi-Fi network.

From the Purchased section of the App Store, you can also redownload any other apps you have previously download. It doesn't matter whether they were free or paid apps. From the bottom of any App Store screen, tap the Purchased button (Figure 8–12).

On the Purchased screen you'll find a list of all the apps you've ever purchased from the iTunes Store. It doesn't matter if you bought them through iTunes on your computer, through the iTunes Store on your iPad, or through the iTunes Store on another iOS device. If you bought any items with the Apple ID you are using on the iTunes Store on your iPad, your entire purchase history appears when you tap the Purchased button.

You can sort through all your purchase history or just your purchase history for items not currently on your iPad by tapping the All or Not on this iPad tab at the top of the Purchased screen.

To redownload any of your previously purchased apps for free, tap the button with the downward arrow in a cloud icon. You will not be charged again for downloading the items you already bought. This is a great feature if you're away from your computer and find you really want an app that you had download but you forgot to sync it to your iPad. It's also a great way to check through all your apps and locate one you may have forgotten about, like a really good game.

The iTunes Store

The App Store is the place to shop if you're looking for games or other software, but what if you want to buy music, movies, or TV shows? That's the purpose of the iTunes app on your iPad (see Figure 8–13).

Figure 8–13. *The iTunes Store. Just tap the iTunes app icon on your iPad to enter it.*

The first thing you may notice is the similarity in the design of the iTunes Store and that of the App Store. The iTunes Store came first and was refined over many years, so Apple took the same concept and applied it to the App Store and the new iBookstore. The iTunes Store has one nice feature the App Store doesn't: previews. To preview any song, video, or movie in the store, tap it. Song previews run for 90 seconds, while video, movie, and TV show previews vary in length.

Both stores have a set of buttons across the top and bottom of the screen. For the App Store, those buttons are New, What's Hot, and Release Date. In the iTunes Store, the buttons are replaced with Featured, Top Charts, and Genius.

Along the bottom of the screen are buttons for all the different types of media you can download from iTunes. The media types consist of Music (single tracks or albums by musical artists), Movies, TV Shows (single episodes or full seasons), Podcasts, Audiobooks, and iTunes U. There's also a button for entering Ping, Apple's media-oriented social network.

The top and bottom buttons work in tandem to show you what's hot in all the different media. I'll explain how they work similarly for music, movies, and TV shows.

Featured

Tapping the Featured button at the top of the iTunes Store when Music is selected at the bottom of the screen displays the now-familiar New and Noteworthy list. This time, of course, we're not talking about apps; instead, we're talking about music. You can find both singles and full albums in New and Noteworthy.

Further down the screen will be buttons linking to special singles and albums, music videos, and items available for pre-order, followed by a section containing content that varies. For example, this section featured "Metal Albums for $7.99" when we were writing this paragraph. The section changes depending on what the iTunes Store staff decides to sell at any point in time, so expect this section title to change often.

At the bottom of the Featured screen is the familiar Quick Links section described in the App Store part of this chapter. The links are different and change frequently. Here's where Apple puts in links for items that are free on iTunes and gives you the ability to complete an album or buy specially priced albums and songs. Finally, the Account, Redeem, and Support buttons once again reside at the bottom of the page, providing much the same functionality that they do in the App Store.

Now, when you tap the Movies button, things change a bit. For example, New and Noteworthy changes to New to Rent or Own. We'll elaborate on movie rentals shortly, but for the time being, it's sufficient to understand that you can either buy or rent movies from the iTunes Store.

Below that is a changing section, similar to that found in the Music section of the store. The Quick Links and various buttons take their usual place at the bottom of the page, although once again they are different from what you see in other parts of the store and change frequently.

By now, you'd expect the TV Shows button to display something similar to what you saw for Music and Movies, and you'd be correct. New and Noteworthy listings appear near the top of the pages, along with the traditional Quick Links and buttons near the bottom of the page. The same is also true for Podcasts, Audiobooks, and iTunes U.

If you're not familiar with iTunes U, it's an innovative section of the iTunes Store that provides educational podcasts and videos from universities around the globe. Yes, you can learn linear algebra, explore concepts in sedimentology and stratigraphy, or follow the history of Rome from Augustus to Constantine, and you can do it all from the comfort of your own home and your iPad.

The Ping button is a gateway to Apple's social network for music. Ping lets you follow artists and friends and displays real-time updates from those people. Through Ping, inform your followers about music you like or reviewed, and comment on their updates. To use Ping, create a free profile with your Apple ID in the Mac or Windows iTunes application by clicking the Learn More button in the upper-right corner. Once Ping is activated for your iTunes account, your friend and artist feeds are visible by tapping the Ping button in the iTunes app on your iPad.

Genres and Categories

At the top of the iTunes screen on the left side, you'll see a button that changes from Genres to Categories, depending on whether you're viewing music, TV shows, movies (Genres), or podcasts or audiobooks (Categories).

In either case, tapping this button displays a list of types of media. For example, podcast categories include arts, business, comedy, and education, to name a few. Music genres include alternative, blues, children's music, and more. Like categories in the App Store, genres and categories in the iTunes Store make it much easier to find what you're looking for.

Movie Rentals

At any time, you can choose to rent a movie from the iTunes Store and view it on your iPad. Rentals differ from purchases in that they have a limited lifetime on your device. When you tap the Rent button, the clock starts. You have 30 days to start watching the movie, so you can preload your iPad with movies before going on a trip. Once you have started watching the movie, you have 24 hours in which to complete your viewing. Want to watch the *Star Trek* movie 10 times during that 24-hour period? No problem.

Once that 24-hour period of obsessive rewatching of the rental is complete or you've reached the end of 30 days without watching the movie, the movie disappears from your library. You can watch the movies you've rented from your iPad only on your iPad, so they can't be transferred to another computer or iPhone. Movies that are purchased on your computer can be transferred to your iPad or iPhone.

If you have one of the optional video-out cables that I discussed in Chapter 1, you can pipe the video that's playing on your iPad into a TV with an HDMI, component, or composite video input. The Apple Digital AV Adapter, Apple Component AV Cable, and Apple Composite AV Cable ($39 each) are perfect for watching video from the little screen (iPad) on the big screen.

When you rent a movie directly from your iPad, consider your network speed. Wi-Fi connections are generally much faster than 3G, so you'll be able to start watching the film sooner when it's downloaded over Wi-Fi.

Season Passes

For ongoing TV series, Apple has created the concept of Season Passes. These allow you to download every episode of a TV season. Current episodes that have previously aired are downloaded to your iPad immediately, while future episodes download after their initial TV airdate the next time you sign into iTunes.

Season Passes are a boon to series fans who don't want to miss an episode of their favorite show, and they make it easy to keep a copy of the show for posterity. As with movies, TV series can be purchased in either high or standard definition.

HD vs. Standard Definition

Many movie titles offer the choice of high definition (HD; see Figure 8–14) or standard-definition downloads. If you're an HDTV fan, you might be disappointed to find that you can't watch your videos in true HD on your iPad. What do we mean by that? The 1024×768–pixel iPad display doesn't match the aspect ratio—the ratio of width to height of a display—of either the common 1080i (1920 pixels wide by 1080 pixels high) or 720p

(1280 pixels wide by 720 high) HDTV formats. The iPad display also lacks the exact aspect ratios found in many movies, commonly 16:9 or 2.35:1.

Figure 8–14. *High-definition video on the iPad lets you see incredible detail even in action scenes. This image shows letterboxing (the black stripes at the top and bottom of the screen).*

That's not to say that you can't display these high-definition video or movies on the iPad—you can, but they'll be letterboxed. That means black bars surround the top and bottom of the video screen, as shown in Figure 8–14. The 720p HD–formatted movies are also downscaled to the width of the iPad screen. On the plus side, video and movies look wonderful on the iPad's display regardless of letterboxing. Part of this is because of Apple's adherence to the H.264 compression scheme, which is able to compress digital video to relatively small sizes without compromising quality.

Standard-definition movies from iTunes are in a format called 720xN Anamorphic. Files are upscaled to fit the width of the iPad screen, resulting in movies that aren't as sharp as those that are HD formatted.

Another major difference between HD and standard-definition iPad movies is the size of the movie file. As an example, *Captain America* is 1.37GB in size in standard definition and 3.25GB in HD (see Figure 8–15). Owners of 16GB iPads might want to stick to standard-definition movies or download only a few movies at a time.

Figure 8–15. *This detailed description of* Captain America *displays the Buy and Rent buttons, as well as the buttons for selecting HD or standard definition. The description displays the size of the file as well, which is important if your iPad is low on storage.*

The rental and purchase prices for movies increase as you go from standard to high definition. An HD movie purchase often costs about $5 more than its SD counterpart, while rentals are usually about $1 more for HD.

Top Charts

Looking at Top Charts while browsing music in iTunes displays two lists: Top Songs and Top Albums. Moving downward on the Top Charts page displays Top Music Videos for your purchasing pleasure.

For movies, Top Charts displays two columns: Top Movie Rentals and Top Movie Sales. In the TV Shows category, Top Charts shows a list of Top TV Episodes and Top TV Seasons. For podcasts, the iTunes Store splits Top Charts into Top Audio Podcasts and Top Video Podcasts.

In the audiobooks category, there's simply a listing of the top 12 audiobooks, and in iTunes U, the Top iTunes U Collections shows you what is popular in the academic world.

Genius

When you're looking at music, movies, or TV shows, there's another button at the top of the page: Genius (see Figure 8–16).

Figure 8–16. *The iTunes Genius is like having your own personal shopper to recommend music or movies. Of course, you'll have to start by telling your personal shopper what you like.*

Have you ever wanted to have your own consultant who could check out what music you like or the movies and TV shows you watch and then suggest new albums to listen to or videos to watch? That's exactly what the iTunes Genius function does for you.

Based on media that you have purchased through iTunes or have moved from your computer to your iPad, the Genius recommends different albums, TV shows, or movies that you may like. You can improve the accuracy of Genius recommendations by occasionally looking at them and voting with a "thumbs up" or "thumbs down."

The accuracy of Genius picks improves with frequency of purchases and rentals. Based on one movie purchase and one rental, the movie Genius did a remarkable job of picking out comedies that we might be interested in, but it also threw in some movies we'd never watch. In the TV area, we had purchased the entire first season of *Star Trek: The Original Series*. The Genius then thought that we would like *Star Trek: Deep Space Nine*, which we loathed. Once again, voting for or against recommended movies is a great idea for improving how well your Genius picks match your true preferences.

The iBookstore

What? You haven't spent enough money yet? You can take care of that quickly with the new addition to Apple's digital stores, the iBookstore. The iBookstore was available on the iPad first and now is available on the iPhone and iPod touch as well.

There's a reason why Apple chose to debut the iBookstore on the iPad. The iPad's book-sized backlit LED screen makes it perfect for reading books in just about any lighting condition. The battery life on the iPad is wonderful, so unless you're planning on doing a marathon reading of *War and Peace*, there should be no need to plug in your device while you're reading.

To take advantage of the iBookstore, you'll need to install the free Apple iBooks app onto your iPad. Probably the easiest way to do that is to tap the App Store icon and then type **iBooks** into the search box. The app should appear at the top of the list of suggestions, and tapping iBooks will display a handful of apps. Look for the free iBooks app, install it by tapping the Free button, and then tap the Install App button. Your iPad downloads the application and installs it.

> **NOTE:** Case doesn't matter when searching in the stores. You can type a search word or phrase in lowercase, uppercase, or mixed-case letters, and you'll get the same results.

Once you've installed the iBooks app on your iPad, launch it. Unlike the App Store and the iTunes Store, iBooks doesn't start in the iBookstore. Instead, you'll see your book library, a beautiful wooden bookshelf with book covers artfully displayed (see Figure 8–17). We'll talk more about iBooks in the next chapter; here we're just concerned with the iBookstore and how to buy books.

> **EASTER EGG ALERT!** An Easter egg is a little treasure hidden in a computer program. To see an example of an Easter egg in iBooks, use your finger to drag down the bookshelves. You should find something very familiar hidden above the top row of books.

In the upper-left corner of the bookshelf is a Store button. That button is your gateway to the iBookstore. Tapping it loads the iBookstore (see Figure 8–18), which looks surprisingly similar to the App and iTunes Stores. It works the same, too; tap the price to see a Buy Book button, and then tap that button to sign into iTunes, pay for the book, and download it.

Figure 8–17. *Your iBooks library displays your books in a familiar place—on a bookshelf.*

Figure 8–18. *Inside the iBookstore. It's very similar to the App and iTunes Stores in both looks and operation.*

Apple made the iBookstore similar to a bricks-and-mortar bookstore in that you can browse books. If you're not sure about a book, check for the Get Sample button that downloads a sizable chunk of the text for you to read. It's like leafing through a book at the bookstore.

To return to your bookshelf, tap the Library button. The Categories button provides a way to narrow down your search to a certain type of book. You know how real bookstores have signs pointing out Mysteries and Thrillers in one area and Cookbooks in another? The iBookstore categories provide the same function as those signs (see Figure 8–19).

Figure 8–19. *Categories are like the departments found in real bookstores. They contain books that are similar by type of content.*

In keeping with the general layout of the iTunes and App Stores, buttons across the bottom of the iBookstore include Featured, NYTimes, Top Charts, and Purchases. The top of the iBookstore has buttons to provide instant listings of only featured books or all books listed by release date. When we were writing this book, the iBookstore contained more than 200,000 books.

Featured

As you'd expect, the Featured button displays lists of New & Noteworthy titles and icons that lead to collections of books about a specific topic or books that the iBookstore team deems must-reads, and then another list of books that changes regularly. As we were writing this, for instance, the list was "Bestselling Bios Under $10," and it featured two books that we ended up buying.

Near the bottom of the iBookstore Featured page, you'll find the familiar Quick Links box, which in this case features not only a link to your account information but also links to book specials (see Figure 8–20).

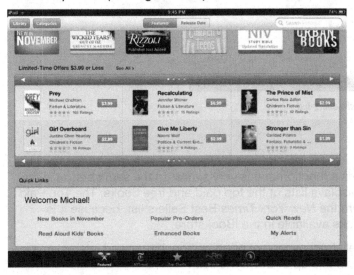

Figure 8–20. *Quick Links are like virtual book clubs.*

At the very bottom of the page you'll find the familiar Account, Redeem, and Support buttons, which perform the same functions that they do in the App and iTunes Stores.

NYTimes

The *New York Times* Best Sellers list is considered to be *the* list of best-selling books in the United States. Published weekly in the *New York Times Book Review* magazine, the best-seller list has been published continuously since 1942.

It's fitting that Apple chose to pick the authority on published books to provide an automatically updated list of fiction and nonfiction best sellers for the iBookstore. Tapping the NYTimes button at the bottom of the iBookstore brings up the lists, which show the top ten books in each category (see Figure 8–21). To see more of the Fiction and Nonfiction Best Seller lists, there's a Show More button at the bottom of the page that will add another ten books to the list each time it is tapped.

Figure 8–21. *The New York Times Best Sellers list*

Top Charts

The Top Charts button provides a function that is very similar to the same button in the App Store. In other words, it displays lists of the top paid and free books. The Top Paid Books list is often different from the *New York Times* Best Sellers list, because it is compiled from the sales of books available in the iBookstore.

The Top Free Books aren't likely to change very often, although renewed interest in a classic book may move a certain title up or down the list.

Purchased

The Purchased screen displays any book that you have bought in the iBookstore. As you'll find out in Chapter 9, you may eventually want to delete some of the books in your personal iBooks library. If you ever want to read those books again, or at least add them back to the library for future reference, Purchased shows a cloud button next to the title (see Figure 8–22) that you can use to reload a previously purchased book.

Figure 8–22. *If you've deleted a book from your library and want to add it back, you can do that from the Purchased screen in the iBookstore. Tapping the cloud button reinstalls the book to its rightful place on your bookshelf.*

When you tap the cloud button, the iBookstore prompts you for your iTunes password in order to validate your request. Upon entering the password and tapping OK, the book downloads and appears in your iBooks library with a "New" banner on it.

Summary

The iPad makes keeping up with your favorite TV shows, finding new music and applications, and watching your favorite movies as easy as tapping a button. Through the App Store, you have access to a large and expanding selection of software written to take advantage of the features of the iPad. The iTunes Store brings a wide variety of audio and visual entertainment to your iPad, while the iBookstore is sure to give traditional paper books a run for their money.

The following are the key points of this chapter:

- The App Store, iTunes Store, and iBookstore all require an iTunes account for billing and validation purposes. Although you can set up the account on your iPad, it's usually much easier to accomplish this feat on your home computer.

- All the stores require an Internet connection over Wi-Fi or 3G.

- The free apps that are portals to the digital App and iTunes Stores come preloaded on every iPad. The iBookstore is accessible through iBooks, which is a free download from the App Store.

- Do you need a hand in picking out movies to watch, music to listen to, or TV shows to follow? The iTunes Genius provides recommendations that get better the more you use iTunes to buy or rent media.

- Be sure to consider the amount of storage in your iPad when purchasing or renting videos and movies from iTunes, because HD content consumes much more space than standard definition.

- Take advantage of the free previews of music and books in the iTunes Store and iBookstore as a way to "try before you buy."

Chapter **9**

Reading Books and Newspapers with iBooks and Newsstand

Your iPad is more than a wonderful device for playing games, surfing the Web, and watching videos. It's also a powerful e-book reader with a library of more than 30,000 free books at your fingertips, as well as thousands more paid books, including many *New York Times* best-sellers. But the iPad's iBooks app doesn't stop there! You can also add your PDFs to iBooks so you can carry them with you on the iPad. This allows you to access all your PDFs from the same library as your books—a great feature for people who regularly work with or receive PDF files. In addition to iBooks, Apple has introduced Newsstand in iOS 5. Newsstand lets you view and buy all your magazine and newspaper subscriptions in one easy-to-access location.

In this chapter, you'll discover how to navigate your iBooks bookshelf and the books themselves. You'll also learn about bookmarking favorite passages from books, creating notes, organizing your books into collections, and even having a book read to you. We'll take you through all the PDF features of iBooks. Finally, we'll explore Newsstand and show you how to shop for an organize all your subscriptions. Let's get started!

The iBooks App

As you discovered in Chapter 8, the iBooks application does not ship on the iPad. To use it, you must first download it for free from the iTunes Store. Once you have done this, the iBooks icon will appear on your iPad's Home screen (see Figure 9–1).

Figure 9–1. *The iBooks icon*

Tap the icon to launch the iBooks app. When you do, you'll be presented with your iBooks bookshelf (see Figure 9–2). The bookshelf will be populated with any e-books you have added to your books library in iTunes (more on that in a moment).

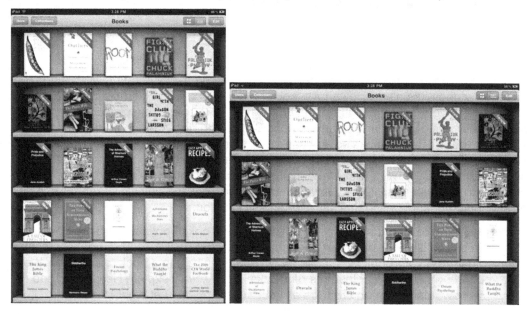

Figure 9–2. *The iBooks bookshelf in Landscape and Portrait views*

Syncing Books

Before you can sync books, you need to first acquire some books to sync. We talked about syncing books to your iTunes library in Chapter 2, but we'll touch on it again here. There are a few ways for you to obtain books to sync to your iPad.

The iBookstore

In the upper-left corner of your bookshelf, you'll see a Store button (see Figure 9–3). Tap this button, and your bookshelf will flip around like a secret passageway. On the backside of the bookshelf, you'll be presented with the iBookstore. In the previous chapter, you learned how to buy books and download free Project Gutenberg books from the iBookstore. Any book you download from the store will appear on your bookshelf and automatically sync with your computer when you connect to it with your iPad. For a complete walk-through of buying books in the iBookstore, see the previous chapter.

ePub Books

A second way to get books on your bookshelf is to download ePub-formatted books from other web sites and then drag them into your books library in your iTunes source list on your computer. Any ePub books you've added to your iTunes library will be automatically synced the next time you connect your iPad to your computer.

What Is ePub?

ePub is a universal e-book file format. Any device capable of opening and displaying ePub files can display the book, no matter where you bought it. In other words, you don't need to buy your books from the iBookstore only. Several sites sell e-books in the ePub format that are compatible with the iPad. ePubbooks (www.epubbooks.com/buy-epub-books) has an excellent list of sites that offer ePub books for sale and for free download. Once you've downloaded an ePub book, simply drag it to your iTunes library, and the book will sync to your iPad on the next connection.

> **NOTE:** Amazon's Kindle bookstore is another popular place to buy e-books. However, Kindle books don't use the ePub format. If you buy an e-book from the Kindle store, you'll need to download Amazon's free Kindle book reader app for the iPad to read those books. You will not be able to read a Kindle book in the iBooks app. Barnes & Noble's Nook for iPad is another way to buy e-books for the iPad, and the BN eReader app supports the standard ePub format. This means you can move books back and forth between various ePub readers.

Navigating Your Bookshelf

OK, you have a bunch of books downloaded and synced. Before you start reading them, let's get a little better acquainted with how to navigate all the books on your bookshelf.

Figure 9–3. *From the title bar of the iBooks bookshelf, you can access the iBookstore, navigate between your collections, and access the View and Edit modes.*

The Title bar in the iBooks bookshelf features five buttons:

> *Store*: As mentioned previously, tapping this will take you to the iBookstore.

> *Collections*: The Collections button displays a list of all your book collections in iBooks. By default, you'll see two collections:

> ■ *Books*: When you tap Books, you'll be presented with your bookshelf. This contains all the e-books you have in the iBooks app.

> ■ *PDFs*: Tapping PDFs will take you to your PDF bookshelf. We'll talk more about the PDF features of iBooks in the second half of this chapter.

> We'll also talk about collections in detail later in this chapter.

> *Icon View*: This is the default view of your bookshelf. The button with four white squares shows you all your books' covers in large, easy-to-see thumbnails.

> *List View*: This is the button next to the Icon View button. It has three white lines in it. Tap it to see a List view of your iBooks bookshelf (see Figure 9–4).

Figure 9–4. *The List view with sorting options by bookshelf, title, author, and category*

When you tap the List View button, you'll notice the genre of the book is displayed next to the book's name. You'll also notice that, at the bottom of the screen, you have four ways to sort your lists:

Bookshelf: Displays your books in the order that they appear in Icon view.

Titles: Displays your books in alphabetical order by title.

Authors: Displays your books in alphabetical order by author name.

Categories: Displays your books in genre groups. Books are arranged alphabetically in each grouping.

List view also displays a search field in the title bar. Tap the search field to open the keyboard and type in your search keywords. You can search through your books library by words in a title or the author's name. Tap a book in the search results to open it. Note that you can search for books in Icon view, too. All you need to do is pull down on the bookshelf, and a search field will be revealed (see Figure 9–5).

Figure 9–5. *The search field in Icon view*

Edit: The Edit button is in the top-right corner of the bookshelf. Tapping this button will cause you to enter Edit mode. Edit mode allows you to rearrange the order of books or delete books from your library completely.

- *Rearranging books*: In Icon view in Edit mode, simply tap and hold a book's cover and drag it to a new position on your bookshelf. This is no different from the way you arrange apps on your iPad's Home screen. In List view in Edit mode, you can only rearrange books in the Bookshelf sorting category. Tap and hold the grip bars on the right of the book's genre and drag the book to your preferred position.

- *Deleting books*: When you tap the Edit button in Icon view, you'll see black and white *X*s appear on the left corner of a book's cover. Tap the *X* to open a deletion confirmation window. Tap Delete to remove the book from your iPad. In List view in Edit mode, you can delete books from any of the four sort views. Simply tap the white minus sign (–) button in the red circle, and then tap the Delete button that appears at the opposite end of the screen to confirm the deletion.

> **NOTE:** Deleting a book from the iPad will not delete it from your iTunes library on your computer. You will be able to resync the book any time you want.

You may notice that some of your books have a blue or red ribbon in the upper-right corner of the cover. The red ribbons say Sample, and they signify the book on your bookshelf is a sample you've downloaded from the iBookstore. Samples will stay on your iPad until you delete them or buy the full book, but they will not sync back to your iTunes books library.

Blue ribbons say New, and they signify that you have not begun reading the book yet. The New ribbon will appear until you've turned at least one page inside the book (see Figure 9–6).

Figure 9–6. *Books with the New and Sample ribbons next to a previously read book*

Organizing Your Books into Collections

iBooks does a wonderful job of displaying your books and PDFs on a digital bookshelf; however, there may come a time when your book collection grows so large that seeing them all displayed on a single iBooks bookshelf might not make for the easiest browsing experience.

Luckily, Apple has a built-in feature called *collections* that allows you to sort your books onto different bookshelves for easier organization. In the upper-left corner of the iBook screen, you'll see the Collections button. Tap it to reveal a list of book collections in iBooks (see Figure 9–7).

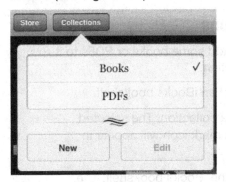

Figure 9–7. *The Collections menu*

Be default you'll see two collections: Books and PDFs. Any e-books you have will appear on their own bookshelf under the Books collection, and any PDFs you have will appear on their own bookshelf under the PDFs collection.

Creating New Collections

If you'd like to create new collections to better manage your library, you can do so easily:

1. Tap the Collections button so the Collections menu appears.

2. Tap the New button.

3. A new collections field will appear (see Figure 9–8); enter the name of
    your new collection.

Figure 9–8. *Creating a new collection*

4. When you have entered your collection's name, click Done, and your
    new collection will be created.

Adding Books and PDFs to Your Collections

Once you've created a new collection, you need to add some books or PDFs to it.
Follow these steps to add books or PDFs to a collection:

1. Tap the Edit button in the upper-right corner of an iBooks bookshelf.

2. Tap the book(s) or PDF(s) you want to add to a collection. The selected
    book or PDF cover will fade, and a blue check mark icon will appear in
    its lower-right corner (see Figure 9–9).

3. Tap the Move button in the top-left corner of the iBooks bookshelf. The
    collections list will be displayed (see Figure 9–9).

4. Choose the collection you want to add the selected books or PDFs to
    by tapping its name. An animation will show the selected books flying
    into the selected collection, and you'll be taken to that collection's
    bookshelf, where you'll now find your selected books or PDFs.

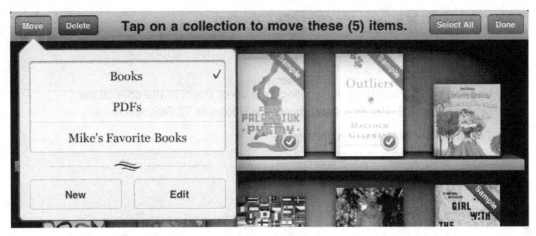

Figure 9–9. *Separating books into collections*

NOTE: You can place a specific book or PDF in only one collection at a time. When you add a PDF or book to a collection, it is removed from its previous collection.

Navigating Between Your Collections

iBooks makes it easy to navigate between your collections. In fact, it gives you two ways to do this:

- Tap the Collections menu and then tap the collection you want to view.

- From any collections bookshelf, drag your finger left or right to swipe to the previous or next collection.

Editing Collections

iBooks lets you edit the names of existing collections, arrange the collections in a specific order, and delete collections.

Follow these steps to edit the name of a collection:

1. Tap the Collections button so the Collections menu appears.

2. Tap the Edit button.

3. Tap the collection that you want to edit the name of.

4. Enter the new name of the collection.

5. Tap the Done button when finished.

Follow these steps to arrange the order of a collection:

1. Tap the Collections button so the Collections menu appears.

2. Tap the Edit button.

3. Use the grip bars to drag your collections up or down in the collections list (see Figure 9–10). You can't move the Books or PDFs collections.

4. Tap the Done button when finished.

Figure 9–10. *Editing collections*

Follow these steps to delete a collection:

1. Tap the Collections button so the Collections menu appears.

2. Tap the Edit button.

3. Tap the red minus sign button (see Figure 9–10).

4. A red Delete button will appear. Tap it to delete the collection. A warning dialog will appear, asking you whether you want to remove the collection's items from the device or move the items the back to their default collections. Tap Remove to remove the items from your iPad, or tap Don't Remove to keep them on the iPad and move them back to their default (Books or PDFs) collections.

Reading Books

The bookshelf displays your books in a gorgeous and easy-to-find layout, but books are meant to be read, not looked at. Let's get started!

To read a book, simply tap its cover. The book will fly forward and open. If it's the first time you've opened the book, you'll be on the first page. If you have opened the book before, it will open on the page you left off on.

While reading a book, you can choose between Landscape or Portrait orientation. Landscape mode shows you two pages side by side, while Portrait mode shows you a single page (see Figure 9–11). You can navigate between the two modes simply by rotating your iPad.

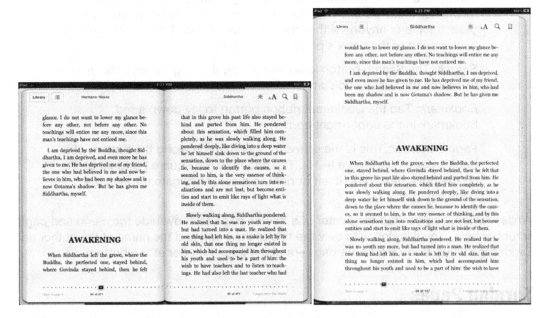

Figure 9–11. *Reading a book in Landscape and Portrait modes*

At the top of any book's page, no matter what orientation you are in, you'll notice a menu that contains a series of buttons (see Figure 9–12).We will get to using all these features momentarily, but let's look at the various menu options first:

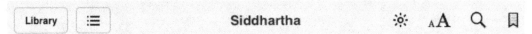

Figure 9–12. *A book's menu buttons*

> *Library*: Tapping this effectively closes the book and takes you back to your bookshelf. The next time you open this book, you'll be taken to the page you were on when you left it.

> *Table of Contents/Bookmarks*: This button is signified by three dots, each with a line after it. Tap this button to be taken to the book's Table of Contents and Bookmarks page.

Buy: This button (not shown) appears next to the Table of Contents button when you are reading a sample book downloaded from the iBookstore. Tapping it allows you to buy the full book.

Brightness: This is the button that looks like the sun and changes the screen brightness while inside the iBooks app only.

Font: This button, symbolized by a small and big *A*, allows you to change the font of the book's text, as well as the font size. This is helpful for those people who need larger text while reading, such as older people or anyone with sight difficulties. It also lets you change the background of the book's page to a sepia tone.

Search: The Search button looks like a magnifying glass and allows you to search through a book's text.

Bookmark: Tap the Bookmark ribbon button to lay down a red bookmark in the upper-right corner.

Page Scrubber: This is the series of dots that run along the bottom of a book's page (see Figure 9–14). Tap and hold the square button that sits on the dots; next, drag it left or right to quickly navigate through the book's pages.

While reading, you can tap the center of a book's page to show/hide the menu and page scrubber bars. You'll be left with only the title of the book and the name of the author (in Landscape view) at the top of the page—and the page number at the bottom.

Turning Pages

You have three ways to move through a book's pages:

■   Tap and hold the side of a page, and then drag your finger across; the page will curl on the screen (see Figure 9–13). When you lift your finger, the page turn will be complete.

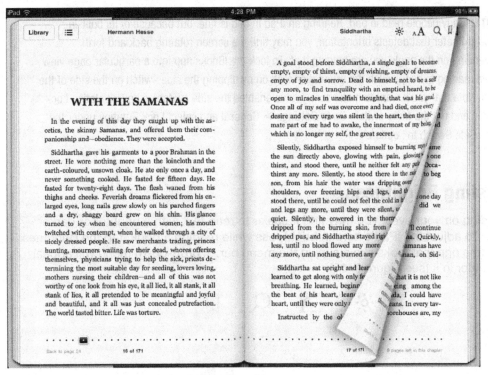

Figure 9–13. *You get cool eye candy when turning a page.*

- Tap the right or left side of the screen to move forward or backward. This accomplishes the same function as the previous one but with less interactive eye candy.

- Tap and hold the page scrubber bar at the bottom of a page (see Figure 9–14) and then slide your finger in either direction. The name of the chapter and the page number will appear above the page scrubber bar as you slide. When you've found the right page, remove your finger from the scrubber, and the page will flip, taking you to the page you've selected. The page scrubber bar lets you go to a specific page number quickly, without having to flip through all the pages of the book.

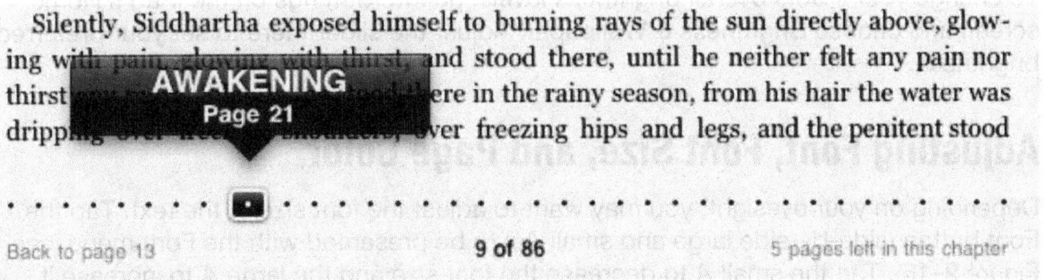

Figure 9–14. *The page scrubber bar shows the page number and chapter title.*

> **NOTE:** Many people read in bed. Reading an iPad in bed is fine, but because of its built-in accelerometer that detects orientation, you may find the screen rotating back and forth, depending on the angle you are holding it at. To lock the iBooks app into a particular page view while reading in bed, switch the orientation lock on by flipping the side switch on the side of the iPad. Note that you'll want to make sure you've enabled the side switch as an Orientation Lock button and not the Mute switch. Go to **Settings ➤ General** and select Lock Rotation under the "Use Side Switch to" option.

Adjusting Brightness

Depending on your eyes, you may find it easier to read text with a brighter or darker screen. To adjust the iPad's screen brightness while reading a book, tap the Brightness button (the one that looks like a sun) in the menu bar. A drop-down menu will appear with a slider in it (see Figure 9–15).

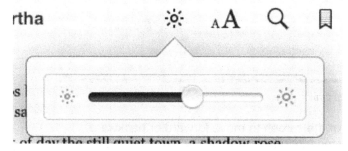

Figure 9–15. *The Brightness slider*

Slide to the left to reduce brightness and to the right to increase it. When adjusting the brightness in the iBooks app, the entire screen will brighten or dim according to your slider settings; however, once you leave the iBooks app, the screen brightness will return to the settings you have specified in the iPad's Settings application. This is a great feature because you can instantly switch between brightness levels when you enter or exit the iBooks app without having to reconfigure them each time.

To change your iPad's overall brightness levels, go into Settings on the iPad's Home screen and choose Brightness & Wallpaper. Adjust the slider there to set your preferred brightness.

Adjusting Font, Font Size, and Page Color

Depending on your eyesight, you may want to adjust the font size of the text. Tap the Font button (side-by-side large and small As) to be presented with the Font menu (see Figure 9–16). Tap the small *A* to decrease the font size and the large *A* to increase it.

Increasing or decreasing the font size will result in fewer or more words on a page, respectively.

Figure 9–16. *The Font panel*

Below the font size controls, you'll see a button that says Fonts. Tap this to select from six font types (see Figure 9–17). Different font types can affect the number of words you see on the screen slightly. Why change the font? Some people have an easier time reading different fonts, especially serif or sans serif fonts. A sans-serif font is like the font of the text of this book; there are no little lines hanging off the letters. A serif font is one like Times New Roman.

Below Fonts, you'll see the Sepia button. Tap to toggle this feature on or off. When On, the entire book will take on a yellow-brown tone, similar to the color pages in an old paper book start to turn after a while. Some people find reading from a sepia screen easier on the eyes because you aren't staring at a bright white background.

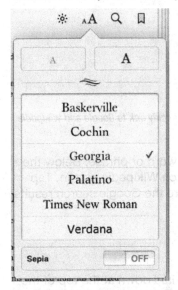

Figure 9–17. *The fonts you can choose from*

Searching Text

You can search for any word or bit of text in the book you are reading by simply tapping the Search icon, which looks like a magnifying glass. A search field will pop up, along with a keyboard. Type any search term you want, and you'll be presented with a list of results, displayed by order of page number (see Figure 9–18). Tap any result to be taken instantly to that page. On the page, your search term will have a brownish yellow bubble over it.

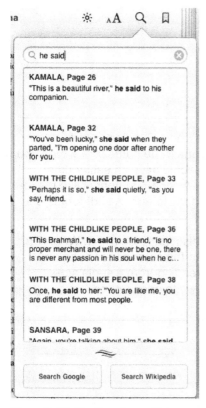

Figure 9–18. *The Search panel lets you perform in-text searches, as well as quickly link to Google and Wikipedia searches on the Web.*

You can also perform a Google or Wikipedia search for your word or phrase. Below the search results, you'll see a Search Google button and a Search Wikipedia button. Tap either to leave the iBooks app. You'll be taken to Safari, where the Google search results or Wikipedia entry page will be presented.

Bookmarking a Page

Tapping the Bookmark icon will cause a red bookmark to be laid down at the top of the page (see Figure 9–19). Laying down a bookmark adds a shortcut of the page to the

Table of Contents/Bookmarks page, so you can quickly access the bookmarked page later. Bookmarking in iBooks isn't really like using a bookmark in a physical book. In the iBooks app, the bookmarking feature is more akin to dog-earing a page on a real book, since you aren't limited to one bookmark. You can bookmark as many pages as you want. To unbookmark a page, tap the red Bookmark ribbon.

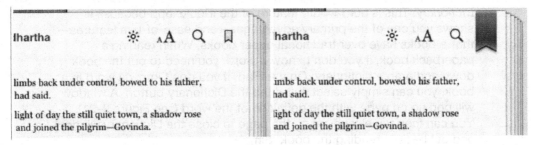

Figure 9–19. *Tap the Bookmark button (left) to lay down a bookmark (right).*

Interacting with Text

Your interaction with the book's text isn't limited to search. What we'll show you next is one of the reasons why e-books are superior to traditional paper books. However, paper books still have a leg up on e-books in many ways. See an article about the two formats here: `www.tuaw.com/2010/05/08/a-tale-of-two-mediums-despite-the-ipad-traditional-books-aren/`. One advantage paper books have over e-books is that they are relatively cheap (especially if you buy them used). Also, you don't need to be afraid to take them to a park or a beach. Sand or dirt isn't going to affect the usability of a paperback the same way it will affect an electronic device like the iPad. Also, while reading in public, paper books are a much lower theft target than Apple's latest gadget wonder.

While on any page, press and hold your finger to the screen, and a Spyglass icon will pop up on the page. To move it around, simply drag your finger. Below the Spyglass icon, a single word will be highlighted in blue. When you've found the word you want, remove your finger from the screen. The Spyglass icon will disappear, and the word will be highlighted with grab bars on either side. Drag the grab bars to select more than one word, such as a sentence or entire paragraph.

With your selection confirmed, you'll be presented with five text-selection tools from the black pop-up menu that appears (see Figure 9–20):

| Copy | Dictionary | Highlight | Note | Search |

voluntarily suffering and overcoming pain, hunger, thirst, tiredness self-denial by means of meditation, through imagining the mind ceptions. These and other ways he learned to go, a thousand tir

Figure 9–20. *The text-selection tools*

Copy: Select to copy the text so you can paste it into another application or the search field. Note that the copy function works only with PDFs and non-DRM (digital management rights) e-books. You will not be able to copy text from any books purchased from the iBookstore because of its copy-protection software.

Dictionary: This is our favorite feature of the iBooks app because it shows you one of the primary advantages—and ease-of-use features—that e-books have over traditional paper books. When reading a paperback book, if you don't know a word, you need to put the book down and grab a dictionary. On the iPad, if you don't know a word in a book, you can simply select it and tap the Dictionary button. A window will pop up on page with the definition of the word (see Figure 9–21). You can then tap elsewhere on the page to close the Dictionary window and get back to reading the book. Simple.

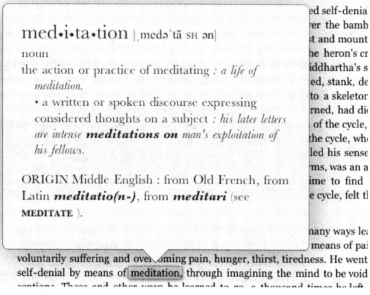

Figure 9–21. *The Dictionary panel*

Highlight: Tapping Highlight will mark the text as if it's been marked by a highlighter (see Figure 9–22). Apple has outdone itself here because the highlighting actually looks the same as it does on physical paper.

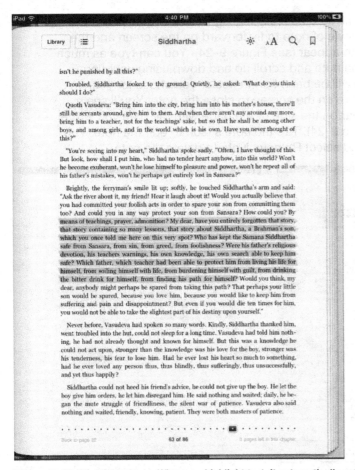

Figure 9–22. *Highlighted text. When you highlight text, it automatically gets added to the Bookmarks page.*

If you tap the colored highlight, another pop-up menu appears that allows you to change the color of the highlight, create a note to go along with the highlighted text, or remove the highlight (see Figure 9–23). Color selections are yellow, green, blue, pink, and purple. Any newly selected text you choose to highlight will be highlighted the color of your last choosing. Any text you highlight will show up in a list on the Bookmarks page (which we'll get to in a moment).

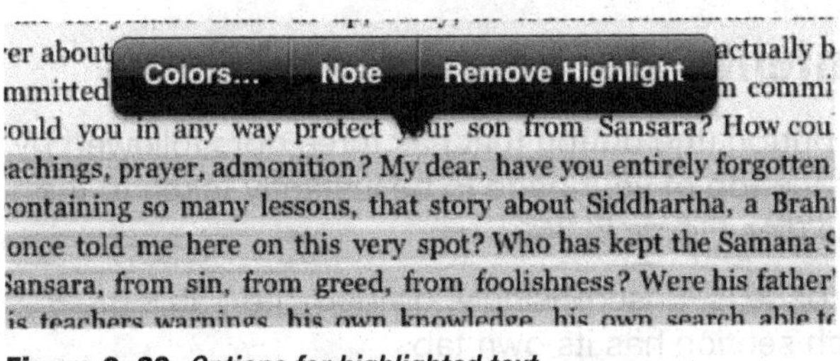

Figure 9–23. *Options for highlighted text*

Note: Tapping Note will automatically highlight the selected text and then cause a Post-it style of note to fly forward on the screen and the on-screen keyboard to appear (see Figure 9–24). You can type as much text as you want in the note and scroll up and down using your finger. The color of the note will be based on the color you chose for your highlight. Tap anywhere on the screen to close the note. You'll see a small Note icon appear on the side of the page with the date you wrote the note on (see Figure 9–24). Tap the note's icon to edit the note. Tap the text's highlight and select Remove Note to delete the note.

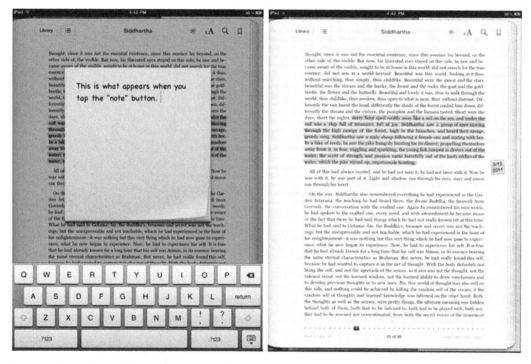

Figure 9–24. *Creating a note and the Note icon in the margin of the page after creation*

Search: Tapping Search will open the Search window (which looks like a magnifying glass) in the upper-right corner of the page. The text you selected will be automatically filled in as the search query.

Accessing the Table of Contents, Bookmarks, and Notes

Tap the Table of Contents/Bookmarks button (the button that has three dots followed by three lines, as shown in Figure 9–12) at the top of your page to be instantly taken to the Table of Contents and Bookmarks page (see Figure 9–25).

The Table of Contents and Bookmarks page is, unsurprisingly, divided into Table of Contents and Bookmarks sections; each section has its own tab.

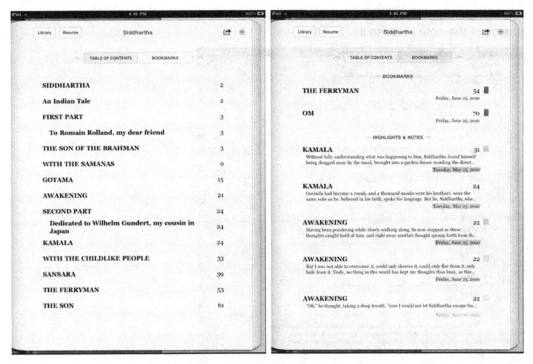

Figure 9–25. *The Table of Contents and Bookmarks page. Switch between the two by tapping the appropriate tab. Return to your last position in the book by tapping the Resume button.*

The Table of Contents tab displays the book's table of contents as a scrollable list. Tap any item in the Table of Contents to be instantly taken to it.

The Bookmarks tab displays all your bookmarks, highlights, and notes. They are divided into two sections: Bookmarks and Highlights & Notes. Under the Bookmarks heading, you'll see a list of chapter names or numbers that hold the bookmark, as well as the page number of the bookmark and the date you bookmarked the page. A red ribbon representing the bookmark lies next to the bookmark's page number. Tap any Bookmark icon to jump to the bookmarked page.

Under the Highlights & Notes heading, you'll see a list of all the highlights and notes you've created. For each highlight and note, you'll see the beginning of the first sentence that the highlight or note appears in, as well as the chapter name or number. You will also see the page number and the date you marked the page. The date is highlighted in the color that you choose to highlight the text in. This is a nice feature if you use different colors for different bookmark classifications, such as quotes from the antagonist in blue and quotes from the protagonist in pink.

Remember than whenever you create a note, a highlight is automatically created. You can distinguish between a highlight and a note easily. Any note has a tiny Post-it style of Note icon in the right margin. To be instantly taken to any highlight or note, tap it in the list. To read a note you've created without leaving the Table of Contents page, tap the Note icon in the margin. The note will spring forward on the screen (see Figure 9–26).

You can then tap the note to bring up the on-screen keyboard to edit it. Tap the area outside of the note to close it.

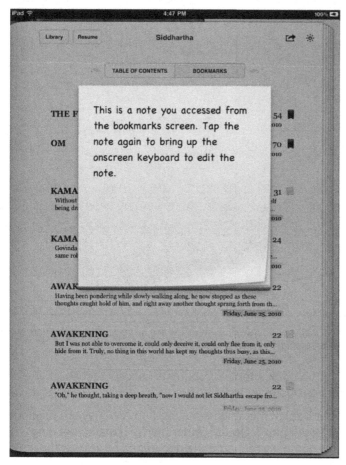

Figure 9–26. *Reading a note on the Bookmarks page*

To exit the Table of Contents/Bookmarks page, tap the Library button to return to your bookshelf or the Resume button to return to your last position in the book.

Sharing Notes

The iBooks app allows you to share the notes you have written in two ways: by e-mailing them or by printing them. To share your notes, tap the Share button at the top of the Table of Contents page. The Share button looks like an arrow breaking out of a box. From the Share menu that appears, tap the Email button to create a new e-mail with all the notes in the body of the e-mail or tap the Print button to print your notes to a wireless AirPrint printer (see Figure 9–27).

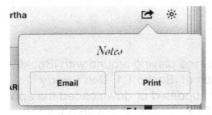

Figure 9–27. *Share notes by e-mailing or printing them.*

Having a Book Read to You

Not only can you read books on the iPad, but you can have the iPad read books to you. Using iPad's VoiceOver screen reader technology, you can make the iPad read any text to you, including the text of an entire novel. We talked about VoiceOver in Chapter 2, but we'll touch on how to activate it for iBook reading. Follow these steps to do so:

1. Turn VoiceOver on. Go your iPad's Home screen and tap Settings, and then choose General ➤ Accessibility ➤ VoiceOver. Triple-click the Home button, and then select Toggle VoiceOver.

2. Return to your book in iBooks. Triple-click the Home button, and a pop-up will appear. Tap Turn VoiceOver On.

3. Now you have two options. To have everything read to you from the top of the page, use two fingers held together and flick up. Everything from the top of the screen down will be read. To have everything read to you from your current position in the text, use two fingers held together and flick down. Everything from the position where you flicked will be read. When VoiceOver reaches the bottom of the page, it will automatically turn it for you and continue reading.

4. To stop VoiceOver reading, tap anywhere on the screen with one finger. It would also be a good idea to triple-click the Home button and select Turn VoiceOver Off now, unless you want to continue using VoiceOver gestures.

Now, you might be wondering why you would have VoiceOver's mechanical voice read you a book when you can just buy an audiobook and sync it to the iPad. The simple answer is because not all books are in audiobook format. It should also be noted that the iBooks VoiceOver ability isn't a feature intended to appeal to a large number of readers; rather, it is an accessibility option to help those who are hard of sight read their favorite books.

> **NOTE:** Some books may not be compatible with VoiceOver.

Syncing PDFs

PDF support was a big feature request when people started playing around with iBooks. Apple listened to them and added it with the introduction of iBooks 1.1. Don't worry about whether you have the latest iBooks app. If you've updated or downloaded the app recently, you've got the latest version, which supports PDF viewing. If you aren't sure, open the App Store application on the iPad to check whether any updates are available for your apps.

You have two ways of syncing PDFs to iBooks on your iPad: using iTunes or using the iPad's Mail app. To sync PDFs via iTunes, simply drag any PDFs you want to sync into your iTunes library. They will automatically be added to the Books section of your iTunes library. The next time you sync your iPad to iTunes, your PDFs will sync as well.

You can also add PDFs to iBooks through the iPad's Mail app. To do this, open Mail and select an e-mail that has a PDF attachment. Tap the attachment in the body of the e-mail to see it previewed full-screen. While previewing it full-screen, you'll see an Open In… button in the upper-right corner. Tap this button and select iBooks from the drop-down list (see Figure 9–28). The Mail app will close, and the PDF will automatically open in iBooks and be added to your PDF bookshelf. When you sync your iPad with iTunes, any PDFs you have added to iBooks in this manner will be added to your iTunes books library.

Figure 9–28. *Opening a PDF in iBooks using Mail*

Navigating the PDF Bookshelf

To see all your PDFs contained by iBooks, open iBooks, tap the Collections button in the iBooks Menu bar, and then tap the PDFs button (see Figure 9–7). Doing so will take you to your PDF bookshelf. As you can see in Figure 9–29, the PDF bookshelf is similar to the regular bookshelf. The PDF bookshelf will be populated with any PDFs you have added to iBooks.

Figure 9–29. *The PDF bookshelf is identical to the regular bookshelf. If you know how to navigate one, you know how to navigate the other.*

Just as with the regular bookshelf, you can choose to view your PDFs as icons or in a list. In List view, you will find you can sort your PDFs by titles, authors, categories, or bookshelf (the way they are arranged in Icon view). List and Icon views also present you with a search field, so you can search your PDFs by name or author. The PDF bookshelf works just like the regular bookshelf when editing and deleting items. Simply tap the Edit button to rearrange or delete PDFs.

Navigating and Reading PDFs

To read a PDF, tap its cover. The PDF will fly forward and open. If it's the first time you've opened the PDF, you'll be on the first page. If you have opened the PDF before, it will open to the page you left off on.

You can view PDFs in Portrait or Landscape mode (see Figure 9–30); however, unlike with books, viewing a PDF in Landscape mode does not show you two side-by-side pages. It's baffling why Apple didn't add this feature (at the time of writing), but most likely it will be added sometime in the future.

Figure 9–30. *Viewing PDFs in Landscape and Portrait modes*

At the top of any PDF's page, no matter what orientation you are in, you'll notice a menu that contains a series of buttons with the name of the PDF document in the center (see Figure 9–31). These buttons will already be familiar to you because they are similar to the ones you see while reading an e-book:

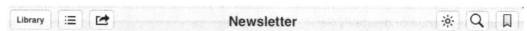

Figure 9–31. *A PDF's menu buttons*

Library: Tapping this closes the PDF and takes you back to your PDF bookshelf. The next time you open the PDF, you'll be taken to the page you were on when you left it.

Contact Sheet: This button is signified by three dots, each with a line after it. Tap this button to be presented with a contact sheet—a series of thumbnails of all the pages in a PDF.

Share: Tapping this button allows you to e-mail the currently selected PDF or print it to a wireless AirPrint printer.

Brightness: This is the button that looks like the sun and changes the screen brightness while inside the iBooks app only.

Search: The Search button looks like a magnifying glass and allows you to search through a PDF's text. It also has *quicklinks* to search Google and Wikipedia for your selected search term.

Bookmark: Tap the Bookmark ribbon to bookmark the current page you are on. Remember that bookmarks in iBooks behave differently than traditional bookmarks for a paper book. Bookmarking a page in iBooks means you have effectively "dog-eared" the page. You can have multiple bookmarks in the same document. To remove a bookmark, tap the Bookmark icon again.

Page scrubber: This is the series of page icons that run along the bottom of a PDF's page (see Figure 9–32). Drag your finger across the thumbnails to quickly navigate through the PDF's pages. You'll see the page number of the page currently selected float overhead. You can also just tap any thumbnail to jump right to that page.

Figure 9–32. *The page scrubber bar at the bottom of a PDF*

While reading, you can tap the center of a book's page to show/hide the menu and page scrubber bars. While on a page, you can double-tap it to zoom in; or, for more control, you can use a pinch gesture to zoom in or out. To navigate the pages of a PDF, simply swipe your finger to the left or right to move forward or backward one page. You can also tap the margins of a page to move forward or backward, or you can use the page scrubber bar at the bottom of the page. Alternatively, you can scroll through the large thumbnails that represent all the pages in the PDF document by using the contact sheet.

Using the Contact Sheet

As you can now see, you already know how to use the PDF menu bar because it is so similar to an e-book's menu bar. The only feature that is slightly different is the Table of Contents button, which has been replaced with a Contact Sheet button (note that both icons are identical—three dots, each followed by a line).

Tap the Contact Sheet button, and you'll see all the pages in the PDF document presented to you in large thumbnails that you can then scroll through with the swipe of your finger (see Figure 9–33). This is useful when you are dealing with a very large document with lots of diagrams or images. It allows you to quickly search the PDF by eye. When you find the desired page, tap it, and you'll be instantly taken to that page in the document.

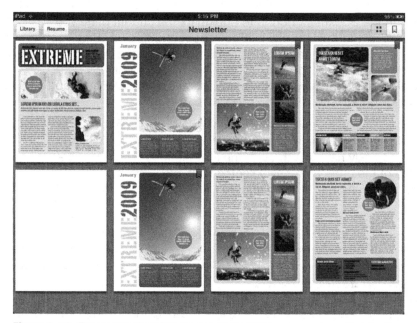

Figure 9–33. *The contact sheet lets you see all the PDF's pages as large thumbnails.*

You'll also notice that some contact sheets might have a little red Bookmark icon in their upper-right corner. This means you've bookmarked that page by tapping the Bookmark button in the PDF menu bar (see Figure 9–31). To see only your bookmarked pages, tap the Bookmark button in the upper-right corner of the Contact Sheet menu (see Figure 9–34). Any page without a bookmark will be hidden from view.

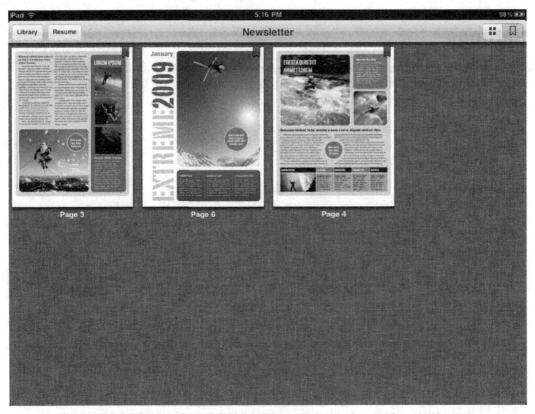

Figure 9–34. *The contact sheet's Bookmarked Pages view*

To leave the contact sheet, you can tap the Library button to return to your PDF bookshelf or the Resume button to return to the page you were on when you navigated to the contact sheet. You can also tap any page to be taken to that page.

> **TIP:** On a Mac, if you can print it, you can turn it into a PDF. Simply choose what you want to turn into a PDF, and then choose Print from the File menu of the application you are in (e.g., Word or Firefox). You'll see a PDF button in the lower-left corner of the Print dialog box. Click it and select Save as PDF... from the drop-down menu. Name the PDF, click Save, and then drag it to your iTunes library. On your next sync, your new PDF will appear in iBooks. If you own a PC, there are several options to turning documents into PDFs. Google "print to PDF" to find the right solution for you.

Settings

There are a few external settings for the iBooks app. Navigate to Settings from the iPad's Home screen and select iBooks from the Apps header on the left side. You'll see five settings (see Figure 9–35):

Figure 9–35. *The iBooks app settings*

Full Justification: When this set to On, the text on a book's page will fill the width of the page evenly. When full justification is set to Off, the text on the right side of the page will be ragged (see Figure 9–36).

Auto-hyphenation: When this is set to On, iBooks will automatically hyphenate words, allowing more words to be displayed on a single page.

Tap Left Margin: You can set this to Previous Page or Next Page. If you set it to Next Page, tapping the left margin of a book will advance you to the next page in a book instead of taking you back one page. This setting might be nice while reading a book on the iPad at odd angles, such as in bed. With Next Page selected, the only way to go back one page in your book is by using the page scrubber bar at the bottom of the page.

Sync Bookmarks: When set to On, this will sync a book's bookmarks, highlights, and notes between devices. This is nice if you are using iBooks on an iPad and iPhone. When you create a note or bookmark in the book on one device, it will appear on the other.

Sync Collections: When set to On, this will sync your iBooks collections. This is nice if you are using iBooks on an iPad and iPhone. When you create or modify a collection on one device, it will appear exactly the same on the other.

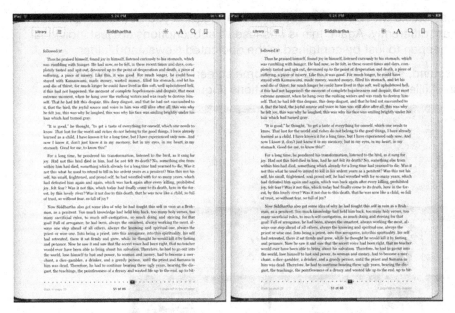

Figure 9–36. *The same page with full justification on (left) and full justification off (right)*

Newsstand

Newsstand is a new feature of iOS 5 that allows you to view and manage all your magazine and newspaper subscriptions in one place. We call it a *feature* because Newsstand isn't technically an app. It looks like an app, but it's actually a folder that resides on your Home screen and holds all your subscriptions.

You can see the Newsstand icon in Figure 9–37. The icon on the left show you what Newsstand looks like with no subscriptions. When you start download subscriptions, they appear in the icon (right).

Figure 9–37. *The Newsstand icon empty (left) and full of subscriptions (right)*

Unlike books in iBooks, magazines and newspapers in Newsstand aren't actually text-based ePub files. Each magazine or newspaper subscription is its own individual app.

This means that, unlike with books in iBooks, each magazine you download and view can look and act differently. Again, this is because all subscriptions are just individual apps; they all happen to just be contained in the dedicated Newsstand folder.

To open Newsstand, simply tap it, and your Home screen splits to display the Newsstand shelf filled with all of your subscriptions (Figure 9–38).

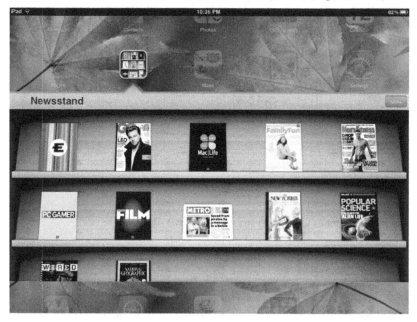

Figure 9–38. *The Newsstand shelf*

The Newsstand store is part of the App Store, and it's where you'll find all of the magazine and newspaper subscriptions you can buy. To quickly get to the Newsstand section of the App Store from your Newsstand shelf, tap the Store button, and you'll be instantly taken there.

Once you have subscribed to the magazines or newspapers of your choice, the newest issues are automatically downloaded as they become available and are placed in your Newsstand. The cover of the most recent issue or the front page of the most recent newspaper is displayed at the top of that periodical's subscription stack on your Newsstand shelf.

To read an issue, tap it, and that periodical's app will open as a normal app would.

Summary

In addition to doing so many other things, the iPad is also a breakthrough e-book and PDF reader. iBooks, the all-in-one application that lets you buy books and read, search, and mark them up, is an elegant yet powerful tool for discovering new titles and taking your entire book library with you, and Newsstand allows you to subscribe to and automatically download the latest issues of your favorite magazines and newspapers. Here are a few key tips for you to carry away with you:

- You aren't limited to buying books from the iBookstore. Many web sites sell books in the ePub format that you can download and sync to the iPad. A great place to start is www.gutenberg.org. Also, Googling *free e-books* will return a host of results for sites that let you download e-books for free.

- iBooks has a powerful dictionary-lookup feature that gives you the definition of a word on the book's page.

- The iBooks bookshelf has many views and a search function to help you navigate your books library. These can also help you organize your books and PDFs into collections.

- Use the iPad's physical Orientation Lock button to freeze your iBooks screen in place, avoiding any unwanted screen rotation while reclining on a couch or reading in bed.

- No audiobook? No problem. You can use the iPad's built-in VoiceOver technology to read any book out loud to you.

- Choose different colors for your notes and highlighting. For example, you might use blue for passages you like and green for something you want to reference later. You can see all your bookmarks, notes, and highlights in one easy place (the Bookmarks page, of course!). You can also tap any one of these to instantly jump to it in the book.

- iBooks isn't limited to reading e-books. It's also a PDF reader. Now you can organize, view, and easily navigate all your PDFs—even while on the go!

- Newsstand automatically downloads your latest subscriptions in the background, so when you wake up in the morning, the day's paper will be there waiting for you.

Chapter 10

Leveraging Your Desk Set

Back in the days before iPads and iPhones, we used what was commonly referred to as a *desk set*. That set varied from year to year but usually consisted of a notebook in which we'd keep meeting notes; a Day-Timer planner where we'd write our appointments; an address book into which we laboriously wrote all of our contact names, addresses, and phone numbers; and a reminders book where we'd jot down to do lists and such.

In the 1990s, many Mac owners were proud owners of a series of Apple Newton MessagePads. These were referred to as *personal digital assistants* (PDAs), and they were the first electronic organizers to synchronize notes, calendars, to-do lists, and contacts to equivalent applications on a desktop computer. Alas, the Newton MessagePad was quite a bit ahead of its time and rather expensive, and Apple dropped the device in 1998.

The PalmPilot took the place of the Newton, followed by several handheld devices running Microsoft operating systems, which were followed by the first series of smartphones. All of these devices had their special capabilities and quirks, and they all had some sort of note-taking facility, a calendar, and an address book.

In 2007, the first iPhones appeared on the market, making life good again for Apple fans and introducing the world to a new form of handheld computing. The iPhone has always had three apps—Notes, Calendar, and Contacts—to perform common desk-set tasks. Now with the introduction of the iPad, the three apps have made the move to another platform. And with the introduction of iOS 5, a fourth app, Reminders, has been added to the desk set bunch.

Notes, Calendar, Contacts, and Reminders really shine on the iPad thanks to the larger-than-iPhone screen. In this chapter, we'll show you how to make the most of these built-in apps and how they synchronize to other devices.

Notes

On the iPhone, Notes is roughly the equivalent of a small pocket notepad. You probably wouldn't want to attempt to take a long set of notes with the app. Even though the note can be scrolled, there isn't a lot of available room. Typing would most likely be done with one finger, slowing down your text entry and making errors more likely.

The Notes app on the iPad is a totally different animal. It's more like a legal pad (see Figure 10–1), both in looks and in how it can be used. In landscape orientation, Notes looks like a leather-bound portfolio, with a small, white, paperlike index list on the left side and a legal pad at the right (complete with margin lines as well as the remnants of torn-off pages at the top).

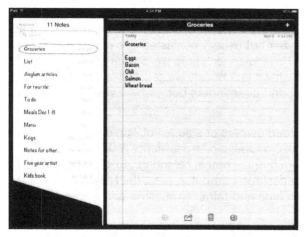

Figure 10–1. *Your iPad's legal pad, the Notes app. The list on the left side displays all the notes you've written.*

When you flip the iPad into portrait orientation, Notes appears to be just a normal legal pad. We personally find the landscape orientation easier to use for data entry in Notes, since we get an almost full-sized keyboard to touch-type on.

When you're using Notes in portrait mode, the index list disappears from the left side of the portfolio, and a Notes button appears at the top of the notepad. To display the index list, just tap the Notes button (see Figure 10–2).

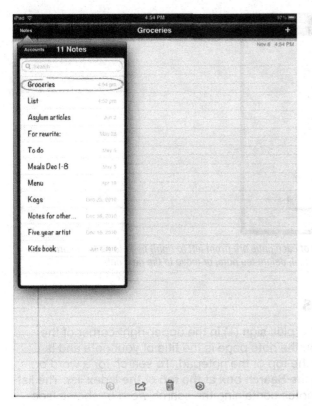

Figure 10–2. *The Notes app in portrait orientation really looks like a legal pad, complete with yellow paper.*

When Notes is being used in landscape mode, touching a note on the white index list highlights it with a red-penciled oval and displays the full note on the legal pad. At the top of each page, whether you're using Notes in landscape or portrait orientation, is the date and time when the note was created, as well as how many days ago it was written. If it was just written, the notebook will display "Today" at the top; if it was written yesterday, it will display "Yesterday." After that, the number changes to the number of days ago that the note was written.

On the bottom of each page are four icons (see Figure 10–3). Tapping the left and right arrow icons flips between pages in the notebook. Tapping the Share icon allows you to e-mail or print the text of the note page, while tapping the trash can icon displays the Delete Note button you see in Figure 10–3. The first line of the note is used as the subject line when sending a note as an e-mail, speeding the process of mailing notes to others.

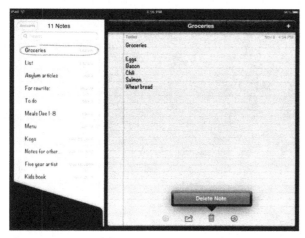

Figure 10–3. *The Notes app icons at the bottom of each page are (from left to right) used to go to the previous note, send the text contained in the note in an e-mail, delete the note, or move to the next note.*

Adding and Deleting Notes

To create a new notebook page, tap the plus sign (+) in the upper-right corner of the notebook. The first line of text typed on the note page is the title of your note and is repeated both on the index list and at the top of the notepad. To search for a word or phrase in any of the notes, type it into the Search box at the top of the index list. The list magically shrinks to show only those notes containing the search word or phrase (see Figure 10–4).

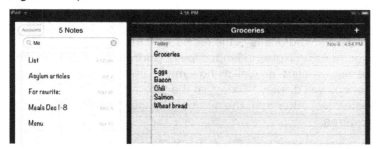

Figure 10–4. *Typing letters or words into the search field narrows the index list to only the notes containing the search criterion.*

You can delete notes in two ways. First, as described earlier, tapping the trash can icon at the bottom of each note displays a Delete Note button. Tap that button to complete the deletion.

The second way to delete a note is to swipe your finger either left or right over the title of the note in the index list. This is easier to do in landscape mode, since the index list is always in view on the left side of the Notes window. In portrait orientation, tapping the Notes button at the top of the notebook displays the index list; then you can swipe to delete a note.

Syncing Notes

If you're writing notes on your iPad, you may want to use them on your Mac or Windows computer. There are a couple of ways to go about moving them to a personal computer—either e-mail them to yourself using the e-mail button we described earlier or use Notes syncing.

To set up Notes syncing, launch iTunes on your computer, and then connect your iPad to the computer using the USB cable, as described in Chapter 2. When the name of your iPad appears in the Devices list on the left side of the iTunes window on your computer, click it, and then click the Info tab. Scroll down the window a bit, and you'll see the cryptic Other heading (see Figures 10–5 and 10–6). Under that heading is the check box you're looking for.

Be sure to take note of the warning displayed in Figure 10–5. If your iPad is being synced to your computer over the air using iCloud and you also decide to perform local syncing using the USB cable, you may get duplicate notes appearing on your computer.

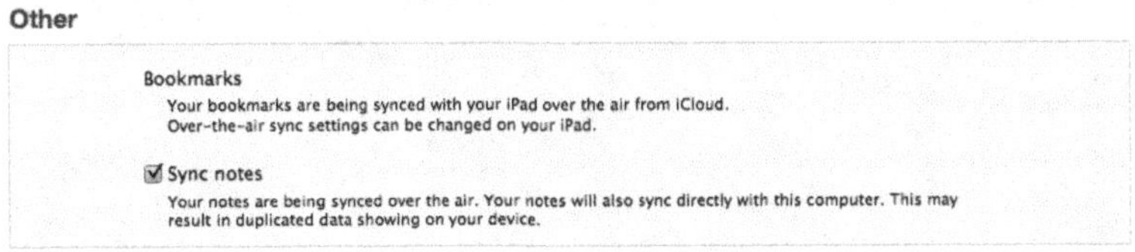

Other

Bookmarks
Your bookmarks are being synced with your iPad over the air from iCloud.
Over-the-air sync settings can be changed on your iPad.

☑ Sync notes
Your notes are being synced over the air. Your notes will also sync directly with this computer. This may result in duplicated data showing on your device.

Figure 10–5. *The Other section under Info in iTunes contains a check box for syncing notes from the iPad to your Mac.*

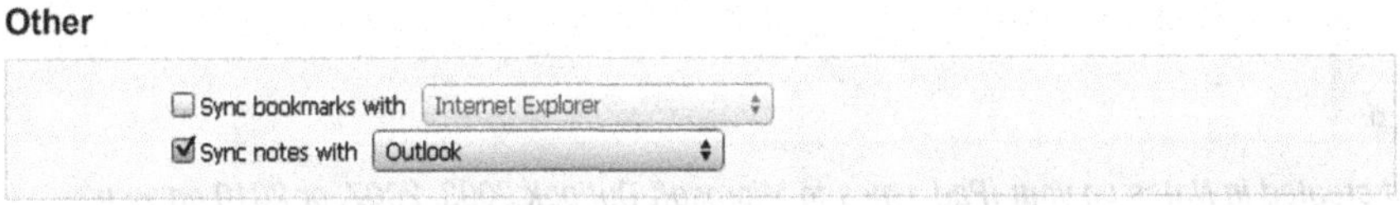

Other

☐ Sync bookmarks with [Internet Explorer   ◆]
☑ Sync notes with [Outlook   ◆]

Figure 10–6. *You can find the check box for syncing notes with Outlook under Other in iTunes for Windows.*

To sync notes to your computer from your iPad, select that box, and then click the Sync button on the bottom-right side of the iTunes window.

So, now you've synced all of those notes to your computer—where are they? Oddly enough, there is no similar app on the Mac, so notes end up in Mail. Launch Mail on your Mac, and then take a look at the sidebar on the left side of the Mail window (see Figure 10–7).

See the Reminders heading? There is a small replica of the Notes icon from the iPad below that. Click that icon, and you'll see two more notepads—one that says "On My Mac" and another that says "iCloud." Click the On My Mac icon, and the notes you've created are there.

On Windows computers, Notes are synced to Microsoft Outlook 2003, 2007, or 2010 (see Figure 10–8). To view your synced notes in Outlook, click the Notes button.

Figure 10–7. *The text created in Notes on your iPad syncs to Mail on your Mac.*

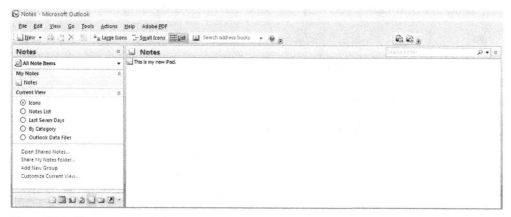

Figure 10–8. *The text created in Notes on your iPad syncs to Microsoft Outlook 2003, 2007, or 2010 on your Windows computer.*

These notes are fully synced, so if you choose to make a change to one of them or create a new one on your Mac or Windows computer, the changes or new file is moved to the iPad the next time you sync. Likewise, any changes, additions, or deletions you make on the iPad are reflected on your computer.

So, what's that iCloud icon all about? If you have an Apple iCloud account, then you can synchronize your notes on all sorts of devices and in various places. Initially, the only way to sync your notes between your computer and iPad was through that hardwired USB connection. Now notes are another type of content that can be synchronized over the air.

Calendar

Like many people who enjoy the layout of the Day-Timer planner, we were thrilled to see how Apple changed the plain-Jane iPhone Calendar app to a thing of beauty on the iPad. In landscape orientation (see Figure 10–9), Calendar looks remarkably like that old Day-Timer.

Figure 10–9. *The iPad Calendar app in Day view looks like a traditional paper appointment book.*

There are five Calendar views, each of which provides a slightly different view of your calendar information. To switch between them, tap Day, Week, Month, Year, or List at the top of the calendar.

The view shown in Figure 10–9 is the Day view, which displays an hour-by-hour listing of what's going to happen during the current day.

On the left side of the Calendar app in Day view, there's a handy month calendar and a list of all the appointments scheduled that day. To turn to the next page in this virtual appointment book, tap the right arrow at the bottom of the page. Moving to the previous page just requires tapping the left arrow. You can also drag a finger back and forth on the days of the current month, which are listed between those two arrows, to navigate to a particular date.

If all of this moving around in Calendar causes you to get lost, there's a Today button in the lower-left corner of the app to quickly jump to the current day. Before we talk about adding or searching for Calendar events, let's take a look at the rest of the available Calendar views.

The Week view (see Figure 10–10) is helpful in mapping out what tasks need to be accomplished during a specific week. Any items listed at the top of the calendar are all-day events, while colored boxes denote the time and duration of your meetings. The days of the week are listed across the top, with the hours of the day on the left side. To scroll earlier or later in the day (the calendar shows only 12 hours of each day at a time), use your finger to scroll up or down.

See that pinhead with the line across from it at about 6 p.m.? That indicates the current time so you can see at a glance how much time you have until your next appointment. Another feature of the Calendar is the Invitations inbox, in the upper left. If someone has used iCal or another calendar application to send you an invitation to an event, it is listed when you tap the Invitations inbox button. It's possible to view the details of the invitation, accept it, or decline it, all from this one place on your iPad.

Figure 10–10. *Using the Calendar app's Week view to capture a week at a glance*

The Week view lists ten one-week periods at the bottom of the page, and you can tap any one of those weeks or slide a finger left or right to look at previous or future weeks.

The Month view (see Figure 10–11) provides the look of those "Month at a Glance"–style calendars that have been sold for years as desk pads. Here, every appointment during the month is designated by a small dot on a particular day. To get details about an appointment, just tap the dot, and a pop-up arrow appears with the time of the appointment and an edit button.

Figure 10–11. *You can look at an entire month's worth of appointments in the Calendar app's Month view. Tap an appointment to open a pop-up arrow for details or to edit the event.*

The area at the bottom of the page changes to a list of the months of a year for jumping to a specific month with the tap of a finger. There are also buttons to navigate to the previous and next months with a tap, as well as links to previous and future years.

The Year view (Figure 10–12) gives you a heat map of all your events in the selected year. The color of the square tells you how many events you have on that day. White date squares have no events scheduled. Yellow date squares have one event. Orange date squares have two events. And red date squares have three or more events.

Figure 10–12. *The Year view gives you a heat map of all your events.*

The last view is the List view (see Figure 10–13), which lists upcoming appointments on a scrollable list on the left side of the page, along with a close-up view of a current event on the right side.

Figure 10–13. *The List view in the iPad Calendar app displays a list of upcoming appointments (left) and details of any appointment you tap (right).*

Tapping any of the appointments in the list on the left displays the details of that event on the right side. Any alerts that were set are listed, as well as notes that are associated with the event. If someone else sent the appointment to you and you accepted it, the detailed view will also show who sent the original appointment and list anyone else who has accepted the event invitation, as well as those who have been invited but have not yet offered a reply.

Adding Calendar Events

Your iPad allows you to add calendar events on the go. This lets you adjust and update your schedule when you are away from your computer. You have two ways to add events. In Day, Week, Month, or List view, you can simply tap and hold on the screen, and a new event bubble appears (Figure 10–14). Drag the grab circles to adjust the times that the event covers. In Week and Month view, you can also drag an event from one day to another.

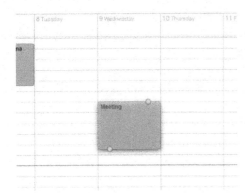

Figure 10–14. *Creating new events by touch*

If you are in the List, Day, Week, or Month view, you can also add a new event by tapping the + button at the lower-right corner of the screen. The Add Event pop-up opens. To enter event information, tap any one of the fields and begin typing on the keyboard. Tapping Start & End, which is used to enter the beginning and ending of an event, displays a date and time picker (see Figure 10–15). Use your finger to roll the start date and time up or down, and then do the same with the ending time of the event. If an event is going to last all day (for example, an all-day meeting or a birthday), then slide the All-day button to On.

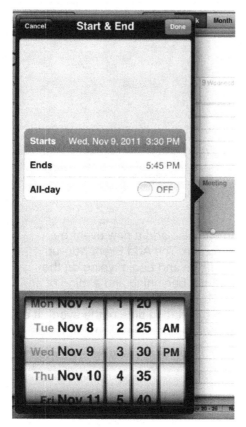

Figure 10–15. *Whenever you're adding events to a calendar, you use the date and time picker to select the starting and ending dates and times.*

If you want to make the event repeat at regular intervals, just tap the Repeat field. You'll be given the choice (see Figure 10–16) of repeating the event every day, week, two weeks, month, or year. A daily repeating event would be useful in reminding yourself to take important medication, while an annual repeating event could save your marriage by reminding you of an impending anniversary.

Figure 10–16. *Any event can be set up to repeat at distinct time intervals that you set.*

Any event can have up to two alerts. Alerts on the iPad are both audible and visual; there is no choice between the two types of alerts like there is on the Mac. Tapping the Alert or Second Alert field displays a list of times before an event at which an alert can go off. Those times vary from five minutes to two days before, or you can have your iPad alert you on the date of the event.

What happens when the alert goes off? A small visual alert appears on the screen (see Figure 10–17), with a Close button that dismisses the alert with a tap and a View Event button that takes you to the calendar to see the details. If you have the sound turned up on your iPad, you'll also hear an alert tone ring.

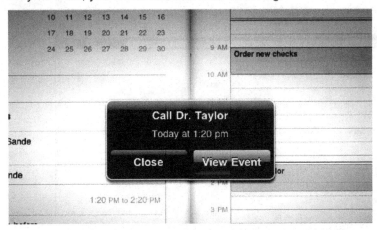

Figure 10–17. *Your iPad alerts you of impending appointments with an alert tone and a visual reminder.*

There are also fields for entering the location of an event or notes about it. When you're done entering the event information, tap the Done button, and the event appears on the calendar.

Syncing Calendar

As with the Notes app, much of the power of Calendar on the iPad becomes apparent when you synchronize to Microsoft Outlook 2003, 2007, or 2010 on your Windows computer, or to iCal or Outlook on your Mac. The method of setting up synchronization is similar to how you set up Notes.

Connect your iPad to your Windows computer or Mac using the Dock Connector to USB Cable, and then launch iTunes if it doesn't start by itself. In iTunes on your computer, click the icon designating your iPad under Devices in the sidebar on the left side of the window. Next, click the Info tab, and scroll down until you see the words *Sync iCal Calendars* (Mac; Figure 10–18) or *Sync Calendars* (Windows; Figure 10–19).

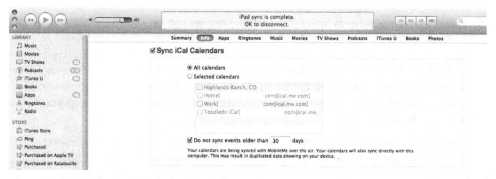

Figure 10–18. *Setting up Calendar syncing in iTunes*

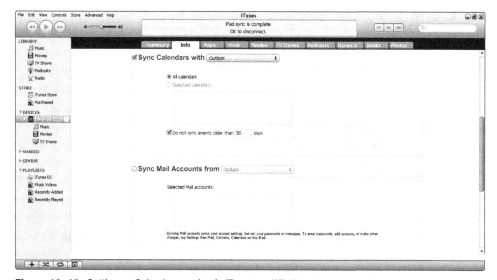

Figure 10–19. *Setting up Calendar syncing in iTunes on Windows*

To set up synchronization of iCal and the Calendar app on your iPad, select the Sync Calendars (Windows) or Sync iCal Calendars (Mac) check box. Below the check box are radio buttons for syncing all calendars on your Mac or Windows computer to the iPad or just selected calendars. You might want to select certain calendars for syncing if you have many calendars on your computer and really don't need to view or edit all of those on your iPad.

You can choose to sync only future and recent events by selecting the "Do not sync events older than 30 days" box. That's very useful if you have many events on your calendar and don't want to waste space on your iPad filling it with calendar debris. The number of days is editable, so if you'd like to only sync events back two weeks and into the future, you can change the number 30 to 14.

To apply the changes and sync your calendar to your iPad, click the Apply button in the lower-right corner of the iTunes window. After the sync is done, launch Calendar on your iPad; then applaud your work! Remember, it's a two-way sync, so any changes or additions you make on your iPad are synced to your computer, and vice versa.

Contacts

The third component of the iPad desk set is Contacts, your electronic address book. On the left side of the address book is a scrolling list of names, while the details of a specific person or company appear on the right side (see Figure 10–20).

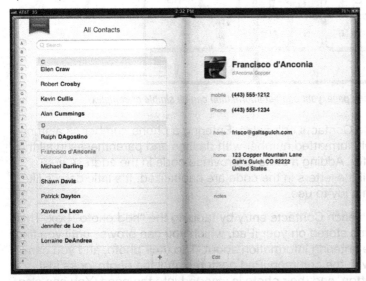

Figure 10–20. *Contacts is your personal address book, synchronized to your Mac or Windows computer and to other devices if you want.*

Compared with Calendar, the Contacts app is very simple. Instead of multiple ways to display the information, there's only one view, which is similar in both landscape and portrait orientations. That's not to say that Contacts isn't useful; in fact, the address list is used by Mail and many other iPad apps to enable sharing of information with other people.

Adding a Contact

To add a contact, tap the plus sign (+) icon on the bottom of the left page. A blank page in the Contacts book appears (see Figure 10–21) with helpful labels to tell you what information needs to be entered into each field. To start entering information into any field, tap it, and the iPad's virtual keyboard appears.

Figure 10–21. *Starting with this blank page, your contact information can be simple or complex.*

Apple did a great job with the Contacts edit fields. Entering a phone number as a string of numbers produces a nicely formatted number with dashes and parentheses in all the proper places for your country. Adding a state or province code in the address area locks the caps key so that all the letters in the code are capitalized. It's little details like this that make the iPad such a joy to use.

You can even add a photo to each Contacts entry by tapping the "add photo" box. This displays a list of photo albums stored on your iPad, which you can browse until you find a photo of the person you're entering information about. Tap their photo, and you can move and scale the image with the common iPad gestures until the photo looks just right. Finally, tap the Use button, and their photo is inserted into the page. You can also use the iPad's camera to take a photo to use with a contact.

Once you're done entering information about a person or company, tap the Done button in the upper-right corner of the Contacts app to see the finished page in your virtual address book.

Should you need to add or change information at any time, tap the Edit button to reveal the edit fields for Contacts. There's also a Share button at the bottom of each Contacts entry that creates an e-mail containing a .vcf (vCard file format) file that can be opened by most address book applications. For those people who have a second- or later-generation iPad, a FaceTime button appears at the bottom of each Contacts entry. With a tap or two, you can video chat with your friends or family.

To delete a contact, tap the Edit button, and then scroll to the bottom of the contact information. There's a large red Delete Contact button there. Tap it, and a small dialog box appears asking whether you want to delete the contact or cancel the deletion. When you tap Delete, the contact is removed from your iPad contacts list.

Groups and Searching

At the top of the left page in Contacts is a small red ribbon bookmark with the word *Groups* on it. Tapping that red ribbon lists all the groups that you have created...but not on your iPad. You cannot create groups of contacts on your iPad. That task has to be done on your Mac or Windows computer.

Why use groups? It's a great way to make it easier to find certain people who you know are in a specific group or to list everyone in a certain group. In other words, instead of searching 2,000 contacts for a person you know is a member of a particular group, you can narrow it down to the people in that group.

Speaking of searching, you can use the Search field at the top of the Contacts left page to look for specific people or companies. Tap in the Search field, start typing, and Contacts provides a list of people or companies that fit the search criteria. As an example, searching for *Steve* produces a list of people with that first name who are included in the contacts list (see Figure 10–22).

Figure 10–22. *The Search field is helpful when you need to find someone quickly in a large number of contacts.*

Syncing Contacts

Remember how you set up syncing of Calendar and Notes earlier in this chapter? That's how you're going to set up syncing of Contacts as well. The companion applications on a Windows computer can be Microsoft Outlook 2003, 2007, or 2010; Windows Address Book (Windows XP), or Windows Contacts (Windows Vista and Windows 7). On the Mac, contact synchronization can be set up with Address Book and Microsoft Entourage 2004 or 2008. Which application should you use? If you use Outlook on your Windows computer, then sync with the Outlook contacts list. If you use web mail or an application other than Outlook for mail, contacts, and calendar, then use either Windows Address Book or Windows Contact depending on which is available in the version of the Windows operating system you're using.

Connect your iPad to your Mac using the Dock Connector to USB Cable, and then launch iTunes if it doesn't start by itself. In iTunes on your computer, click the icon designating your iPad under Devices in the sidebar on the left side of the window. Next, click the Info tab and scroll down until you see the words *Sync Address Book Contacts* (Mac; Figure 10–23) or *Sync Contacts* (Windows; Figure 10–24).

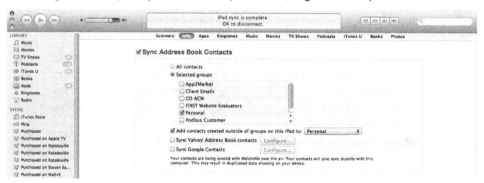

Figure 10–23. *To sync Contacts with your Mac, select the Sync Address Book Contacts box.*

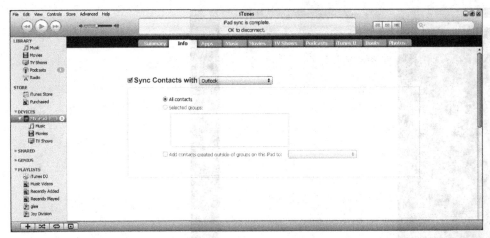

Figure 10–24. *To sync Contacts with your Windows computer, select the Sync Contacts in iTunes box.*

As with syncing calendars, you have the choice of either syncing all your contacts to the iPad or just selected groups. There are several other check boxes to consider when setting up address book syncing.

First, you may want to add contacts that you create on your iPad to a specific group. That's what the "Add contacts created outside of groups on this iPad to" check box is for. Select the box, and then select a group. Any new contacts created on the iPad are automatically added to that group.

Apple also built in synchronization with other address books. The next two check boxes are used to set up synchronization with Yahoo! Address Book or Google Contacts. Checking either of the boxes displays a legal agreement allowing iTunes to synchronize with Yahoo! or Google. You can either agree or disagree with the statement, but realize that you won't be able to sync with these services without clicking the Agree button.

Once you've agreed to allow the sharing of information with Google or Yahoo!, a configuration screen appears requesting your user ID and password for that service. Entering that information and then clicking Apply in the lower-right corner of iTunes ensures that your Contacts information is synced between your iPad, your computer's address book or Contacts application, and either Yahoo! Address Book or Google Contacts.

Setting Reminders

Reminders is a new app included on every iPad. It's a to-do app that lets you create lists and set reminders so you never forget anything again. To launch Reminders, tap its icon on your Home screen. When you launch the app, you'll first see a loose-leaf piece of paper with the title "Reminders" at the top. This is your main reminders list (Figure 10–25). To create a reminder, tap the + button and enter a name or description for the reminder. Tap Done when you have finished naming the reminder. In Figure 10–25, one of our reminders is to "Buy flowers."

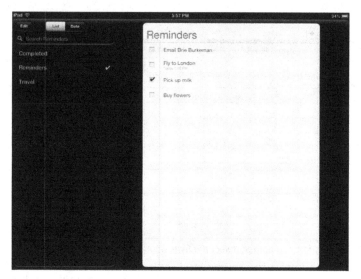

Figure 10–25. *The Reminders app*

The lists button appears at the top-left corner of the screen. Tap it to reveal all your lists. Tap a list to jump right to that list. To create a new list, tap the edit button on the list screen and then tap Create New List. Multiple lists can be very handy. You can create one for work, one for groceries, one for your personal life, and so on.

But Reminders isn't just an app that helps you create lists. It's called "Reminders" for a reason. You can set a number of ways to be reminded to do something on your list. Reminders reminds you of your to-do list items via the Notification Center, and you can set reminders to notify you based on date and time.

To set details and notifications for your reminders, tap an item from your reminders list. On the details screen that appears (Figure 10–26), you can set the time and date for your reminder, set whether the item on your list is a one-time or repeating event (such as weekly), set when to end the repeating reminders, set the priority of the to-do item (None, Low, Medium, High), set the list the reminder should be on ("travel" or "family," and so on), and even add notes to the reminder to give it more details.

Figure 10–26. *Setting the details of a Reminders event*

When you are done entering details about a reminder event, tap the Done button. To delete a reminder, tap the red delete button that appears at the bottom of the details screen.

Besides viewing your reminders as a list, you can also view them by date. Tap the Date button at the top of the screen (Figure 10–25), and you'll be taken to the date view (Figure 10–27). Tap any date on the calendar to be taken to its date page to view the reminders on that date.

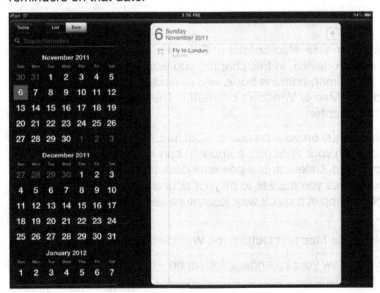

Figure 10–27. *Browsing Reminders by date*

When you complete an event in your reminders list, tap the box to mark it off. The event is removed from your Reminders list and added to your Completed list (Figure 10–28). To view your Completed list, tap its name in your Reminders list.

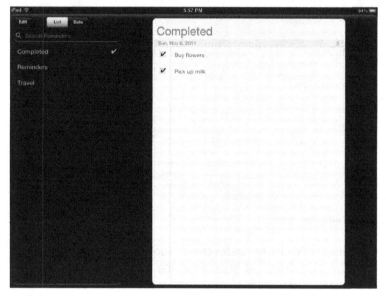

Figure 10–28. *The Completed list*

Reminders syncs with iCal on the Mac and Outlook 2007 and 2010 on a PC.

Summary

Some of the most useful apps on your iPad consist of Calendar, Notes, Contacts, and Reminders—the desk set of your device. In this chapter, you learned how to use your iPad as a digital notepad, Day-Timer, address book, and reminders list, as well as how to sync that information to your Mac or Windows computer. These are several important topics to remember from this chapter:

- The desk-set application(s) on your computer (iCal and Address Book on your Mac, Outlook on your Windows computer) can sync with similar apps on your iPad. Calendar is a powerful desk calendar on the iPad, while Contacts gives you access to all your address book information. The Notes app is a quick way to capture text and move it to your computer.

- Notes sync to Mail on the Mac and Outlook on Windows computers.

- There are five ways to view your calendar information—Day, Week, Month, Year, and List views.

- Reminders is a wonderful app that can help those of us with poor memories remember when things need to get done.

- Although you can't create groups of contacts on your iPad, Contacts does support groups that have been created in Address Book or Outlook. Groups are a powerful tool for organizing large numbers of contacts.

Chapter 11

Setting Up and Using Mail

E-mail. It's our connection to the world, our way of being part of a larger society. It occupies huge chunks of our days and, even more than phone calls, may be the primary way people touch base with and update each other. Ask most people what they'll be using their new iPad for, and a good number of them will instantly reply "e-mail." Being able to step away from your desk and still be able to keep in touch while on the go is a hugely valuable component of iPad use.

The iPad uses the Mail app to compose, send, and receive electronic communications. It provides a handy way to drop a note, share a file, and view material that others have shared with you. Many iPad apps also use Mail as a conduit for sharing documents or files with others, so Mail is a good app to know.

In this chapter, you'll learn how to set up e-mail accounts on your iPad, discover what's involved in composing and organizing mail, and see how Mail works with other iPad apps to help you share information with others.

Setting Up Mail Accounts

The iPad Mail app is instantly recognizable with its white paper envelope floating upon a blue-sky background. By default, Mail's icon is placed in the Dock at the bottom of the iPad screen. The Dock ensures that Mail is easily accessible from any one of the panes of the Home screen. At times you'll see a red bubble with a number appear on top of this envelope/sky icon. That bubble lets you know how many new messages have arrived and are waiting for you to read them.

Chapter 10 discussed how you could synchronize your calendar, contacts, and notes between your iPad and computer. The iPad and iTunes make it just as easy to transfer accounts to your computer. If you already have multiple e-mail accounts set up on your Mac or Windows computer, there's no reason to reenter all of the information to set them up on your iPad. You can use the same process used in Chapter 10 to sync Mail accounts to your iPad for a quick method of setting up Mail, or you can set up the accounts on the iPad—it's your choice. The next two sections show you how to do both.

Syncing Mail Accounts

Synchronizing mail accounts using the Info tab in iTunes provides the fastest way to set up all of your e-mail accounts on your iPad with your Mac or Windows computer. Connect your iPad to your Windows computer or Mac using the Dock to USB Connector Cable, and then, if it's not already open, launch iTunes on your computer. In iTunes, locate your device in the source list, which is the blue column at the left side of the screen. Click the icon designating your iPad and then open the Info tab at the top of the screen. The Info tab provides a simple way to synchronize information from your computer to your device, including mail accounts, address book contacts, and calendars. Scroll down until you see Sync Mail Accounts (see Figure 11–1).

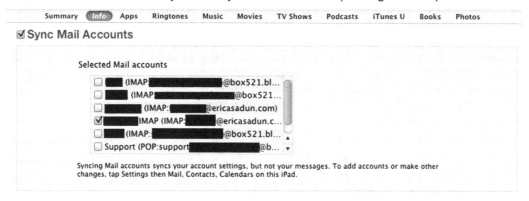

Figure 11–1. *Already have multiple e-mail accounts set up on your Mac or Windows computer? iTunes offers a simple-to-use interface for synchronizing those mail accounts to your iPad for fast and reliable setup.*

A check box appears to the left of each account name. To enable mail account syncing between your computer and iPad, select the Sync Mail Accounts check box (see Figure 11–1, at the top left of the screen capture), check the box for each mail account that you want to set up on your iPad, and then click the Sync or Apply button at the bottom-right corner of the iTunes window.

One important thing to remember about syncing Mail accounts is that this process synchronizes only your account *settings*, not the *messages* that may be stored on the mail server for your account. This is important because the way your iPad retrieves mail varies by the protocol it is set up to use.

Post Office Protocol 3 (POP3, often just called POP) mail accounts are typically configured to download e-mail to your computer or device and remove it from the mail server. This download-then-delete process means that when you receive POP-based e-mail on your iPad, you'll never see it on your computer.

In contrast, when your mail account isn't set up to remove the message from your mail server (as with most default IMAP or Exchange account setups), you'll retain a copy on both the iPad and the computer, and removing it from one machine won't remove it from the other. You can read the message on one device or on the other, and the only thing that changes is the message status, from unread to read.

Apple's iCloud mail, like other Internet Message Access Protocol (IMAP) mail systems, retains messages until you delete them. That means, with iCloud, you will see the message on multiple devices, and they'll all have the same status. Unopened messages will be that way on all devices, and read messages show up as read on all devices.

Microsoft's Exchange Server is widely used in business, so it's important to know that Mail provides excellent support for this e-mail standard. Exchange provides push mail capabilities (discussed later in this chapter) for almost instantaneous receipt of incoming mail. iPad fully supports Exchange Server 2003 and Exchange 2007 synchronization and supports Exchange 2010 as well, with up to ten devices per account.

Although setting up Exchange accounts on the iPad is no more difficult than configuring other types of e-mail, it's comforting to know that most organizations that use Exchange can also provide technical support to iPad-toting clients if you run into problems.

If you're interested in using Exchange for your iPad e-mail hosting but don't have the technical expertise available to configure and maintain Exchange Server, there are many Exchange hosting services available worldwide. An Internet search of *Exchange Server* displays many companies that host Exchange for you.

Setting Up Mail Accounts Directly on the iPad

When you have only one or two e-mail accounts to establish and you either cannot (for example, when you're away from your office) or don't want to synchronize account information between your iPad and your computer, you *can* set up mail accounts directly on the iPad. This isn't as easily accomplished as simply synchronizing accounts over from your computer, but it's not so hard that you cannot set up an account on the go when you need to.

Before you begin setting up your accounts, make sure you have the following information on hand. This information is often found on your Internet service provider's support pages under a section about configuring your e-mail.

> *Name of your e-mail service provider*: Common providers include Apple's own iCloud service, Google's Gmail, Yahoo! Mail, AOL, or Internet service providers such as Comcast and Time Warner.

> *Your e-mail address*: All e-mail addresses are set up in the common myname@domain.tld format, where myname is a name or pseudonym for an individual or company, domain is the domain name being used by an organization, and tld is the "top-level domain" for the domain (.com, .gov, .edu, and so on).

Your e-mail password: This is the most critical piece of information for setting up an e-mail account, but surprisingly few people remember what their password is! That's because many IT departments create particularly difficult passwords that include numbers and symbols in order to increase overall security. The end result is, of course, that many people write down that difficult password on a sticky note and attach it to their monitor, defeating the entire purpose of the "difficult password" exercise.

You may want to either contact your Internet service provider or IT department to retrieve your password if you don't remember it or have the password reset to something more memorable. Once set on your iPad, you will not need to reenter it. It is stored securely in your system's "key chain," a private way that your iPad remembers important information.

Server information: Some accounts will be set up automatically by Mail. In other words, it will know whether your server is an Exchange server, POP server, or IMAP server, and it will adjust settings accordingly. However, it's a very good idea to get this information before you start and keep it for your records.

The information to gather includes server addresses (your e-mail provider may refer to this as a server URL) for both your incoming e-mail server (usually prefaced with POP or IMAP) and your outgoing (usually SMTP) server. The e-mail provider may also require that your mail be channeled through specific Internet Protocol ports for security reasons, so requesting port information prior to setup can save headaches later.

Although port 587 is a standard for secure SMTP connections, some connections use ports 25 (SMTP), 110 (POP3), 143 (IMAP), 993 (SSL-encrypted IMAP), 995 (SSL-encrypted POP), and 465 (SSL-encrypted SMTP), among others. Exchange setup also requires a domain name, which can be as simple as a word—HOST—or as complicated as host.admin.mycompany.com.

The following steps demonstrate how to set up a Gmail account, one of the most common types of e-mail accounts available. Although each brand of e-mail account may vary in the amount of information required for setup, the setup procedure for all brands is basically the same on the iPad, so you should be able to follow these steps to set up an account other than Gmail:

1. Always make sure that your iPad is connected to the Internet through a Wi-Fi or 3G connection before attempting to set up or otherwise interact with mail.

2. In Settings ➤ Mail, Contacts, Calendars, look for Accounts; then tap Add Account. Alternatively, if you have no other accounts set up, you can open the Mail application and be greeted by the same setup.

3. Choose the proper account type from the list that appears (see Figure 11–2). This example uses Gmail. If you don't see your e-mail service provider listed here, tap Other. Using a predefined account style simplifies setup, because you generally do not need to add extra information like server addresses. Yahoo!, Gmail, iCloud, and AOL server information is provided automatically for you.

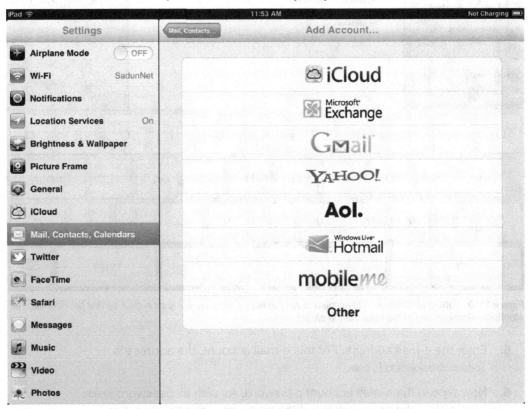

Figure 11–2. *When you're using any of these major e-mail service providers, Mail does most of the setup work for you.*

4. After selecting a preset service, enter your information into the setup window (see Figure 11–3). Specify the name that you would like recipients to see. For example, if your name is John Appleseed, you can enter that, John, Mr. Appleseed, or the Apple Tree Guy, and recipients will see your choice as the "real name" of the person who sent them e-mail.

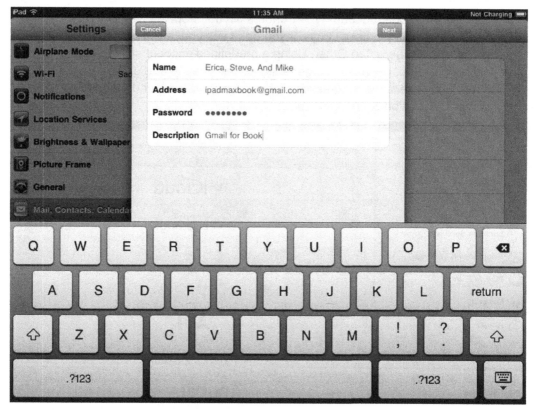

Figure 11–3. *Setting up a new e-mail account is easy in Mail, especially using an e-mail service provider like MobileMe, Gmail, or any of the others listed earlier.*

5. Enter the e-mail address. For this e-mail account, the address is ipadmaxbook@gmail.com.

6. Now type in the e-mail account password. As with all password fields on the iPad, the password is hidden by a series of dots almost as quickly as you type it in.

7. Enter a description of the account. This example uses "Gmail for Book" to describe the purpose and use of that e-mail address. Always add a meaningful description for each e-mail account, especially when you use many accounts on the same device. These short, descriptive names show up in the list of accounts in Mail on your iPad and allow you to distinguish which mail corresponds to which account. A description like "Gmail" alone is not useful when you use five or six separate Gmail accounts.

8. Tap the Save button. At this point, your iPad enters a validation process to make sure that there is an account with that e-mail address, that the password is correct, and that the settings have been properly made for that account. A progress wheel will let you know that the process is ongoing. If your iPad cannot establish the account, you'll know within a few minutes, but you do need to be patient during this step.

9. If everything checks out properly, you'll be presented with a list of account services (see Figure 11–4). These services vary by provider and allow you to choose which services you want to be able to sync over the air. Select your services, and click Save at the top right of the services pop-up. Once you have selected your services and returned to the list of e-mail accounts in Settings, the new account appears, added at the bottom of the list.

Figure 11–4. *Account services vary by provider. Gmail allows you to activate Mail, Calendar, and Note services with your account.*

In case of a setup discrepancy, your iPad notifies you of the error. In most cases, the e-mail address or the password was mistyped or, if setting up an account manually using the Other option, a server address was incorrectly entered. Mail does an excellent job of making e-mail setup easy to do on the iPad, so in most situations you'll be done with setup in a few minutes. After setup is complete, most people never need to update their account any further. But what if you need to change settings at a later date?

You'll find a button for each e-mail account listed under Settings ➤ Mail, Contacts, Calendars on the iPad. Tapping that button opens a detail display view, offering a review of enabled services. Tap the Account line for account information settings, as well as a further link to Advanced options (see Figure 11–5).

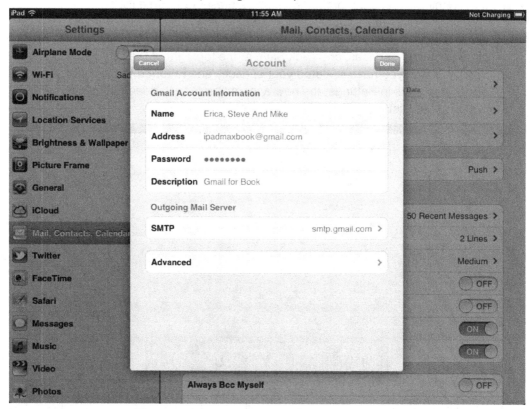

Figure 11–5. *Account information, including the name that is displayed to recipients, the name of the account in Mail, and the full e-mail address, is listed for each account in the account information screen. Tap SMTP or Advanced to adjust your account setting details.*

When you're in a low-bandwidth situation and want to turn off services, whether e-mail accounts, calendar, notes, or other over-the-air services, open the settings for each account by tapping the account name in the Mail, Contacts, Calendar screen. An account detail screen appears. Slide the service button, Mail for example, from On to Off. After doing so, Mail no longer checks the e-mail server for that account, and the account shows up as Inactive. (The status appears under the name of each account in the Accounts list.) To reverse the process, just slide the Mail button to On.

Occasionally you may be asked by your Internet service provider or IT department to change some settings for the e-mail servers, or you may run into issues sending, receiving, or configuring Mail. We recommend using Apple's handy cheat sheet, available from http://support.apple.com/kb/HT1277, to help you solicit the proper e-mail account settings from your e-mail providers and to document them in a way that offers an easy-to-use, well-organized reference.

Under Outgoing Mail Server for a specific e-mail account, it's possible to edit the settings. The SMTP option indicates the Simple Mail Transport Protocol server used as the primary server for outgoing e-mail. Tapping that option and then tapping the primary server name displays the settings for the server (see Figure 11–6). When the settings are grayed out like in Figure 11–6, then they are preset, correct, and cannot be edited. When editable, you can use your cheat sheet to change the settings to their proper values.

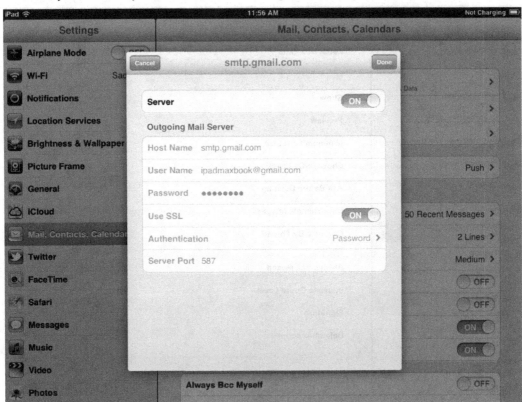

Figure 11–6. *When the Outgoing Mail Server settings are grayed out as they are in this figure, then your settings are correct for the server presets and should not be changed.*

For security reasons, most mail servers now use authentication and specific server ports. Standard ports include 110 for POP3 servers and 995 for POP3 over TLS/SSL, 143 for IMAP and 993 for POP3 over TLS/SSL, 587 for submission of password information, and 25 for SMTP (outgoing) mail.

Authentication means that Mail must submit a username (usually your e-mail address) and a password to the mail server before being allowed to download mail to your iPad. There are four common types of authentication: MD5 Challenge Response, NTLM, HTTP

MD5 Digest, and Password. As always, check with your mail provider for this information if your password is not accepted properly.

Other Mail Settings

You will find many more settings (see Figure 11–7) in Settings ➤ Mail, Contacts, Calendars that you can edit to suit your personal preferences. Most of these settings never need to be touched, but it's comforting to know you can change them if necessary. The following sections introduce some of these settings and discuss how they affect the way you use e-mail on your iPad.

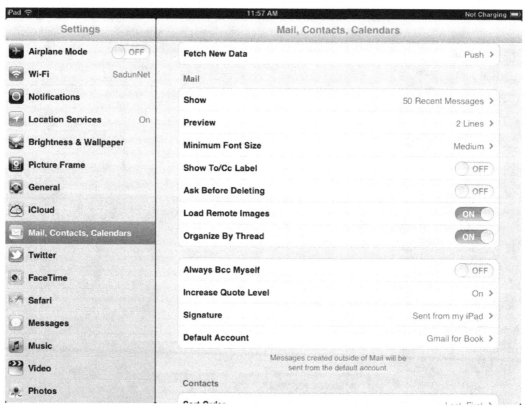

Figure 11–7. *Mail settings can be changed to make reading and sending e-mail more enjoyable and productive.*

Fetch New Data

The Fetch New Data button appears just below the last e-mail account listed (Figure 11–7 shows the right pane scrolled down past the Accounts list). Some e-mail accounts, like MobileMe's IMAP service, allow you to set up what is called *push* service. When push is enabled, new e-mails immediately transfer to your device when the e-mail server receives them. Although this is a great way to get mail as quickly as possible, it also requires more communications between the iPad and the e-mail server. That can reduce battery life, but even more importantly, it increases the amount of bandwidth used by your device.

Although this isn't an issue if you're on a Wi-Fi network, 3G network data plans are costly, particularly if you are using a metered account, which is the standard offered by most iPad carriers. With a metered account, you are granted a certain bandwidth allotment, such as 250MB per month. Exceed that bandwidth, and you may be cut off, charged again for another allotment, or possibly charged at an exorbitant out-of-plan rate; details vary by the plan you have selected and the carrier you have signed up with.

The alternative to push, and the method that is used most often for e-mail accounts, is *fetch*, otherwise known as *pull*. With this method, your iPad checks for new mail on the server only when you tell it to or at preset intervals. You can set the schedule to have e-mail accounts check for mail every 15 minutes, 30 minutes, 60 minutes, or manually. Manually means that the account doesn't check for mail until you open the inbox in the Mail app or tap the Refresh button that is found at the bottom of most mailboxes. This is a great way to save bandwidth (especially when traveling out of country), but you may miss important messages that arrive between checks.

For most purposes, we recommend leaving push notification turned on for MobileMe accounts and any other e-mail accounts, such as Exchange, that can provide push notification. For other accounts, it's your choice depending on whether you want to have new mail waiting for you when you open your inbox or want the iPad to fetch it at the time you actually open the inbox.

The **Settings** ➤ **Mail, Contacts, Calendar** ➤ **Fetch New Data** ➤ **Advanced** button provides configuration for each individual e-mail account on your iPad. Each account's separate button leads to an option to choose between Fetch and Manual. Pick Fetch to add the account to the iPad's automatic routines, or pick Manual to keep your account offline until you decide to retrieve mail.

Be aware that you cannot individualize polling times; the polling time you select in the Fetch New Data screen applies to all fetched accounts. For example, if you select 15 minutes, all polled accounts will be checked four times an hour.

Show

The next section of the settings page is more about the look and feel of the Mail application. The first button, Show, provides a choice of how many recent messages you'll see in your inbox at any time. The default value is 50 messages, but you can also select 100, 200, 500, or 1,000 messages.

If you don't receive a lot of e-mail, setting the value to 50 messages is fine. When you receive a ton of e-mail or don't check your inbox for a while, you can always pull more messages down from the server by tapping the Load More Messages link at the bottom of your inbox. Some people prefer a cleaner look and are willing to load more messages when needed. Selecting a bigger number of messages means your mailbox will always be more cluttered but avoids the wait involved when fetching additional mail batches.

Preview

Each message in a Mail inbox can include a short preview of the contents so that you can see not only the sender and subject but also a small preview of the content. The Preview button allows you to set the length of the preview from none (no preview) to five lines.

Mail's message display updates to reflect the preview size you set here. As the preview gets larger, you can see fewer items on-screen at once. As it gets smaller, you see more. With the iPad's generous screen size, this choice affects you less than it would if you were managing mail on a smaller device like the iPhone or iPod touch, where this setting becomes more critical in use. The iPad's default setting includes two lines of the message, which is usually sufficient to see whether the message is important.

Minimum Font Size

If you wear bifocals or otherwise have issues with reading small text, you're going to love the next setting. Minimum Font Size lets you change the size of text in Mail from Small to Giant, with three other sizes in between. Unlike the iPhone or iPod touch, increasing the font size on the iPad, with its large screen, doesn't affect usability, so don't be afraid. Being able to put your iPad down on a table and refer to it while standing is a wonderful thing, even if your eyes are otherwise quite strong.

Show To/Cc Label

When the Show To/Cc Label button is enabled (set to On), a small label appears next to every message in an inbox indicating whether the message was sent directly to you or you were cc'd (carbon copied) on an e-mail sent to another person. If you leave this option disabled, you can still access the feature while composing your mail—it just takes an extra tap or two. This option simply sets the default, how your mail will start out when you're starting to compose it.

Ask Before Deleting

On occasion, you may accidentally delete an e-mail. Enabling Ask Before Deleting forces you to validate that you do indeed want a mail message to be deleted. iPad owners who frequently have to perform mass deletions of e-mails should probably disable this setting to avoid getting bogged down in validations. If the consequences of losing an e-mail may be more serious for you, then enable this option.

Load Remote Images

When you're on a slow Internet connection, receiving e-mails with lots of images can be a recipe for frustration because it takes a while for those images to load. When you're in a location with a weak 3G signal, the radio in the Wi-Fi + 3G iPad reverts to much slower cellular networks like EDGE or GPRS. Even a Wi-Fi network can be connected to a slow Internet connection. As an example, many cruise ships provide Wi-Fi networks onboard yet are reliant on one very slow satellite connection over which all shipboard Internet traffic must pass.

Images also eat up bandwidth, which is an issue if you're trying to manage your cellular data usage. Because of this, you may want to skip image loading while on the go and view those items only when you're back at your desk, away from the metered Internet.

Load Remote Images enables and disables the capability of Mail to autoload images. Instead of loading them right away, they are replaced with an image stand-in. You can still view each image by manually downloading it with a tap. That way, you can skip all the snapshots from your company picnic while still enjoying the pictures of your sister's baby.

Organize by Thread

This option allows you to organize the mail you view by thread, grouping items together that share the same message history. When enabled, items appear in the inbox with a count, showing how many messages make up that threaded discussion.

Always Bcc Myself

Do you want a copy of every e-mail you send to be sent to yourself as well? Setting Always Bcc Myself to On automatically sends a blind carbon copy (bcc) to your inbox. This setting is particularly handy for anyone who wants to keep a record of outgoing e-mail and whose account does not automatically do that for them. Although many modern e-mail services offer a "sent mail" archive, there are still providers who do not offer this option.

What does *blind carbon copy* mean? It just means that the recipients of the e-mail don't know that you're also getting a copy of it. When you want to send copies of e-mails to co-workers but don't want the original recipient to know that you're sending those copies, bcc is very useful.

Increase Quote Level

This option, when enabled, adds a new level of indentation whenever you reply to a message, letting your recipient know which items are being quoted and what is new material that you've added yourself.

Signature

Have you gotten e-mail from someone with an iPad, iPhone, or other iOS device? You'll usually know it right away because of the "Sent from my iPad" signature that appears at the end of each message. On your iPad, you can easily tailor that default message for your outgoing mail, changing it to whatever text you like.

Many people like to add a quick note to their signature that explains the brevity of their messages ("so please excuse the terseness of my reply"), and possibly excuse any typographic mistakes (our technical editor Dave Caolo signs his messages, "Please excuse typos. I have big fingers. Not comically large, mind you, just average for a 6' guy").

Some iPad users who use POP e-mail and forwarding accounts have their signature reflect that situation as well ("Sent from my iPad's e-mail forwarding account. Please do not respond to this address. Use my normal work e-mail instead, thanks!"). Still others use their signature for general contact information, to allow lawyers to earn their pay ("This e-mail, including attachments, is intended for the person(s) or company named and may contain confidential and/or legally privileged information") or to simply gloat about their iPad ("Sent from my iPad. I have the best toys. I win!").

To customize your e-mail signature, tap the Signature button. Unlike most Mac or Windows e-mail programs, Mail on iPad doesn't offer a separate signature for each mail account. Instead, you create a generic signature that is used by every account. Edit the default "Sent from my iPad" text as desired. You can change it to add your name, web site address, or anything else you want. Keep in mind that if you include a name in your signature, it appears across all accounts. That's not a problem when all accounts belong to the same user. When both Jon and Suzie share the same iPad, a signature saying "Best, Jonny" will appear at the bottom of Suzie's e-mails as well. For that reason, you may want to avoid names in shared signatures.

Default Account

The Default Account setting allows you to pick the account you want to send outgoing messages from. When you compose messages using other applications on your iPad, they'll always be sent from the default account. Tap the Default Account button to view a list of the accounts on your iPad, and then select the account you want to use.

Viewing and Managing Your Incoming Mail

After you set up Mail on your iPad, you'll start to receive e-mail messages automatically, assuming you haven't set everything to "manual." Your first indicator of a new e-mail message is the New Mail sound. Although it's nice to have an audible indication that you're getting mail, it can get a little obnoxious if you receive a lot of mail every day or if you're in a meeting and receive a message. To switch off the New Mail sound, visit **Settings ➤ General ➤ Sounds**; then slide the switch to Off.

Your iPad also provides a slick little indicator to notify you that you have unread e-mail messages in your inbox or inboxes. The Mail app icon displays a small red oval containing the number of unread items in your inboxes (see Figure 11–8). This number encompasses all inboxes, so if you have 10 messages waiting in one account and 5 in another, the red oval shows that you have 15 unread messages.

Figure 11–8. *You've got mail! It looks like it is time to tap that Mail icon and take a look at those 57 unread messages in your various mailboxes.*

You can adjust the way iOS notifies you about new mail by selecting **Settings ➤ Notifications ➤ Mail**. In this settings pane, you can enable Mail to be presented to you as part of Notification Center (choose On for yes or Off for no). If you use Notification Center to alert you, select whether you want to be presented with a pop-up alert or if you want the information to appear in the center's slide-down banner.

What's more, you can enable/disable the badge from Figure 11–8 here, decide whether to show new mail alerts on your lock screen, and toggle whether you want to see a small preview of the message in the alert.

Launching and Viewing the Mail App

You launch the Mail application by tapping its icon. Once launched, what you see depends on whether you've launched the device in portrait orientation or landscape orientation. That's because Mail uses an iPad feature called *split views*. If you hold your iPad with the wider dimension from side to side (landscape mode), there's enough room on-screen to see both a list of mailboxes and accounts on the left and messages on the right.

Flip the iPad to its side, with the long side going up and down (portrait mode), and that list of mailboxes and accounts pops into an Inbox button. You can only view that list by tapping the Inbox button at the top left of your screen. The small window that opens is called a *pop-over* screen element, in that it pops over the window from the button that you tap.

Figure 11–9 shows the iPad screen in both orientations. As a rule, Mail is *much* easier to use when you hold the iPad in landscape mode. You don't have to keep opening the pop-over list from the top-left button. Instead, you see everything on-screen at once.

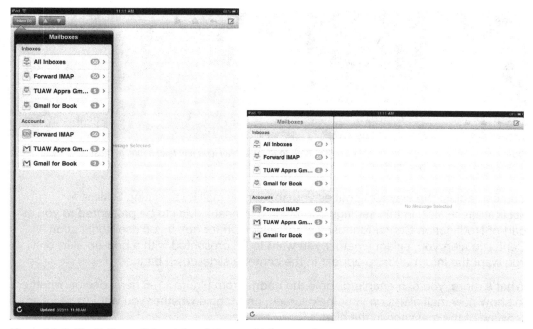

Figure 11–9. *The Mailboxes list contains all the e-mail inboxes and accounts currently set up on your iPad, as well as the number of unread e-mails for each. When you hold your iPad in portrait orientation (left), you can view that list only by tapping the Inbox button at the top left of the screen. In landscape mode (right), that list is integrated into the screen, displayed to the left of any selected content.*

To view the messages in any one of the inboxes or accounts, tap the item in the Mailboxes list. If you have set that particular e-mail account for manual fetching of messages, the iPad will check the server for new messages at this point. There's also a small refresh icon in the bottom-left corner of the list of mailboxes and accounts. Tapping this icon forces Mail to check the server immediately and retrieve any new messages that have arrived. This allows you to bypass any normal fetch intervals and check for mail whenever you desire.

> **WARNING:** With IMAP accounts, sent mail can be saved on the server. With POP3 accounts, however, this may not be the case. If you find that sent messages are not being saved and you want to keep an archive of outgoing mail, use the blind carbon copy feature to send yourself a copy.

Notice the All Inboxes item that appears at the top of your Inboxes list. All Inboxes joins together all items from all accounts, allowing you to read new messages in a single location. It's new to iOS and is one of the many great improvements recently added to Mail.

The Inboxes list is different from the Accounts list in that the former contains *only* the inbox for each account—that is, the folder of messages that your account has received. Most mail accounts allow you to create other folders, for filing and organizing your messages, allowing you to declutter your inbox without deleting archival mail. Each entry in the Accounts list takes you not just to the account's inbox but to a complete set of folders for that account, which usually consists of other items, as shown in Figure 11–10. These might include a Trash folder for deleted items, a Sent Mail folder for outgoing mail, a To-do folder for action items, and so forth. Default folders for a Gmail account include Personal, Receipts, Travel, and Work.

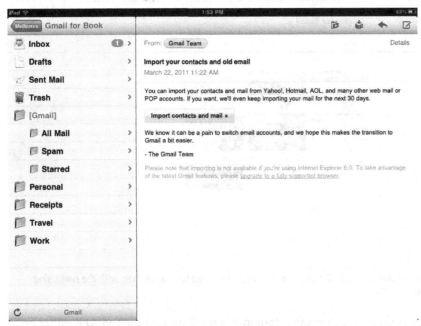

Figure 11–10. *The inbox for this example Gmail account contains an unread message, with the remaining e-mail being selected and viewed.*

Although the Inboxes screen provides quick and ready access to all new messages, using the Account presentation is particularly handy when you need to organize your mail by moving messages to other folders. It allows you to view all your folders in one place, which simplifies the selection of a destination folder for a message. You'll read more about editing mailboxes later in this chapter.

Browsing Your Mail

You can quickly determine which mail you have already viewed and which items remain unread by looking to the left of each listing in any mailbox. A blue dot appears next to each message that you haven't viewed, as shown in Figure 11–11, in which two of the three messages have not been read. The top of the inbox shows the number of unread messages in parentheses.

Figure 11–11. *The inbox for this example Gmail account contains two unread messages, with the remaining e-mail being selected and viewed.*

To read a message, you tap the message item in the mailbox and then view it either on the right side of the screen (in landscape mode) or full-screen (in portrait mode). You can navigate through the message by scrolling up and down.

The Details option at the top right of your message allows you to expand the header to see more information about whom the mail was sent to. When expanded, you can then tap Hide to return to the original presentation.

Viewing and Opening Attachments

Most people use e-mail to send documents or other files between computers. Let's say that somebody wants to send you a PDF file for you to view, or a Microsoft Word .doc file so that you can make changes to it on your iPad. You'll need to know how to receive that attachment, view that attachment, and possibly then open it in the appropriate app to make your changes.

When the e-mail arrives with the attachment, it appears in the inbox with a tiny paper clip icon denoting an attached file. In the e-mail itself, attachments are represented as small icons and are not downloaded to your iPad until you tap them. This reduces the amount of data automatically transferred to your iPad. You will see the name of the file, its size, and an icon, as shown in Figure 11–12.

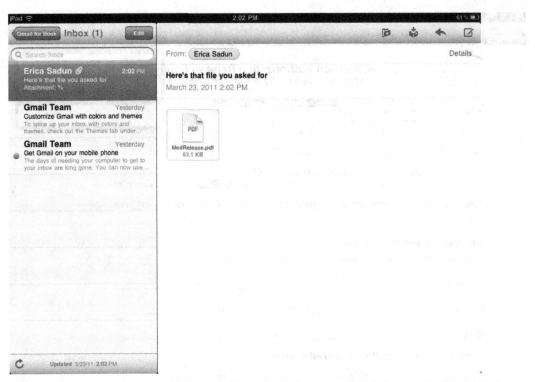

Figure 11–12. *A small paper clip icon indicates the message has an associated attachment, a file that has been sent in addition to the core e-mail. Attachments appear in your message with their name, size, and icon. Tap the icon to try to download and view the attached file, or tap and hold the icon for a pop-up menu of other options.*

Depending on file type (not all attachments can be viewed), tapping the icon typically allows you to open the file in an in-Mail viewer (called the Quick Look viewer), as shown in Figure 11–13. The viewer allows you to scroll through documents, play back media, and otherwise get a quick overview of the material that has been sent to you, but the viewer does not allow you to make changes to a file. For many attachments, you won't need to do anything further with the file, in which case you can tap the Done button to return to your inbox. Otherwise, you can open the file in another application (to edit a Word document, for example), which you can do from the Open In menu. You can access this menu in either of two ways.

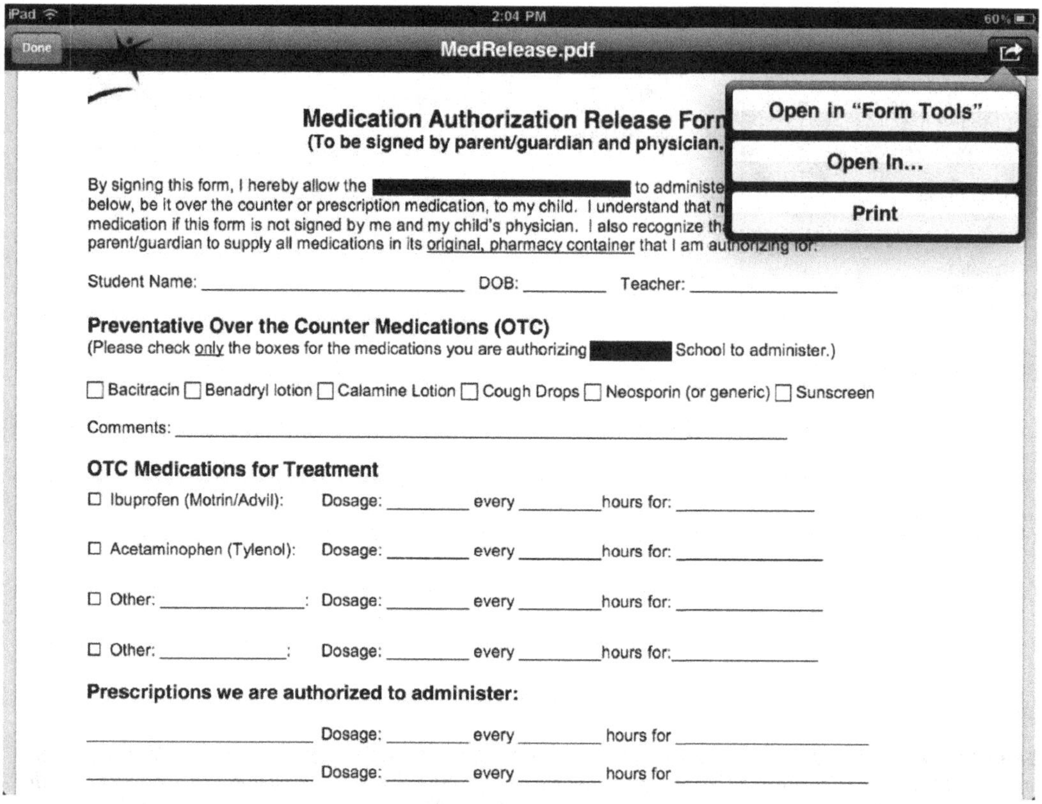

Figure 11–13. *Mail's Quick Look attachment viewer allows you to view many types of files sent as mail attachments. When you are done viewing, you can tap Done to leave the viewer or use the action menu at the top right to open the item in another application or perform other system functions. Here, Mail will allow you to print the PDF form to any supported AirPrint printer.*

iPad Mail offers two ways to redirect an e-mailed item to another application. As Figure 11–13 shows, you can tap the Action menu button at the top right of the Quick Look viewer screen. This presents a pop-over menu that includes one or more options (such as Form Tools in Figure 11–13) for opening the attachment in a specific application, an Open In option (which you can tap to see a list of possible applications to open it with), and a Print option.

Alternatively, you can just tap and hold the file attachment icon in the e-mail itself. A similar Open In pop-up appears over the attachment, offering the same choices (plus a possible Quick Look option, if the file is viewable). The names on the buttons vary depending on the file type of the attachment and by the applications you have installed on your iPad. Tapping Quick Look, if available, gives you the same quick look at the document in a viewer that you can get if you tap the icon directly (see Figure 11–13). You can't make changes to the document or do anything else; you can just view it.

If you ever have problems getting Mail to open the attachment in the correct app, try opening the document in Quick Look and then tapping the Open In button in the upper-right corner of the Quick Look window. It lists all apps currently installed on your iPad that are capable of opening and editing files of that particular type.

Editing Your Mail

The Edit button at the top right of the mailbox listing provides a way for you to apply batch deletions or moves of the e-mail that populates your mailbox. Consider Figure 11–14, which shows the mailbox after tapping Edit. Next to each message, you'll find either an empty circle or a red-filled, checked circle. Initially, these circles are empty. Tapping a message either adds that item to the collection (filling the circle with a white check mark over a red background) or removes it from the collection (returning the circle to empty).

In batch mode, you always start by choosing which items you want to work with. As you do so, a "stack" of messages appears to the right, as shown in Figure 11–14, giving you a simple visual overview of the most recently selected item and a rough indication of how many items you've chosen.

To delete all of the selected messages, tap the red Delete button at the bottom of the window. If you are using Gmail, the Delete button is replaced by the Archive button (as shown in Figure 11–14), because Gmail has its own "never delete data" policy that the iPad supports. Regardless of whether you are using a Gmail account, deleted items are removed from your mailbox. They are automatically moved to the account trash can, moved to an archival folder (as with Gmail), or possibly removed and disposed of completely. It all depends on how your mail account is set up and how your mail provider handles deletion.

To remove individual messages in any mailbox outside of edit mode, swipe your finger left or right over the message. A red Delete button appears, which you tap to send the message to the trash. You will not receive a delete confirmation alert unless you choose that option in Settings, as discussed earlier in this chapter.

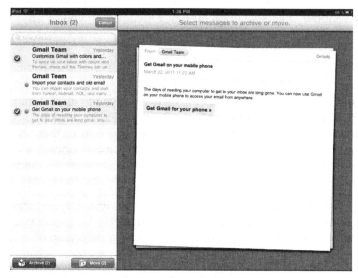

Figure 11–14. *To bulk-delete messages, tap the Edit button at the top of the message list; then tap the circles on the left side of the message list to mark the e-mails for deletion. Finally, tap the Delete button (or Archive in Gmail, which stores all your mail).*

Recovering Deleted Items

Did you accidentally delete messages? Your ability to retrieve those deleted items depends on your mail provider. In some situations, you don't need to worry, since you may be able to retrieve them from another mailbox such as the Trash mailbox, which is used by many IMAP mail accounts. In other cases, you may need to hunt around the mailbox a bit to find out where deleted items went, such as into an archival folder. In still others, your mail will actually be gone permanently. So, always check with your account provider to see how deleted messages are handled for your e-mail account.

If your account uses the Trash mailbox, you can open the mailbox from the list of mailboxes for the account (as shown earlier in Figure 11–10) and use the same management tools described in the previous section. Tap the Edit button, mark the messages that you want to recover by tapping the empty circles next to them, and then tap the Move button at the bottom of the window. That displays the list of mailboxes so you can move the selected mail items back to a destination mailbox that you select, such as the account's inbox. Alternatively, tap Cancel instead of tapping a mailbox to leave the messages in the Trash mailbox.

Navigating Mail

You'll find several buttons at the top of every Mail window that are important to know about. In portrait orientation, up and down arrows on the top-left side of the window let you navigate to the previous or next message. On the top right side of the window are buttons for moving the message to another mailbox, deleting the message, replying or forwarding the message, or creating a new message.

The Move and Delete Buttons

The Move button looks like a folder with a downward-pointing arrow. To its right you'll find either a standard Delete button (trash can icon) or, in Gmail, an Archive button (an arrow pointing into a box).

Tapping the Move button displays the list of mailboxes; navigate to a mailbox and then tap it to move the message from its original location into the selected mailbox. Tapping the Delete/Archive button provides a simple way to remove the current message. If supported, the message will move to the account's Trash/Archive mailbox, where either it will be deleted eventually or you will retrieve it if you've deleted it in error. With certain POP accounts, the message will be deleted immediately.

Reply/Reply All/Forward/Print

The Reply/Forward button looks like a curved, left-pointing arrow and appears to the right of the Move and Delete/Archive buttons. When you tap the arrow, a small pop-up menu appears with Reply, Forward, and Print options (see Figure 11–15). Each option allows you to choose an action associated with the currently displayed e-mail.

Tapping Reply opens a new message addressed to the original sender, containing the content of the original message, and allowing you to write your reply at the top of the original message. The message subject is also repeated, with the word *Re:* listed at the beginning to let the original sender know you're sending a reply.

If a message was addressed to you and several other people, another button appears—Reply All. Tapping this button sends the reply to the original sender and all of the other recipients of the e-mail as well.

The Forward button forwards the message to third parties, not limited to the parties included in the original message. Forwarding allows you to pass messages along to anyone who might be interested in their contents. For example, you might forward some family pictures to friends or send along an amusing joke to your colleagues. When you tap Forward, the message appears in a new window with an empty address list. The subject is repeated with the word *Fwd:* to indicate to the recipient that you're forwarding someone else's e-mail to them, and then there's a place for you to write a short note to the new recipient of the message.

The Print option allows you to wirelessly print from your iPad to a supported AirPrint printer. Apple has a list of supported printers in its AirPrint 101 knowledge base (see http://support.apple.com). This list is continuously updated, so search for the newest version. In addition, a number of third-party solutions like Printopia for OS X and AirPrint Activator for Windows let you print to most network-connected printers, even if they're not officially AirPrint capable.

Figure 11–15. *You can reply to or forward any e-mail by tapping the Reply/Forward button at the top of the Mail message window.*

Composing a New E-mail

The rightmost button at the top of the mail window looks like a pencil poised over a piece of paper. This Compose Message button allows you to compose new e-mail messages. Tapping the button opens a blank message with an empty address list in the To line, an empty Subject line, and a content area showing only your signature (see Figure 11–16).

To address an e-mail to someone, simply start typing the name in the To field. As you type, a pop-up appears with a list of all names from your contacts list or received e-mails that contain the letters you've typed. The letters may match the real-world name *or* the e-mail address. In the example in Figure 11–17, note that a list of people appears after typing in only the letters *jo.*

Figure 11–16. *Composing a new message in Mail. Your default signature and e-mail address are entered by Mail.*

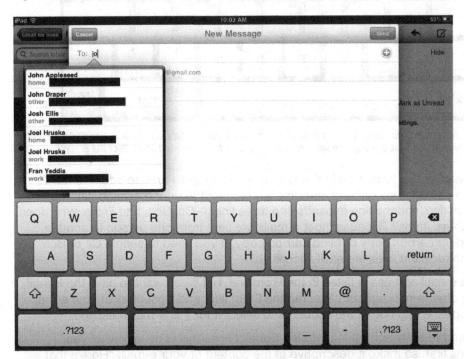

Figure 11–17. *As you type a name for the recipient of a mail message, a list of possible names and associated e-mail addresses appears.*

If you're addressing the e-mail to one person and that person appears on the pop-up list, tap their name to add it to the To line of the e-mail. What if you want to send the e-mail to more than one person or to a group? Tap the circle containing a plus sign (+) at the right end of the To line. That displays your contacts (see Figure 11–18), and you can search for individuals by typing their names in the search box or by scrolling the list with a flick of your finger. To jump to a certain letter in the alphabet (for example, all people with last names beginning with S), tap the letter from the list on the right side of the pop-up.

Figure 11–18. *You can add as many contacts to your To list as you want by tapping the plus sign and then adding one name at a time. If you have a group you want to send an e-mail to, tap Groups and select the group name.*

As with the names that appeared in the search list, just tap a name to add it to the To list. To add a carbon copy or blind carbon copy recipient to your message, tap the Cc/Bcc, From line, and the line expands into three lines—Cc, Bcc, and From. Why does Apple hide these items? Because most e-mails are sent from one person to another, with no need for carbon copy or blind carbon copy. If you need to send a Cc or Bcc message, the recipient lines are easily accessible.

Your default e-mail address is listed in the From line, but if you want to have the e-mail sent from another e-mail account, just tap the From line, and a list of all of your e-mail accounts appears. Tap one of the accounts to select it for this e-mail message.

Next, you need to enter something into the Subject line. This is usually what your recipient sees first, so make it descriptive of the content of your e-mail. "Here's that article for you" or "Friday Lunch" is a little more helpful than "Hi" or "From me."

Finally, type your message into the body of the message. When you're ready to send the message, tap the Send button in the upper-right corner of the message. If you're currently connected to the Internet over a Wi-Fi or 3G connection, the message immediately attempts to move to the server. If you do not have an Internet connection, have quit Mail, or have shut off your iPad, the message is placed in an Outbox mailbox. The next time the iPad connects to the Internet, Mail will attempt to send any messages waiting in Outbox mailboxes.

Using Mail in Other Apps

You can send e-mail from many of the other apps, both Apple apps and third-party apps, on your iPad. Generally, the app displays either an envelope icon or a Share icon, the latter appearing like a piece of paper with an arrow coming out of it. This section discusses some of the common Apple apps and how they integrate with Mail to let you share information with others.

Contacts

You can share address cards in Contacts through Mail. A Share Contact button appears at the bottom of each address card. Instead of sending someone a laboriously typed list or copy/pasted version of a person's contact information, it's much easier to tap the Share Contact button and send them a vCard. Each vCard contains every bit of contact information that you've captured for that person, including telephone numbers, addresses, e-mail addresses, URLs, and even a photo if one has been added to the contact.

Tapping Share opens a new, unaddressed message that contains the .vcf file for the person whose information is being shared. Address the message to someone, type in a subject line ("Steve's address information," for instance), and then send the message.

Anyone receiving this e-mail on an iPad can tap the .vcf icon that signifies the file is attached to the message, and a small pop-up appears (see Figure 11–19) showing the information contained in the file as well as an option to either create a new contact or add that information to an existing contact (handy for when people get new cell phone numbers or e-mail addresses).

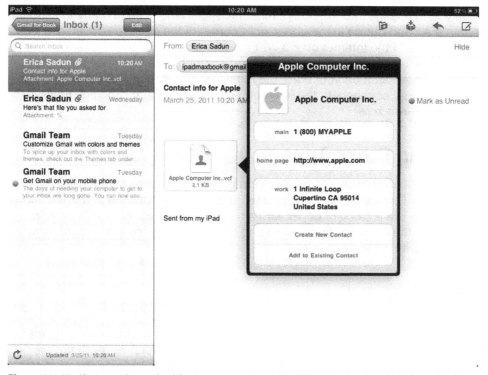

Figure 11–19. *If you receive a vCard from someone, tap and hold the icon to view the information it contains. You also have a choice of creating a new contact or adding this information to an existing contact.*

Likewise, the .vcf file, when clicked in an e-mail message on a Mac or Windows computer, will launch the appropriate application on the computer and ask the recipient whether they want to add the card to their address book.

To share contact information with others quickly and easily, send vCards through Mail.

Notes

As mentioned in the "Notes" section of Chapter 10, it's easy to send a copy of one of your iPad notes to yourself or others from this app.

Tap the envelope icon at the bottom of a page, and a new Mail message appears. The Subject line is filled in with the name of the note, the note is copied as text into the body of the message, and all you need to do is address the message and send it.

YouTube

There's nothing like finding a funny or thought-provoking video on YouTube and then sharing that clip with friends.

When you find a video in the iPad's YouTube app using the search function, a Share button appears just above the video sample on the page. Tap the Share button, and a new message appears with the name of the video as the subject and a link to the video in the body of the message. Type in an address, and tap Send to let your friends share in the fun.

iTunes

iTunes includes a quick link for telling friends about movies, music, TV shows, podcasts, or other items that you've found in the store. Tap the Tell a Friend link found in the upper-right corner of each listing in the iTunes Store to create a nicely formatted e-mail complete with any images that accompany the store item, a button that links the recipient to the item in the store, ratings, and more.

If the recipient doesn't have iTunes, they can use the automatically included link to download and install the program on their computer.

App Store

Once you own an iPad, it's tempting to let the world know about all the wonderful apps available for the device. Apple makes it easy to spread the word about fun or useful apps by including the same Tell a Friend link on every app description in the App Store. Like iTunes, the e-mail generated by the Tell a Friend link includes a picture of the app icon, the app rating, a button that links the recipient to the app in the App Store, and a link for downloading iTunes.

iBooks

If the other two stores on the iPad—iTunes and the App Store—include Tell a Friend links, then you might imagine that the iBookstore also provides a similar link. You're correct—for every book listing in the iBookstore, the Tell a Friend link appears in the same location (upper-right corner of the listing) that it occupies in iTunes and the App Store.

iWork for iPad

All three of the iWork for iPad apps—Keynote, Pages, and Numbers—include a Share button on the main page. The main page displays all the presentations, documents, or worksheets that you've created in one of the apps.

To share a file with a friend or co-worker, drag it to the center of the page, and then tap the Share button below the image of the document. A pop-up appears, with Send via Mail as the first of three actions you can choose.

Tap the Send via Mail button, and a dialog box appears asking which file format you want to convert the file to before sending. For Keynote, the choices are Keynote or PDF.

For Numbers, you can select either Numbers or PDF. There are three file format choices for Pages—Pages, PDF, or Microsoft Word .doc format.

Once you've selected the file type, the document is formatted and then attached to a new e-mail message with the document name as the Subject line. Enter an address or two in the To line, tap the Send button, and your work moves on to another person.

Photos

There's nothing more fun than sharing photos with friends and family, and the Photos app on your iPad makes it simple to send one or more pictures to anyone with an e-mail address.

When viewing photos in any photo collection, album, or event, our familiar friend the Share button lurks in the upper-right corner of the window. Tapping the button adds Email, Copy, and Delete buttons to the upper-left corner of the window. To add up to five photos as attachments to an e-mail message, tap the photos you want to send, and a check mark appears on them. When you've selected the photos, tap the Send button to embed them in an e-mail.

Like many actions you can perform on an iPad, there's more than one way to send a photo in Mail. While you're browsing your photos, you may see an image that you want to share. Tap and hold the image until a Copy pop-up appears. When it does, tap the pop-up to copy the image. Paste that image into a Mail message, address it, and mail it to share the picture.

Why can you send only five photos? It's all about the size of the images. Depending on the image resolution of the camera that takes the photos, it's not uncommon for photos to be many megabytes (MB) in size. Photos transferred to your iPad are downsampled to the maximum resolution of your iPad's display, which is 1024×768 pixels. That creates a file size of about 900KB. It doesn't sound like much, but embedding five photos in an e-mail message increases the file size to approximately 5MB.

To facilitate the sending of pictures from the iPad, Apple set a limit on the number of pictures. Just about any e-mail system will accept an incoming message with a 5MB file; double or triple that size, and many e-mail servers reject the message as being too large.

What if you have a lot of smaller images to mail to someone? Use the copy and paste method we described earlier to add as many photos as you want, but be cognizant of the fact that the recipient's mail system may reject your message if it is too large.

What happens to photos sent to your iPad in e-mail messages? When the messages appear in your inbox, you may see the photo or an icon that designates that the photo still needs to be downloaded to your iPad from the e-mail server.

Any photo sent to you can be either saved to Photos or copied for pasting into another app. To save or copy the photo, tap and hold it, and a pop-up appears with two buttons—Save Image and Copy. To save the image to Photos, tap Save Image. The iPad copies the image to your Camera Roll in the Photos application. If you're going to paste the image directly into another document, tap Copy, which moves the image to the clipboard for pasting.

> **TIP:** Have you ever wondered how we got the wonderful screen shots for this book? To take a screenshot of whatever is on your iPad display, just press and hold the Home button and then push the Sleep/Wake button. Your screen "flashes," and a shutter sound tells you that the screenshot has been captured to your photo library.

Summary

As the primary conduit for electronic mail on your iPad, the Mail app is arguably one of the most important pieces of software on the device. Setting up Mail is easy, with the app handling much of the configuration work behind the scenes with a minimum of assistance required from the iPad owner.

This chapter showed you how to set up the app and then use it to send or receive e-mail. We discussed how Mail works with many other applications on the iPad to provide a way to share information with others. These are the important points to take away from this chapter:

- To use Mail, accounts must first be configured in the app. An easy way to move account information to the iPad from another computer is to sync Mail settings from iTunes on the computer.

- When you're setting up Mail accounts on the iPad, it's helpful to use Apple's Mail "cheat sheet" to capture all the settings necessary to successfully configure the accounts.

- Upon receiving an e-mail with attachments, tap and hold the attachment icon in the message to view or open the file on the iPad.

- Send vCard files from the Contacts app to quickly share contact information with others. vCard is a nearly universal file format that works well for Windows, Mac, and Linux users.

- All of the electronic storefronts on your iPad—the iTunes Store, iBookstore, and the App Store—include Tell a Friend links for sending friends detailed information about items in the store that you think deserve their attention.

- Only five photos at a time can be sent from the Photos application to avoid conflicts with message size limits on mail servers, but it's possible to work around this limit by copying and pasting photos into Mail.

Working with Maps

The iPad has a powerful mapping application called Maps. It uses Google Maps to interactively find and display locations using map and satellite imagery. With Maps, you can get directions, view traffic, and more.

In this chapter, you'll discover how to navigate maps, bookmark locations, "walk down" a street in Street view, and even use your iPad as a compass. Maps isn't just a powerful app; it's a fun one, as well. Let's get started.

Launch the app by tapping the Maps icon (see Figure 12–1). It looks like a small map that shows a section of Interstate 280. The pin on the icon just happens to be where Apple's headquarters is located in Cupertino, California. This takes you into the Maps application, where you can view and explore geography from around the world.

Figure 12–1. *The Maps icon*

Maps Screen

Tap the icon to launch the Maps app. When you do, you'll be presented with your Maps screen (see Figure 12–2).

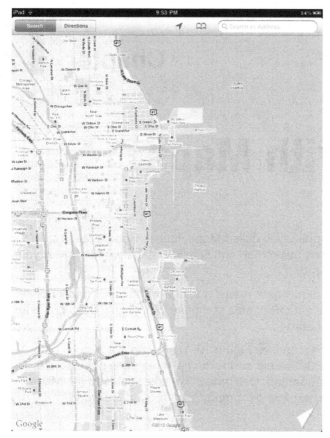

Figure 12–2. *The Maps screen. Note the page curl at the bottom right of the screen.*

At the top of the Maps screen, you'll see the Maps toolbar (see Figure 12–3).

Figure 12–3. *The Maps toolbar*

The Maps screen, including the toolbar, shows the basic Maps interface, which consists of the following:

> *Search/Directions tab*: This tab allows you to switch between the search and direction functions of the Maps app. You can search for local business, attractions, and specific addresses. You can also easily get directions to and from those locations.

Current Location: This button, which looks like an arrowhead, finds your current location on the map by using the iPad's built-in positioning tools. These built-in tools vary, depending on which iPad you have. The iPad Wi-Fi + 3G uses both the Global Positioning System (GPS) and Skyhook Wi-Fi positioning to locate you. Skyhook Wi-Fi positioning uses known wireless hotspot locations to triangulate your current position. The iPad Wi-Fi only uses Skyhook Wi-Fi positioning because there is no GPS chip inside the iPad Wi-Fi.

Bookmarks: The Bookmarks icon at the left side of the search field links to your saved locations. From the Bookmarks pop-up that appears when you tap the Bookmarks icon, you can edit your bookmarks, see recently viewed locations, or choose a location from your contacts list.

Search field: Marked with a spyglass, the search field allows you to enter addresses and other queries. You can type an entire address (*1600 Pennsylvania Avenue, Washington, DC*); you can find addresses for contacts (*Bill Smith*) or landmarks (*Golden Gate Bridge*); and you can even find pizza places in any ZIP code across the country (*Pizza 11746*). When in Directions mode, the search field will turn into two search fields, so you can enter beginning and end points.

Map: The map itself takes up the rest of the screen. It's fully interactive. You can scroll by dragging your finger along the map, or you can zoom in and out using pinches and double-taps.

Page curl: In the lower-right corner of the map (see Figure 12–2), you'll see the corner is curled up a bit. Tap the curl, or tap and hold and then drag the curl with your finger to reveal map settings. This allows you to change map views, get traffic conditions, and drop pins.

Navigating Maps

The iPad Maps app makes it so you can explore the world from the comfort of your couch. As with any other app, you navigate the map using gestures. You can also view the map in different modes.

Gestures

On maps you use gestures to zoom in, zoom out, pan, and scroll:

Zoom in: You have two ways of zooming in. Either pinch the map with two fingers; or, using one finger, double-tap the location on the map that you want to zoom in on. Double-tap again to zoom in even closer.

Zoom out: You can zoom out in two ways. Either reverse-pinch the map with two fingers; or, using two fingers, double-tap the map. Double-tap with two fingers again to zoom even further out.

Panning and scrolling: Touch and drag the map up, down, left, or right to move the map around and view another location.

Changing Map Views

The default map view is Google's standard road map with orange, yellow, and white streets. But the Maps application also allows you to look at the map in four additional views, as well as with a traffic overlay (see Figure 12–4).

Figure 12–4. *Four map views, from left to right: Standard, Satellite, Hybrid, and Terrain*

To access these features, tap, or tap and drag the page curl at the bottom of the Maps screen. The map will curl up, and you'll be presented with the settings page (see Figure 12–5). Your settings include map views, overlays, and a special Drop Pin feature, which places, or *drops*, a pin anywhere on the map. These dropped pins let you easily mark a business, street corner, beach, or any other kind of location on a map.

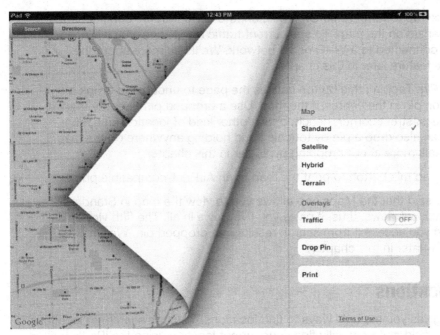

Figure 12–5. *The Maps setting page lies behind the page curl in the map.*

Here are the basic map views and what they do:

Standard: This is the default map view. It uses Google's standard road map.

Satellite: This view shows you the world using satellite imagery. It's perhaps the coolest map view because you can zoom in on streets and see little blips of people walking about on the day that the satellite imagery was taken. No labels appear in Satellite view.

Hybrid: This view combines the Standard and Satellite views. You see the map in satellite imagery, but it has labels, roads, and borders overlaid on it.

Terrain: This view shows you the terrain of a given map, including relief maps of the terrain. The Terrain view also overlays roads, borders, and labels. This view is great if you're thinking of doing a cross-country cycle—you'll be able to see how hilly areas of your route are.

TIP: The Standard view uses orange, yellow, and white to color streets. Orange indicates interstate highways, yellow indicates state highways and county parkways, and white indicates local and private streets.

Traffic: Tap to turn Traffic On. While on, the current traffic conditions will be overlaid on the map. To see current traffic conditions, you will need to be connected to a Wi-Fi or 3G network. We'll talk more about the Traffic feature later in this chapter.

Drop Pin: Tapping this button causes the page to uncurl and drops a location pin in the center of the map. Use a dropped pin to easily mark a business, street corner, beach, or any other kind of location on a map. You can also drop a pin by touching and holding anywhere on the map. We'll talk more about dropping pins later in this chapter.

Print: Tap this button to print the map to an AirPrint-compatible printer.

You'll notice we said that the Maps app allows you to view the map in Standard view, as well as four additional views; thus, it gives you five views in all. The fifth view is called Street view, and you access it from search results or a dropped pin. We'll talk more about Street view later in this chapter.

Finding Locations

The Maps app gives you multiple ways to find locations. You can search for locations using the search field, automatically find your current location using the iPad's built-in GPS or Skyhook location services, or even just zoom in and browse the map like a bird flying overhead.

Depending what you are looking for, some types of search are better than others. For example, if you are looking for your favorite spot on a beach, chances are it doesn't have an address or name, so your best bet is to navigate to the beach and then zoom in and scroll around in Satellite view until you find that favorite spot.

Search

You'll find most of your locations through the search function in the toolbar at the upper right of your screen (see Figures 12–2 and 12–3). Tap the search field, and a Recents pop-up window and keyboard appears (see Figure 12–6). Remember that if you have a hardware keyboard synced to your iPad, the software keyboard will not appear on the screen.

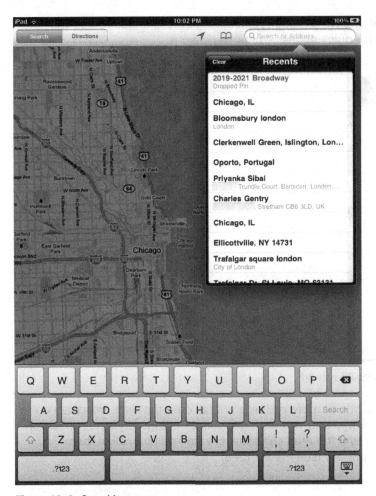

Figure 12–6. *Searching maps*

There are many ways to search for a location on your iPad. You can enter an entire address (*1600 Pennsylvania Avenue, Washington, DC*); you can find a contact's address by typing in the contact's name (*Bill Smith*); or you can find the address for a landmark by entering its name (*Eiffel Tower*). You can even find pizza places by entering your local ZIP code and the keyword *pizza* (*Pizza 60605*).

The Recents pop-up window shows you all your recent searches, including recent directions (see Figure 12–7). Tap any of the results in the Recents list to be taken to its location. Tap the Clear button in the Recents pop-up window to clear the Recents results list. Clearing the Recents list ensures that no one else who uses your iPad will be able to see the locations you have searched for. For example, if you looked up directions to a special restaurant that you are taking your wife to for her birthday, you don't want her seeing it. Clearing the Recents list ensures she won't. Be careful not to clear the list if you are going to be frequently pulling up the same directions, however. The Maps app can save any kind of location, whether or not it has an address; however, it does not have the ability to permanently save direction routes. Regardless, those routes will remain in the Recents list—for quick access—until you clear it.

Figure 12–7. *The search field with the Recents list*

Enter your search query, and one or more red pins will fall onto the map. Imagine you're taking a trip next week to Chicago and you want get some Chicago-style pizza. Search on the criteria *Pizza Chicago*, and the map will show several red pins, all of them representing pizza places in the city (see Figure 12–8).

Figure 12-8. *Search result pins on the map*

When you touch one of the red pins, you get the pin's Information bar (see Figure 12–9). The Information bar tells you the name of the establishment (a pizzeria, in this case) and displays an icon on either side. Those icons represent the Information window and Street view.

Figure 12-9. *A search result pin's Information bar shows the name of the establishment with a Street View icon on the left and an Information icon on the right.*

You can also view your search results as a list. After the pins fall onto the map, a gray circle with three lines appears in the search field next to your queried search term. Tap the circle, and your results will be presented in a drop-down list (see Figure 12–10). You can then keep tapping names in the list and see their locations bounce to life on the map.

Figure 12–10. *The search results list*

The Information Window

Tap the white and blue *i* on the pin's Information bar to make the Information window slide open. The Information window (see Figure 12–11) displays information for the establishment, such as its phone number, web page, and physical address.

Figure 12–11. *The Information window*

The Information window provides the following options for a given location on your iPad:

Image: Depending on the establishment, you may see a thumbnail icon of the establishment's Street view in the Information window. You can tap this thumbnail to be taken to Street view. You'll see more on that in a bit.

Directions To Here: Tap here to be taken to the Directions toolbar. The address of the establishment will be populated in the second (end destination) directions field. We'll talk more about directions later in this chapter.

Directions From Here: Tap here to be taken to the Directions toolbar. The address of the establishment will be populated in the first (origin destination) directions field.

Phone: This displays the establishment's phone number. Touch and hold to copy the number to the clipboard. Tap the phone number to initiate a FaceTime call. FaceTime calls work only if the number is a valid FaceTime number.

Home page: This displays the establishment's web address. Tap it to close Maps and be taken to the web address in Safari.

Address: This displays the establishment's address. Touch and hold to copy the address to the clipboard.

Add to Contacts: Tapping this button will add the name of the establishment and its phone number, web address, and physical address to a contact. This contact presents you with two options: Create New Contact and Add to Existing Contact.

If you choose Create New Contact, a New Contact window will slide up (see Figure 12–12) in the Information window, populating contact fields with information and also allowing you to add more information to the contact. Tap Done to save the new contact.

Figure 12–12. *The New Contact window lets you add a search result's information to your address book from within the Maps app.*

If you choose Add to Existing Contact, a list of all your contacts from your address book will slide up in the Information window. Tap the contact you want to add the information to. The information will be added, and the contacts list will slide away.

FaceTime: If you have chosen to look up the address for a friend you already have in your address book, you'll see a FaceTime button instead of an Add to Contacts button. Tapping the FaceTime button will bring up a dialog box that asks at which number or e-mail address you want to FaceTime the person at. Tap which one you want, and FaceTime will open and proceed to call your contact. Check out Chapter 15 for more on FaceTime.

Share Location: Tapping this button will allow you to e-mail a link of the establishment's name, add a Google Maps link, and attach a vCard (a virtual business card the receiver can choose to add to an address book).

Add to Bookmarks: Tapping this button will allow you to save the location to your Maps bookmarks. You'll be able to name the bookmark, so you can change "Edwardo's Natural Pizza Restaurant" to "My favorite pizza joint." We'll talk more about bookmarks in a moment.

Tap anywhere on the map to close the Information window.

Street View

Street view is the fifth way to view maps that we mentioned earlier. Street view uses Google technology to display 360-degree panoramic views of a given location. To enter Street view, tap the white and orange Street View icon in the pin's Information bar (see Figure 12–9), or tap the picture thumbnail in the Information window (see Figure 12–11). Your map will begin to zoom in on the pin; it will then tilt up and present you with a street-level panoramic view (see Figure 12–13).

Figure 12–13. *Street view fills the entire screen. Tap the white Arrow icon on the road to move forward down the street. Tap the map's Navigation icon to return to Map view.*

Google has had Street view available on the Web for some time, but using it on the iPad brings it to a whole different level. The fact that you can touch and drag and pinch and zoom around the street gives Street view an immediacy it never had previously.

While in Street view, drag your finger around to experience the 360-degree panoramic views. Pinch or double-tap the screen to zoom in. Reverse-pinch to zoom back out. To "walk" down the street, find the big white arrow icons at the end of a street label and tap them. You'll then move in that direction.

The small circular Navigation icon sits at the bottom right of a Street view map. It shows you the direction you are looking in. Tap the icon to return to your last Map view location.

Street view isn't available in all cities yet, but it is in most major North American and European ones. Street view is a wonderful tool because it lets you check out what a place or area looks like in advance. Thinking of moving to a new area of town? You can virtually scroll down the street in Street view to see whether you like the looks of it before you take the time and trouble to start searching for houses in the neighborhood.

Current Location

Curious about where you are in the world? The Maps app allows you to find your current location with a tap of a button. The Current Location button is in the toolbar at the top of the screen (see Figure 12–3). It looks like an arrowhead. Tap it to jump to your current location on the map.

The Current Location feature works by using the iPad's built-in positioning tools. These built-in tools vary depending on which iPad you have. The iPad Wi-Fi + 3G uses both GPS and Skyhook Wi-Fi positioning to locate you. The iPad Wi-Fi uses only Skyhook Wi-Fi positioning, because there is no GPS chip inside the iPad Wi-Fi.

GPS uses satellite-location technology to pinpoint your location with an accuracy of up to 16 feet (5 meters). Skyhook Wi-Fi positioning uses known wireless hotspot locations to triangulate your current position with an accuracy of 60 to 100 feet (20 to 30 meters).

As mentioned earlier, if you have an iPad Wi-Fi + 3G, it will use both technologies to pinpoint your location. Even though GPS has a much more accurate range, there are some areas where Skyhook has an advantage over GPS, namely, in urban locations. Tall buildings can obscure GPS satellite signals, so Skyhook's wireless network triangulation has an advantage there.

Your current location is signified by a blue dot, as shown in Figure 12–14. If the Maps app can't determine your exact location, a blue circle appears around the dot. The circle can range in size—its size depends on how precisely your location can be determined. The circle means you are somewhere in the vicinity of that circle on the map. The smaller the circle, the more precise the current -location marker.

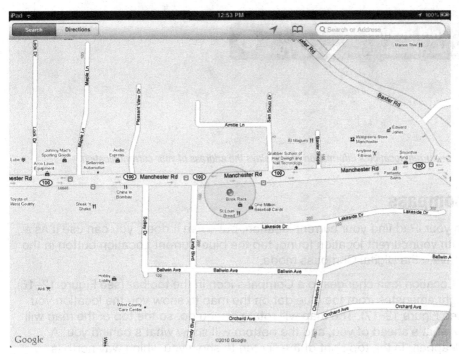

Figure 12–14. *The blue dot surrounded by the circle represents your approximate location.*

> **NOTE:** Location Services must be turned on for your iPad to find your current location. To turn on Location Services, go to **Settings ➤ Location Services** and make sure the switch is set to On.

When you are in Current Location mode, the Current Location icon in the toolbar turns blue. After you've found your current location, if you drag the map around, you can simply tap the Current Location button again to have the map center back on it.

You can tap the blue current location dot on the map to open the current location's Information bar (see Figure 12–15). The address of the current location will be displayed. Tap the *i* button to get the Information window for the location, including the ability to get directions to/from the location, bookmark it, add it to contacts, or e-mail the location. Tap the Street View button to enter Street view (if available in the area).

Figure 12–15. *The current location's Information bar displays the address of your current location.*

Digital Compass

Not only can your iPad find your current location, but when it does, you can use it as a compass. With your current location found, tap the blue Current Location button in the toolbar to activate the Digital Compass mode.

The Current Location icon changes to a Compass icon in the toolbar (see Figure 12–16), and a headlight emanates from the blue dot on the map to show you the location you are facing (see Figure 12–17). The map will rotate as you do, so the top of the map will always show what's ahead of you, and the bottom will show what's behind you. A compass will appear in the top right of the screen to show you which way north is.

Figure 12–16. *The Current Location button (left) turns into the Digital Compass button (right) when you tap it twice.*

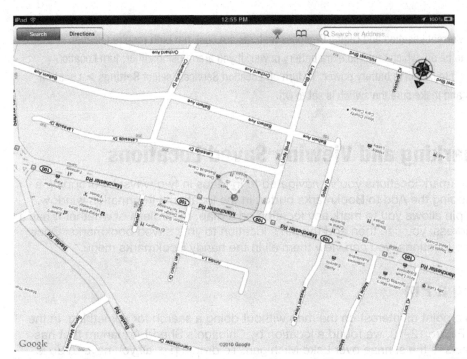

Figure 12–17. *Digital Compass mode. This is the same image as in Figure 12–14, but with the Digital Compass turned on. Notice how the map is pointing the other direction; that's because the iPad is facing that direction, which in this case is south. Note the compass pointing north in the upper-right corner and the "headlight" emanating from the blue current location dot.*

The first time you use Digital Compass mode, you'll need to calibrate the compass. A gray icon will appear on the screen telling you to move your iPad in a figure eight (see Figure 12–18). Doing so will complete the calibration. Lots of metal and magnets (like those found in a car's speaker system) affect compasses. You may need to calibrate the compass from time to time, but the iPad will tell you when calibration is needed.

Figure 12–18. *The Digital Compass calibration notice*

TIP: The Current Location and Digital Compass features are cool, but both require Location Services to be on, which requires extra battery power. If you aren't using either, turn Location Services off to conserve battery power. To turn off Location Services, select **Settings** ➤ **Location Services** and make sure the switch is set to Off.

Bookmarking and Viewing Saved Locations

You can bookmark locations you've navigated to in Maps in two ways: by dropping a pin or by tapping the Add to Bookmarks button in the location's Information window. Dropping a pin allows you to mark any location on a map, regardless of whether it has a physical address; you can then add the pin's location to your saved bookmarks. Once you've saved locations, you can view them all in the handy Bookmarks menu.

Dropping a Pin

Navigate to a point of interest on the map without doing a search for something. In the example in Figure 12–19, we found a location by Chicago's Shedd Aquarium that has beautiful views of the sunrise over Lake Michigan. To drop a pin, all you have to do is press and hold your finger on the map where you want to drop it. After a second or two, a purple pin will fall and stick in the map.

Figure 12–19. *A dropped pin and its Information bar with the approximate address*

The pin's Information bar will appear with the approximate address of the pin, as well as the usual icons for Street view and the Information window. If the pin's location isn't exactly where you want it, you can tap and hold the purple pin's head and drag it to the location you want. Remove your finger to sink the pin into the map.

Tap the *i* button to bring up the Information window for the pin's location (see Figure 12–20). This window's options include the ability to get directions to/from the location, bookmark it, add it to contacts, or e-mail the location. You can also tap the Street View button to enter Street view (if it's available in the area).

Figure 12–20. *A dropped pin's Information window lets you find directions, add the location to contacts and bookmarks, or share the location.*

You can also drop a pin in the center of the map by accessing the Maps settings page behind the page curl in the lower-right corner (see Figure 12–6). Tap, or tap and drag the page curl at the bottom of the Maps screen and then tap the Drop Pin button. The settings page will uncurl, and a pin will drop in the center of the map. You can then tap and drag the pin to move it to anywhere you want on the map.

Dropping pins might seem like a nice but unnecessary feature at first. If you can search maps with the app's powerful search features, you might wonder why you would want to manually add locations. Again, dropped pins are great because they allow you to mark locations that do not have a fixed address, like a good trail in the mountains, the site of your first kiss (for the romantics among you), or even the location of your favorite bench in Central Park.

Bookmarking

So far in this chapter, we've shown you several ways to bookmark locations, whether it be by a dropped pin or the Information windows of a business, friend, or address you looked up. But where are all those bookmarks you've saved? In the Bookmarks window, of course!

Tap the Bookmarks icon in the Maps title bar; the icon looks like a book folded open (see Figure 12–3). The Bookmarks window will appear, presenting three views: Bookmarks, Recents, and Contacts (see Figure 12–21).

Figure 12-21. *The Bookmarks window displays your bookmarked locations, recent locations, and contact locations.*

The different views of the Bookmarks window behave like this:

Bookmarks: This view lists all the bookmarks you've saved in the Maps app. Tap any bookmark to jump to it on the map. Tap the Edit button to delete a bookmark, move it up or down the Bookmarks list, or change the name of the bookmark.

Recents: This view lists all the recent search queries, driving directions, and dropped pins you've made (see Figure 12-22). Tap any item on the list to jump to it on the map. Tap the Clear button to remove all items from the list. Remember, clearing your Recents list will ensure that people who use your iPad can't spy on locations you've searched for. Be aware, however, that it will also clear your direction routes. Routes can't be bookmarked, so the only way to quickly access them is through the Recents window. If you clear the window, you'll need to perform your route searches from scratch.

Contacts: This list shows you all your contacts (see Figure 12-22). Tap any contact on the list to jump to its address on the map (provided you have the contact's address in your contacts book). If a contact has more than one address, you'll be asked to choose which address to navigate to. Tap the Groups button to navigate through your contact groups.

Figure 12–22. *The Bookmarks windows for Recents and Contacts*

> **TIP:** To close any pop-up window, such as the Bookmarks window or a search results list, tap anywhere on the map. The pop-up window will fade away.

Directions and Traffic

The iPad Maps app lets you search for directions and view current traffic conditions. Like the Maps app itself, directions and traffic require an Internet connection. If you have an iPad Wi-Fi + 3G, this won't be an issue if you're using it to find directions while on the road. If you have an iPad Wi-Fi only, you'll need to look up the directions before you leave home.

Directions

To get directions, tap the Directions tab in the Maps toolbar (see Figure 12–3). You'll notice that the search field becomes a double field to enter your start and end locations (see Figure 12–23). The Maps app will make your current location, if available, the starting location. If you don't want to use your current location as the starting address, tap it into the first search field anyway. From there, you can tap the X to remove it or choose another location from the Recents pop-up list that appears.

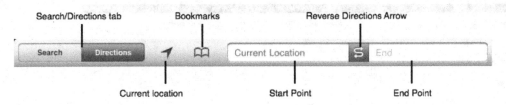

Figure 12–23. *The Maps toolbar changes to accept directions input when you tap the Directions button.*

> **NOTE:** You can also begin a directions search from any pin's Information window.

To enter an address from one of your contacts, tap the Bookmarks icon, and then choose a contact. You'll be asked to choose Directions to Here or Directions From Here. Choose the one you want, and the contact's address will be populated in the appropriate directions field. To reverse the start and end points, tap the curvy *S* arrow to switch the points (and get reverse directions). The reverse directions feature is nice because sometimes the route you used to get somewhere isn't the quickest route back. Reverse directions will show you whether another route home is quicker.

When you have selected both a start point and an end point, one or more blue lines will appear on the map showing suggested routes you can take. Tap the route label (Route 1, Route 2, and so on) to select a route (see Figure 12–24). A green pin represents your starting location on the map, and a red pin indicates your end location. You'll also notice that a blue Directions bar has appeared at the bottom of the screen (see Figure 12–25). The Directions bar lets you choose between driving (a Car icon), public transit (a Bus icon), or walking (a Person icon) directions. These different modes of transportation may give you different direction routes on the map between the same two locations. This is because people aren't allowed to walk on highways, and cars aren't allowed to drive on pedestrian streets or on certain bus routes, depending on the city you live in.

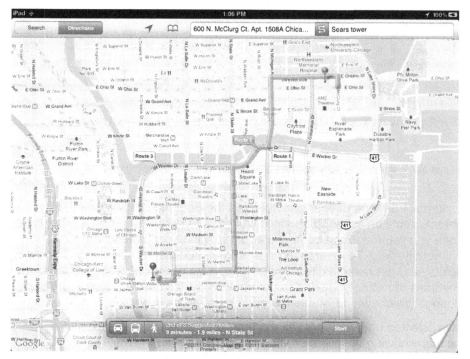

Figure 12–24. *The map with the directions route*

Figure 12–25. *The Directions bar allows you to switch between driving, public transit, and walking directions.*

Driving or Walking Directions

Tap the icon for either driving or walking. You'll see the length of the route and the estimated time it will take to get there. If traffic data is available, the estimated journey time will adjust accordingly.

To navigate through the directions step by step, tap the blue Start button. The Directions bar will change to the one shown in Figure 12–26. Tap the icon of the three dots with lines trailing after them to see the directions displayed in a list format (see Figure 12–27). Tap any step in the list to be taken to that part of the route on the map. To return to the Directions bar, tap the blue icon in the top-left corner of the Directions List window.

Figure 12–26. *Tap the left arrow or right arrow icon to move through the directions step by step.*

If you'd like to navigate through the directions step by step in the map, tap the right arrow icon on the bar. Each subsequent tap will bring you forward one step in the route. To move back a step, tap the left arrow icon.

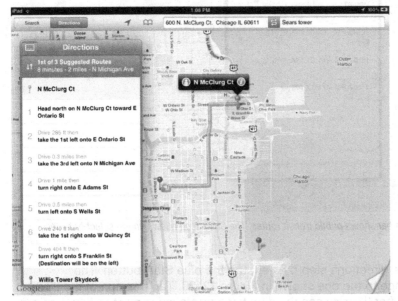

Figure 12–27. *Directions presented in a list format. Note the map displays a circle to show you what step of the route you are on.*

Public Transit Directions

Tap the Bus icon to select the public transit option. In the blue Directions bar, you'll see the estimated time it will take to get there. If traffic data is available, the estimated journey time will adjust accordingly.

Tap the Clock icon to display a pop-up list of departure times and schedules (see Figure 12–28). Tap Depart to choose a date and time. The depart field defaults to the current date and time unless you change it. Below the depart time, you'll see a list of alternate schedules. Select one, and then tap the Done button.

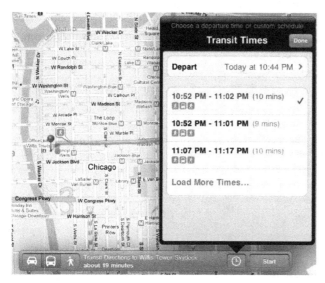

Figure 12–28. *The Directions bar shows public transit routes. The Clock icon allows you to select between different transit schedules.*

To navigate through the directions step by step, tap the blue Start button. The Directions bar will change to the one shown in Figure 12–29. Tap the icon of the three dots with lines trailing after them to see the directions displayed in a list format. Tap any step in the list to be taken to that part of the route on the map. To return to the Directions bar, tap the blue icon in the top-left corner of the Directions List window.

Figure 12–29. *Tap the left arrow or right arrow icon to move through the public transit route step by step.*

If you'd like to navigate through the directions step by step in the map, tap the right arrow icon on the bar. Each subsequent tap will bring you forward one step in the route. To move back a step, tap the left arrow icon.

> **NOTE:** We've mentioned it before, but unfortunately you can't bookmark routes. That's a pity because it would be nice to be able to quickly pull up traffic conditions on your favorite routes. Ideally Apple will add this feature in the future.

Traffic

The Maps app can display traffic conditions that help you when planning an immediate journey. To turn on traffic conditions, tap or tap and drag the page curl at the bottom of the Maps screen and switch Traffic to On (see Figure 12–6). Back on the map, you'll notice that green, yellow, and red lines have appeared over some of the roads (see Figure 12–30).

Just how on Earth does the Maps app know what the current traffic conditions are? Most major U.S. cities have sensors embedded in the highways and major roads. These sensors feed data back, in real time, to the Department of Transportation (DOT). The DOT uses this information to update digital traffic signs that report local traffic conditions (such as those bright Broadway-like signs that hang from overpasses on major metro highways that tell you how long it will take to get to a certain exit). The DOT also shares this data, which Google collects and uses to display near real-time traffic maps.

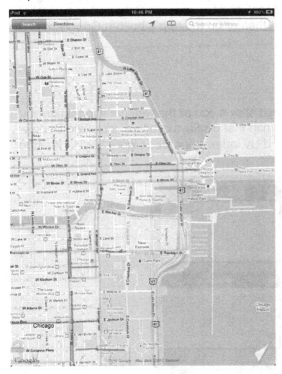

Figure 12–30. *Traffic overlays on the map*

Green lines indicate traffic is flowing at least 50 mph. Yellow lines mean that traffic is flowing between 25 and 50 mph. Red highways mean that traffic is moving below 25 mph. A gray route indicates that traffic data is not available for that street or highway.

The traffic feature is limited to certain regions, mostly major metropolitan areas in the United States, France, Britain, Australia, and Canada; however, new cities and countries are frequently added. If you don't see traffic conditions, try zooming out on the map. If you still don't see any, they aren't available in your area yet.

Maps in Other Apps

You aren't limited to using the Maps app only if you want to see or use maps on the iPad. Several other iPad apps allow you to navigate and search their own maps, as well as use maps for other things. Here are just a few.

Flixster

Flixster is a popular iPad app that allows you to look up movies in your area. Among its many features, the app shows you a list of theaters near you—based on your current location—and shows you the location of the theater on the app's built-in Google map. It is free in the App Store.

The Weather Channel

The Weather Channel app is a versatile app that shows you all the weather information you could dream of. It also uses a built-in Google map that displays overlays, including Doppler Radar, cloud coverage, temperatures, rain, and UV index maps (see Figure 12–31). It's free in the App Store.

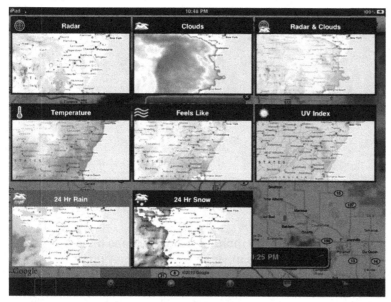

Figure 12–31. *The Weather Channel app's map overlays*

Ndrive US HD

Ndrive is a powerful navigation app for the iPad. It uses its own built-in mapping software and stores map data on your iPad, so you can use it without an Internet connection. You can use the app to plan routes, get step-by-step directions, and locate more than 1.5 million points of interest. It's $4.99 in the App Store.

UpNext 3D Cities

UpNext gives you maps of New York City, Washington D.C., and San Francisco, among others, in 3D. Swipe and zoom on the 3D maps, and touch a building to find out what businesses are inside (see Figure 12–32). It's an amazing app and shows you where the future of personal mapping apps is going. It's free in the App Store.

Figure 12–32. *Touchable 3D buildings in UpNext 3D Cities*

Find a Lost iPad

Have you lost your iPad? Don't worry! Apple has created a free app called Find My iPhone. Yes, it says "iPhone," but it works for iPads and iPod touches, as well. Using this app, you can locate all your iDevices from any iPhone, iPad, or iPod touch, or by logging into your iCloud account at www.icloud.com.

Before you can find a lost iPad, you need to make sure you've installed and set up the Find My iPhone app on the device. Therefore, it's best to do that as soon as you get your iPad. Once you've set up Find My iPhone to work with your iPad and other iOS devices, launch the app and sign in. You'll then be presented with the screen shown in Figure 12–33.

Figure 12–33. *The Find My iPhone app shows you where your iPad and other iOS devices are at any given time.*

From the Devices button in the top-left corner, you can choose what iOS device you want to see the location of. Select a device, and it will be located on the map. An iPad will be represented by a tiny iPad icon. Tap the icon to see the name of the device, and then tap the blue Info button to display a pop-up window that shows you the various actions you can perform with the device (Figure 12–33):

> *Play Sound or Send Message*: This lets you display a text message on your iPad or play a sound at full volume for two minutes (even if the iPad is muted). The sound feature is great if you don't know where in the house you have left your iPad or iPhone.

> *Remote Lock*: Use this to set up a remote passcode lock on your device or initiate your current passcode lock. This will keep anyone out of the device who doesn't know the passcode.

> *Remote Wipe*: This is a worst-case scenario feature. If your iPad has been stolen and you don't want to play detective and track it to the perpetrator's house, you can remote wipe your iPad. Remote wiping your iPad will permanently erase all your personal data on it, ensuring that whoever has or finds your iPad can't commit identity theft against you.

Find a Friend

Your iPad is so amazing that not only can it help you find other iOS devices and Macs you own, it can help you find friends as well! Well, not "find friends" as in make new ones, but it can help you find the friends you already know. It does this through an app (and iCloud service) called Find My Friends (Figure 12–34).

Figure 12–34. *The Find My Friends icon*

Using Find My Friends, you can instantly see the location of any of your friends who have iPhones, iPod touches, or iPads. That is, you can see where they are as long as they've given you permission. The Find My Friends app allows you to also share your location. It's a great way to see where you are in location to your friends. Perhaps you're out shopping and you're thinking of grabbing a coffee. Just open Find My Friends and looks for any buddies that are near you to meet up for a quick drink.

As you can see in Figure 12–35, all your friends who have allowed you to know their location show up in a list. Tap the friend's name to get the address of where they are and also view their location on a map.

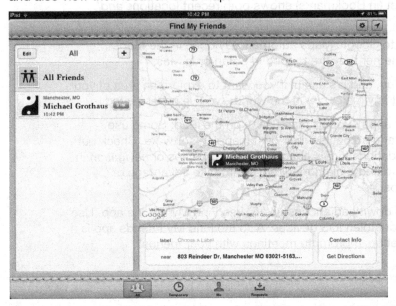

Figure 12–35. *The Find My Friends app shows you a list of the locations of all your friends.*

And for those of you concerned about privacy know that Apple has built in a great many privacy options. For instance, you can choose to share your location for only a certain period, such as three hours; or a certain time of day, such as from noon to 5 p.m. You can also revoke all location invitations at any time, which will disable any of your friends from following you.

The Find My Friends app is a great new social networking app that's a free download in the App Store. The only requirement is that you have a free iCloud account. Get one at www.icloud.com.

Summary

The Maps app puts the world in your hands. With it, you can find directions to your favorite pizza joint, get an instant fix on your current location, or check out what the tops of the Pyramids of Giza look like without leaving your living room. You've learned how to use maps to find public transport times and routes, to get current traffic conditions, or just to virtually stroll down the street of a neighborhood you are thinking of moving to. Here are some tips to take away with you:

- When a person or business is in your contacts list, save yourself some time. Don't type in the entire address, but instead enter a few letters of the name and select the contact.

- Tap individual items on the directions list to jump to that part of your route.

- The Recents list (in Bookmarks) shows both recent locations *and* recent directions.

- URLs that link to Google Maps automatically open in the Maps application, whether they are tapped in Safari or in Mail.

- Street view is fun, and it's useful if you want to explore an area of your city—or almost any major city in the world—you've never visited.

- Plenty of other apps support map usage on the iPad. Some use Google Maps, and some use their own mapping software. Check out the recommendations in this chapter, or search *maps* or *navigation* in the App Store to find a plethora of apps that take advantage of interactive maps.

- Don't forget to download and install the free Find My iPhone app. Use it to track lost or stolen iOS devices. Also the Find My Friends app is a great way to set up impromptu meetings with your friends!

Touching Your Digital Photos

With the iPad's Photos application (launched from its icon, shown in Figure 13–1), you can free your photos from your home computer and pass them around the room like you used to do with photos of old. Hand your iPad to your friends, and they can swipe through your photos in their hands without the need to huddle around a desktop computer. In this chapter, you'll discover how to navigate your photo collections, share them with friends and family, use the iPad as a digital picture frame, and even edit your photos right on your iPad.

Figure 13–1. *The Photos app icon*

Getting Photos onto Your iPad

Before you can view your photos on the iPad, you first need to put them on it. There are six ways you can do this: syncing photos from your computer, importing photos from a digital camera directly into the iPad, saving photos from e-mailed messages, saving images found on web pages, adding photos via iCloud's Photo Stream, and taking photos with the iPad's built-in camera. We talk about the various ways you can capture photo's with the iPad's camera in Chapter 15.

Syncing Photos from Your Computer

We discussed syncing photos to your iPad in Chapter 2, but let's touch upon it briefly again. iTunes can synchronize your iPad with pictures stored on your computer. This allows you to bring your photo collection with you and share it using the iPad's unique touch-based interface. Who needs to carry around thick and heavy physical photo albums when you have an iPad with its thin body and vibrant display?

To get started, connect your iPad to your computer, and launch iTunes. Select your iPad from the source list (the blue column on the left side of the iTunes window), and open the Photos tab. Select the "Sync photos" box, and then choose the location of the photos you want to sync. Your choices depend on your operating system.

On the computer, your options will be Adobe Photoshop Elements 3.0 or newer or any folder on your computer, such as My Pictures. On the Mac, your options will be iPhoto 4.0.3 or newer, Aperture 3.0.2 or newer, or any folder on your computer.

After you choose where to sync your photos from, select whether to sync your entire photo collection (a good choice for relatively small libraries) or individual albums (better for large libraries that might not fit on the iPad's limited storage space). In the latter case, pick only those albums you want to copy to your iPad.

If you are using a Mac and iPhoto or Aperture, you'll have the option to sync faces (iPhoto '09 or newer), events (iPhoto '08 or newer), and albums (see Figure 2-38). Faces are smart photo albums that contain all the photos that have a selected individual's face in them. It does this by using iPhoto's built-in facial recognition software. Events are another type of smart album that group photos together that were taken on the same day. This helps eliminate clutter and keeps your photo library organized.

To finish, click Apply to save your changes, and then sync.

Importing Photos from a Digital Camera or iPhone

You can also import photos to your iPad directly from any camera that can connect via USB or that uses a SD card. To do this, you will need to purchase the iPad Camera Connection Kit ($29 at the Apple Store). The kit includes two adapters—one for connecting a camera through a USB 2.0 cable and the other for reading SD memory cards (see Figure 13–2).

The iPad supports standard photo formats, including JPEG, GIF, TIFF, PNG, and RAW. You can connect most cameras to your iPad through the USB adapter in the iPad Camera Connection Kit, including an iPhone so that you can do direct iPhone to iPad photo transfers. You can even connect the popular line of Flip cameras to the iPad, but because of USB power issues, you will need to connect the Flip camera to an external power source before you connect it via USB to your iPad.

You can also import video clips taken by your camera through the iPad Camera Connection Kit if those video clips are in one of the video formats the iPad supports.

Supported iPad video formats are M4V, MP4, MOV, MPEG-4, and H.264. The iPad does not support many popular video formats such as AVI and WMV, but there are countless applications that let you convert AVI and WMV files to iPad-compatible formats. Google *WMV to iPad* or *AVI to iPad* to see all the software that offers conversion capabilities.

Figure 13–2. *The iPad Camera Connection Kit features a USB adapter and an SD card reader.*

To import photos, plug either the USB adapter or the SD card adapter into the iPad. When using the USB adapter, connect your digital camera to it using the USB cable the camera came with, and switch the camera into transfer mode (see your camera's manual for details). To import photos from your iPhone's camera, plug the iPhone into the USB adapter using the iPhone's Dock Connector to USB Cable. Make sure the iPhone is turned on. When importing using the SD card adapter, plug the adapter into the iPad, and insert the SD card into it.

Once your camera or SD card is attached, unlock your iPad by sliding the unlock bar on the bottom of the lock screen. The Photos application automatically appears, displaying the photos available for importing. You now have two options: import all the photos by tapping the Import All button (see Figure 13–3) or import only a selection of photos.

Figure 13-3. *Import all your photographs by tapping the Import All button at the bottom of the screen.*

To import selected photos, tap each photo you want to include. A check mark appears on it (see Figure 13-4). When you are done selecting photos, tap Import and select Import Selected.

Figure 13-4. *Importing some of your photographs*

After a successful import, the iPad prompts you to decide whether to keep or delete the photos you imported from the device you imported them from (see Figure 13-5).

Figure 13–5. *Choose to save or delete the imported photos on the external device.*

Newly imported photos appear in an album called Last Import (see Figure 13–6) and in a new event, which contains the last imported photos. After you have imported photos more than one time, you'll also see an album called All Imported.

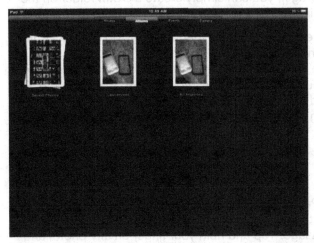

Figure 13–6. *Photos imported directly to the iPad from a digital camera or SD card will show up in the Last Import album.*

Once you have transferred your photos, you can disconnect the camera connection adapter from the iPad.

To export transferred photos from the iPad back to your computer, connect your iPad and open a photo application such as iPhoto or Image Capture on a Mac or Adobe Elements on a Windows computer.

Using a USB Thumb Drive to Transfer Photos to the iPad

You may find yourself in a situation where you quickly want to add some photos from your computer to the iPad. You want to avoid an entire synchronization procedure. Wouldn't it be great if you could quickly import images to the iPad using a USB thumb drive?

Good news! You can *unofficially* use the iPad Camera Connection Kit to attach some types of USB thumb drives for quick and easy transfer of photos from your computer to the iPad. To do this, you have to trick your iPad into thinking your thumb drive is a camera.

DCIM (Digital Camera Images) is a universal standard used by camera manufacturers to organize photos on your camera by a defined file system and structure including the file naming specification, file formats, and metadata information. Before the iPad connects to your camera or SD card, it looks for a DCIM folder on the device. The presence of this folder from the folder.

A camera's SD card automatically creates a folder labeled DCIM when you take the first picture. Since there's not much difference between an SD card and a USB thumb drive (both are just forms of solid-state storage), you can simply create a DCIM folder on the thumb drive to trick your iPad into thinking it's a camera.

The easiest way to do this is to create a new folder on your desktop and name it DCIM. Drag that folder to the USB thumb drive. Once the folder is on the thumb drive, find and drag whatever photos you want from your computer into the DCIM folder on your thumb drive. After the photos are copied, plug the thumb drive into the USB adapter in the iPad Camera Connection Kit, and the iPad will see the photos in the DCIM folder and think it's talking to a camera, thus allowing you to import those pictures from the thumb drive into the iPad Photos app.

Saving Photos from Mail and Safari

You can also store photos on your iPad without importing them from your computer or camera. If someone e-mails a photo to you, in the iPad's Mail app you'll see the photos appear in the body of the e-mail message. Tap and hold your finger on any photo, and you'll see a pop-up appear that allows you to save that one photo or all the photos contained in the e-mail (see Figure 13–7). The photo or photos you've selected to save will appear in an album labeled Saved Photos in the iPad's Photos app.

Similarly, in the iPad's Safari web browser, you can tap and hold your finger on any photo in a web page and select the Save Image button from the pop-up that appears (see Figure 13–7). That photo will be saved to a Saved Photos album in the iPad's Photos app.

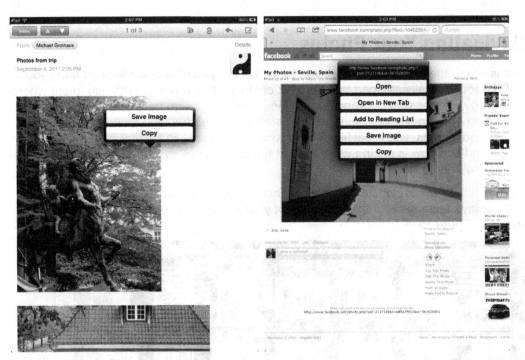

Figure 13–7. *Saving photos from an e-mail (left) or a web page (right)*

> **NOTE:** Many third-party apps (such as web browsers and magazines) also allow you to save images to your iPad. Some apps may have their own, unique way of saving images, but most should be fairly similar to the way you save images in Mail or Safari.

Photo Stream

Alongside iOS 5 Apple introduced a new cloud-based service called iCloud. iCloud seamlessly syncs all your documents, e-mails, and photos across all of your devices (Mac, PC, iPads, iPhones, and iPod touches).

The photo syncing portion of iCloud is called Photo Stream. If you have a free iCloud account, the 1,000 most recent photos and videos you take on your iPad will automatically be pushed to your other iOS devices and Macs and PCs.

Photo Stream relies on a Wi-Fi connection, but once you have that, the second you take a photo on your iPad, it will also appear in your iPhoto library on your Macs, in your Pictures libraries on your PCs, and in the Photos app of every iOS device you own. Photo Stream is a pretty cool way to share all your pictures with all your devices simultaneously.

iCloud and all its benefits are free. To set up an account go to www.icloud.com. You can turn on Photo Stream by navigating to **Settings ➤ Photos**.

Navigating Your Photos

This is where the fun begins. When you touch your digital photos for the first time, you feel like you've finally stepped into the 21st century—that promised utopian future where technology merges with our fondest memories and we can go back and relive and explore them like never before. When you start pinching, dragging, and expanding your photos and albums, you'll feel like a child who has just spread his first bag of marbles on the ground and now is staring wide-eyed at the array of colors, shapes and sizes that he can control before him.

To launch the Photos app, tap its icon on the Home screen. Once launched, the Photos app displays thumbnails of the beginning of your photos in your Photos library, as shown in Figure 13–8.

Figure 13–8. *The Photos app*

Running along the top of the app, right above the thumbnail photos, you'll see the menu bar (see Figure 13–9). This bar displays tabs that allow you to switch between the different ways your photos are organized. To select a view, tap its tab in the menu bar. Note that you may not see all the tabs, depending on how you've synced your photos. For instance, those who sync only a single album won't see Events. Similarly, those whose photos lack geotag data won't see Places.

Figure 13–9. *There are different ways your photos are organized on the iPad.*

Photos: This is the first view you see when you launch the Photos app for the first time. Subsequent launches will display what was active the last time the app was run (the Places tab, for example). On the Photos tab (see Figure 13–8), your pictures aren't grouped into any kind of albums at all. They are displayed in a sequential order by date taken. If you have lots of photos synced on your iPad, scrolling through this list can take quite a while.

Albums: This view displays your photos in their albums as you've arranged them on your computer (see Figure 13–10). You will also see a Saved Photos album if you've saved images from the Web or that you've received in an e-mail on your iPad. Also, as mentioned earlier, if you've imported photos directly to the iPad from a digital camera, you will see them in a Last Import album.

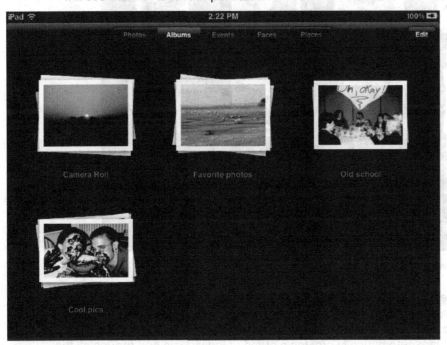

Figure 13–10. *Albums view*

> **NOTE:** If you are using iCloud's Photo Stream feature, you'll see another tab titled Photo Stream. Any photo you take with your iPad will appear here and be pushed to your other iOS devices and Macs and PCs automatically. Also, photos taken on your other iOS devices will automatically be pushed to your iPad and show up on the Photo Stream tab.

Events: This view displays your photos in Events (see Figure 13–11). Events are used in Aperture 2 and iPhoto '08 and newer as a way to automatically arrange your photos according to the date they were taken. This helps people automatically keep large photo libraries in easy-to-navigate shape. The Events tab is a Mac-only feature. You will not see this tab if you are using a Windows computer to sync your iPad.

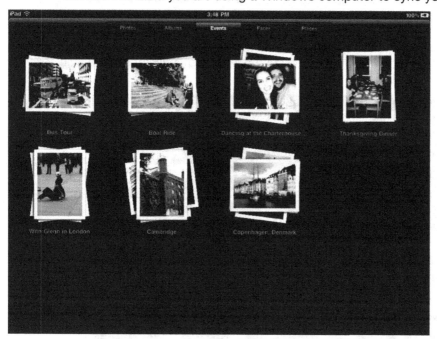

Figure 13–11. *Events view*

Faces: This view displays your photos grouped into an individual's "face" album (see Figure 13–12). If you are using iPhoto '09 or Aperture 3 on a Mac, the programs have facial recognition software built in. The Mac software automatically creates albums of individuals and groups all the photos they appear in. It's an amazingly fun way to see all the photos a certain friend or family member is in. Faces also works to some extent on cats and dogs. You will not see this tab if you are using a Windows computer to sync your iPad with; Faces is a Mac-only feature.

Figure 13–12. *Faces view*

Places: Many cameras today feature *geotagging*, which codes the photo with the location coordinates where it was taken. What the Places tab does is take your photo's coordinates and display them on a Google map (see Figure 13–13). This is arguably the coolest feature of Photos on iPad because it lets you navigate your photos on a map that you can view from a global level to a street level. It's an especially cool feature for travelers: you can see at a glance where you have been and just how much of the world is left to explore.

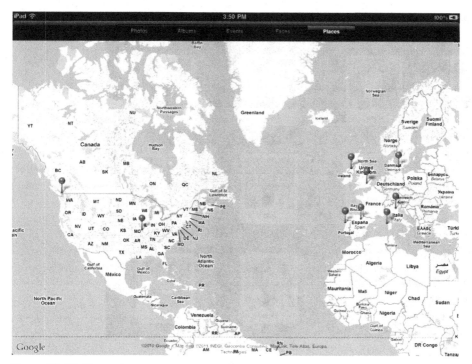

Figure 13–13. *Places view*

Red pins appear on the map that signify the geographic location of
your photos. You can pinch and zoom on the map to get closer. As
you do, you may see more pins appear on the map (see Figure 13–14).

Figure 13-14. *Note that more pins appear as you zoom in to an area of the map signifying greater accuracy of the photo's coordinates.*

Tap a pin to see an album pop-up appear (see Figure 13–15). You can then explore all the photos that were taken in that location. Places requires an Internet connection to display the Google map.

Figure 13–15. *Tap a pin to see an album thumbnail of every photo that was taken at that location.*

As you can now see, the iPad's Photos app organizes your photos into five views for easy navigation. It is important to note that you may not see all the views on your iPad. The view categories you see depend on whether you are using a Mac or Windows computer, whether you have chosen to sync albums from each category view, and whether your photos are tagged with geocoordinates.

As long as you have one photo on your iPad, you'll always see the Photos tab. Most likely you will see the Albums tab too, especially if you've imported photos from a digital camera onto the iPad (a Last Import album is automatically created) or if you've saved an image you received in an e-mail or saw on the Web (a Saved Photos album is automatically created). To see other albums, events, or faces, you'll need to sync them from your computer. You don't need to do anything to sync Places; its tab will appear automatically if you have any photos tagged with geocoordinates.

Touching and Viewing Your Albums and Photos

Now that you know how to navigate your photo collections, you'll learn how to touch and view them. Remember all the gestures covered in Chapter 4? When viewing a collection of albums or a single image full-screen, the iPad allows you to interact with that album or photo using a number of these gestures.

Touching and Viewing Albums

For this section, an *album* will refer to a regular album, an event, or a faces album, since interacting with these are all the same. As you can see in Figure 13–11, there are a series of event albums. An album appears as a pile of some of the photos that are contained in the album. To open the album, you have two options to expand, or open, the photo album:

■ Tap the album once to cause the photos in it to spread out and expand.

■ Starting with two fingers together on an album, slowly spread them apart in a reverse-pinch motion, and you'll see the album's photos start to spread out (see Figure 13–16). Remove your fingers to expand the album fully.

Figure 13–16. *An album being expanded by a reverse pinch*

You'll notice the menu bar at the top of the screen has changed once you are in an album (see Figure 13–17). It now displays the name of the album, a back button on the left that takes you to the category view you were previously in, a Slideshow button, and a Share button, which allows you to present your photos and share them with others (we'll talk about the Slideshow and Share buttons a little later).

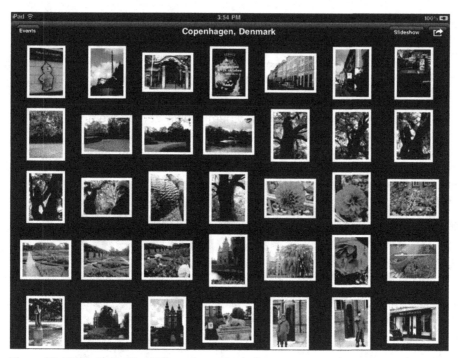

Figure 13–17. *Photos inside an album*

To exit the album, tap the back button (which will be named after the category the album is in; in Figure 13–17, the album *Copenhagen, Denmark* is contained in the Events category, so *Events* is the name of the back button in this example) or pinch the photos of the album together. They will collapse on each other, and you'll find yourself back on the album screen.

While on the Places tab, the red pins on the map act as albums containing all the photos taken there. Tap the pin to be presented with an album thumbnail (see Figure 13–15); then tap the thumbnail, or reverse-pinch it, to expand the photos of that location onto the screen (see Figure 13–18).

Figure 13–18. *Expanding a series of photos taken in the same location in Places view*

Touching and Viewing Photos

When in an album, you will see thumbnails of the photos it contains (see Figure 13–17). To view a photo full-screen, you have two options to expand, or open, the photo:

- Tap the photo once to cause the photo to fill the screen.

- Starting with two fingers together on a photo, slowly spread them apart in a reverse-pinch motion, and you'll see the photo start to grow. Remove your fingers to expand the photo fully to fill the screen.

Once you display a photo full-screen, you have several ways to interact with it:

- Pinch to zoom into and out of the photo.

- Double-tap to zoom into the photo. Double-tap again to zoom out.

- When your image is displayed at the normal zoomed-out size, swipe to the left or right to move to the previous or next image in the album. When zoomed into an image, dragging the photo pans across it.

Tap any image once to open the image overlay, as shown in Figure 13–19. The image overlay features a menu bar at the top of the screen and a scrubber bar at the bottom.

Figure 13–19. *Viewing a photo. Note the image overlay bars.*

The image overlay menu bar at the top of the screen shows you the number of the selected image out of the total number of images in the album, the back button to return to the album, the Edit button, a Slideshow button, and a Share button. If you're in range of a Wi-Fi network that also has an Apple TV and you're running iOS 4.3 or newer on your iPad, you'll see the AirPlay button here as well (discussed in the next section). Slide your finger across the photo thumbnails in the scrubber bar at the bottom of the screen to quickly scan through your images (see Figure 13–20).

While viewing a photo in the Saved Photos album, you'll notice a garbage pail icon next to the Share button. This garbage pail icon shows up only in the menu bar of images in the Saved Photos album. Tapping this button will delete the selected photo. We talk more about deleting photos later in this chapter.

Figure 13–20. *The scrubber bar*

While viewing individual photos, flip your iPad onto its side to have your photo reorient itself. If the photo was shot using landscape orientation, it fits itself to the wider view.

You can tap a full-screen image once with two fingers to return to album view.

Viewing Your Photos over AirPlay

New to iOS 4.3 and newer, AirPlay support allows you to send music, photos, and videos wirelessly to Apple-supported devices. In the case of images, that is limited to Apple's newly updated Apple TV media presentation device and to some custom third-party applications like Erica Sadun's Banana TV for OS X.

The AirPlay icon, which you can see toward the right in Figure 13–21, looks like an outline of a rectangle with an upward-pointing triangle within it. When tapped, it presents a list of available receivers. The TV icon to the left of each name indicates that the receiver can receive photos and videos. When you tap any item other than the first, which corresponds to your iPad, the photo will wirelessly echo out to the selected device and display there, as will any photos that you slide to as you navigate through your album.

To disable AirPlay echoing, select the first iPad option. Once checked, AirPlay transmission ceases.

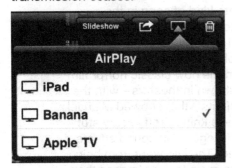

Figure 13–21. *The AirPlay selection menu lets you redirect photos from your iPad to an Apple TV or third-party application running on a computer.*

Viewing Your Photos as a Slideshow

When viewing the contents of any album or a single image in any album, you'll see the Slideshow and Share buttons in the upper-right corner of the screen (see Figure 13–22). As the name suggests, the Slideshow button displays the contents of a photo album, one image after another. We'll discuss the Share button after the Slideshow button.

Figure 13–22. *The Slideshow and Share buttons display in the right of the menu bar when viewing a single photo or the contents of any album.*

Slideshows are an awesome way to share your photos with your friends and family. Remember, however, that our images are associated with our personal memories, so they are always going to be more pleasant for us to watch than for others. All you have to do is remember a time you were stuck looking at someone else's photos and the seconds ticked by as if they were hours. To keep slideshows exciting for your viewers, keep a few things in mind:

Shorter is better: The average shot (a clip of video displayed between cutting away to another shot) in a movie or TV show is less than two seconds nowadays. Back in the 1950s, the average shot was 30 seconds long. Watch an episode of *Friends* and then an episode of *I Love Lucy*, and you'll see exactly what we mean. *Lucy* seems to trudge along so slowly by today's standards. As the world—and media—got faster, our attention spans shrunk. This applies to viewing still images too. People can take in a lot from an image in just two or three seconds. If they are forced to look at an image any longer, they start to get bored. Keep the time a single image is displayed short. Also, keep the entire length of the slideshow short. When you watch a movie trailer in the cinema, its time is exactly 2 minutes and 20 seconds, which is considered a perfect length to whet the appetite, show people the best shots, and leave them feeling fulfilled but not exhausted.

Music always helps: Playing the appropriate kind of song in the background of a slideshow really adds a lot of ambience and power to a slideshow. Music is a powerful tool for conveying the emotion and sense of place and situation. In film school, one of the authors had an editing class where we watched clips from the now classic horror film *Halloween*. We watched a clip, as it was shown in theaters—with the soundtrack score, dialogue, and sound effects—that showed Michael Myers chasing his victim with a big butcher's knife. Pretty scary stuff. Then we watched the same clip with the dialogue and sound effects only—the soundtrack's score was removed. The clip went from being scary to being almost comical. Music adds more to your images than you realize.

Transitions help too: A transition is the effect that occurs when moving from one image to the next. It adds some visual flair to the change of images. Photos' slideshows allow you to choose between five transitions. Use them as eye candy to keep your audience entertained.

Use your TV: If you are having a party, a great way to show off your photos without wrangling up all your guests and forcing them to sit and watch is to project your slideshow on a TV and set it to repeat. That way, your slideshow is constantly playing in the background, and your guests can continue to catch glimpses of it as they mingle. Images on slideshows playing in the background are great conversation starters and allow you to play much longer slideshows and display individual images for longer, since you don't have to worry about a captive audience. If you are going to play your slideshows in the background, you can choose to show several thousand images for as long as five or ten seconds each; that way, the entire show could run for hours, and it won't get boring or tedious.

To begin a slideshow, tap the Slideshow button. A drop-down menu appears that presents several slideshow options (see Figure 13–23). At the top, if you have an Apple TV, you'll find the same AirPlay receiver list you saw in Figure 13–21. Starting with iOS 4.3, the iPad allows you to play slideshows wirelessly to Apple TV and other AirPlay receivers. This AirPlay option is in addition to your ability display slideshows on-screen or to use a connected cable via the HDMI, VGA, or other video adapters to mirror the iPad to a TV screen. These branded adapters are available from the Apple Store, starting at $29.

Figure 13–23. *The Slideshow Options drop-down menu*

Below the AirPlay receiver list are the following options:

> *Transitions*: Transitions provide a visual effect when moving between images. Available transitions depend on the capabilities of the selected output device. The onboard transitions include wipes, ripples, and dissolve among other options. Apple TV adds a number of slick extras including Ken Burns, Sliding Panels, Origami, Reflections, and more.

> *Play Music*: When switched to On, this option will play music in the background while the slideshow runs.

> *Music*: Tap this button to navigate through all the songs in your iPad's music library. Once you find the song you want, tap it to select it.

> *Start Slideshow*: Tap this button to start the slideshow. The image overlays disappear, and the slideshow plays, whether directly on-screen for local slideshows or on a remote device with AirPlay. With AirPlay, your screen turns black, and a message appears telling you that "This slideshow is now playing" via AirPlay. To stop the slideshow at any time, touch the screen. This stops the slideshow and places you in the full-screen photo display. To start the slideshow again, tap the Slideshow button and tap Start Slideshow.

Slideshows display each slide for a set period of time, which you can set. As mentioned, you can export your slideshow to a TV screen by purchasing a special cable from Apple that connects your iPad to your TV. Apple offers a number of different cables, which are discussed in Chapter 7.

To customize how your iPad displays its slideshows, go to your Home screen, and navigate to **Settings ➤ Photos**. As shown in Figure 13–24, this settings screen allows you to specify exactly how you want your slideshows to display:

Figure 13–24. *The Slideshow settings*

> *Play Each Slide For*: Here, you can set the slide duration. Your choices are 2 seconds, 3 seconds (the default, which works really well for most people), 5 seconds, 10 seconds (which starts to get boring fast), and 20 seconds (which is probably recognized officially by Amnesty International as torture for most humans; seriously, don't do this to your friends and family).
>
> *Repeat*: Set this to On to make your slideshow loop.
>
> *Shuffle*: Show your pictures in a random order by switching Shuffle from Off to On. When Shuffle is disabled, your pictures display in album order.

Sharing Your Photos

You have a number of ways to share photos you have on your iPad. To access all the ways you can share your photos, bring up a photo full-screen and tap the Share button, which looks like an arrow breaking free from a small box. You'll be presented with a drop-down menu of sharing options (see Figure 13–25):

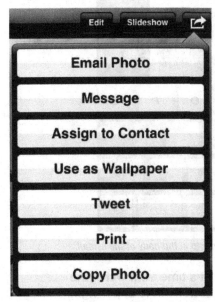

Figure 13–25. *The Sharing drop-down menu*

Email Photo: Tap this to see an e-mail compose window appear on the screen. You'll notice the photo has been copied into the body of the e-mail already (see Figure 13–26). Enter the recipient's e-mail address, a subject, and body text; then tap Send, and your photo is on its way!

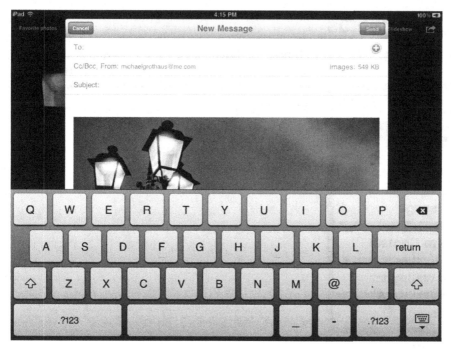

Figure 13–26. *The new message compose screen appears with the photo in the body of the e-mail.*

Alternatively, you can e-mail up to five photos at a time from within the Photos app. While in an album, tap the Share button in the upper-right corner (Figure 13–19) and you'll see the album menu renamed to Select Photos. Tap up to five photos that you want to send, and then tap the new Share button in the upper-left corner (see Figure 13–27). From the drop-down menu that appears, tap Email. An e-mail compose window will appear on the screen with the photos in the body of the message. Note that although you are limited to e-mailing five photos at a time from the Photos app, you can actually copy as many as you want and then open the Mail app, compose a new message, and paste them all in the body of the e-mail.

Figure 13–27. *You can e-mail up to five photos at a time from within the Photos app.*

Message: Messages is a new iPad app that lets you send text messages between iPhones, iPads, and iPod touches. You can also attach photos and videos to messages. To send a photo from the Photos app via Messages, tap the Share button, and then tap Message. A window will appear with the photo embedded in the message. You can write a note with it if you want (see Figure 13–28). When you are done composing your Message, tap Send. You can also send multiple photos by following the steps for sending multiple photos by e-mail above and then tapping the Message button in the Share drop-down menu (Figure 13–27).

You can read more about the Messages app in Chapter 11.

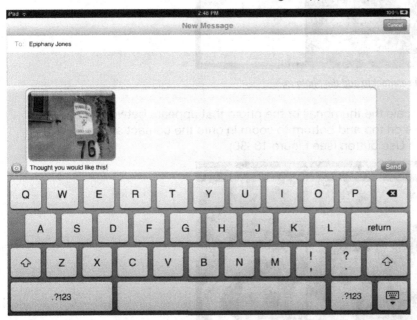

Figure 13–28. *Sending a photo in a message*

Assign to Contact: This option allows you to assign a photo to an address book contact. Tap Assign to Contact, and then select the contact's address book entry from the drop-down menu (see Figure 13–29).

Figure 13–29. *Select the contact to add the photo to.*

Move and scale the thumbnail of the photo that appears between the opaque bars on top and bottom to zoom in onto the contact's face; then tap the Use button (see Figure 13–30).

Figure 13–30. *Move and scale the contact's photo.*

The next time you view the contact in the iPad's Contacts app, the image you selected for them will appear next to their name. This image will sync with their contact information in Address Book and Entourage on a Mac and Outlook on a Windows computer.

Use as Wallpaper: Tap this button to use the selected image as wallpaper on your iPad. From the menu bar (see Figure 13–31), you'll be able to select whether you want to use the image for the iPad's lock screen, the Home screen, or both. This isn't the only way to set your iPad's wallpaper options. We'll talk about the other way in a bit.

Figure 13–31. *The wallpaper menu bar options let you select which screen you want to use the photo as wallpaper for.*

Tweet: Tapping Tweet will open a Twitter upload screen. This allows you to Tweet your picture directly to your Twitter account. You can also add a short message and your current location to the photo (see Figure 13–32).

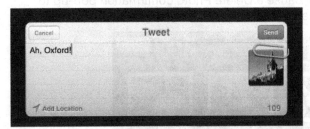

Figure 13–32. *Tweeting a picture*

Print: This allows you to print your photo to an AirPrint-compatible printer. Tap Print and then select the printer you want to print to and the number of copies you want to print. We talk about AirPrint and printing from your iPad in Chapter 3.

You can also print multiple photos at a time. When viewing an album, tap the Share button. You'll see the album menu renamed as Select Photos. Tap as many photos as you want to print. A check mark will appear on each selected photo (see Figure 13–27). After you have selected all your photos, tap the Print button in the upper-left corner and then select the printer you want to print to and the number of copies of each photo you want to print.

Copy Photo: Tap Copy Photo to copy the image. This saves the image to your clipboard for use in pasting into other things (such as an e-mail or document) later.

You can also copy multiple photos at a time. When viewing an album, tap the Share button. You'll see the album menu renamed as Select Photos. Tap as many photos as you want to copy. A check mark will appear on each selected photo (see Figure 13–28). After you have selected all your photos, tap the Copy button in the upper-left corner. These photos can then be batch copied into an e-mail or other applications.

Deleting Your Photos

Apple made it so you can only delete photos on your iPad that are part of the Camera Roll album. This album contains any photos you have saved from the Web or an e-mail on the iPad plus photos and videos taken with the iPad 2's camera. Apple disabled deletion of photos from your other albums synced to your iPad because it didn't want users accidentally deleting photos they had stored on their computer.

To delete the photos, navigate to your Camera Roll album and tap the Share button. Tap the photos you want to delete, and a check mark will appear on them; then tap the red Delete button (see Figure 13–33). Alternatively, while displaying a photo full-screen in your Saved Photos album, you'll notice a trash can icon next to the Share button (see Figure 13–34). Tapping this button will cause a Delete Photo confirmation pop-up to appear. Tap Delete Photo to delete the selected photo from your iPad.

Figure 13–33. *You can delete photos on the iPad only from the Saved Photos album.*

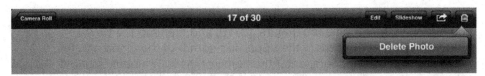

Figure 13–34. *The trash can icon in the upper-right corner of a photo in the Saved Photos album*

To delete other photos on your iPad, you must delete them on your computer first and then resync the iPad.

Managing Photo Albums

As previously discussed, the Albums tab (Figure 13–10) contains all the photo albums on your iPad. However, you aren't limited to just the albums you've imported from your computer. You can create new albums right on your iPad and add photos on your iPad to albums other than the ones in which they currently reside. This is handy if you want to manually manage your photo albums on your iPad and not your computer.

> *To add photos to an existing album*: Go into a photo album or event and tap the Share button. Tap all the photos that you want to move to an existing album. A check mark will appear on each selected photo (see Figure 13–35). After you have selected all your photos, tap the Add To button in the upper-right corner of the screen. The pop-up menu shown in Figure 13–35 will appear.

Figure 13–35. *Adding photos to new or existing albums*

> To add photos to an existing album, tap Add to Existing Album, and then choose the album you want to add your photos to from the album viewer that appears on the screen.
>
> *To create a new album*: You can create entirely new albums on your iPad. To do so, tap the Add to New Album button that appears beneath the Add To button, and then enter the name of the new album in the dialog box that appears. The new album will then show up in your album viewer.

You can also create a new album directly in the Albums tab. Tap the Edit button in the Albums tab (Figure 13–10) and then tap the New Album button that appears in the upper-left corner of the menu bar. In the dialog box that appears, enter the name of the new album. A photo selection screen will appear (Figure 13–36). Tap the photos you want to add, and then tap the Done button.

Figure 13–36. *Adding photos to a new album*

To delete an album you've created: On the Albums tab, tap the Edit button in the Album tab, and then tap the *X*s that appear next to each album you've created on the iPad (Figure 13–37). Confirm that you want to delete the album in the pop-up notification that appears. The photos from any deleted albums are returned to their original locations. Note that you cannot delete albums that were not created on your iPad. Tap the Done button when you are finished deleting albums.

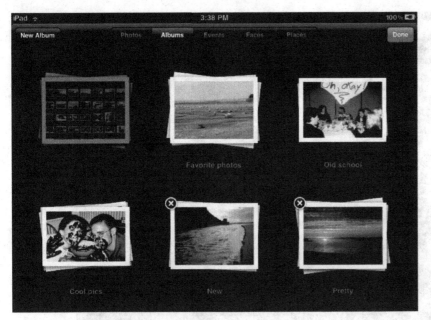

Figure 13–37. *Deleting albums on the iPad*

NOTE: Did you know you can take screen shots of your iPad? A *screen shot*, or a *screen capture*, is an image taken of whatever appears on the iPad's screen at the moment you are taking it. To take a screen shot, press and hold the power button on the iPad, and then press and release the Home button while still holding the power button. The iPad's screen will flash white, and you'll hear a shutter-click sound effect. Once you hear the sound, you can let go of the power button. The captured screen shot will appear in the Saved Photos album. You can use screen shots to save images of entire web pages or show off that high score in a video game. Most of the images in this book were taken using the iPad's screen capture function.

Picture Framing

On the iPad's lock screen (the screen that appears when you turn on your iPad or wake it from sleep), to the right of the Slide to Unlock bar, you'll notice there is a small icon of a flower inside a box (see Figure 13–38). This is the Picture Frame button. Tap this to turn your iPad into an awesome digital picture frame. The picture frame turns your iPad into an interactive piece of furniture in your office or living room and is a great way to still "use" the iPad while you're doing other things. You can buy one of the many stands that supports the iPad to make best use of the Picture Frame feature.

Figure 13–38. *The iPad's lock screen with Picture Frame button in the lower right*

To start the picture frame, lock the iPad by briefly pressing the power button. Press the power button or Home button on the iPad again to be taken to the lock screen. Tap the Picture Frame button to enter picture frame mode. The icon will change to a blue color, and the screen will fill with a photo, displaying one after the next. To pause the slideshow, tap the screen. The current image will pause in the background as the lock screen fades into view. To disable the picture frame, tap the blue picture frame icon, and you will return to the lock screen with its selected wallpaper displayed.

You have several options for the Picture Frame feature, described next, which can be configured from within the iPad's Settings app. Navigate to your iPad Home screen, and tap the Settings icon. Select Picture Frame (see Figure 13–39).

Figure 13-39. *Picture Frame settings*

Transition: Choose between Dissolve and Origami to flow from one photo to the next.

Show Each Slide For: Choose from 2, 3, 5, 10, or 20 seconds.

Zoom in on Faces: When this is set to On, photos that display in the picture frame will focus on faces in the picture. It knows which faces you like because of the Faces feature built into the Photos app. If more than one face is in a picture, it will choose one at random to focus on. Face zooming is only an option when transitions are set to dissolve.

Shuffle: When set to On, your photos will show in a random order.

The Picture Frame feature will display all the photos from your Photos app by default. You can select to show only photos from certain albums, faces, or events by selecting their category and then selecting the one you want to show.

Changing the Wallpaper Without Using the Photos App

We showed you how to set your wallpaper from a photo in the Photos app, but you can also set it from within the iPad's Settings app. To do this, navigate to your iPad Home screen, and tap the Settings icon. Select Brightness & Wallpaper. You'll see two images, one representing your iPad's lock screen and the other its Home screen (see Figure 13–40). The pictures you see on each image show you the wallpaper you have selected for each one currently.

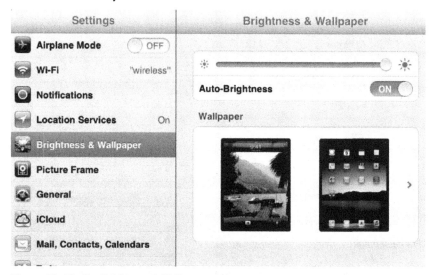

Figure 13–40. *The Brightness & Wallpaper settings*

Tap the images to be taken to the wallpaper selection screen (see Figure 13–41). Here you'll see a list of every album in your Photos app and also a new album labeled Wallpaper.

Figure 13–41. *You can select from Apple's included wallpapers or use any photo you have on your iPad as wallpaper.*

Wallpaper includes images Apple included on the iPad to be used as wallpaper. Select an image from any album, and you'll get a full-screen preview of it. Then tap Set Lock Screen, Set Home Screen, or Set Both to use the image for the background of the lock screen, Home screen, or both the lock screen and Home screen (see Figure 13–31). If you choose to use the image just for, say, the lock screen, you can go back and select another image for the Home screen.

Editing Your Photos

With iOS 5, Apple has introduced photo-editing features to the Photos app. The photo-editing features aren't too advanced, but they do allow you to make some nice adjustments to your photos. Apple has including four editing tools: rotate, enhance, redeye reduction, and cropping. To edit a photo, select a photo from your albums, and then click the Edit button in the top-right corner to enter Edit mode.

Figure 13–42. *Editing a photo. The tools, from left to right: rotate, enhance, redeye reduction, and crop.*

Figure 13–42 shows you what edit mode looks like in the Photos app. Your four editing tools are displayed along the bottom of the screen (close-up, Figure 13–43).

Figure 13–43. *Your editing tools, from left to right: rotate, enhance, redeye reduction, and crop.*

Rotate: Rotating a photo is something almost everyone has done or needs to do. Usually when a photo needs to be rotated it's because you took it in portrait, or vertical, orientation with your camera, but it was imported in the standard landscape, or horizontal, orientation. Tap this button (it looks like a curved arrow) to rotate the photo in 90-degree increments. Click the yellow Save button when finished rotating your photo.

Auto-Enhance: Sometimes you might take a beautifully composed photo but the color may be off, or the photo may appear too light or too dark. When this happens, there's no need to panic! The Photos app has a one-click fix for most photos with ailments such as poor saturation or contrast; it's called the Enhance button, and it works almost like magic. Tap the Enhance button (it looks like a magic wand) to auto-enhance your photo. Enhancing a photo can really bring out details that would normally have remained hidden without doing advanced manual adjustment techniques on it in a dedicated photo editing app. Click the yellow Save button when finished enhancing your photo.

Red-eye reduction: Ah, red-eye. The scourge of photographers everywhere. We're all familiar with red-eye. It's the thing that makes us look like demons in photographs: the red halo that appears in people's eyes that is caused by the makeup of the human eye and the camera's flash. Luckily, most of the cameras on the market today offer built-in red-eye reduction, but the iPad's camera does not. However, if your iPad takes photos where your friends look like they're about to unleash some heat vision, the Photo app's red-eye reduction tool makes it easy to remove their red-eyes.

To eliminate red-eye in your photos, tap the red-eye tool (it looks like a red dot with a line through it). Next, tap each eye of the person (Figure 13–44). Like magic, their red eyes will become natural colors. Click the yellow Apply button when finished.

Figure 13–44. *Reducing red-eye in your photos. In this photo, the left eye has had red-eye reduction applied, while the right eye has not.*

Crop: You can crop your photos to remove unwanted portions of them. To crop a photo, tap the crop button (it looks like a square) and you'll see crop gridlines appear (Figure 13–45). Simply drag the gridlines around until you've selected the portion of the photo you want to crop. Click the yellow Crop button to apply the crop.

Figure 13–45. *Cropping a photo*

You can also constrain the aspect ration of the crop so you'll know the exact size of the
photo once you are done cropping it. To constrain a photo's crop aspect ratio, click the
Constrain button at the bottom of the crop screen (Figure 13–45). The constrain screen
will appear (Figure 13–46).

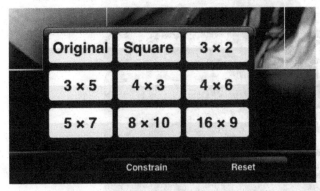

Figure 13–46. *Constraining a crop's aspect ratio*

Tap the desired aspect ratio. That will lock the crop box to that specific ration. You can then drag the constrained crop box around knowing that no matter where you crop, the photo will have the selected ratio. Tap the yellow Crop button when ready to crop your photo, and then tap the yellow Save button to save your cropped photo.

Don't worry if you make a mistake while editing your photos. None of your changes save until you tap the yellow Save button in the top menu bar of the edit screen (Figure 13–47). From this menu bar you can also tap Undo to undo the last edit you made or Revert to Original to undo all the edits you've made to the photo and revert it to its original state.

Figure 13–47. *Saving or undoing your edits*

Viewing Videos

With the iPad 2, Apple added front and rear cameras that, among other things, allow you to record video (see Chapter 15 for all the things you can do with the iPad 2's cameras). You can also import recorded video from a digital still camera using the iPad Camera Connection Kit (see earlier in the chapter). All recorded or imported video is stored in the Camera Roll album. To view any video you have recorded or imported onto the iPad, simply tap its thumbnail in the Camera Roll. The video will appear with a big play button in the center. Tap any area of the screen once to bring up the on-screen video controls (see Figure 13–48).

Figure 13–48. *Displaying video from the Camera Roll. Tap once to bring up the on-screen menus.*

Once you display a video full-screen, you have several ways to interact with it:

- Tap the video once to play it. Tap the play/pause button in the upper-left corner to pause it.

- Scrub through the video by tapping and holding the silver drag bar in the scrubber bar. The scrubber bar shows you segments of the video represented by thumbnails for those segments.

- Hold your finger on the scrubber bar for a few seconds, and you'll see the scrubber bar stretch out. This gives you finer control over finding a specific spot in the video.

The video overlay menu bar at the top of the screen shows you the back button, labeled Camera Roll, to return to the main Camera Roll. You can tap the Done button to exit the Camera Roll and return to the Camera app. You'll also see the Share button and the trash can icon, which will bring up a deletion confirmation menu. Tap the red Delete Video button to delete the selected video.

Editing Your Video

Apple has included limited video-editing functionality in the Camera app. Video editing isn't exactly the right word, though. *Trimming* is more accurate because you can shorten, or *trim*, the video at the front and end of the clip.

To trim a video, bring up the video menu overlays (see Figure 13–48). Next, grab the beginning of the scrubber bar, and pull it to the right. This activates trim mode (see Figure 13–49).

Figure 13–49. *Video trim mode*

In trim mode, you can drag the ends of the scrubber bar, now outlined in yellow, toward the center. Dragging the ends shortens the clip at the beginning and the end.

Trimming is a great feature that allows you to highlight just the really good portions of your video clips. When you've adjusted your trim commands, tap the yellow Trim button to bring up a Trim pop-up (see Figure 13–50).

Figure 13–50. *The Trim pop-up lets you trim the original or save the trim as a new clip.*

The Trim pop-up gives you two options:

Trim Original: This actually changes the original video recording. It will permanently delete the sections of video you have trimmed out.

Save as New Clip: This leaves your original video intact and creates a completely new video file of just the trim you specified.

To cancel a trim, simply tap anywhere outside of the Trim pop-up. Remember that if you choose to keep the original clip, storage space on your iPod can quickly fill up. A one-minute clip took up a whopping 120MB of space on our iPad.

Sharing Your Video

While viewing any single video clip, you have several sharing options. To bring up the sharing menu, tap the Share button, which looks like an arrow breaking free from a small box. You'll be presented with a pop-up of sharing options (see Figure 13–51):

Figure 13–51. *The video-sharing options*

> *Email Video*: Selecting this option will compress the video clip as a QuickTime movie file. A new message window will appear with the movie clip attached to the body of the message.
>
> Depending on the length of your video clip, you may get an error message that says "Video is Too Long." If you see this, your iPad will ask you whether you want to select a smaller clip from the video to e-mail. Tap OK, and you'll enter trim mode, which will allow you to cut down the length of the clip.
>
> What's interesting about trim mode is that the yellow trim selection bar is fixed to 54 seconds. You can shorten it or drag the 54-second trim selection bar around, but you can't increase the trim to longer than 54 seconds. So, as of now, 54 seconds seems to be the longest a clip can be that you can e-mail. Apple can always change this with a software update in the future, however.
>
> Once you have trimmed your video, tap the yellow Email button above the scrubber bar. A blank e-mail with the video in the body of the message should appear.

Message: Messages is a new iPad app that lets you send text messages between iPhones, iPads, and iPod touches. You can also attach photos and videos to messages. To send a video from the Photos app via Messages, tap the Share button and then tap Message. A window will appear with the video embedded in the message. You can write a note with it if you want. When you are done composing your Message, tap Send.

You can read more about the Messages app in Chapter 11.

Send to YouTube: Selecting this option will allow you to upload your video to YouTube right from your iPad. On the screen that appears (see Figure 13–52), enter a name and description for your video, select to upload it in standard or high definition, add tags, select a YouTube category, and then tap Publish. You must have a YouTube account to upload videos to YouTube.

Figure 13–52. *Publishing a video to YouTube*

Copy Video: Tap Copy Video to copy the video. This saves the video to your clipboard for use in pasting into other things (such as an e-mail or document) later.

You can also copy multiple videos at one time. When viewing an album, tap the Share button. You'll see the album menu renamed as

Select Photos. Tap as many video (and/or photos) as you want to copy. A check mark will appear on each selected item. After you have selected all your videos and/or photos, tap the Copy button in the upper-left corner. These videos and photos can then be batch copied into an e-mail or other applications.

Summary

This chapter introduced you to the iPad's Photos app and showed you how to navigate your photo collections, share them with friends and family, change the iPad's wallpaper, use your iPad as a digital picture frame, and even edit your photos. Once you view your digital photos on the iPad, you might find that you'll never want to navigate and view them on a computer monitor or laptop screen again.

Here are some final thoughts for this chapter:

- The iPad's Photos application offers some of the most instantly appealing ways to show off the power of your iPad. You can scroll through your albums, zoom in and out with a pinch or double-tap, and flip the unit on its side. These features all deliver the iPad "wow" factor.

- You can import photos directly from a camera onto the iPad. This is a huge help for professional photographers who might be out in the field shooting. They can load their images on the iPad and instantly see what they look like on a bigger screen. They can even zoom in to see more detail.

- Consider investing in an inexpensive business card holder and a cheap speaker. They make watching slideshows on your iPad a lot easier, especially for more than one person at a time. A video-out cable from Apple increases the fun by sending the slideshows to a TV screen.

- The Photos app also allows you to view recorded or imported video. You can even trim your video clips and easily send those clips to YouTube or e-mail them to your friends.

- You aren't limited to just viewing photos on your iPad, you can also apply simple edits to them to make them look their best!

- With iCloud's Photo Stream feature, the photos you take with your iPad are automatically pushed to your other Macs, PCs, and iOS devices the moment you take them, provided your iPad has a Wi-Fi connection.

Chapter 14

On the Go with iWork

In this book, we've discussed apps that can help you get organized, let you communicate with others, or enjoy media in the form of music, books, videos, and photos. Now we're going to talk about three apps that turn your iPad into a powerful work platform.

The three apps are Pages, Numbers, and Keynote, together known as iWork for iPad. These Apple-produced apps can be purchased in the App Store for $9.99 each, and they provide much of the functionality that productive workers need while they're on the go. With that, we'll add a caveat: for serious work, you should consider using your iPad to remotely control your "real" work computer. Apps such as LogMeIn Ignition and iTeleport make this possible, although a detailed explanation of their configuration and use is not included in this book. In this chapter, we'll cover the basics of each app only, because a detailed dig into iWork could easily be the subject of another book.

Buy and Install iWork for iPad

Unlike many of the apps built into your iPad, iWork for iPad apps must be purchased and installed on your iPad. In Chapter 8, we told you about the App Store app and how it works on your iPad to assist you in browsing, purchasing, and installing iPad software.

You don't need to purchase all three of the apps if you don't need some of the functionality. For instance, if you just need a good word processing app and don't do any work that requires spreadsheets or presentations, you can just buy Pages. Presenters might just want to purchase Keynote, and budget managers could just pick up Numbers.

Here are some things you may choose to use each app for.

Pages:

- Writing letters
- Creating or updating a résumé
- Developing a project proposal

- Writing a term paper
- Making creative posters, greeting cards, invitations, or flyers

Numbers:

- Creating checklists
- Making comparisons of mortgages or other loans
- Developing a budget
- Creating expense reports and invoices
- Logging business and personal auto mileage
- Drawing charts and graphs from data

Keynote:

- Developing business presentations
- Creating class presentations by both students and instructors
- Making strikingly attractive personal slideshows
- Using your iPad as a teleprompter for giving speeches

Launch the App Store app, and then type the word **pages** into the search box in the upper-right corner of the App Store. Tap the Search button on your keyboard, and a list of apps with *pages* in their names appear. Under iPad Apps, look for Pages (listed in the Productivity category), and then tap the price button. That button turns into a green Install App button. Tap it, and you'll be asked to enter your Apple ID. Pages downloads to your iPad and then automatically installs itself. The same process works with both Numbers and Keynote.

These apps are big—more than 20MB each—so be sure to have your iPad connected to a Wi-Fi network prior to installation. If you try to install any of the iWork apps while connected to a 3G network, a message will ask you to either install while you're on a Wi-Fi network or install the app through iTunes on your computer. Our recommendation is to purchase and install the iWork for iPad apps through iTunes on your computer.

Pages

Pages is more than a word processing app for iPad—it can be used to create sophisticated page layouts with graphics, tables, charts, and numerous text styles. The Mac version of Pages evolved over its lifetime to become a powerful writing and desktop publishing tool, but the iPad version was born with many of the same capabilities. The app is optimized for use with the touch interface of the iPad, making it a joy to use.

In this section, we'll familiarize you with the user interface and some of the functionality of Pages.

Creating a New Document

Launching Pages for the first time, you're greeted with a document with the title Tap to Get Started with Pages. It's more than just a pretty set of pages; it's an interactive tutorial into many of the features of the app. It coaxes you to use common iPad interface gestures to move, rotate, scale, and delete images, restyle text, and add objects to your documents.

The My Documents page, the first thing you see in Pages, looks like a piece of gray cloth on which all of your documents are nicely laid out side by side. To open a previously created document, tap it once.

To start with a blank piece of paper or perhaps a template, you can either tap the New Document button in the upper-left corner of the Pages window or tap the plus sign (+) icon in the middle of the bottom of the window. Tapping the plus sign below an existing document in the My Documents window gives you a choice of creating a new document from scratch or duplicating the existing document.

If you tap either of the New Document buttons, the first thing you see is a Choose a Template screen with a number of useful document types (see Figure 14–1). You can choose to start with a wide-open piece of paper or a well-designed document template. Templates help when you want to create a professional-looking document quickly or when you're faced with writer's block and need some ideas to launch your imagination.

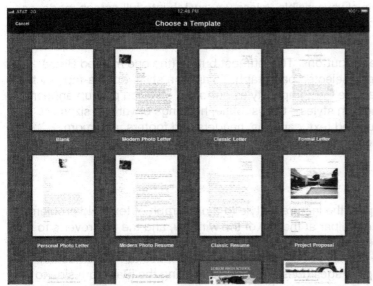

Figure 14–1. *Creating a new document in Pages for iPad provides the option of starting with a blank page or using a professionally designed template.*

For the purposes of this book, we'll start with a blank page. Tap the blank page in the upper left of the Choose a Template window, and you're ready to start writing. Before you begin, we'll explain a bit about what's on the top of the Pages window, as shown in Figure 14–2.

'You've got to find what you love,' Jobs says

Figure 14–2. *The Pages Style ruler*

The Pages Style Ruler

Apple named the ruler-like user interface element shown in Figure 14–2 the *Style ruler*, because it provides both a way to style your text and a ruler for aligning page elements. You can make the Style ruler disappear from your page by tapping the circled *X* in the upper-right corner, and you can make it reappear by double-tapping the barely visible edge of the ruler at the top of the screen.

The Style ruler is different from the toolbar just above it. The toolbar includes a button for returning to My Documents, an Undo button (for reverting to previous versions of a document), and a set of buttons on the right side that we'll describe in a moment. Unlike the Style ruler, the toolbar is always visible unless you switch into full-screen mode, as described later in this chapter. Full-screen mode hides all elements except the document.

The ruler features a number of buttons. The leftmost button (the one marked Body) applies styles to any currently selected paragraph. To apply a style, double-tap any text in a paragraph, and then tap the Paragraph Styles button. A scrolling pop-up appears with a list of common paragraph styles—title, subtitle, headings of various sizes, subheadings, body text, bulleted text, captions, headers and footers, and more. Selecting one of those styles applies it to the entire paragraph of text.

Undo/Redo

Did you just accidentally apply the incorrect style to a paragraph of text? No problem. Tap the Undo button on the toolbar at the top of the window, and the text reverts to the original style. If you later decide that you really meant to make a specific change, tap the Undo button again. A pop-up may appear allowing you to choose to redo an action. Unlike many other iPad apps, Pages does not support shaking the iPad from side to side to undo/redo.

Common Styles

The next set of buttons—B, I, and U—apply common styles to characters. B stands for bold, I for italic, and U for underline. To select a word, double-tap it. When you select a word, it's highlighted with a light blue background and gains a pair of selection handles, one at each end (see Figure 14–3).

Figure 14–3. *Double-tapping any word in a Pages document selects it, adds selection handles to either side to expand the selection, and displays a pop-up menu of actions.*

Expand your selection by dragging the handles left or right, or select an entire paragraph by triple-tapping it. A pop-up also appears, showing actions that can be applied to the text. The most widely used actions—Cut, Copy, and Paste—appear in the pop-up. Tapping the More button provides several more actions—Copy Style, Replace, and Definition.

Cut, Copy, Paste, and Copy Style

Cut, Copy, and Paste work just like they do in any word processing program on a Mac or Windows computer. It's possible to cut a word or phrase out and paste it somewhere else or to copy text to paste in another location. Copy Style copies the existing style of the text. For example, if you create your own style for a word by using bold and underlining it, you can apply bold and underlining to any other text by copying the style of the word and then pasting the style (which appears when you've copied a style) to another selected word or phrase.

Replace and Definition

Replace assumes that you've misspelled a word and displays possible replacements to apply. Tapping one of the replacement words inserts it in place of the existing word. Definition provides a one-tap dictionary lookup. When you select Definition, a pop-up appears with the dictionary definition of the word (see Figure 14–4).

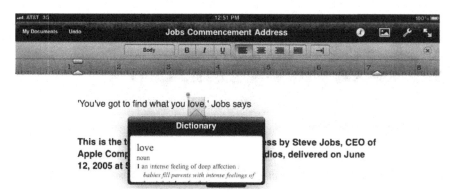

Figure 14–4. *Definition provides a way to determine the meaning of any word without needing to quit Pages and move to another app.*

Justifying Text

Moving down the Style ruler, you come upon a set of icons covered with lines. From left to right, these are left-justify, center, right-justify, and fully justify text. The final button, the one that looks like an arrow pointing at a wall, pops up a menu from which you can apply tabs or breaks (see Figure 14–5).

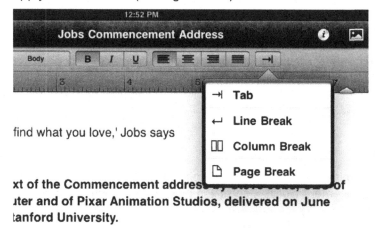

Figure 14–5. *The final button on the Style ruler is used to apply tabs, line breaks, column breaks, and page breaks.*

Applying a tab to the beginning of a line of text can be used to indent the text by half-inch increments. A line break ends the existing line of text and moves the insertion point (where new text appears) down a line. Column breaks work only when you have set up the document with more than one column, in which case applying a column break moves text located after the insertion point to the next column. Finally, a page break starts writing text on a new page.

NOTE: If you're using an external Bluetooth or USB keyboard or the Apple Keyboard Dock, you can use the Tab key in place of the Tab button. Other buttons on the top of the keyboard provide varying functions, including setting sound volume and increasing or decreasing the brightness of the iPad display.

If you'd like to set tabs at various points on the ruler, just tap the ruler and then drag the tab to the appropriate point. Now when you tap the Tab button several times in succession, it will jump between the tab points that you have set. A right tab, meaning that text is moved to the right of the tab point, is set by default. Double-tapping a tab once turns it into a center tab (text centered around the tab point), and double-tapping a tab twice converts a tab into a left tab (text aligned to the left of the tab).

The Style ruler also displays adjustable margins and a first-line indent tool. The small upward-pointing arrows (see Figure 14–6) indicate the margins, which default to 1 inch from each side of a traditional 8.5×11-inch sheet of paper. Those margins can be moved left or right depending on your needs. The first line of a paragraph can be indented by dragging the indent tool (the small rectangular block above the left margin indicator on a new page) to the right.

'You've got to find what you love,' Jobs says

This is the text of the Commencement address by Steve Jobs, CEO of Apple Computer and of Pixar Animation Studios, delivered on June 12, 2005 at Stanford University.

Figure 14–6. *Indent the first line of a paragraph by dragging the indent tool (the rectangular tool at 1.5 inch) to the right. Several right tabs are visible in this image as well.*

Renaming a Pages Document

Moving back to My Documents by tapping the My Documents button, you can rename the "Blank" document by tapping the name that shows up beneath the image of the document. Type a new name, and then tap Done to save the name (Figure 14–7).

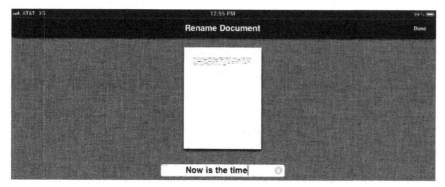

Figure 14–7. *Renaming your document helps identify it uniquely in the My Documents view in Pages.*

The Pages Toolbar

Now let's look at some of the other tools on the toolbar above the Style ruler. As we mentioned earlier, the Undo button lets you correct mistakes. In fact, it can correct a lot of mistakes—each time you tap Undo, another earlier action you took in Pages is undone.

After you read the following descriptions of the many other tools available to you in Pages and begin working with the app, you'll discover how powerful this iPad word processor and page layout tool can really be.

Info

Migrating across the toolbar past the document name, you come to a small round icon that looks a lot like the international sign for information—a lowercase *i*. Apple calls this the Info button, and depending on what is currently selected on your iPad, text or an object, it provides different capabilities.

For text, the Info button gives you the tab choices of Style, List, and Layout, as shown from left to right in Figure 14–8.

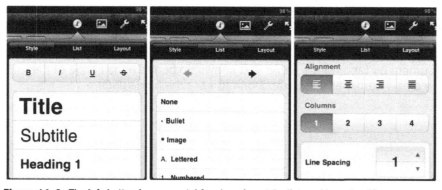

Figure 14–8. *The Info button is your portal for changing style, list, and layout settings.*

The Style tab reiterates the text styles you saw earlier; it allows bolding, italicizing, underlining, or striking through text and also (at the very bottom; they're not visible in Figure 14–8) text options such as size, color, and font. The List tab sets lists as bulleted, lettered, numbered, or bulleted with an image. Use the large arrows to increase or decrease the indentation of list items in formatted outlines. The Layout tab is another way to apply alignment to a document, set it up with up to four columns, or adjust the line spacing.

For objects (images, charts, tables, or shapes), the Info button changes to show the Style, Text, and Arrange tabs (see Figure 14–9).

Figure 14–9. *Objects and text can be styled or arranged using the Info button.*

When applied to an object, the Style tab adds a variety of frames, shadows, and reflections to provide a sense of depth to the object. The Style tab provides a number of options, including turning an image border on or off, scaling the border, changing the line type from whole to dashed, and choosing from a dozen different frames. The Text tab applies styles to text that is entered into an object. The Arrange tab moves an object backward or forward compared to other objects, allows you to flip an object vertically and horizontally, allows you to do some in-document cropping of images with masks, and allows you to set how text wraps around the object.

When we discuss Numbers, you'll learn about some other uses of the Info button, such as for setting options for charts and shapes.

Insert

The Insert button looks like a little drawing of a landscape. It inserts media from your Photos library, tables, charts, or shapes into your document (see Figure 14–10).

The Media tab adds pictures in the Photos app to your document. Tables provides a number of attractive and colorfully shaded preformatted tables for displaying tabular information in your document. With Charts, there's a choice of bar, column, area, line, scatter, and pie charts in six bright colors to add to your document. Double-tapping a chart you've inserted displays a simple spreadsheet for editing the charted information. Finally, if you need to add a box, a cartoon balloon, a line, or geometric shapes to your Pages document, just tap Shapes.

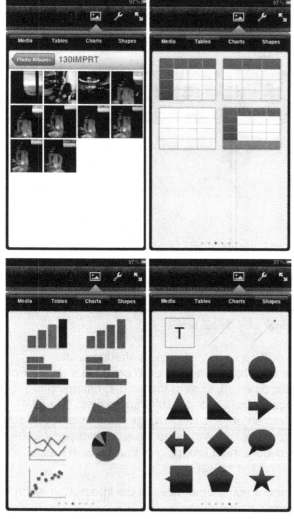

Figure 14–10. *Use the Insert button to add images, tables, charts, or shapes to your Pages document.*

Once you've added a table, a chart, or a shape to a document, tapping that element and then tapping the Info button displays a pop-up that makes changing options for that element a snap. We'll describe the table and chart options in more detail when we talk about Numbers.

Tools

The little wrench-like icon that's next on the toolbar is the Tools button (see Figure 14–11). It's used to change settings that apply to the document as a whole and is also where to go if you want to print a Pages document.

Figure 14–11. *The Tools button in Pages provides features that apply to a complete document, not just a word or paragraph.*

Do you need to find and replace a word or phrase in a document? Find searches your entire document for a set of characters, replaces them (if you've chosen the Find and Replace option), and can even match case or complete words if you need a more finely tuned search (see Figure 14–12).

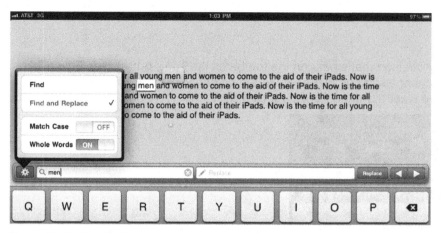

Figure 14–12. *The Find function under the Tools button in Pages is a powerful tool for making global replacements throughout a document.*

Printing was added to the iPad with the release of the iOS 4.2 operating system in late 2010. An Apple feature called AirPrint browses for compatible printers on your Wi-Fi network and then displays those printers when you tap on the Print item under Tools. Selecting the number of copies for printing and tapping the Print button sends the current iWork document to the chosen printer.

Unfortunately, at the time of publication, very few printers were compatible with AirPrint right out of the box. However, several software vendors have developed applications for Mac and Windows that make any shared printer compatible with AirPrint.

Ecamm Network developed Printopia ($9.95, www.ecamm.com/mac/printopia/) for Mac, which gives Mac owners an opportunity to select the printers they want to share with iPads on their networks (see Figure 14–13). Those who own Windows computers or Mac owners who want the ability to send photos directly to iPhoto can try Collobos FingerPrint ($7.99 for Mac, $9.99 for Windows, www.collobos.com/). Both applications also have added features, such as the ability to send documents to your PC or Mac or save them to the popular Dropbox cloud storage service.

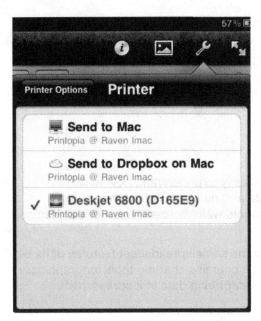

Figure 14–13. *Print, found under the Tools button on the Pages toolbar, displays printers or print-to-file services hosted by applications such as Printopia or FingerPrint.*

Tapping the Document Setup button on the Tools menu displays a blueprint-like layout of the document on which you can tap and edit headers and footers or move the document margins.

The Settings button under Tools provides access to settings such as turning center and edge guides on or off. What are center and edge guides? If you have more than one object on a page, dragging one of them will display alignment guides so you can see when the center or edges of the objects line up. Turning edge guides off means that only the center guides appear when moving objects, while disabling center guides makes only the edge guides visible. If you don't need alignment guides, you can disable them. There's also a word count feature that, when enabled, displays a running total of words in a document.

The last tool under Settings enables or disables the real-time spelling checker. As you type in a Pages document, words that might be misspelled appear with a red dotted underline. Tapping the word displays any possible replacements, and tapping one of those inserts the replacement word. If you find the constant reminders to be annoying, disable the spelling check.

Tapping the final button under Tools, Go to Help, starts up Safari and points you to Apple's online help for the iWork for iPad suite. There's a surprising amount of information contained in the online help, so if you get stuck using a certain feature in Pages, Keynote, or Numbers, be sure to check it out.

Full-Page Display

Coming to the final icon on the toolbar, one that looks like a pair of arrows pointing diagonally, you find the control that can display a full page without the toolbar, Style ruler, or anything else. This is most useful when you're reading a document and want to see as much of it as possible.

Numbers

Once you're familiar with Pages on the iPad, it's easy to understand how to use Numbers. For people who need to organize data and numbers, the Numbers app creates, opens, and saves spreadsheets compatible with Microsoft Excel or the Mac version of Numbers.

Not only does Numbers for iPad contain a lot of the same spreadsheet features of its big brothers on Windows computers and Macs, but it contains charting tools for graphically representing information and even form tools for capturing data in a spreadsheet.

Follow along as we introduce you to Numbers.

My Spreadsheets

Does Figure 14–14 look familiar? It should. My Spreadsheets is the Numbers equivalent of My Documents in Pages. In fact, everything about the user interface in My Spreadsheets is identical to My Documents. The Sharing, New or Duplicate Spreadsheet, and Delete icons below the image of a spreadsheet perform the same tasks as their Pages counterparts, and you can tap the name of a spreadsheet to rename it.

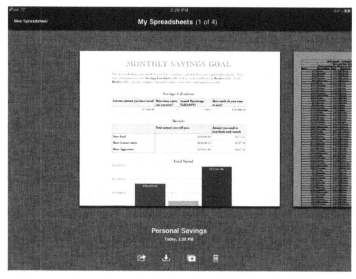

Figure 14–14. *My Spreadsheets is analogous to My Documents in Pages. It's used to create new spreadsheets, rename them, delete them, and share them with others.*

The New Spreadsheet button opens to a window that's the Numbers version of the New Document window. As with Pages, you can either select a blank spreadsheet or choose from a number of templates thoughtfully provided by Apple.

The Numbers templates (see Figure 14–15) range from simple checklists to mortgage calculators and from weight loss and running logs to class attendance sheets. Although not everyone may need a GPA calculator, it's available. Many of the templates exist to give you a taste of the range of tasks you can perform with Numbers.

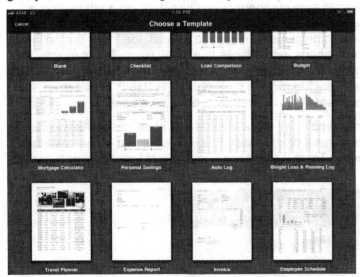

Figure 14–15. *Apple includes 16 templates with Numbers, many of which can be used to perform useful calculations.*

One unique Numbers user interface feature is the concept of tabs. As shown in Figure 14–16, tabs define different sheets or forms for a spreadsheet. As an example, a Numbers spreadsheet could consist of one sheet to describe how to use the spreadsheet, a form to capture data, and another sheet to perform calculations on the data you captured. Each of those pages displays its own tab at the top of the spreadsheet, making navigation between the pages as simple as tapping a tab.

Figure 14–16. *Use tabs to name individual sheets or forms in a Numbers spreadsheet file.*

If you're familiar with Microsoft Excel, just think of tabs as sheets and the group of sheets as an Excel workbook. To add a new tab, just tap the rightmost tab. It's marked with a plus sign, and tapping it displays a pop-up with two buttons—New Sheet and New Form. Any tab can be renamed by double-tapping the existing name and then typing a new name.

As in Pages, there's a very helpful Getting Started document that is a thinly disguised interactive Numbers tutorial. For iPad owners just getting started with Numbers, it is well worth the time and effort to go through the Getting Started pages.

Adding Elements to a Spreadsheet

A blank spreadsheet isn't very useful. Although even the "Blank" template contains a generic table that you can begin to type numbers or text into, tapping a tab creates a totally blank sheet. Where are the rows and columns you're used to? In Numbers, you need to add a table to the sheet to begin using it. As you'll recall, the Insert button in Pages let you add media, tables, charts, and shapes to a blank page. That's exactly what the Insert button does in Numbers as well. The Tables tab is slightly different, but Media, Charts, and Shapes tabs are identical to their siblings in Pages in that they provide a way to add pictures, create charts, or draw shapes on a page.

In Figure 14–17, we've added a simple five-column table to a blank sheet. As you can see, the first column contains a check box for each row, while the rest of the columns are blank. The table has a name—Table 2—and some things that look like scrollbars to the top and left of the table.

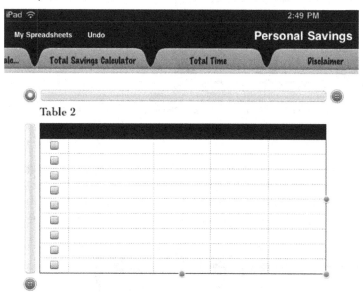

Figure 14–17. *A blank table added to a blank sheet in Numbers*

See those little things at the end of the scrollbars that look like buttons on a shirt? Dragging one of those to the right or down adds another column or row to the table. Dragging a button up or to the left removes a row or column from the table. To move the entire table around on the sheet, drag the button in the upper-left corner of the table.

The dark dots on the right and bottom edges of the table stretch the table when dragged, increasing the width of all the columns and rows without adding any new columns or rows. Likewise, you can make the table smaller by dragging those "handles" up or to the left.

Although we won't go through the details of the many spreadsheet functions that you can choose from in Numbers, let's talk about how you enter information into spreadsheet cells. Double-tapping a cell on the spreadsheet highlights it with a dark blue border, and a light green data entry field appears on the screen along with an appropriate keyboard (see Figure 14–18) and four buttons in a toolbar. On the far left you'll see a button with "42" on it, which indicates that you use this button to enter numbers into the cell. The numbers can be formatted as plain numbers, as currency (using the dollar sign button on the data entry keyboard below), as a percentage (using the percent sign button), as a star ranking from 1 to 5 (using the star button), or as a check box (0 or 1, using the check box button). Buttons on the right side of the keyboard take you to the next cell to the right or to the next cell down for quick navigation around the spreadsheet.

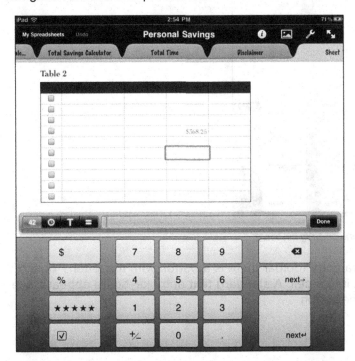

Figure 14–18. *The numeric data entry keyboard*

> **SUBTLE JOKE ALERT!** Are you wondering why the numeric entry button has "42" on it? In the classic science fiction series *The Hitchhiker's Guide to the Galaxy*, 42 is the answer to the ultimate question of life, the universe, and everything. We're speculating that someone on the Numbers development team is a sci-fi fan.

Use the next button (to the right of 42), which looks like a clock, to enter dates, times, or durations into spreadsheet cells. The keyboard looks different as a result of tapping this button (see Figure 14–19), featuring the months of the year on the keypad and buttons for denoting whether you're entering a date and/or time or a duration. What's the difference between a date or time and a duration? A date is a specific date, for example June 10, 2010, and a time is a specific time, like 4:32:06 p.m. A duration is a length of time that can be measured between two time points. One of our writers has a lifetime measured with a duration of 53 years, 7 months, 29 days, 1 hour, and 22 minutes at the time of writing this sentence.

Figure 14–19. *The date, time, and duration entry keyboard*

Moving further down the data entry toolbar there is a button with the letter *T* on it. Use this button to enter text into a cell. A standard text entry keyboard appears (see Figure 14–20) after tapping the button.

Figure 14–20. *The text entry keyboard*

The last button has an equal sign (=) on it. Tapping this button displays the formula entry keyboard (see Figure 14–21). A formula operating on data contained in cells, using functions entered through the functions key, is typed into the data entry field and applied to the cell by tapping the check mark button at the end of the field. The keyboard also contains a set of mathematical operators (parentheses, plus, minus, multiply, divide, exponents, and logical operators) for use in spreadsheet formulas.

Figure 14–21. *The formula entry keyboard is used to enter both simple and complex formulas into spreadsheet cells.*

The Info Button

Remember the Info button in Pages? Numbers has one, too. Tapping the Info button when selecting a table displays a pop-up for changing table settings (see Figure 14–22).

The first tab, Table, applies a choice of different shading colors and types to a table from a palette of six prepackaged types. The Table Options button on this tab provides options for disabling the table name, deleting the border of the table, shading alternating rows in the table, turning off lines in the table grid, and changing the font and text size for any text or numbers in the table.

The Headers tab adds header rows, header columns, and footers to a table. You can choose to freeze header rows and columns so that they're always visible, even when you have scrolled the table down or to the right.

Figure 14–22. *The various tabs displayed by the Info button when a table is selected*

The Cells tab applies formatting to text cells on the table and is very useful for configuring header rows. The last tab, Format, applies special formats to cells or ranges of cells in the table. A cell can be formatted as a number, currency, a percentage, a date and/or time, a duration, a check box, a star rating (one to five stars), or text.

Tapping the Info button while an image is selected causes the same three tabs (Style, Text, and Arrange) to appear that we described in the earlier section about Pages. When a chart is selected, tapping the Info button displays an entirely different pop-up (see Figure 14–23).

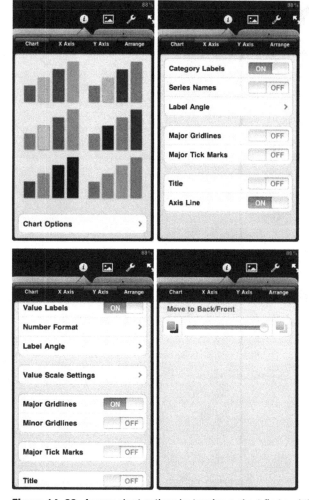

Figure 14–23. *Access chart options by tapping a chart first and then the Info button.*

The Chart tab provides some preset options for the color of your chart. Tapping the Chart Options button at the bottom of this tab displays controls for enabling or disabling the chart tile, legend, and border; changing the text size and font; turning value labels on and off; or changing the type of chart.

The X Axis tab is available only when your chart displays both x- and y-axes—it wouldn't make sense on a pie chart. It controls the visibility of category labels and series names; allows you to orient the labels along the x-axis of your chart horizontally, diagonally, or vertically; allows you to add gridlines or tick marks for the axis; and lets you enable or disable an axis title.

The Y Axis tab is similar to the X Axis tab but controls the options for the vertical axis of your chart. The Arrange tab moves your chart forward or backward in relation to other objects on the same page.

When you tap shapes that have been added to your sheets, the Info button displays the familiar Style, Text, and Arrange tabs (see Figure 14–24).

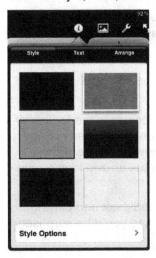

Figure 14–24. *There is more to the Style tab than meets the eye. The Style Options button provides a set of fills, borders, and effects to modify shapes.*

When the Style Options button is tapped, another set of tabs appears (see Figure 14–25). Fill provides a number of color and grayscale fills, Border enables or disables a border around the shape and changes the border's style, and Effects creates a shadow and determines the opacity of the shape. Believe it or not, you can actually use a transparent color shape as a "filter" for exciting image effects.

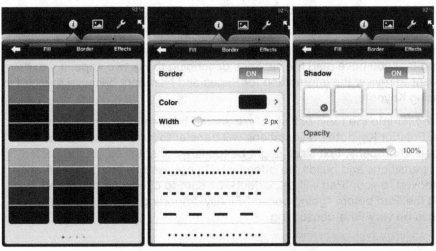

Figure 14–25. *Tapping Style Options displays the Fill, Border, and Effects tabs displayed here. Note that these same tabs appear in Pages and Keynote when a shape is selected and the Info button is tapped.*

For example, suppose you'd like to add a colored highlight to a photo to call out a certain object in the picture. Creating a red oval shape, setting it to be transparent, and then dragging it over the object in the photo makes a functional and professional-looking highlight.

The two other tabs that accompany Style in Figure 14–24 are Text and Arrange. The Text tab adds text styles to text typed into the shape, while Arrange once again places the shape in front of or behind other objects on the page.

The Tools Button

The familiar wrench icon, otherwise known as the Tools button, resides in the toolbar of Numbers and acts as your gateway to Tools. Choices for Tools are fewer than in Pages, with only Find, Go to Help, Edge Guides, and Check Spelling showing up. As with Pages, there's a full-page mode in Numbers enabled by tapping the arrows icon on the far right end of the Numbers toolbar.

Remember, you can't really hurt anything by creating a new spreadsheet and playing with Numbers. It's a great way to become familiar with the app, and you'd be surprised what you can learn just by creating fun or useful spreadsheets.

Keynote

If you have read the chapter up to this point, you are familiar with Pages, Numbers, and all of the many common features available in those two apps. Now you'll learn about Keynote, which is the presentation app of the iWork for iPad suite. Keynote is the only iWork app that can be used with the various video-out cables for the iPad for the purpose of projecting your presentation, so it is a powerful tool for teachers, businesspeople, and anyone else who needs to get their message across to groups of people.

This part of the chapter is shorter than the sections for Pages and Numbers, because we are assuming that you have read the sections describing those two apps. If you have not, you may want to review the information for Pages and Numbers because much of it is relevant to using Keynote.

Before we get too far into the topic of Keynote, it should be mentioned that not all imported PowerPoint or Keynote presentations will transfer to Keynote for iPad cleanly. Images may scale improperly, text sizes might be too large or small on your imported document, and transitions and builds are often lost. Do not assume that a presentation that has been moved to your iPad will be perfect—be sure to check the converted presentation on the iPad before "going public." Finally, importing and converting large presentations can be very time-consuming.

My Presentations

Launching Keynote by tapping it, the first thing you see is My Presentations (see Figure 14–26). This is analogous to My Documents in Pages and My Spreadsheets in Numbers. Also, like its siblings in iWork for iPad, Keynote comes with a Getting Started presentation document that is useful in learning how the app works. It's interactive, teaching you how to work with Keynote as you follow the instructions provided in the presentation.

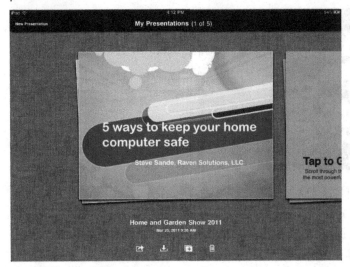

Figure 14–26. *The My Presentations window is very much like the My Documents window in Pages and My Spreadsheets window in Numbers.*

When you tap the New Presentation button in the upper-left corner of the My Presentations window, you're asked to choose a theme (see Figure 14–27). Apple provides a dozen themes that range from plain white to fancy.

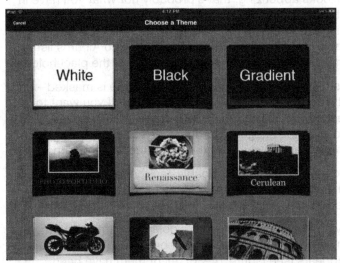

Figure 14–27. *Pick a theme from one of the dozen professionally designed themes built into Keynote for iPad.*

Tapping any one of the themes displays the first slide in your presentation deck, which by default is a title slide. Figure 14–28 shows the title slide and toolbar for the Renaissance theme.

Figure 14–28. *The default title slide for the Renaissance theme. Both the text and the image are placeholders that you replace with your title, subtitle, and image.*

Editing and Adding Slides

Although the risotto on the slide looks appetizing, that's probably not what you have in mind for your presentation. That's OK, since that image is just a placeholder, just like the "Double-tap to edit" text is waiting for you to edit it. To change the title slide image, tap the small circular image icon that is in the corner, and the familiar Photo Albums list is displayed. Select an image from your photos, and it takes the place of the placeholder.

The image placeholder may be smaller than your image, so your image is masked—part of it is made transparent so that it appears that the image is cropped. If you want to change the way the photo is masked, double-tap it, and the entire image appears (see Figure 14–29). Use your finger to slide the image up or down, or scale the image using the slider control. When things look the way you want them, tap the Done button.

Editing the text placeholders is done the same way. Double-tap them; the placeholder text disappears, and a standard iPad keyboard appears. Type in your new title and subtitle to make your title slide shine.

Unless you plan on giving a very short presentation, you're going to want to add more slides. That's what the plus sign at the bottom of the left sidebar is for. Tap the button, and a pop-up palette of slides appears (see Figure 14–30). All of them have been designed to match the colors, fonts, and general look and feel of your title slide.

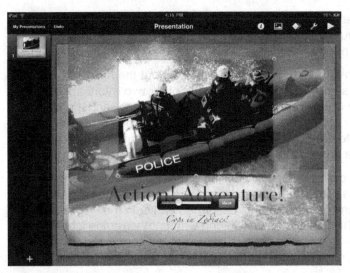

Figure 14–29. *Masking an image is useful in making sure that your audience is focused on the most important details of your image.*

Figure 14–30. *The Add a Slide pop-up presents a graphical representation of eight different slide types. Tap any one of the slide images to add a new slide to your presentation, and then edit the slide to your requirements.*

Some of the slides show bulleted text, some are blank or nearly so, others are designed to display images, and several slides show text and images side by side. Tap the appropriate slide type for your next slide, and it is added to the slideshow under the title slide.

Like your title slide, the other slide types all contain placeholders. Double-tap text to edit it, and tap the image icon on an image to replace the placeholder image with your own picture. You don't have to add an image; since the tools in Keynote are similar to those in Pages and Numbers, the Insert button can provide you with a way to add tables, charts, and shapes as well. You edit and configure all of these objects using the same tools discussed earlier in the chapter.

Not only does the Insert button appear in the Keynote toolbar, but the Info button is there as well, and it works the same way that it does in the other two iWork apps. Our familiar friend the Tools button is also represented by the wrench icon, and it provides access to Find, Print, Presenter Notes, Settings, and Go to Help. When tapped, Presenter Notes displays a yellow lined notepad upon which you can write notes to jog your memory while delivering a presentation.

Settings provides a number of controls. Check Spelling turns spell checking on and off, and Slide Numbers enables the placement of small numbers on the bottom of each slide in a presentation deck. Edge and Center Guides, described earlier in the Pages section of this chapter are present in the Settings as well, along with another guide labeled Guides at 10%. When enabled, this places snap-to guides at horizontal and vertical locations every 10 percent of the slide width and height.

The Animation Button

The other button that is unique to Keynote is the Animation button, which looks like a diamond and is found in the middle of the pack of buttons at the right end of the Keynote toolbar. The Animation button is used to add animated slide transitions to your slideshow, something that can really increase the impact of your presentation. The transitions available to you as a Keynote user vary by theme.

To add a transition to a slide, tap the slide in the sidebar to select it, and then tap the Animation button. A black arrow, initially marked with the word *None*, appears and is pointing at the slide you're adding the transition to. Tap the blue circle on the arrow, and a Transitions pop-up appears (see Figure 14–31). This scrolling list contains a number of different animated transition effects, all of which add life to otherwise dull presentations. To see how a specific transition works with your slide, tap the name of the transition, and it is demonstrated for you.

The Options button (see Figure 14–32) on the Transitions pop-up sets options such as direction, speed, delay, and when to start the transition. Each transition effect is a bit different, so each has its own options to set. Once you've changed option settings, you can see how the changes affect your transition by tapping the small Play button in the upper right of the Transitions pop-up.

Figure 14–31. *The Transitions pop-up contains a comprehensive list of eye-catching animations to use in transitioning between slides.*

Figure 14–32. *Each effect has a separate set of option controls to customize the speed, delay, direction, and other factors.*

If you're familiar with setting up presentations in either Microsoft PowerPoint or the Mac version of Keynote, then you know that slide transitions aren't the only animations available to spice up your presentations. Animated builds, which add movement to slides by moving or spinning graphics or adding text bullets one at a time, can also rivet the attention of your audience.

To add a build effect to an object (graphic or text) on a slide, tap the Animation button, and then tap the object or text. A double-sided pop-up appears (see Figure 14–33) for adding a build-in (a transition where text or a graphic is being added to the slide) or build-out (a transition to remove text or a graphic from the slide).

Figure 14–33. *The Build pop-up. Tap the plus button on the left to create a text build to add one bullet at a time, and tap the button on the right side to create a build that removes the build when moving to a new slide or object.*

Tapping the plus sign on the pop-up allows you to select the effect and change options. Two other buttons on the Build pop-up weren't on the Transitions pop-up—Delivery and Order. Delivery is usually available only for bulleted text, and it determines whether the text appears all at once or one bullet at a time. If you're using multiple builds on your slide, Order allows you to set the order in which the builds appear.

Although slide transitions and builds can be useful in creating an attractive presentation, be sure not to overuse them to the point of distracting from the goal of your slides— providing information to an audience.

The Play Button and Presenter Display

At the far-right end of the toolbar is the Play button. When it is tapped, the toolbar and sidebar disappear, and your presentation is displayed in full-screen. To advance slides or build bullet points in the presentation, tap the screen or swipe your finger to the left. Returning to a previous slide or bullet is accomplished by swiping your finger to the right. When using a video-out cable to project your presentation, the iPad display can provide a lot of useful information (see Figure 14–34).

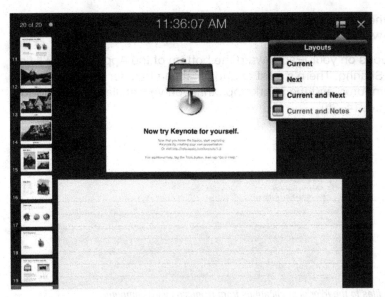

Figure 14-34. *The Keynote Presenter Display. When you're giving a presentation from the iPad, this screen is a great assistant. The Presenter Display provides a view of upcoming and previous slides, what is currently on the projection screen, how long you've been talking, and even notes you've written.*

At top left is a green light indicating that your presentation is being sent to the projector, along with a slide counter. In the figure, we're on the last of 20 slides, and a vertical strip showing your slides appears on the left side of the screen. You can see the current time at the top of the presenter display; tapping it displays a timer showing how long you've been talking.

There's a small Layouts button at the top right, which displays four different presenter layouts when tapped. Current shows just the current slide, Next displays just the next slide in your presentation, Current and Next displays both the slide that is being projected and the next slide in your deck, and Current and Notes shows the current slide and any notes you may have written using the Presenter Notes tool. By the way, if you forgot your laser pointer back in the office, Keynote will save the day. Holding down your finger on the iPad screen creates a red virtual "laser pointer" that is useful in highlighting items on slides.

When your presentation is finished, tap the X button to return to the Keynote slide editor.

Importing Documents from a Computer

Many times, you may want to work on documents that you already created on your computer or that someone else sent to you through e-mail. In Chapter 11, we showed you how to open attachments that have been sent to you in Mail, so e-mailing documents to your iPad is one way to work on them while mobile.

Another method is to transfer the documents to your iPad by using iTunes on your computer. With your computer and iPad connected by the Dock Connector to USB cable, launch iTunes on the computer. When the iPad appears in the Devices list in the left sidebar in the iTunes window, click it, and then click the Apps tab.

Scrolling past the list of apps on your iPad toward the bottom of the Apps tab, you'll find an area with the title File Sharing. There's a list of apps that can transfer documents between the iPad and computer, and the iWork apps that you've installed on your iPad will be in that list (see Figure 14–35).

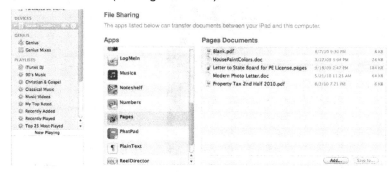

Figure 14–35. *You can transfer files to the iWorks applications from iTunes on your computer.*

To transfer documents from your computer, click the appropriate app name on the left, and then click the Add button on the right side. A standard file Open dialog box for your computer appears, and then you can select one or more documents to transfer. Once the document files have been added to the list on the right side, clicking the Sync button in iTunes transfers the documents to your iPad.

Within any of the iWork apps, tapping the folder icon in the top-right corner of the My Documents, My Spreadsheets, or My Presentations window displays the documents stored on your iPad, and tapping the filename opens the file in the app.

A number of iPad file manager apps, like Air Sharing Pro and GoodReader, provide another way to move files to your iPad. These apps connect to MobileMe's iDisk, Dropbox, and other servers; allow you to view the files on the server; and then download and open them in iWork for iPad. With iPad printing support built into Air Sharing Pro, it makes a wonderful companion to iWork.

Moving documents out of iWorks is not as simple, because there is no common file store for these file managers to retrieve files from. In many cases, the only choices you may have for exporting documents are through e-mail (see Chapter 11), saving the documents to iWork.com (Apple's online repository for sharing iWork documents), or using iTunes as described earlier.

Using iCloud to Sync Your Documents Between Devices

If you are using iCloud, any document you create in an iWork app (Pages, Numbers, or Keynote) on your iPad will automatically be available to you on all your other iOS devices. Also, any changes you make to a document will be instantly changed on your other iOS devices.

The documents will also be available for easy download to your Mac or PC by going to www.icloud.com in your web browser, logging in, and selecting the iWork icon. From the bar at the top of the screen (Figure 14–36), select the app the document was made in. Next, move your mouse cursor over the thumbnail document and click the download button. A drop-down menu will appear asking you to select your download format. You can choose from between the iWork app document, PDF, or Microsoft Word format.

Figure 14–36. *Using a desktop web browser to access your iWork documents via iCloud*

Once you've downloaded the document, you can open it up in the appropriate app on your computer. Simply click the cog icon and choose "Upload document" from the menu. You can also upload documents from your computer to iCloud. Any uploaded documents will appear on all your iOS devices.

Summary

The iWork for iPad trio of Pages, Numbers, and Keynote is a powerful set of apps for creating documents for work or pleasure while you're on the go. These optional Apple apps work well with their Mac counterparts and, to a more limited degree, Microsoft Office.

In this chapter, we've provided a look at the user interface and major capabilities of Pages, Numbers, and Keynote. Although a more detailed discussion of each app could easily fill another book, we've given you the information you'll need to get started using iWork for iPad. Some important points to remember from this chapter include the following:

- Pages, Numbers, and Keynote do not come with your iPad. To purchase the apps for $9.99 each and then install them, use the App Store app on your iPad while you're connected to a Wi-Fi network or purchase the apps in iTunes and then sync the iPad to your computer.

- All three of the iWork for iPad apps include a page (My Documents/My Spreadsheets/My Presentations) displaying your existing documents, and you can choose to create a new document on a blank page or with a professionally designed theme or template.

- The user interface is consistent between all three of the apps. If you become familiar with one of the iWork apps, you'll understand how to use the other two in no time at all.

- Pages can be used both as a traditional word processor and as a page layout application, depending on your needs.

- Numbers tabs are similar to sheets in an Excel workbook. Each tab can have one or more tables (spreadsheet) on it, as well as media (images), charts, and shapes.

- Add transitions and builds to your Keynote presentations to make them more interesting and vibrant to your audience.

- Transferring documents from your computer to your iPad is a great way to work on the go. You can transfer them by e-mail, through iTunes, or through a growing number of file management utilities.

Chapter 15

Using the iPad Cameras with Camera, Photo Booth, and FaceTime

Perhaps the most significant upgrade to the second-generation iPad is represented in its two cameras. These cameras introduce new and compelling features to the formerly cameraless iPad: the ability to take photos and record high-definition video, the ability to play with those videos using Photo Booth, and the ability to place and receive FaceTime video calls.

Are you lucky enough to own one of the latest iPads? If not, this chapter is really not for you, at least until you're ready to upgrade. But if you've been able to purchase a newer-generation iPad, then this chapter will teach you great ways to take photos and record video.

The Camera Hardware

The iPad 2 features two cameras—one in the front and one in the rear. These cameras allow you to snap photos and record video. The cameras aren't created equal, however. As you'll see, each one has been designed for different uses.

Front Camera

The front iPad camera is located at the top of the device, directly in the center of the iPad's upper bezel, across from the unit's Home button. If you own a white iPad, the tiny dot is quite obvious to see; it's less conspicuous on black models. Behind this dot lies the front-facing camera.

This front camera is meant primarily for FaceTime video calls, but you can also take photos and record video with it. For example, you might use the front-facing camera to snap a profile picture for your Facebook account or to record yourself and a friend singing "Happy Birthday" to a special someone. With the front camera, there's no shooting pictures in a bathroom mirror or turning a camera around and hoping you frame yourself into the shot. The front camera allows you to see and compose the shot as you take it.

The front-facing camera isn't as powerful as the rear camera; it cannot record high-definition (HD) video. HD video is video that has at least 720 lines of resolution. With video, the more lines of resolution you have, the sharper the picture will be. Although the front camera can record video, its resolution is limited to standard-definition (SD). SD video, also called video graphics array (VGA), uses a resolution of 640x480. VGA refers to an old computer monitor standard and is actually a higher resolution than the 525 lines that was originally broadcast over commercial television stations in the original NTSC standard.

Why didn't Apple use an HD camera in the front? Well, it would be unnecessary. The front camera was designed for FaceTime video calling, not recording video. The image quality while video calling on a portable device like the iPad is more than good enough using an SD camera.

Rear Camera

The iPad's powerful rear camera allows you to take photos, record video, and work with third-party augmented reality applications. When you flip your iPad over, you can easily spot the rear camera in the top-left corner of the device.

The rear camera records videos in 720p HD resolution at 30 frames a second; that's 1280x720 pixels wide. Although its still-camera capabilities are better than the front-facing camera, the rear-facing camera is still limited to taking still pictures at 960x720 resolution. If that doesn't sound like a lot, it's because it isn't. 960x720 resolution isn't even equivalent to a 1-megapixel camera; or, if you want to get specific, the iPad's still capabilities record photos in 0.69 megapixels. That's far less than you expect with most point-and-click digital cameras you buy on the market today.

The iPad's sub-megapixel resolution is fine for simple snapshots for e-mailing or posting to Facebook, but when you are at an important event like a wedding or a child's birthday party and want to take some good quality pictures suitable for framing, leave the iPad at home and bring your point-and-shoot digital camera.

> **NOTE:** What's the *p* stand for in 720p, you ask? It means progressive. When HD video is displayed on a screen, it shows either all 720 lines of resolution at a time or just half of them. If it shows only half of them, this is known as *interlace video* and is denoted with an *i*. Simply put, progressive video generally looks sharper, because it shows you all the data (or lines of resolution) in a single frame at a time, and interlace shows you only half the data at a time (followed quickly by the other half). Interlace video used to be the norm when bandwidth issues were more of a factor for television reception, but as bandwidth increased, progressive video slowly took over.

Real-World Use

In real-world use, the iPad does an acceptable job at recording HD video in good lighting conditions. While developing this chapter for the book, the video shot outdoors in the daytime or inside with good lighting showed up watchable when played it back on our HDTVs. Like the newer-generation iPod touch, whose camera system the iPad basically shares, the iPad uses a light-sensitive sensor, which can be used in a wide range of lighting situations. This sensor allows for the best video quality the hardware can record. Because of this sensor, even in low-light conditions, the video quality was usable, but it can appear somewhat grainy as illumination decreases.

As for taking still images, the iPad is convenient to have around when you're out and about and might not necessarily have your digital camera on you. Because of its 0.69-megapixel images and lack of a camera flash, the iPad is in no way a replacement for your standard digital point-and-shoot camera or even the quality camera shipping on the iPhone 4 and newer. That being said, Apple didn't set out to design the best camera possible; Apple set out to design the best iPad possible at the best possible price—and at that, Apple excelled. The iPad isn't about capturing great art; it's about social use, especially in situations where you normally bring your iPad along with you. So, it's a trade-off. If you want a really good camera, then buy a camera or a newer-model iPhone. Because with its large form factor and awkward handling, the iPad isn't all about photos. It's about integrating cameras and photography into the iPad user experience.

Navigating the Camera App

To launch the Camera application, tap the Camera icon. It's a silver-gray button with a camera lens on it (see Figure 15–1). The camera can be used in either portrait or landscape mode. Simply rotate your iPad to switch between the two orientations.

Figure 15–1. *The Camera app*

Figure 15–2 shows the standard layout of the Camera app. With the exception of the Switch Camera button in the top-right corner, all the camera controls reside in the gray bar at the bottom of the screen in portrait orientation. When you rotate into landscape orientation, the Switch Camera button remains in the top-right corner, but the camera control bar shifts to the left (or right) of the screen. The icons on the control bar rotate to match your iPad's orientation.

Switch between front and rear camera

Switch between still and video camera

Camera Roll   Shutter/Record button

Figure 15–2. *The camera controls*

The camera controls are as follows:

>*Switch between still and video camera mode*: A tiny slider appears at the bottom right of the screen. The slider has two icons, a still camera and a video camera. To toggle between recording modes, tap this slider. The slider's button rests below the icon whose mode is selected. When it is to the left, your iPad is in single-shot mode. On the right, you are ready to record video. In Figure 15–2, the slider is below the still camera, so you know that you are in still-camera mode.

>*Switch between cameras*: Tap the Switch Camera icon in the top right of the screen to switch between the front and rear cameras. The icon looks like a traditional still camera with swirling arrows on either side. You'll see a 2D animation of the screen flipping between cameras.

Shutter button: Tap the oval button with the icon of a traditional still camera in the center of the control bar to snap a still photograph. This button changes to an oval button with a pulsing red dot in the center when you are in video camera mode. Tap the button to record video. Tap again to stop recording. If you have your finger on the Shutter/Record button but then change your mind about photographing or recording your subject, you can slide your finger off the button and no image will be taken, nor will video begin being recorded.

Access the Camera Roll: Tap the square button on the left of the control bar. The square will be filled with an icon of the last image or video recorded. Once tapped, your Camera Roll will slide up on-screen. This is a great feature for reviewing your last photo or video. It saves you a lot of time, because you don't have to leave the Camera app to check out your Camera Roll in the Photos app. Tap Done to return to the camera from the Photos app Camera Roll.

Taking Still Pictures

Taking a still photograph couldn't be easier. Point your camera at what you want to photograph and tap the shutter button. You'll hear a shutter click sound effect and see a cool animation of a lens's iris quickly closing and then opening. After that, the still image you just took will jump down into the Camera Roll icon.

One of the rules for good composition is truly "classic." The ancient Greek and Egyptian philosophers discovered an important feature about beauty. Much of what we find attractive and beautiful incorporates a specific ratio, which is approximately 3:2. They called this ratio Phi (rhymes with "tie"), the "golden ratio," or even the "divine ratio." You can find this mathematical relationship abundantly in nature, such as in the way a tree grows, flowers bloom, or our body parts (fingers, hands, arms, and so on) are laid out.

The ancients incorporated this idea into their art and architecture. It was this transference from nature into art that came to be known as the rule of thirds. Basically, the rule is that things that are split into thirds, with features placed at the one-third mark and/or two-thirds mark, look better than things with more arbitrary placements. It's as simple as that.

We personally like to enable the grid overlay when composing pictures on my iPad. To do this, tap the background, choose Options and switch Grid to On. This creates an overlay that floats over the image, letting you use the grid lines to follow the rule of thirds when composing pictures. By placing features along the rule-of-thirds lines, especially at the four intersections, you'll end up with better-composed scenes.

NOTE: Some people find that tapping the on-screen shutter button to take a still photo causes their composition to get messed up. A neat trick Apple included to counteract any accidental nudging when you tap the shutter button is this: tap and hold the shutter button and *then* compose your shot. When you are ready to take the photo, simply remove your finger from the shutter button, and the shot will be recorded.

Changing the Exposure

You can set the exposure of the camera by tapping anywhere on the screen. You'll see a white box with crosshairs quickly appear. The iPad's camera reads the exposure setting of the part of the image inside the box and adjusts the camera sensors accordingly.

Setting the exposure helps when you are shooting an image of a cloudy sky, for example. If you want the sky to appear other than blinding white, tap the area of the image on your iPad's screen, and the exposure adjusts to better emphasize the lighting conditions at that point.

Zooming In and Out

When you tap the screen to set the exposure, you'll also see a zoom bar appear along the bottom (Figure 15–3). This zoom bar allows you to adjust the digital zoom settings of the photograph; it lets you zoom in and out on your subject. Digital zoom, unlike optical zoom, does not actually increase the fidelity of your image. Instead, it blows up a smaller section of your image using whatever data is already there. Because of that, the more you zoom, the lower quality your image will be. Slide your finger along the bar to zoom in or out. You can also tap the + or – button to zoom in increments.

Figure 15–3. *The zoom controls appear above the control bar when you tap the screen in still-camera mode.*

NOTE: You can only zoom on while in still camera mode using the rear camera. You cannot zoom using the front-facing camera. There is also no zoom while in video camera mode.

Recording Video

To record video, set the slider in the control bar to video camera mode. The camera's shutter button will be replaced with a recording button (see Figure 15–4). Tap the record button to begin recording your video. The red dot on the record button will begin to glow, and a time code stamp will appear in the upper right of the screen showing the hours, minutes, and seconds that have elapsed since recording began. To stop recording, tap the record button again.

Just how much video can you record on your iPad? That depends on the size of your iPad and how much space you have available. If you have a 32GB iPad but have only 10GB of free space on it, you'll be able to record only 10GB of video.

Here's a simple rule of thumb: 720p/30fps video works out to about 120MB per minute. If you think in terms of gigabytes, one hour of 720p/30fps video will occupy about 7GB of space on your iPad. One hour of video is a lot, but so is 7GB of storage space, especially if you own one of the lower-end iPad models with less onboard space. If you are going to be recording a lot of video, it's helpful to be close to your computer or have your laptop with you so you can easily dump your video onto your computer's hard drive and then wipe it from your iPad, freeing up space for more video.

Do you travel without a laptop? At this time you cannot use the iPad's Camera Connection Kit to offload video to an SD card while on the go, although it's a feature that Apple might add in future iOS updates. You can, however, use the kit to move data between one iOS device to another. If you have extra room on a noncamera unit, you can transfer media between devices.

Whether you want to do this at all is another matter. Transferring data using the Camera Connection Kit to clear up space on your iPad is probably all a little more work than it's actually worth, but if you're quickly running out of space and you want to keep taking pictures and videos, it's a workaround that could help you out when space gets tight.

Figure 15–4. *The video-recording screen shows the time elapsed while recording at the top left corner. The red record button at the bottom center will pulse during video capture.*

> **TIP:** If you are going to be using the recorded video in a movie or be viewing it on your TV, you probably want to make sure you record in landscape mode. Although you can also record in portrait mode, portrait mode provides a weird aspect ratio to view videos in and, if you use the iMovie on your iPad, to edit videos in. What's more, the iPad is a bit big and cumbersome to hold up in portrait mode, especially if you want to have a finger free to be able to tap the stop/start recording button.

Changing the Exposure

As with still images, you can set the exposure of recorded video. You'll see a white box with crosshairs quickly appear. The iPad's camera reads the exposure setting of the part of the image inside the box and adjusts the video's exposure settings accordingly. This optimizes the recording for the quality of the scene at the point you touch.

Viewing Your Camera Roll

To view all the photos you have taken and the videos you have recorded, tap the Camera Roll icon at the left of the bottom control bar. The last image or video you recorded is integrated into the look of the button as a little reminder. You can just barely see this in Figure 15–4, where the last image of a cloudy day was rather similar to the view being shown in the viewfinder.

Tap the Camera Roll arrow to be taken to the Camera Roll (Figure 15–5). You can instantly detect which items are videos and which are still images. Videos appear with a small "video camera" icon (a rectangle with a triangle lens image to its right) and a time indicating the duration of the video that has been shot. The fifth item (second to last) in Figure 15–5 is a five-second video segment.

Figure 15–5. *The Camera Roll contains all the photos and videos you have taken with the iPad's camera.*

As Figure 15–5 shows, the tabs located at the top of the Camera Roll interface allow you to sort through your recordings in the following three ways:

> *All*: Shows you all your photographs taken and videos recorded

> *Photos*: Shows you just the photos you have taken

> *Videos*: Shows you just the videos you have recorded

To view any individual photo or video, simply tap its thumbnail. The item you select will zoom out, and you will be able to view or play it back.

Viewing Individual Photos

When in your Camera Roll, you will see thumbnails of the photos it contains (see Figure 15–5). To view a photo full-screen, tap the photo once. As you can see from Figure 15–6, you can view the photo in portrait or landscape mode, depending on how you hold your iPad.

If the image was shot in the opposite mode to the current iPad orientation, as demonstrated in the image on the right, the Photos application will use letterboxing or pillarboxing to pad the image as it presents it. In Figure 15–5, pillarboxing adds black columns to each side of the portrait photo, allowing you to view the entire image in its original aspect. Letterboxing, which is used for landscape photos presented in portrait orientation, adds black rectangles above and below the image.

Figure 15–6. *Viewing a photo in portrait and landscape modes*

Once you display a photo full-screen, you have several ways to interact with it, as discussed in more detail in Chapter 13. These include the following:

- Pinch to zoom into and out of the photo.

- Double-tap to zoom into the photo. Double-tap again to zoom out.

- When your image is displayed at the normal zoomed-out size, drag to the left or right to move to the previous or next image in the album. When zoomed into an image, dragging the photo pans across it.

While viewing individual photos, you may flip your iPad onto its side at any time. The photo will automatically reorient itself. If the photo was shot using landscape orientation, it will size itself to a wider view; if the photo was shot using portrait, it will resize to a longer one.

Tap any image once to bring up the image overlay, as shown in Figure 15–6. The image overlay features a menu bar at the top and a photo-selection slider at the bottom of the screen.

The image overlay menu bar at the top of the screen shows you the number of the selected image out of the total number of items in the Camera Roll and shows you the back button, here labeled Camera Roll, to return to the album of items shot on this device. You can tap the Done button to exit the Camera Roll and return to the Camera app.

You'll also see the Share button (it looks like an arrow breaking free from a small box), the Airplay button (it's a rectangle with a triangle inside it), and the trash can button. Tapping the trash can button will bring up a deletion confirmation menu. Tap the red Delete Photo button to delete the selected photo.

The Slideshow button presents options for showing your images as a local slideshow or remotely using AirPlay wireless connections. If you have connected your iPad to a TV using any of the many dock connector adapters (these include HDMI, VGA, Composite, and Component video adapters), you can play your slideshow back on that bigger screen.

AirPlay not only offers a wireless solution, assuming you either have an Apple TV on-hand or have purchased a third-party solution like Banana TV for the Mac (http://bananatv.net) but also (in the case of Apple TV) provides a wider range of slideshow presentations for more eye-catching displays.

See Chapter 13 for more details about slideshow presentations with your iPad and for sharing your photos and videos with others.

Viewing Videos

To view any video you have recorded, simply tap its thumbnail in the Camera Roll. The video will appear with a big play button in the center. Tap any area of the screen once to bring up the on-screen video controls (see Figure 15–7).

Figure 15–7. *Displaying video from the Camera Roll. Tap once to bring up the on-screen menus.*

Once you display a video full-screen, you have several ways to interact with it.

- Tap the video once to play it. Tap again to pause it.

- Scrub through the video by tapping and holding the silver drag bar in the scrubber bar at the top of the screen. The scrub bar shows you segments of the video represented by thumbnails for those segments.

- Hold your finger on the scrub bar for a few seconds, and you'll see the scrub bar stretch out. This gives you finer control over finding a specific spot in videos longer than a few seconds in length.

- Adjust the video's in- and out-points by dragging the sliders at each end of the video overview slider. As you adjust them, these will turn golden in color. A Trim button will appear, allowing you to keep the selected segment of the video and to discard the rest. You can trim the original video in-place or to save the trimmed version as a new clip. Using a new clip keeps the original video intact but takes up extra room on your iPad (see Figure 15–8), up to 120MB per minute. Tap the Cancel button to return to the Image/Video browser without applying your edit.

- Use the AirPlay menu to redirect the video to an AirPlay-capable device. During AirPlay playback, your screen goes dark and a message will appear, letting you know that the video is being sent to that AirPlay destination.

- Use the Sharing menu to e-mail your video (if it is short enough), to send it to YouTube, or to copy your video to the system pasteboard for use in other applications. If you are a Mobile Me customer, you'll find an option to post your video to a Mobile Me gallery from this menu. See Chapter 13 for more details about sharing your videos and images with others.

The video overlay menu bar at the top of the screen shows you the back button, labeled Camera Roll. Tapping this returns you to the main Camera Roll on your iPad. From there, you can tap the Done button to exit the Camera Roll and return to the Camera app.

Other items you may see on-screen include the trash can button, which brings up a deletion confirmation menu and an asset slider, which appears at the bottom of the screen. Dragging along the slider lets you select what image or video you want to view, for easy navigation through your Camera Roll library.

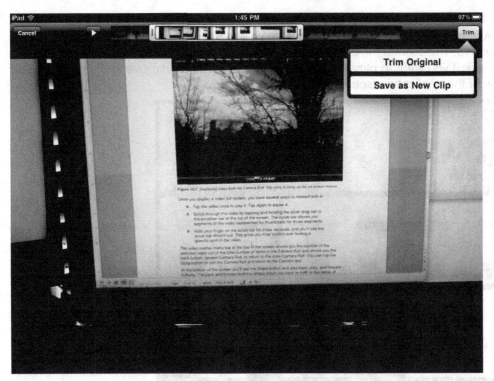

Figure 15–8. *Video-trim mode. Yes, that is a video of the writing of this book. See if you can spot where in the chapter it was recorded.*

Having Fun with Photo Booth

With its bright red curtain, it's hard to miss the cheerful icon that represents the Photo Booth application (see Figure 15–9). Photo Booth lets you apply special effects to pictures *as you are taking them*. Working with both the front- and back-cameras, Photo Booth isn't about to cure cancer or create world peace, but it will offer a lot of fun for playing with your cameras and the pictures you take.

Figure 15–9. *The iPad's Photo Booth icon leads to a fun application for playing with your pictures.*

Photo Booth lets you select an effect that distorts or otherwise changes images in real time. At first launch, you're presented with a selection of those special effects, as shown in Figure 15–10. Choose the effect you want to work with (undistorted/normal is right in the center, if you want to play things safe) and tap it. You then move to the photo-taking portion of the application (see Figure 15–11).

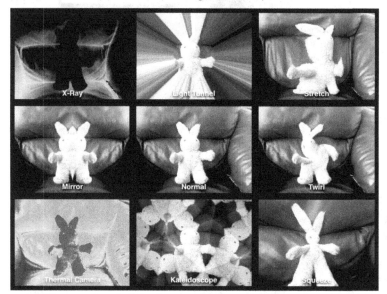

Figure 15–10. *Select one of eight image effects (or the center for Normal undistorted imagery) from Photo Booth's effects screen. Effects include X-Ray, Light Tunnel, Stretch, Mirror (not reverse, the center mirrors out to either side), Twirl, Thermal Camera, Kaleidoscope, and Squeeze.*

Here, as shown in Figure 15–11, is where you can manipulate, select, and share your photos. You can return to effect selection at any time by tapping the kaleidoscope-looking button at the bottom left of the Photos/Camera screen.

Figure 15–11. *The Photos/Camera screen of Photo Booth allows you to snap new photos (tap the gray camera button at the bottom middle); to control the camera you're using (tap the camera selection button at the bottom right); and to select, view, and share your photos.*

Snapping Photos

Initially, you're presented with a live camera preview. When working with live effects, you can sometimes stroke your finger across the screen—up and down or side to side—to affect the way the special effect is applied to the image.

Adjustments are not available for every effect; for example, they do not work with the "thermal" images, but they do set the center of the light tunnel and the position of the mirror effect. It's best to explore by touching to see how you can affect your results during the live preview.

To snap a photo with Photo Booth, just aim the camera you want to use at your subject and tap the camera button. You'll hear a shutter sound, indicating the picture has been captured. Switch between the front and back cameras by tapping the camera flip button at the bottom right of the screen.

Each time you take a picture, the Photo Booth library adds a new image to the row just above the buttons at the bottom of the screen. You can view each image by tapping on it. When selected, the live camera preview stops, and the selected image appears on-screen. Figure 15–12 shows what Photo Booth looks like during image viewing.

To delete an image, tap the circled *X* that appears to the top left on selection (see Figure 15–12). A red Delete Photo confirmation menu will appear. Tap Delete Photo to remove the photo from the library or anywhere else on the screen to cancel and dismiss the menu.

Tap the black Photo button at the bottom center to return from the static display of library images back to the live camera preview.

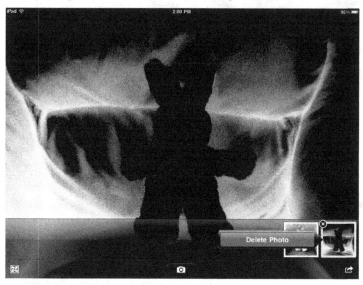

Figure 15–12. *Tapping on any item in the library list displays that photo on-screen in image-viewing mode. Tap the blackened camera icon at the bottom center to return to the live preview mode or tap the manage button (bottom right) to manage your entire Photo Booth library at once.*

Managing Photos

While displaying any image, you can tap the Manage button at the bottom right of Figure 15–12 to select photos. The Manage button looks like a rectangle with an arrow coming out from it. When in library management mode, you can tap any photo select it. A check mark appears to indicate your selection, and the display changes (as shown in Figure 15–13) to a pile of photos. Tap a photo again to remove it from your selection. A check mark will disappear.

Once you've assembled your selection—the number of items you have chosen is listed at the bottom of the screen—choose to e-mail, copy, or delete that collection. By choosing e-mail, the iPad composes a new message and adds your images. Remember that you can attach up to five photos to any e-mail. Copy will, as the name suggests, copy the images to your iPad's system pasteboard, ready to be pasted into other applications. Delete, once confirmed, removes all selected images from your library.

Be aware that Photo Booth coordinates with your main Photo application library. When you snap a picture in Photo Booth, it's automatically added to your main library. When you delete a Photo Booth image, it's also deleted from the main library as well. At this time, Photo Booth images are not collected into a separate album in Photos, although Apple may move that way in the future.

Uploading Photo Booth Pictures to Your Computer

Although you can e-mail photos to yourself, it's generally easier to upload photos directly when connected to your computer. On the Mac, you can use iPhoto's Import and Download buttons. Under Windows, you need to follow the instructions that shipped with the photo application you're using.

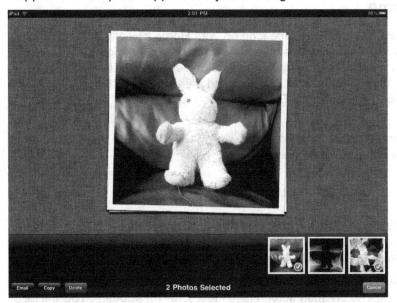

Figure 15–13. *Create a collection of images by tapping the Share button and adding images from the scrolling library at the bottom of your screen. Checks indicate that images have been selected for the collection.*

Using FaceTime to Chat

This chapter has already introduced the iPad's front and rear cameras. These cameras signify a major hardware upgrade for the iPad. They aren't just for taking pictures and recording video: you can also use them for FaceTime, a technology that brings easy and intuitive video calling to the masses.

With the FaceTime app on the iPad, you can video call anyone whose computer or device also runs FaceTime. This includes second-generation or newer iPads, fourth-generation or newer iPod touches, iPhone 4 or newer, and Mac computers that are running FaceTime software. Ideally, FaceTime will soon arrive on Windows as well.

Apple wants to make FaceTime the de facto standard for video calling, and in order to do so, Apple has made the FaceTime technology an open standard. That means other phone manufacturers can build the technology in their phones, so one day, ideally, you'll be able to FaceTime video call on your iPad to someone on an Android phone.

To use FaceTime, besides your iPad, you'll need to have a Wi-Fi Internet connection and an Apple ID. The person who you are calling must also have a Wi-Fi connection, even if you are calling them on an iPhone 4. At the time this book was being written, iPhone 4 owners could use FaceTime only over Wi-Fi, not over their service provider's data network. The service providers and not Apple most likely put this limitation in place. Streaming live video over a cellular network takes a lot of bandwidth—something that is very costly for a service provider. It's also very taxing on the network itself.

Opening FaceTime

To begin using FaceTime, tap the FaceTime icon on your Home screen. The icon looks like a white video camera with a blue lens on a metallic background (Figure 15–14). If this is the first time you've launched the app, you'll be presented with the FaceTime Get Started screen (Figure 15–15). Enter your Apple ID and password and then tap Sign In to get started. If you do not have an Apple ID, you will need to tap Create New Account instead.

If you click the "Learn more about FaceTime" link, Safari will open, and you'll be taken to Apple's iPad FaceTime page on Apple's web site.

Signing In

To sign in with your existing Apple ID, fill in the e-mail and password fields, and tap Sign In. You already have an Apple ID if you use the iTunes Store, the App Store, or the iBookstore. You also have an Apple ID if you have an iCloud account.

If you do not already have an Apple ID, you can set up a new account from FaceTime. Tap Create New Account. The creation screen (see Figure 15–16) appears. You will be prompted to enter your name, a valid e-mail (which will act as your new Apple ID), a password, and other security information.

When you sign in for the first time, whether creating a new account or using an existing ID, Apple notifies you that people will call you using your e-mail address. You are asked which e-mail address you would like to use. You can keep the same e-mail address that is your Apple ID, or you can enter another e-mail address.

Once you have entered the e-mail address you want associated with FaceTime calls, tap the Next button. A short verification screen appears as Apple verifies that your e-mail address is authentic. Then a Check Mail button will appear; tapping it will navigate you to your selected e-mail account in the iPad's mail app.

Look for an e-mail with the subject "Please verify the contact e-mail address for your Apple ID." Tap the Verify Now link in this e-mail. A Safari window opens, taking you to the My Apple ID page. There you'll need to enter your Apple ID and password to verify your FaceTime e-mail address.

Once you are presented with the "E-mail address verified" web page, return to the FaceTime app. You'll be presented with a list of contacts, similar to the Contacts application on your iPad's Home screen.

NOTE: Apple now requires e-mail style Apple IDs. If you are used to using an older account name style (such as firstname_lastname), you will be prompted to associate an e-mail address with your existing account. After doing so, you will need to log in using the e-mail in future, not your original account name.

Figure 15–14. *The FaceTime icon*

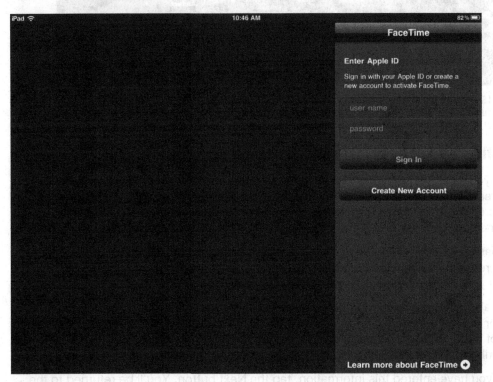

Figure 15–15. *The FaceTime Get Started screen. You will generally see a live front-facing camera preview in the area to the left.*

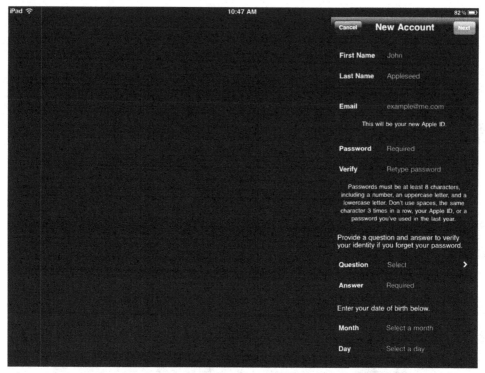

Figure 15–16. *Use this screen to create a new Apple ID to use with FaceTime. The account creation and authorization procedure for FaceTime is subject to change as Apple evolves its software.*

Creating an Account

When you have not previously established an Apple ID, you can create one by tapping the Create New Account button. The New Account screen (Figure 15–16) appears. On this screen, you will enter your first and last name, your e-mail address (which will become your new Apple ID), and a password of at least eight characters.

This password does not have to be the same as the password for your e-mail account. Apple requests that you include a number, an uppercase letter, and a lowercase letter as part of your ID to increase the security of your password.

You'll also need to choose a security question and enter the answer. This question and answer is used in case you forget your Apple ID password. Finally, enter your month and date of birth, choose which country you reside in, and select whether you want to subscribe to the Apple e-mail list.

Once you have entered this information, tap the Next button. You'll be returned to the Sign In screen with your Apple ID and password already entered, and signing in will commence.

You'll need to go through the same e-mail verification process described in the previous section. A short verification screen will appear as Apple verifies that your e-mail address is authentic. Once verified, you can return to FaceTime and sign in.

Navigating Your FaceTime Contacts

Each time you launch the FaceTime app, once you've established your identity and signed into your account, you are presented with a list of contacts. The contacts screen is divided into three sections, accessible by tapping the buttons in the contact bar at the bottom of the screen.

> *Favorites*: This screen allows you to add your favorite contacts to it. It's handy as a shortcut to the people you call the most.

> *Recents*: This screen lists the recent FaceTime calls you've made or received.

> *Contacts*: This screen lists all the contacts in your address book.

Here's a closer look at each of these contact sections.

Favorites

The Favorites screen (Figure 15–17) allows you to create and maintain a list of your favorite contacts. Favorite contacts generally are the people you call the most, such as family and friends and important work contacts. This screen acts as a shortcut to their FaceTime e-mail addresses or phone numbers.

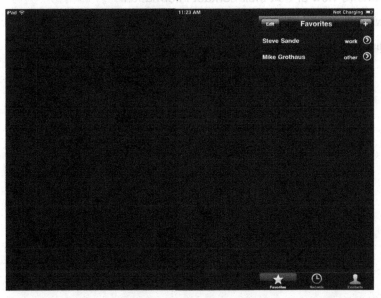

Figure 15–17. *The Favorites screen (left). Selecting the e-mail or phone number of a Favorites contact (right).*

Adding a contact to Favorites: Tap the + button in the upper-right corner, and then select your contact from the address book list that slides up on the screen.

Choosing the contact's FaceTime info: From your selected contact's information screen, tap the FaceTime e-mail address or phone number for the contact. If your contact is using an iPad, you must choose their associated FaceTime e-mail. If you contact is using an iPhone 4, you can choose their iPhone 4 phone number. Once you have chosen your contact's FaceTime info, a blue star appears by their FaceTime e-mail or number.

Calling a Favorite: Once you have set up your favorites, simply tap their name in the Favorites list, and a FaceTime call will be initiated.

You can tap the chevron next to a favorite's name to view or edit their contact information.

Recents

The Recents screen (see Figure 15–18) gives you a list of recently made or received FaceTime calls. This list can be sorted into the following two categories via the tabs at the top of the screen:

All: Shows you all the FaceTime calls you have made, received, or missed. Missed calls show up in red. The time of the call is shown to the right of the name of the person called. You can tap the chevron next to a favorite's name to view or edit their contact information.

Missed: Shows only the FaceTime calls you have missed.

To clear your Recents list, tap the Clear button in the upper-right corner of the screen.

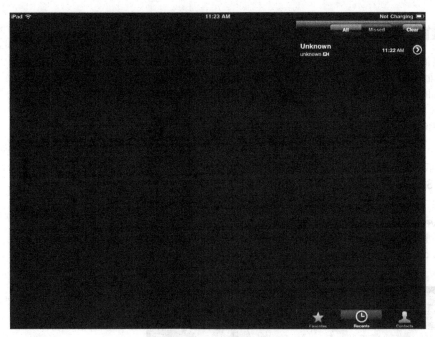

Figure 15–18. *The Recents list*

Contacts

The Contacts screen features your entire address book. It works just like your stand-alone Contacts application. When you find the contact you want to call, tap their name, and their contact information card will be displayed. Tap their FaceTime e-mail or FaceTime phone number, and your call will begin (see Figure 15–19).

Figure 15–19. *Placing a FaceTime call from your iPad. A front-facing camera preview appears on-screen as the call is being placed. Tap End to terminate the call without connecting.*

Placing and Receiving a FaceTime Call

To make a FaceTime call, select a contact from your Favorites, Recents, or Contacts list. Tapping a name in the Favorites or Recents list will initiate the FaceTime call (Figure 15–11). To start a call using your Contacts list, you'll need to tap the contact's name and then tap either a FaceTime phone number or e-mail. To cancel a call before the person has picked up, tap the END button shown in Figure 15–19.

> **NOTE:** You can change your incoming FaceTime ringtone by navigating to the Settings app and then choosing **Sounds ➤ Ringtone**.

When you receive a FaceTime call, a message will appear on-screen telling you that a friend would like FaceTime with you (Figure 15–20). The front camera automatically activates so you can see what you look like. To accept, slide your finger along the "slide to answer" area.

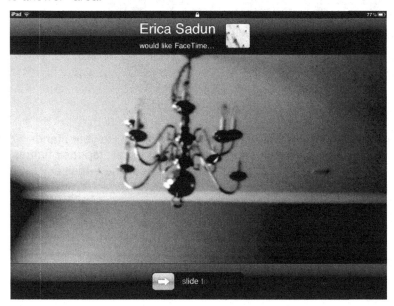

Figure 15–20. *Receiving a FaceTime call*

Figure 15–21 shows you what it looks like when you are in a FaceTime call. The speaker's image takes up a majority of the screen, while your image appears in a rectangle at the corner of the screen. Below your image is the FaceTime control bar. This gives you several options.

Figure 15–21. *A FaceTime video call*

Mute: Tap the microphone icon to switch between muting and unmuting a call. While you call is muted, you can still hear the person you are calling, but they cannot hear you. While a call is muted, the other person can still see you, so be careful what you do!

Switching cameras: Tap the Switch Camera icon in the bottom right of the screen to switch between the front and rear cameras. The icon looks like a traditional still camera with swirling arrows on either side. Switching cameras changes what the person you are talking to sees. When the camera is switched, your friend will see what the rear camera on the iPad is pointed at.

Switching cameras during a call is a handy feature. It allows your friend to see what you are looking at, like your newborn crawling on all fours, for example.

Ending the call: To end a FaceTime call, tap the End button.

NOTE: You know that the iPad has two cameras, but did you know the front one has been specifically designed for FaceTime? Apple made sure it has just the right focal length and field of view to focus on your face at arm's length.

Other FaceTime Calling Options

FaceTime gives you several advanced options while on a call that help with its usability features:

> *Change orientation*: You can rotate your iPad into landscape mode, and the image your caller sees will change to match. Landscape mode while FaceTime calling is useful if you want to show your caller a wide shot of something using the rear camera, like a beautiful sunset from your backyard.

TIP: To avoid unwanted orientation changes as you move the camera around, lock your iPad in portrait orientation by pressing the Home button twice and flicking right until you see the portrait lock button. You can also set the switch on the side of the iPad, normally used for muting, to work as an orientation lock in Settings. Choose **Settings ➤ General ➤ Use Side Switch to: ➤ Lock Rotation**.

> *Moving picture-in-picture*: That little square in the corner that shows you what your caller is seeing can be moved around. Tap and hold the square and drag it to any of the four corners of the screen. This is useful if the square is blocking something on the screen that you want to see.

> *Multitasking during a FaceTime call*: You can use any app on your iPad while on a FaceTime call. To do so, while in a FaceTime call, press your iPad's Home button once to be taken to the Home screen. You can then launch any app you want. To return to your FaceTime call, tap the glowing green "Touch to resume FaceTime" bar at the top of the screen (Figure 15–22).

Figure 15–22. *You can use other apps while on a FaceTime call. Touch the green bar at the top of the screen to return to the FaceTime call when you're done.*

The multitasking feature is particularly nice when you are on a FaceTime call. It allows you to check the Yelp app for restaurants while you're making dinner plans with your FaceTime caller, for example.

While you are multitasking, you can still talk to your FaceTime caller, but neither of you can see the other.

FaceTime Settings

FaceTime has several settings. You can find them in the Settings app under FaceTime (Figure 15–23).

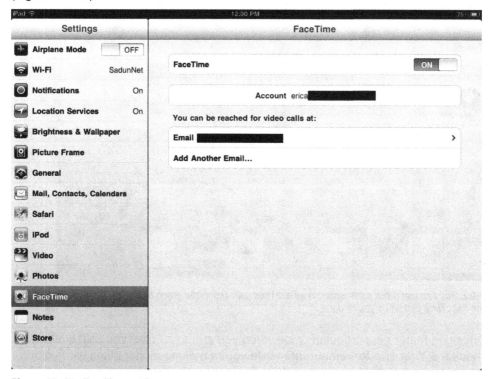

Figure 15–23. *FaceTime settings*

Switch FaceTime on or off: Tap the FaceTime switch to On or Off. While off, you cannot make or receive FaceTime calls, which means you may miss a special treat while you are busy getting work done. When enabled, however, other people can call you, interrupting whatever you are doing.

Change your FaceTime geographic location: Tap your blue Account e-mail. From the pop-up menu, tap Change Location. Choose your location's new region from the list of regions.

View your FaceTime account settings: Tap your blue Account e-mail. From the pop-up menu, tap View Account. Sign in with your Apple ID and password. The account settings screen from Figure 15–6 will show up on-screen. Tap any field to change your account settings, such as your name or security question.

Sign out of FaceTime: Tap your blue Account e-mail. From the pop-up menu, tap Sign Out. This will immediately sign you out of FaceTime without any more warnings. To sign back in, reenter your Apple ID password on the Sign In screen.

Remove a FaceTime e-mail address: You can dissociate your FaceTime e-mail address by tapping it and then tapping the Remove This E-mail button.

Adding more e-mail addresses: FaceTime allows you to associate more than one e-mail address with your FaceTime account. This is handy if you use several e-mails for different purposes in your life. For example, you might have one for friends and one for work colleagues, and so forth. When multiple e-mails are associated with your FaceTime account, people can initiate a FaceTime video call with you using any one of them.

To add additional e-mails, tap the Add Another Email button, and then enter your other e-mail address. Repeat this step for each e-mail address you have. With each e-mail added, you'll need to check that e-mail account for the FaceTime verification e-mail from Apple and click the link in that e-mail before the e-mail address can be added to your FaceTime account.

Summary

The front and rear cameras add some nice features to the iPad. The HD video-recording capabilities are amazing, but the still photography leaves something to be desired, even if you take Photo Booth into consideration. In addition, FaceTime is an awesome feature, and its popularity is sure to grow as more devices become FaceTime-compatible. Here are a few more tips for using your camera and FaceTime:

- Do *not* leave your regular digital still camera at home when going on vacation. Yes, you can take still photos with the iPad, but it's more for social use, such as taking quick snaps of friends or self-portraits. If you want to catch that beautiful sunset over the ocean, do it on a point-and-shoot camera or on a cool new iPhone 4S. Want to distort your face and send it on to your pals? The iPad plus Photo Booth is the answer.

- You can zoom in while in still camera mode using digital, but not optical, zoom, but there is no zoom option while recording video.

- One minute of 720p video takes up about 120MBs. Keep this in mind if you are going to be recording a lot of video because you'll need a lot of free space on your iPad.

- Apple has limits size when e-mailing videos. In our tests, a video clip must be 54 seconds long or shorter in order for you to e-mail it. If it's 55 seconds or longer, you'll be asked to trim the clip before you e-mail it.

- When you are taking pictures or recording video within range of a Wi-Fi network or if you own a GPS-enabled 3G iPad, the iPad's Camera app can tag your photos and videos with geodata. Applications such as Apple's iPhoto can then display your photos on a map. If you are planning to make a lot of FaceTime calls at home or in the office, you may want to invest in an iPad dock or a simple picture stand so you don't have to keep holding your iPad at arm's length. A dock helps you eliminate those horrible up-the-nose and double-chin points of view that happen when we hold the iPad out.

- Use FaceTime from the sky! If you're on a plane that offers Wi-Fi service, you can use FaceTime to talk to your friends and family back on the ground.

- Don't forget to use the rear camera to show your caller what you are looking at. You don't have to turn your iPad around to show them!

- FaceTime is an amazing feature for those who can't speak. The screen resolution is big enough and crisp enough where sign language can easily be read.

- Watch out for bright backgrounds. If light is glaring in through the window behind you, it's likely to cause your viewer to see you in silhouette. To fix this, move your iPad's camera just a tiny way away from the light source, and your face should show up just fine.

Chapter **16**

Other Great Ways to Use Your iPad

Throughout this book, we've shown you how to use your iPad to listen to your music and watch movies, write e-mails and documents, navigate with maps, and show off your photos, but all of that (and it's a lot!) is just the start.

In this chapter, we show you just some of the many other ways you can use your iPad in everyday life, including as a helper in the kitchen, as a teaching tool, as a gaming device, as an artist's canvas, and more!

NOTE: All prices of apps and games mentioned in this chapter are current as of the time of this writing. App and game prices are subject to change at any time, however.

The iPad as a Game Machine

The iPad is a great device when you just want to kick back and unwind. You can listen to music, watch your favorite TV shows, and flick through photos of your last vacation with ease. Another way to unwind on the iPad is by playing games.

Whether you're into card games, adventure epics, or sports, there's a game for you. As a matter of fact, as of the time of this writing, more than 4,000 dedicated iPad games are available in the App Store, and that's not including the 90,000+ iPhone games that play on the iPad as well.

Here we spotlight just some of the types of games you can play on the iPad.

Pinball HD

Pinball HD (see Figure 16–1) harkens back to the times when games existed in three dimensions in the physical world and not on a computer screen. You'll quickly forget that you aren't playing on an actual pinball machine, however, because the level of realism in Pinball HD is amazing. You can choose from three pinball tables, including the Wild West, a jungle, and the deep ocean. The app is a steal at $2.99.

Figure 16–1. *Pinball HD*

Doodle Jump

Doodle Jump (see Figure 16–2) was the first runaway hit game for the iPhone. It's taken almost a year and a half, but now Doodle Jump is also available for the iPad. In Doodle Jump you use the iPad's built-in sensors to tilt Doodle the Doodler left or right as he jumps from platform to platform making his way up a sheet of graph paper. Along the way, Doodler must get past enemies and access accessories that help him jump higher. If the game sounds simple, that because it is. But it's also the most addictive iPad game you'll ever play. Best of all, it's only $2.99.

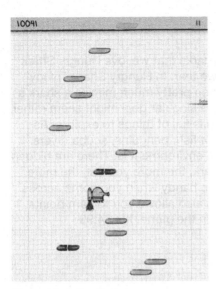

Figure 16–2. *Doodle Jump*

iFish Pond HD

This isn't a game in the traditional sense. Oh, you interact with it as much as you would any game, but iFish Pond HD (see Figure 16–3) can be fun even if you don't touch it. The game gives you a virtual fishpond on your iPad screen. Tap the water, and watch it ripple. See the colorful fish scurry away from your fingers, only to slowly come back to the calm of the pond. Add dragonflies, frogs, and pond lilies as you like; then sit back and enjoy the tranquility of nature on your iPad. It's $2.99.

Figure 16–3. *iFish Pond HD*

Hungry Shark Trilogy

Maybe it's because we have an unreasonable fear of sharks that we love Hungry Shark Trilogy so much. It allows us to control the very thing we fear. In Hungry Shark Trilogy (see Figure 16–4) you play as the shark, and your mission pretty much mimics a shark's real life: your only goal is to eat and keep eating. While a singular goal might seem rather monotonous, it's anything but. The Hungry Shark world is full of things to explore. As you chomp and bite your way though dozens of kinds of fish, penguins, scuba divers, and seagulls, you'll discover just how rich the undersea environment is. There are hidden caves, sea mines, and secret objects galore. As the shark, the more you eat, the more you grow and the stronger you become, which comes in handy when you come across the best boss of any iPad game—the giant crab. Eating also allows you to earn points, which unlocks other Hungry Shark episodes, or levels, in the game. It's $4.99.

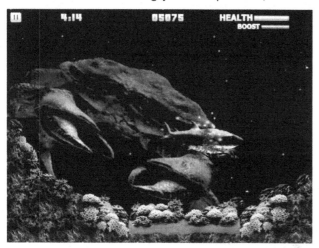

Figure 16–4. *Hungry Shark Trilogy*

Mirror's Edge

Major game developers are releasing games for the iPad in droves. One of the biggest game developers in the world, Electronic Arts, has a host of games out already. Mirror's Edge (see Figure 16–5) was originally released for the Xbox 360 and PlayStation 3, and Electronic Arts has successfully ported it to the iPad, which goes to show just how powerful of a gaming device it can be. You play Faith, a "runner" who must get secret information past totalitarian police. Using nothing but your fingers and the iPad's built-in tilt sensors, you pilot Faith through her world by making her flip, slide, jump, and run. It's one fun game and is just a hint of the kind of action games you can expect to see coming to the iPad in the future. It costs $9.99.

Figure 16–5. *EA's Mirror's Edge*

The iPad as a News and Weather Center

The iPad is an awesome device that puts the Internet in your hands. You'll always be able to open the Safari web browser and check out any news site in the world. However, web sites are different from physical newspapers. They have a different layout, and you interact with them differently. Many major newspapers make apps for the iPad that enable to you to navigate the newspapers in the format you are used to in their physical counterparts. In addition, there are weather apps designed specifically for the iPad that show you the weather forecast in a nicer and faster way than if you looked it up on the Web. Here we'll touch on just some of the news and weather apps available for the iPad.

News Apps

It seems that there's a new news app added to the App Store every day. We've sorted through the clutter and present to you here four of our favorites. There are many more out there—some very good—so browse through the App Store to find others that deliver the latest headlines to your iPad as well.

MarketDash by Yahoo! Finance

Yahoo! Finance is one of the most popular finance sites on the Web. It took a while, but Yahoo! Finance has finally released an iPad app in the form of MarketDash (see Figure 16–6). MarketDash presents to you all the information that you find on Yahoo! Finance in an elegant and interactive package so you can keep up with up-to-the-minute news on financial markets around the world. It offers news, stock quotes, price charts, and more. You can create a list portfolio of stocks to track, monitor market currencies, and even sign in with your Yahoo! ID to automatically track all the portfolios you track online. MarketDash by Yahoo! Finance is free in the App Store.

Figure 16–6. *MarketDash by Yahoo! Finance*

Huffington Post for iPad

The Huffington Post is the Internet-only newspaper that's taken the Web by storm. The "paper" has regular staff writers but also features article by experts across a myriad variety of fields.

Huffington Post for iPad offers a selection of the latest news, opinion, and features from every section of the paper (see Figure 16–7). The app is nice because it doesn't try to do too much. Sure, you can look at photo galleries and videos in the app, but it also has a terrific interface that mimics the layout of an actual newspapers. The Huffington Post knows that most people still like to read their news, and it presents text to you in an easy-to-view layout. The app is free in the App Store.

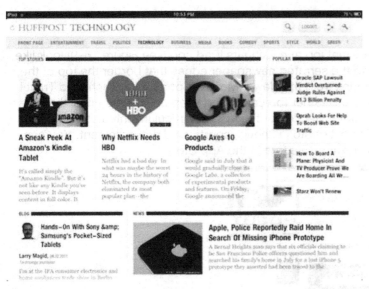

Figure 16–7. *Huffington Post for iPad*

BBC News

The BBC News app (see Figure 16–8) takes the best of the BBC's web site and news channels and rolls it into one beautifully designed iPad app. Scroll through the latest news in Top Stories, Technology, Business, Science & Environment, Regional, and more than a dozen other categories. Listen to live BBC Radio from within the app with the tap of a button; watch short video news clips; share articles easily via e-mail, Facebook, and Twitter; and even read news articles in other languages including Russian, Chinese, Arabic, and Portuguese. It's free in the App Store.

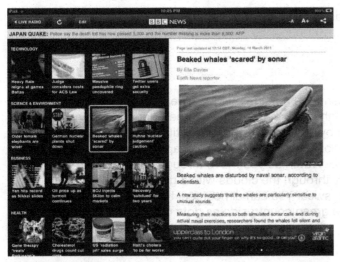

Figure 16–8. *BBC News*

USA Today for iPad

USA Today has done an excellent job at making its iPad app (see Figure 16–9) look like the real paper—right down to the serrated newspaper edges that border the top of the screen. Browse and read stories from the News, Money, Sports, Life, Tech, and Travel sections; see local and national weather forecasts; and keep up-to-date on all the latest sports scores. The Day in Pictures section of the app is particularly interesting. It lets you swipe through the day's best photos in news, sports, and entertainment. You can also play the images as a slideshow. It's free in the App Store.

Figure 16–9. *USA Today*

Weather Apps

Just like with news apps, there are myriad weather apps for the iPad, but these are two of our favorites.

Weather HD

Weather HD (see Figure 16–10) isn't the most full-fledged weather app, but it is among the most beautiful. Browse through your selected city's three-hour and seven-day forecasts while being captivated by some of the most beautiful 3D animated landscapes representing the current weather outside. The Weather HD app shows you just how beautiful your iPad screen can be. Watch as you move through a field of lush green grass and tall wind turbines or fly through the clouds with a glorious moon rising in the distance. Raining outside? You'll swear you can almost feel the drops mist your face as Weather HD glides you through a green countryside as dots of rain float in the air. It's a steal at $0.99 in the App Store.

Figure 16–10. *Weather HD*

The Weather Channel

Although it lacks the beauty of Weather HD, the Weather Channel's official iPad app more than makes up for it in features. The Weather Channel for iPad (see Figure 16–11) delivers in-depth weather reports for current, 36-hour, and 10-day forecasts. Watch the latest weather-related news stories and a selection of Weather Channel original programming right in the app. You can even navigate weather maps by pinching and zooming. See Doppler radar, cloud coverage, Feels Like, and even UV Index maps. It's the weather of the world in your lap. Best of all, it's free in the App Store.

Figure 16–11. *The Weather Channel*

The iPad as an Artist's Canvas

As you've seen, the iPad isn't just a tool to consume data; you can also use it to create things such as documents, spreadsheets, and presentations. But the ability to create content on the iPad isn't limited to those who work in the business world. The iPad is a wonderful artist's tool. It's quite literally a blank canvas that you can use to create masterpieces Picasso would be envious of. Although there are several iPad artist apps, here are two that are our favorites.

Brushes

Brushes got its start on the iPhone and has since moved to the next level on the iPad (see Figure 16–12). Brushes is a powerful tool for creating original works of art using your iPad's Multi-Touch display. Drag and swipe your fingers to create brush strokes on a blank canvas. Use the advanced color picker, myriad brushes, layers, the eyedropper tool, undo and redo controls, and more to create whatever your mind can conceive. Do you think creating artworks on the iPad isn't for "serious" artists? Artist Jorge Colombo famously created the June 1, 2009, cover of *The New Yorker* entirely using Brushes…for the iPhone. Now imagine what he—and you—could do with a digital canvas the size of the iPad's screen. The app costs $7.99, but think of how much money you're going to save by not having to buy replacement canvases and paints.

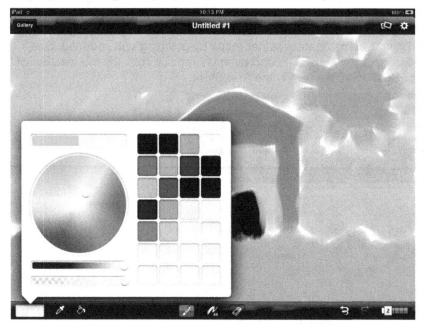

Figure 16–12. *It looks like it was drawn by a 2 year old, but it was actually created by one of the authors in about 30 seconds. Try your own hand at creating art on the iPad with Brushes.*

Adobe Ideas

If Brushes is a canvas, Adobe Ideas is a sketchpad (see Figure 16–13). Using the tips of your fingers, sketch that latest idea you have for the dress that is going to take New York and Milan by storm, test designs for next year's most popular new superhero, or even use it as a whiteboard for coffee-table meetings in Starbucks. A nice feature of this app is that you can export any image you create as a PDF and e-mail it to yourself or others for editing in Adobe's professional apps like Illustrator and Photoshop or for viewing with any PDF viewer. Adobe Ideas is free in the App Store.

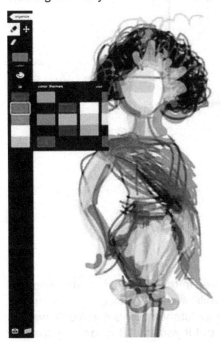

Figure 16–13. *Adobe Ideas lets you get your ideas down on paper...er, Multi-Touch screen.*

The iPad as a Phone

When the iPad was first unveiled, some people joked that it was nothing more than a big iPhone. As you can now tell, they couldn't have been more wrong. However, you can actually use your iPad as a phone. All you need to do is download the free Skype app (see Figure 16–14) from the App Store, and you can make calls from your iPad to any phone in the world.

To use the app, you'll need a free Skype account, which you can set up at www.skype.com. You'll also need to be connected to a Wi-Fi network since Skype uses VoIP (calls made over Internet lines) to make phone calls.

Once you log in to the Skype app on your iPad, you can make free iPad-to-computer calls with other Skype users. If you buy Skype credit, you can make iPad-to-landline or cell phone calls. One of the writers uses Skype on his iPad in London to call his mother on her house phone in the United States because it is much cheaper than regular international rates or even buying a calling card. So, the iPad is not just an oversized iPhone, but it can make calls like the iPhone can.

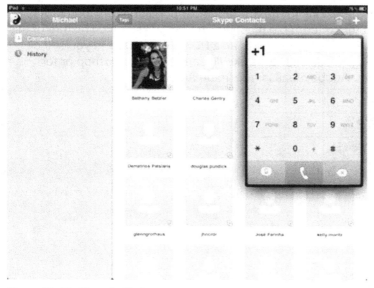

Figure 16–14. *Skype for iPad*

The iPad as a Kitchen Helper

It may sound strange, but the iPad is very much at home in the kitchen. Whether you're using it as an electronic cookbook, surfing the Web while waiting for water to boil, or listening to music while you cook, the iPad is the perfect kitchen computer. You'll want to make sure that your iPad isn't near liquids or heat, but if you treat it with the respect of a beloved cookbook, you're probably fine.

A good way to keep your iPad safe from splashes or smears when it is on the kitchen counter is to put it into a resealable zipper-type freezer bag. Chef Sleeve (www.chefsleeve.com) also makes reusable bags that are the perfect size for an iPad, made of a much more transparent plastic, and come in a box that doubles as an iPad stand.

Since you'll be chopping veggies and slicing meat, using a case with a built-in stand to keep the iPad in an upright position is a good idea. It takes up less counter space that way, and with a quick glance at the screen, you can find out what ingredient you need to add next to your recipe. Apple's iPad Case works very well to place your iPad in the proper position. We also suggest setting Auto-Lock (**Settings ➤ General ➤ Auto-Lock**) to Never so that you're not constantly having to turn the iPad back on. With those hints in mind, let's explore some kitchen-friendly apps.

Food Network In the Kitchen

If you're not sure about using your iPad in the kitchen, then Food Network In the Kitchen (see Figure 16–15) is the perfect app to install to try your device as a kitchen helper. The $1.99 app calls upon recipes from various Food Network stars to provide thousands of recipes, all of which are rated by users. The list of featured recipes changes by season, and holiday specials are always useful for family get-togethers.

Figure 16–15. *The $1.99 Food Network In the Kitchen app turns your iPad into an intelligent cookbook with recipes for every occasion.*

The In the Kitchen app provides a way to change the font size, so if you want to set your iPad a bit farther away from your stove, you should still be able to read the screen from across the kitchen. There's a built-in kitchen timer and a unit converter, and each recipe has a shopping list icon; tapping that icon pushes the ingredients to a shopping list. Once you're ready to go to the store, it creates a combined shopping list that can be e-mailed to your iPhone, since you probably won't want to carry your iPad around the grocery store. When you want to share recipes with friends, you can e-mail them or send links to Facebook or Twitter.

BigOven

Another electronic cookbook to spice up your iPad is BigOven (see Figure 16–16). The app searches more than 170,000 recipes in the BigOven.com database by name, by keyword (such as *rutabaga*), and even by what leftovers you have around the house.

Figure 16–16. *BigOven is another wonderful resource for the iPad-toting chef. The ability to search for recipes that use up your leftovers is priceless.*

The recipes display in both an overview format and a prepare format. The latter lists ingredients in one column and preparation instructions in the other.

A BigOven Pro membership ($15.99 per year) includes powerful syncing functions to make your grocery list and other information available on your iPad, on your iPhone, and on the Web.

My Recipe Book

Sometimes recipes don't come from an electronic source but are provided to you in the normal manner, such as scrawled on a note card by your Aunt Minnie in her indecipherable handwriting. Once you get a chance to sit down with her to translate the recipe, consider entering it into My Recipe Book (see Figure 16–17).

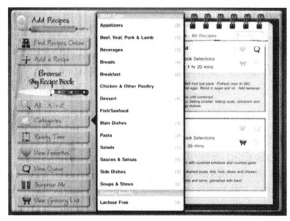

Figure 16–17. *Finally, My Recipe Book provides a place to organize all of those handwritten recipe cards you've been collecting over the years.*

This $2.99 app is just the thing for organizing recipes that would otherwise clutter up a recipe box or get stuffed into a kitchen drawer. My Recipe Book includes a way to search by preparation time and even includes a kitchen timer.

Serving Sizer Pro for iPad

Have you ever become so good at making a particular recipe that you're "volunteered" to cook it for thirty people instead of four? Serving Sizer Pro for iPad (see Figure 16–18) can help.

Figure 16–18. *Serving Sizer Pro for iPad is a great tool for upsizing or downscaling recipes for various size groups.*

After entering a recipe into Serving Sizer Pro for iPad for a set number of servings, the $4.99 app not only keeps your recipe but can scale it to any number of portions.

Wine.com for iPad

There is an old French proverb that says "Un jour sans vin est comme un jour sans soleil," which means a day without wine is like a day without sunshine. For people of many countries, wine is a welcome accompaniment to meals, and there's nothing better than a really good bottle of wine with a special meal.

The free Wine.com for iPad app provides names of good wines, ratings, a photo of the label on the bottle, recommendations on food pairing, a flavor profile, and the price. If you live in a state that allows delivery of wine by mail, there's even a way to purchase your favorite vintages.

The iPad as a Presentation Tool

Teachers, presenters, and people who need to get a point across to an audience have a compact and low-cost tool available in the iPad. Rather than needing a dedicated Windows computer or Mac to drive a projector, presenters can use an iPad with inexpensive software to produce professional, good-looking presentations or course materials.

Keynote

We talked about Keynote in Chapter 14, so we won't belabor the point in this section. It's just important to understand that Keynote for iPad can display both Keynote for Mac and PowerPoint presentations on a computer projector.

Many presentations created on Macs or Windows computers work perfectly when transferred to the iPad. Be sure to test those presentations and any video-out savvy apps in advance before you have a live audience, and make sure that all transitions, builds, and fonts transfer to the iPad properly. Another plus is that Keynote documents sync across all your iOS devices via iCloud.

Sadun's Whiteboard

There's only one flaw with using an iPad as a teaching tool, or should we say there *was* one flaw? There was no way to just write on a slide and have it displayed through the video output cables.

One of the authors of this book, Erica Sadun, wrote the aptly named Sadun's Whiteboard (see Figure 16–19) app to resolve this issue. The $2.99 app starts off displaying a plain white background on which you can use black, red, blue, and green markers to draw or write on a virtual whiteboard. Sadun's Whiteboard supports video-out, so everything you put on the whiteboard is displayed on an attached computer projector.

If that's not enough functionality for you, Sadun's Whiteboard also displays your Keynote slides, and you can "write" on them. It also has a built-in web browser, perfect for demonstrating sites or web apps, and once again, you can mark up the sites with your virtual markers.

Figure 16–19. *Sadun's Whiteboard is an inexpensive electronic whiteboard that is perfect for teachers or presenters who need to display handwritten notes or marks on a virtual whiteboard, on a web page, or on a Keynote presentation.*

The Education Category in the App Store

If you're a teacher or a parent who wants to give your child an advantage in school, take some time to search the large and growing list of education apps for iPad. Launch the App Store on your iPad, tap the Categories button at the bottom of the page, and then tap the Education button.

What is displayed (see Figure 16–20) is every educational iPad app written for iPad. When we were writing this book, there were more than 8,500 apps in the Education category in the App Store.

Figure 16–20. *The Education category in the App Store has something for everyone, from preschoolers to graduate students. Many apps are available for free.*

Depending on the topic and type of app, you may be able to download many education apps for free.

iTunes University

Although it's not iPad-specific, we would be remiss in discussing educational content for the iPad without discussing iTunes University (see Figure 16–21). Accessible from the iTunes U button at the bottom of the iTunes app (not the App Store) is a vast collection of free video courseware made available by prestigious organizations throughout the world.

Figure 16–21. *iTunes University provides a wealth of free courseware about almost any topic.*

The videos range in topics from farming to astrodynamics and range from content for kindergartners to content for graduate students. iTunes University is the perfect destination for anyone who desires to further their knowledge.

The iPad as a Travel Computer

Whether you travel for business or pleasure, your iPad is a lightweight and unobtrusive traveling companion. If you're used to lugging a laptop and all of the sundry accessories (power supply, extra battery pack or two, Ethernet cable, and the laptop case) on your trips, you'll be surprised at how useful and powerful the iPad is as a fully functional travel computer.

Business travelers are usually interested in being able to track and book travel, communicate with people at home or back at the office, and determine whether weather is going to affect their travel plans. For leisure travelers, those requirements are usually the same, with the addition of being able to edit or retouch photos and video. Let's take a look at a handful of iPad apps that are perfect for travelers.

FlightTrack

FlightTrack (see Figure 16–22) is a handy app for determining the status of most flights, domestic or international, and in its free version displays beautiful maps showing the location of a flight in progress, departure and arrival times, and other important information.

Figure 16–22. *The free FlightTrack app for iPad is a fascinating tool for tracking the status of your flight. The $9.99 FlightTrack Pro app adds a significant amount of functionality, including synchronization with TripIt.com itineraries.*

Upgrade to the $9.99 Pro version, and you add a whole new level of functionality. FlightTrack Pro synchronizes itineraries with the TripIt.com travel planning service, so your flight information is automatically entered into the app. If you have multiple flight segments planned for a trip, FlightTrack Pro tracks all your flights on one screen for easy updates on flight status.

If a flight is delayed or canceled, a notification is pushed to your iPad even when the app isn't open. For those canceled flights, FlightTrack Pro finds alternate flights with a tap. Even when you're on a plane and have your device in airplane mode, FlightTrack Pro's maps will still work, showing your location on a detailed map. Weather information is available at a glance, with live radar maps showing any storms along your flight path.

Kayak HD for iPad

Kayak.com's motto is "Search one and done," meaning that one search finds the best possible airfare between two airports. Although you can't actually book the flights that are found in an exhaustive yet fast search, the free Kayak HD app (see Figure 16–23) provides a link so you *can* book the flights on Orbitz, CheapTickets, and airline web sites. In many cases, you're even provided with the number of seats left at a certain price on a particular flight.

Figure 16–23. *Rather than making you search a lot of airline web sites for the best air fare deals, the Kayak HD app does it all for you. Enter the departure and arrival airports and add a few details, and within seconds you have the lowest possible fares.*

If you need a hotel or rental car, Kayak HD links you to the appropriate web sites.

Urbanspoon HD for iPad

Man does not live on airline food alone, so the traveler needs restaurants to survive on the road. Urbanspoon HD (see Figure 16–24) is a popular free app for finding popular and good restaurants in almost every cuisine.

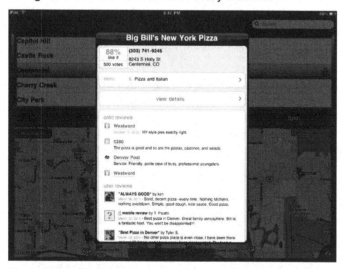

Figure 16–24. *The Urbanspoon HD app is a fun way of exploring restaurants in your local area or in any major city, all from the screen of your iPad.*

The app lists every restaurant in an urban area; in locations such as New York City, it's not uncommon to see 25,000 restaurants highlighted. To help you make a decision, there's a Popular button to narrow down the list to only those restaurants that have gained success through positive reviews and diner feedback. Urbanspoon also provides a way to narrow your search to individual neighborhoods, cuisines, and cost.

A fun thing to do is to use the Spin button to have Urbanspoon randomly pick a restaurant for you. Once you've decided whether the restaurant is actually a place you really want to try, tap the map for an address and phone number, the menu of the restaurant, and more reviews and information.

Don't be stuck with room service food when you're traveling; find out where the locals eat with Urbanspoon, and go enjoy yourself.

Built-in iPad VPN Support

Business travelers who need a secure Internet connection back to the services available in their offices often rely on virtual private networks (VPNs). A way to describe VPNs is that they create a secure, encrypted tunnel between your iPad (possibly sitting in a hotel room on an open Wi-Fi network) and your office.

Your network or IT support group has probably created a VPN portal for your company. You'll need to know the following information in order to configure your iPad:

- Type of VPN: L2TP, PPTP, IPsec
- Server address
- Account name
- Whether or not you're using an RSA SecurID fob
- Password (if not using RSA SecurID)
- Secret
- Proxy server information (if required)
- For PPTP: encryption level
- For IPsec: group name, and whether a certificate is being used

Once you have this information in hand, go to Settings ➤ General ➤ Network ➤ VPN. Add a VPN configuration, and enter the information in the appropriate places before saving the VPN configuration.

To connect to the VPN, make sure that you have a working Internet connection, and then turn on VPN and select your configured network. The iPad negotiates a secure connection, and you're free to work on your office network as if you were actually sitting there instead of next to the pool.

Getting the VPN configuration set up properly can be difficult, so ask your IT department for assistance if you run into any problems.

Photography/Videography Apps

It's common to see travelers using small digital cameras or iPhones to take pictures and video while they're visiting faraway places.

Your iPad can serve as a portable digital backup tool and editing suite. Use the iPad Camera Connection Kit to transfer your digital photos or video to the Photos app, and your digital imagery is backed up to another device. Next, you can use one of these apps to retouch or edit your work before sharing it with friends back home.

Photogene

Photogene (see Figure 16–25; $1.99) is a powerful iPad tool for making your good photos even better. Pull an image from your photo library, and Photogene's tools let you crop or rotate it, adjust the resolution of the photo, add preset filters, adjust colors, remove red-eye from pictures of people, and even add frames and annotations.

Figure 16–25. *Photogene's palette of preset effects and filters is useful in making good photos shine.*

Once you're done creating your photographic masterpiece, Photogene makes it easy to share the photo through Twitter, Facebook, Flickr, Dropbox, and e-mail. Your retouched photos can be saved to your photo library for posterity and eventual syncing to your Windows or Mac computer.

Masque

Another photo-editing and enhancement app is Masque (see Figure 16–26, $5.99). It also takes your work from the photo library, but it performs some different functions. For example, you can apply gradient effects to your photos and stack filters to create completely unique images.

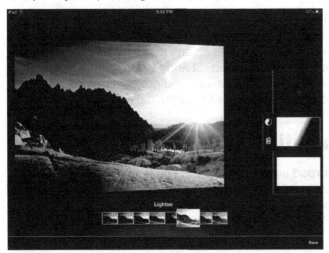

Figure 16–26. *The Masque toolset is different from Photogene's, and the two apps complement each other.*

iMovie for iOS

Apple's iMovie for iOS (see Figure 16–27, $4.99) is an incredibly easy-to-use video-editing app for iPad. You won't want to edit your next feature-length documentary on the iPad, but iMovie is perfectly suited for making short movies to share with family and friends.

Figure 16–27. *Whether you're editing a video presentation for a business meeting or just compiling clips for a family video, iMovie for iOS is an iPad-based film studio in an app.*

We could easily write a short book on how to use iMovie on your iPad, so we'll just describe the major features instead. To use iMovie for iOS, load video from a camera or iPhone into the photo library using the Camera Connection Kit, or shoot video with the cameras on newer iPad models. In iMovie, create a new project, and begin adding film clips to it. Move the clips around on the timeline, trim or split them, and then add transitions, a soundtrack, and titles.

When the edited product is done, iMovie renders the video into a playable movie incorporating all the elements you added. The finished product is sharable through e-mail, although the relatively large size of most movies means that you'll probably want to sync them to your Windows computer or Mac instead. Sharing videos through YouTube, Vimeo, Facebook, and CNN iReport is a button tap away, and projects can be sent to iTunes to be imported into the Mac version of iMovie for additional editing.

Remote Desktop Computing

An iPad is a tech support guru's or road warrior's dream. Being lightweight and unobtrusive, it's easy to carry around while fixing technical issues or trying to work on another computer a few offices—or continents—away. Several apps can help you do work back in the office or support local or remote users without needing to be tied to a desktop or laptop computer.

The first two tools discussed in this section are used for remote control of Mac or Windows computers. In both cases, the app has a counterpart that must be running on the target machine that you want to control.

Splashtop Remote

Splashtop Remote (see Figure 16–28; $4.99) is an excellent example of what is known as a *virtual node controller* (VNC) client. With a free piece of software (Splashtop Streamer) running on a Mac or Windows computer, an iPad can take over control of a remote machine.

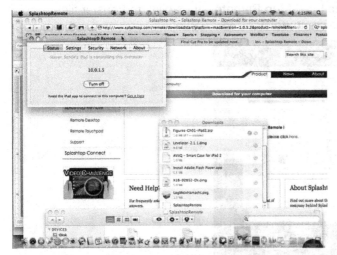

Figure 16–28. *Splashtop Remote's features are fast and easy to set up to provide remote control or support of Mac or Windows computers.*

An onscreen button displays the iPad's virtual keyboard for text entry, and your finger on the iPad screen acts as a "mouse" on the remote PC.

LogMeIn Ignition

LogMeIn Ignition (see Figure 16–29; $29.99) is another remote-control app. It's a product of LogMeIn, a company specializing in secure control of computers of any type. For large IT shops using LogMeIn, LogMeIn Ignition provides a way for support personnel to take over control of remote machines for troubleshooting purposes. The app also has a feature not found in Splashtop Remote—the ability to transfer files between the iPad and the desktop computer.

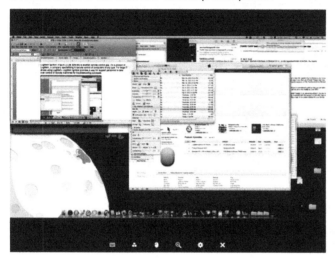

Figure 16–29. *LogMeIn Ignition is better suited for larger organizations with more computers to control.*

Between Splashtop Remote and LogMeIn Ignition, the former is best used in situations where there are few computers to control, while LogMeIn Ignition is better suited for individuals who must have access to a large number of computers or need to transfer files between their iPad and desktop computers.

As with Splashtop Remote, your finger acts as a mouse on the remote machine, and you can use the familiar two-finger zoom gesture to look at details on the screen.

NetTools

Many times computer problems are not the fault of the computer. Instead, the network is causing issues. For that reason, most tech support personnel become very familiar with tools that allow them to troubleshoot network problems.

NetTools (see Figure 16–30; $3.99) places three of the most popular network tools— Ping, Traceroute, and DNS—on your iPad. Ping is used to determine whether another device is actually visible on a network, Traceroute looks at the various network hops between your iPad and another machine, and DNS provides information about the Domain Name Service (DNS) server corresponding to an Internet address.

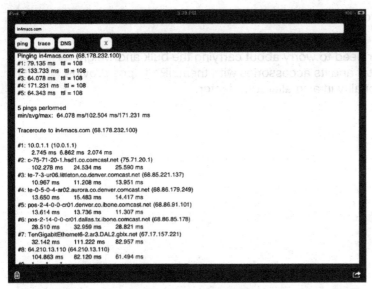

Figure 16–30. *Pinging networked devices, running a Traceroute, or looking up DNS entries is simple with NetTools. Any of the test results can be e-mailed or printed.*

Although it's not the most powerful network toolkit on the market, NetTools has just enough functionality to make it useful for IT support people who are using an iPad.

Summary

In this chapter, we discussed a variety of use cases for iPad owners. Whether you're a gamer, a traveler, an artist, a foodie, or an IT geek, or you just like to see what's going on in your world, there's probably an app for you.

Don't just stop here—your iPad is an incredible tool and toy that changes with every app. Make a quick look at the App Store part of your everyday routine, and you'll find more delightful and useful apps to enjoy. These are some of the key points to remember from this chapter:

- There are more than 4,000 iPad-specific games, and your iPad can also run more than 90,000 iPhone games.

- Free or inexpensive news and weather apps are easily available for your iPad, and they often rival or surpass their web-based counterparts in capability and speed.

- Your iPad isn't a phone, but it can make VoIP calls using the free Skype iPhone app that also works on iPad.

- iPads are the perfect kitchen helper. Just be sure to protect your iPad from heat and liquids.

- The Dock Connector to VGA Cable is a useful accessory for iPad-toting educators.

- Travelers no longer need to worry about carrying the bulk and weight of a laptop computer and its accessories with them. iPad apps provide laptop-type functionality in a smaller form factor.

Index

Printed in the United States
By Bookmasters